GEORGE SANTAYANA

*. . . learn to love, in all things mortal, only
What is eternal.*

GEORGE SANTAYANA

By

George W. Howgate

. . .

A Perpetua Book
A. S. Barnes & Company, Inc.
New York

Copyright 1938

UNIVERSITY OF PENNSYLVANIA PRESS

Manufactured in the United States of America

PERPETUA EDITION 1961

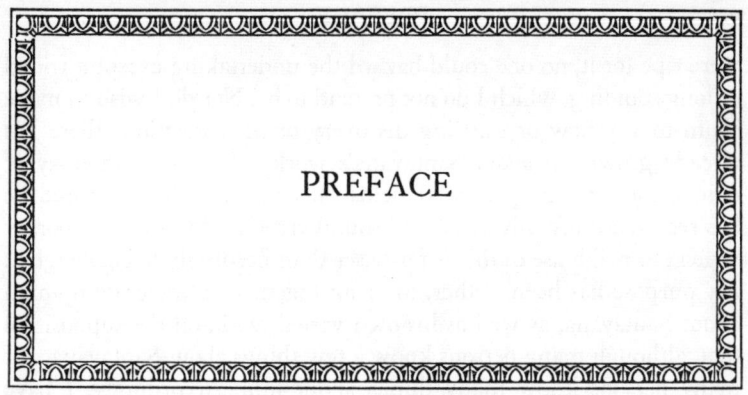

PREFACE

Prophecies are always hazardous, but it seems increasingly clear that we shall have had in George Santayana one of the remarkable men of this generation. Not only has the wisdom of his philosophy great significance for the modern world, but he has also managed to combine a rare intellect with a rare gift of expression, so that his works have an interest for the general reader and student of literature as well as for the professional philosopher. And now that he has been writing for many years and his work has approached a state of finality, it is perhaps fitting to stand off and view his unique contribution to the literature and to the culture of our times. The years have brought into relief the various sides of Santayana's genius, and it is not premature, I believe, to study these—the poet, the critic, the moral philosopher, the master of prose, and the metaphysician—in their interrelationship and in their underlying unity, for all these are manifestations of a central, consistent view of life and a love of the beautiful wherever found. I believe the reader will find that the artistic and philosophic sides of Santayana illuminate each other; that the poems, soliloquies, dialogues, and novel contain Santayana's philosophy in its most fluid, personal form, and that the philosophical treatises not only clarify the former, but also have themselves a beauty of conception and an artistry of execution. In bringing the manifold expressions of Santayana's art into closer relationship and in seeking for the central vision which animates them, I have tried to do something, however inadequately, which has seemed to me for some time to demand the undertaking.

I do not claim for the present study the scope and method of biography, certainly not in any gossipy, intimate sense of the word. Even if Santayana's work could be approached in this way, and the time were ripe for it, no one could hazard the undertaking except a friend of long standing, which I do not pretend to be. Nor do I wish to make claim to any new or startling discovery or interpretation; there has already grown up about Santayana's work a kind of orthodoxy of opinion, and in the particular fields into which he has ventured he has received unusually acute and sound criticism for a contemporary writer; to make use of this is far wiser than needlessly to challenge it. My purpose has been, rather, to bring together, to integrate opinion about Santayana, as well as his own varied work, on the supposition that, although many persons know a few things about Santayana, not many persons know many things about him. Accordingly, I have supplied sufficient information regarding his life and philosophy, I hope, to dispel the many mysteries which have accumulated about his name, and to present his accomplishment as a man of letters in its proper setting. With this last intention in mind, I have tried at least to suggest the many traditions and cultures which leave a rich residuum in his work, with the hope that scholars more competent in their respective fields than I, will investigate further some of these influences and parallels. I have frankly approached my subject from a literary rather than a technically philosophical point of view, and thus have subordinated, perhaps out of its proper proportions, Santayana's metaphysics; some selection was necessary, and inclination determined my choice. I have, however, felt it necessary to devote a chapter to this material because it rounds out Santayana's work and has an aesthetic interest in its own right. Santayana's tendency to confine his efforts at certain periods of his life to certain themes and literary forms has made it possible to arrange the present volume topically and at the same time to follow a roughly chronological order. Thus the chapters may be read consecutively or as separate studies of particular problems.

To the many reviewers and critics of Santayana, past and present, I have expressed my indebtedness in the numerous footnotes at the end of the book. To those who have given me aid and encouragement by word of mouth or through correspondence I wish to give thanks: to Professor Arthur H. Quinn, of the University of Pennsylvania, for helpful guidance from beginning to end; to Mr. William A. Leahy, Mr. Bentley Warren, and Miss Margaret Münsterberg, of Boston, for information concerning Santayana's boyhood and youth; to Mr. Lee J. Dunn, of the Boston Latin School, for material relating to Santayana's activities at the school; to the late Professor George Herbert Palmer, Dean LeBaron Russell Briggs, and Professor Ralph Barton Perry of Harvard University, for information regarding Santayana's activities at Harvard as student and teacher; to Logan Pearsall Smith, Esq., for comments on Santayana's residence in England; to Professor Harry Hayden Clark, of the University of Wisconsin, for research concerning Santayana material in the libraries of Paris; to Professor Domenico Vittorini, of the University of Pennsylvania, for suggestions concerning Santayana's relation to the Italian poets; to Dr. José Zozaya, of Gladwyne, Pennsylvania, for remarks concerning his friendship with Santayana and general advice; and last, but by no means least, to Mr. Santayana himself for his willingness to talk freely about himself and to subject the opinions of the present writer to his cordial criticism. In making these acknowledgments, I would have none of these persons held responsible for the judgments and opinions voiced in the book, and I certainly exonerate them from any share in its shortcomings.

I am deeply grateful to Professor Wendell G. Farr, of Wilmington College, and to Mr. Edward H. O'Neill, of the University of Pennsylvania, for their careful reading of the manuscript. I am also grateful to the authorities of the libraries at Harvard University, the University of Pennsylvania, Ohio State University, the University of Cincinnati, and the British Museum for the use of their respective facilities. Finally, I am grateful to the editorial department of Charles Scribner's Sons for permission to quote frequently from Santayana's works; without these excerpts the present undertaking would be seriously handicapped.

For permission to use copyrighted material, I wish to thank the following publishers:

The Macmillan Company, for excerpts from Santayana's "Brief History of My Opinions," in *Contemporary American Philosophy;* for several other brief selections from the same volume; for several selections from *Essays in Critical Realism;* for a quotation from H. O. Taylor's *The Medieval Mind;* for two excerpts from the poetry of Lionel Johnson; and for a passage from Walter Lippmann's *A Preface to Morals.*

The Harvard University Press (by permission of the President and Fellows of Harvard College), for numerous excerpts from Santayana's *Three Philosophical Poets.*

Little, Brown & Company, for excerpts from the correspondence of Santayana and William James, in R. B. Perry's *The Thought and Character of William James.*

The Boston Latin School Association, for selections from Santayana's work in the *Latin School Register.*

Dodd, Mead & Company, for eight lines from Ernest Dowson's "Carthusians."

The American Mercury, for selections from Margaret Münsterberg's "Santayana at Cambridge."

The New Republic, for selections from Santayana's articles in that magazine.

Thomas Y. Crowell Company, for excerpts from D. W. Prall's *Aesthetic Judgment.*

Willett, Clark & Company, for a passage from Van Meter Ames's *Proust and Santayana.*

Alfred A. Knopf, Inc., for selections from Lorna de' Lucchi's *Anthology of Italian Poems.*

Charles Scribner's Sons, for selections from J. A. Symonds' translations of the sonnets of Michelangelo.

The Oxford University Press, for selections from Robert Bridges' *The Testament of Beauty* and from Lorna de' Lucchi's *The Minor Poems of Dante.*

Dunster House, Inc., Cambridge, Mass., for brief extracts from Santayana's *Lucifer.*

Lee Furman, Inc., for passages from *American Philosophy Today and Tomorrow.*

G. W. H.

Wilmington, Ohio.

CONTENTS

Chapter		Page
	PREFACE	v
I	EARLY YEARS	1
II	THE POET	40
III	THE MORAL PHILOSOPHER	87
IV	THE CRITIC AND ESSAYIST	142
V	THE METAPHYSICIAN	227
VI	SANTAYANA AND AMERICA	257
	NOTES	297
	APPENDIX	327
	BIBLIOGRAPHY	349
	INDEX	353

CHAPTER ONE
EARLY YEARS

One of the many paradoxes connected with George Santayana is that he is most widely known for something that never took place at all. Those who have heard little else about him will tell you knowingly that one fine spring morning Santayana looked out of his classroom in the Harvard Yard, felt the call of a new world freshly green, laid down his book, and without further ado left the campus, never to return. As a matter of fact Santayana's leave-taking was leisurely and entirely premeditated, but for all that the story is less a falsehood than a myth. It persists perhaps because it relates the kind of thing one would like Santayana to have done; somehow it squares with his insistence upon the right of the free soul to follow its inclinations fancy-free. And it was only natural for legend to surround the one event of Santayana's life which must have seemed to many of his friends and readers unexpected, even unaccountable. In the words of Margaret Münsterberg, daughter of one of Santayana's most famous colleagues, "Of course the academic world was astonished. To leave Harvard in order to contemplate in Spain, in Paris, in Oxford and on the banks of the Cam was to cut off an enviable career for idle musing. . . . Besides, after so much admiration had been lavished upon him, it seemed ungrateful to scatter the incense to the breeze. And, really, how could one leave Harvard and Boston by choice?"

Except for this incident, Santayana's life has been so concealed from the public eye that the average reader of his books is often ignorant of where he lives at the moment and even of where he was born. And being naturally curious about such things, the reading public is only too ready to find mystery and complexity in what is really a simple matter of reticence and seclusion. The facts of Santayana's life are briefly stated: He was born in Madrid, December 16,

1863, spent the first nine years of his life in Spain, came to America in 1872, and for the most part remained in this country for the next forty years—throughout grammar school, high school, college, and twenty-two years of teaching. After leaving Harvard in 1912, he returned for a short time to Spain, but the years of the World War found him in England, and during the last decade Italy has claimed him. Thus Spain, England, and Italy share with America almost the entire life of Santayana up to the present.

Yet when all is said and done, Santayana's eyes have been turned upward and inward rather than outward, so that the particular place in which he finds himself matters little if it affords him comfort and leisure. It is significant that he has admired and written about the sky, the clouds, and the stars rather than about the earth and its foliage; landscape seems to him a thing of shreds and patches; nature itself is only a backdrop for human nature, or a subject for speculation, or a congeries of forces. Even human nature is but "a theme for reflection," for Santayana has not been "tempted into the by-ways even of towns, or fascinated by the aspect and humours of all sorts and conditions of men," as he tells us in the preface to his collected poems. It matters little to him who rules his land or what form of government he must submit to. He says, "I have found, in different times and places, the liberal, the Catholic, and the German air quite possible to breathe; nor, I am sure, would communism be without its advantages to a free mind, and its splendid emotions." For are not nationality and religion "like our love and loyalty towards women: things too radically intertwined with our moral essence to be changed honourably, and too accidental to the free mind to be worth changing?"

And is not the free mind the philosopher's goal: to be reasonably detached, to stand a little apart from the press of the world's business, to view life from the vantage point of the ideal spectator, sympathetic but disinterested? Detachment is the most striking single attribute of Santayana; it is the key to his temperament and to his philosophy. To it have contributed his nationality, his religion, his residence in America, his profession, and, perhaps more basic than these, the inclination of his own personality. If absorption in philosophy deepened the contemplative vein in Santayana, that vein already existed to lead him to philosophy.

The influence of place upon Santayana is nevertheless distinguishable, however aptly he has been likened to an archangel because of his sublime detachment. And surely Spain has the first claim to Santayana, a claim based upon his ancestry, birth, and early childhood. His father and mother were both pure Spanish, and he remarks of all his family, "We were not emigrants; none of us ever changed his country, his class, or his religion." He has always looked upon Spain as a sort of fatherland, at least a place to return to at some time, if only, as he says in one of his sonnets, to die there.

One may detect the Spaniard immediately in Santayana's appearance. Margaret Münsterberg, who saw him frequently when Santayana and her father were both young instructors at Harvard, writes:

In his dark Spanish eyes there was a sudden illumination, an extraordinary focusing of light rays having the effect of a blaze of pure spirit. His face was handsome, delicate, pale against the black hair and small mustache; it seemed the face of a dreamer rather than of a scholarly thinker. But his eyes had sprites in them and a light from fairy-lands forlorn. . . . And then his laugh! He laughed not with his lips only, but with his whole face. His was a laugh to delight a child's heart, the laugh of Peter Pan, brimming over with pure merriment.

Age is a great leveler; Santayana's hair has thinned and grayed, his features seem less Spanish. But his eyes are still the badge of his nationality; in other Spaniards I have seen the same dusky pigment glowing as if with an inner luminence; too, no one but a Spaniard could smile with such a merry and yet ironic twinkle.

Of course, after coming to America, Santayana soon lost the more external of his Spanish traits. At the close of his freshman year at Harvard, when he returned to Spain for the first time, he felt "like a foreigner . . . more acutely so than in America, although for more trivial reasons: my Yankee manners seemed outlandish there, and I could not do myself justice in the language. Nor was I inclined to overcome this handicap, as perhaps I might have done with a little effort: nothing in Spanish life or literature at that time particularly attracted me."

To this day Santayana speaks without a trace of Spanish accent, has never written a book in Spanish, and has seldom referred to Spain in his writings. One looks in vain for "Soliloquies in Spain" (as there were *Soliloquies in England*) paying tribute to the picturesqueness and variety of Spanish life, to market-place, cloister, and festival. Neither the peasant nor the grandee finds a place in Santayana's work. One poem is addressed to Spain, but it is a rhetorical piece, chiding Spain for her dreams of world supremacy and for the evils which attended the colonization of America. "Overheard in Seville" records a bit of local color; "Avila" celebrates the uplands which were the scene of Santayana's early life; there are also an essay on Spanish drama, a discussion of Spanish opinion during the World War, an article on Cervantes, and an "imitation" of Calderón. Seven pieces are a small number, though, for a man of letters to devote to his native land; in turn, his work is little known in Spain, only a few articles having been translated into Spanish.

I wonder sometimes if the part of Spain Santayana lived in did not deprive him of a close acquaintance with the antiquity and the charm of Spanish provincialism. Madrid has not the tradition, the sense of the past, which like a delicate fragrance hangs over Seville or Cordova. John Hay in *Castilian Days* says that it lacks that "mysterious and haunting memory that peoples the air with spectres in quiet towns like Ravenna and Nuremburg." Around it is the Castilian Tableland, gaunt and bleak, in Santayana's words,

> Realm proudly desolate and nobly poor,
> Scorched by the sky's inexorable zeal.

In the small town of Avila Santayana spent much of his childhood, but it was only later in England that he came to see nature in softer mood and to know the loveliness of the countryside. He remarks of his poetry, "I am city bred, and that companionship with nature, those rural notes, which for English poets are almost inseparable from poetic feeling, fail me altogether." Certainly whenever he mentions Spain in his verse, it is a Spain lonely and sad, elemental and unyielding, that he pays tribute to, a country of "castled hills and windy moors," in whose skies the "eternal brooded" among "unfathomed oracles of woe." This is his native Spain, the Spain he feels exiled from. But, Salvador da Madariaga reminds us, "The Castilian Tableland is a country with a grandeur and a majesty which make it the worthy companion of the great scenes of Nature—seas and skies—and of the great moods of the spirit—poetry and contemplation."

The effect of place upon character is of course a matter of conjecture, but one Castilian at least was to become a poet with a boundless respect for Nature in all her strength and severity. Señor Madariaga contends further that it is the Spaniard's nature to be detached and philosophic. Since his "turn of mind is realistic and apt to pierce through words till it strikes the bedrock of things," he is likely to "consider motion as a mere bridge between two shores of immobility." He "conceives life as a drama and judges things and people from the point of view of a spectator." What is sometimes called Oriental in Santayana, that intimation of a wisdom very old and profound, that ironic refusal to "take every phase of art or religion or philosophy seriously, simply because it takes itself so," may be in reality Spanish.

Santayana's early life accentuated what Count Keyserling calls in the Spaniard these "incarnated basic tones." His parents, before their marriage, had both lived in the Philippines, where, during the eighteen-forties and fifties, Santayana's father and his maternal grandfather had been officials in the Spanish civil service. These had been for both parents "their more romantic and prosperous days." Santayana's mother had been, in his own words,

. . . rather the grand lady, in a style half Creole, half early Victorian. Virtue, beside those tropical seas, might stoop to be indolent. She had given a silver dollar every morning to her native major-domo, with which to provide for the family and the twelve servants, and keep the change for his wages. Meantime she bathed, arranged the flowers, received visits, and did embroidery. It had been a spacious life; and in our narrower circumstances in later years the sense of it never forsook her.

Santayana's father, who had been around the world three times, supplied the more vigorous side of Eastern life with his tales of ships and the sea, of the ports he had visited and the customs of the natives. A broad panorama was thus unfolded before the growing boy, a spaciousness of outlook he has never lost. As Santayana says:

From childhood I have lived in the imaginative presence of interminable ocean spaces, coconut islands, blameless Malays, and immense continents swarming with Chinamen, polished and industrious, obscene and philosophical.

Perhaps because he saw it only with the mind's eye, this panorama finds little concrete expression in his later work. Its chief effect on his thought seems to have been to give him an "ironical background enormously empty, or breaking out in spots, like Polynesia, into nests of innocent particoloured humanity." Every reader must have felt at some time in Santayana's work this background, this presence of something immeasurably vast and immeasurably old underlying the shell of civilization.

Upon such an "ironical background" was superimposed an intimate family life which did much to determine the direction of Santayana's later interests. Living in Spain, he learned his catechism and prayers, and particularly through the example of his Spanish relatives, who were devout believers, came to love the forms and ceremonies of the church; an attachment was set up which has lasted even to this day, though he has become intellectually estranged from Catholicism. There was in his parents, indeed, a vein of free thought, a leaven of irony, which did much to counteract, though it never quite succeeded in destroying, Santayana's religious sentiment. In other ways, though, his parents influenced him considerably. Santayana's mother had been taught by her father "to revere pure reason and republican virtue and to abhor the vices of a corrupt world. But her own temper was cool and stoical, rather than ardent, and her disdain of corruption had in it a touch of elegance." From his mother Santayana may have received the sterner elements of his nature, his uncompromising loyalties, perhaps a certain intellectual austerity. His father, too, though he had more respect for material greatness, possessed a "seasoned and incredulous mind, trained to see other sorts of excellence also." As a boy "he had worked in the studio of a professional painter of the school of Goya, and had translated the tragedies of Seneca into Spanish verse." Later in life, too, in spite of his official duties and his many travels, he found time to write a book about the topography and inhabitants of the island of Mindanao. Thus Santayana found in his own home a respect for art and literature and a stimulus to creative work. Even after he had come to America and throughout his school days, he says:

The most decisive influences over my mind . . . continued to come from my family, where, with my grown-up brother and sisters, I was the only child. I played no games, but sat at home all the afternoon and evening reading or drawing; especially devouring anything I could find that regarded religion, architecture, or geography.

I was quick to discern an ethereal beauty in the landscapes of Turner. Furgueson's *Cathedrals of England,* too, and the great mansions in the Italian style depicted in the eighth edition of the *Encyclopedia Britannica,* revealed to me even when a boy the rare charm that can envelop the most conventional things when they are associated with tender thoughts or with noble ways of living.

America could not break up this leisurely rhythm of family life, although it did subject the Santayana household to certain strains,

EARLY YEARS

separating Santayana first from his mother and next from his father. At the time of her residence in the Philippines Santayana's mother had been the wife of an American merchant of Manila named Sturgis. Mr. Sturgis, the son of a Bostonian, had always planned for his children a typical Boston education, and upon his death in 1857 his widow settled in Boston, where his plans might be carried out and where the children had relatives and a little property. But during a visit to Madrid in 1862 she met and married Augustin Santayana, who had been a friend of the Sturgises in the Philippines. This second marriage, however, did not interfere with the original Sturgis plans, even if the education of the children in time necessitated a separation of husband and wife, "friendly, if not altogether pleasant to either party." Mr. Santayana "recognized the propriety of that arrangement," and when the question of his own son's education arose, he bundled him also off to America, feeling that the prospects he could offer his son "in his modest retirement" were "far from brilliant." Thus, says Santayana, "by a sort of pre-natal or pre-established destiny" was determined "my connection with the Sturgis family, with Boston, and with America."

The Santayana family spoke at home "a Spanish more or less pure," but fortunately for one who was to grow up in a strange land, Santayana was sent the first winter in Boston to a "kindergarten, among much younger children, where there were no books," with the result that he "picked up English by ear before knowing how it was written." He attributes to this circumstance his ability to speak English without a foreign accent; learning English by ear kept him also from the idiomatic faults so common in the English of even highly educated foreigners.

After kindergarten Santayana attended the Brimmer elementary school, but in the fall of 1874 his real school life began when he entered the Boston Latin School. In the halls of this oldest of American public schools Santayana spent eight years, and was subjected to an old-fashioned mental discipline which was no doubt good for him. The course regularly covered six years, but during Santayana's attendance at the school was for a time lengthened to eight, so that it stretched back into the grade-school years. As a result, instruction, in the foreign languages for instance, could be gradual and thorough; Latin was begun the first year and Greek the fourth. There was also a wholesome correlation of studies; ancient history accompanied ancient languages, and credit for translation was apportioned between the English and the foreign language departments. Neither were the arts neglected, special instruction in music and drawing being provided. Particularly significant in view of Santayana's later attainments was the school's attitude toward English. A catalogue of 1880 calls attention to the increased emphasis laid upon the study of the English language "in its literary rather than its literal features" and upon the students' obligation to translate the classics at sight into idiomatic English. Constant practice in original composition and in translation encouraged Santayana's natural interest in both, and constituted invaluable training for a foreigner.

His school work was brilliant in those subjects which were to his taste. His name is not to be found among the lists of students cited for general honors or all-round ability, but it appears frequently during his last three years in connection with prizes for sight translation in French and Latin, for reading and declamation, for an English poem, and for a poetical translation from Horace. In recalling his school days Santayana mentions only one of the masters, Byron Groce, who, he says, instilled into him an enduring love for the English poets.* He must have felt, too, the far-reaching influence of an able scholar in Greek, Arthur Irving Fiske, who later became headmaster of the school.

But when Santayana thinks back over his schooldays, neither the masters nor the studies come to mind.

There is one image above all others that survives from the wreckage of my school days: the picture of the old Bedford Street Schoolhouse. There is no beauty in it, and little intrinsic interest; but for me it has become a symbol; a part of one of those Great Companions, one of those friendly worlds or countries of the imagination, which accompany a man through life. . . . The Bedford Street Schoolhouse was, or seemed, a vast rickety old shell of a building, bare, shabby, and forlorn to the point of squalor; not dirty exactly, but worn, shaky, and stained deeply in every part by time, weather, and merciless usage. . . . No blackboard was black; all

---

* The reader may be interested in a statement by Groce of the reforms he brought about in the teaching of English at Boston Latin. "No longer would a rapid survey of the history of English Literature do; the best English Literature itself must be read in wholes and must be studied to be fully enjoyed. . . . No longer would rules of grammar and rhetoric suffice; . . . power to express oneself accurately, clearly, and forcibly was to be prepared for by constant observation of good models, constant practice, and careful coaching." *Latin School Register*, XXXIV (1915), 19. On the other hand, I have the word of certain graduates of the school that Groce could have given Santayana nothing he did not already possess.

were indelibly clouded with ingrained layers of old chalk; the more was rubbed out, the more was rubbed in. Every desk was covered with generations of inkspots, and cut deeply with lines and letters and grotesque drawings. A ramshackle staircase wound up through the heart of the building, to the fourth storey, where the Hall was; and down those steep and dangerous curves the avalanche of nail-hoofed boys would come thundering down, forty or eighty or two hundred together. However short your legs might be, it was simpler and safer to rush down with the avalanche, trusting to luck, rather than to hold back or fall out, and be trampled upon or deserted.*

One can see descending that stair a boy not overly tall or robust, but straight and agile (for Santayana in his last year at school led the school battalion in military drill). Dark and handsome in appearance, quiet and restrained in manner, he must have been conspicuous among his schoolfellows. Perhaps to them he was somewhat of an oddity, not because he was foreign, but because in temperament and habits he was so different from the New England schoolboy of his age. Yet those who knew him at school insist that he was not unsociable, nor unpopular with his classmates, though few knew him intimately.

Santayana's first literary effort to see the light of print reveals him as anything but a solitary misfit among his schoolfellows. The members of his class had formed a kind of social club, and when the school moved from the Bedford Street schoolhouse to newer quarters, the club decided to celebrate the occasion in verse. Santayana, being the most poetically gifted of the group, was pressed into service and responded with "Lines on Leaving the Bedford Street Schoolhouse." One morning at assembly members of the club stationed themselves prominently in the aisles to see that no student failed to secure bills on which was printed the poem, anonymously of course. Now this proceeding would have been inoffensive enough had not the poem contained caricatures, none too gentle, of the ·masters. Through the action of Dr. Moses Merrill, headmaster, says one of the culprits, "we were placed under the ban of disapproval, where we remained for some time." But not before Santayana's poem had won a much wider circulation. One member of the class with newspaper connections saw to it that the verses, caricatures and all, met the delighted gaze of Bostonians over their morning breakfast table. And so through

* Reprinted by courtesy of the Boston Latin School Association.

a schoolboy prank Santayana the poet was, however anonymously, brought before his first reading public, a public greater in numbers at least than any he was to reach for many long years.

The verses are good schoolboy work, showing metrical proficiency and at times a knack of witty comment. The remarks on the masters seem harmless enough today; in fact, the more impressive parts of the poem are where in serious vein Santayana regrets to leave the building with its store of fond associations. The first stanza may serve as illustration.

> Forth from the seed by its first founders sown,
> With rolling years, our good old School has grown;
> And, for the brighter future that now nears,
> Its fifth and noblest home the City rears.
> We hasten thither, with high hopes elate,
> And leave the older schoolhouse to its fate.
> No more shall those familiar sights and sounds,
> There oft repeated, cheer its lonely bounds;
> No classic name shall henceforth greet its ear,
> No Greek or Latin on the board appear;
> No sudden thunder the old stairs shall shake,
> And with a palsied tremor make them quake;
> Month after month will pass, and yet no more
> Shall be heard tales so often told before
> Of Spartacus, Bozzaris, and the rest,
> Or Toussaint l'Ouverture, of all the best.
> The hum of voices during the recess;
> The romping that the teacher would repress;
> The merry groups that round the windows gather
> Of all the day's events to talk together;
> The cheated silence, when the opening door
> Let in one of the boys—and nothing more;
> All these will disappear, and in their place,
> Business this classic site will soon disgrace.*

In the fall of 1881 a group of the more talented boys decided to publish a school magazine that would "both benefit and amuse." Thus came into being the *Boston Latin Register,* which for fifty-one years has upheld the traditions of the school and encouraged the student body to express itself. Santayana was one of the original board of editors, though he says with characteristic modesty,

---

* Reprinted by courtesy of the Boston Latin School Association.

When I search my memory for details about the first issue of *The Latin School Register,* I find a complete blank. The fact is I can have had little to do with it; neither the idea nor the requisite energy could have been mine, and the credit for launching so wonderfully long-lived and prosperous an undertaking must belong entirely to the business manager and the other contributors. I have often written since for other periodicals, and I observe that almost invariably they have soon stopped publication.

At any rate, Santayana's contributions to the early issues were a history of his class, a parody of the *Aeneid,* and a "sonnet" on President Garfield. The history begins auspiciously, in clear, unaffected prose, but after a few anecdotes of the early years of the class, running through two issues of the magazine, it suddenly breaks off with an unfulfilled promise to resume in a later issue. The parody is mostly schoolboy humor, depending upon incongruities and anachronisms and seldom venturing very far from the jokes of the Latin class. Fun for its own sake has never been Santayana's forte; there is more wit when he turns to satire, as in the passage where Venus receives Aeneas disguised as a servant of Dido and remarks that he is "the embodied form of woman's rights or ladies' dress reform," or where the Greeks in the wooden horse are said to be badly off

> For, although men were tougher than at present,
> The question had not yet been agitated,
> How dwellings should be drained and ventilated.

The generally smooth versification contrasts strangely with the boyishness of idea and imagery, as in the following extended figure:

> As when among a crowd of idle boys
> At times arises playfulness and noise,
> And spit-balls fly around and beans and chalk—
> For mischief lends them weapons,—if in walk
> By chance a teacher, each his glee restrains
> The noise is hushed and guilty silence reigns,—
> So, at the sight of Neptune's awful form,
> Did sudden calm succeed the sudden storm.

Better than anything in the parody is the tribute to Garfield:

> A child of Fortune, taught in Freedom's school
> To serve his country and himself to rule,
> Heard the glad accents of the people's voice
> Proclaim him monarch of the people's choice.
> But fiendish malice struck a blow, and then

> The dying patriot heard that voice again:
> He heard the murmur of the nation's ire;
> He heard the whisper of her long desire;
> And when his heart with hers no longer throbbed,
> The widowed nation with the widow sobbed;
> Unwoven still, she strewed upon his bier
> The laurels plucked to crown a long career.
>
> Now in his native land there is a tomb,
> And in his home there is a silent gloom;
> There is a bond of union in his fall;
> In his brave life, a lesson to us all;
> And, in the annals of his country's fame,
> A withered hope, a sorrow, and a name.*

Santayana in a letter to the present writer maintains that this poem is "not merely rhetorical froth," and explains that his interest in President Garfield's illness and death was the result of his friendship with Bentley Warren, now a distinguished Boston lawyer, who at the time of the composition of the poem lived with the Garfield boys at Williams College. Certainly the sonnet, in its quaint eighteenth-century style, is no worse than many other tributes to deceased presidents.

It is obvious from the preceding quotations that Santayana was not a literary prodigy, nor will one find from his pen the exotic effusions which mark many preparatory school and college journals. He kept himself within familiar bounds, with a resulting boyishness as wholesome as it is genuine. Meanwhile he was constantly perfecting his style, as if aware that some day it would stand him in good stead. Boston Latin marks the literary apprenticeship of George Santayana; for when we meet his work again in college, we find it has become singularly mature.

Boston Latin marks, too, the span of his boyhood, impressionable years of adjustment to a new world and a new way of life. Keenly sensitive to his environment, he saw Boston as a "red-brick world," in a sense an extension of the Boston Latin schoolhouse,

> ... mean and shabby-genteel, with an atmosphere of whimsical, ineffectual Bohemia.... Later I found the same sentimental Bohemia, in the same red brick setting, still surviving in some circles in England, for instance, in the Inns of Court, and in the more modest corners of Ox-

---

* Reprinted by courtesy of the Boston Latin School Association.

ford and Cambridge. It was the world of Hogarth and Cruikshank, of Dickens and Thackeray, romantic but sardonic, poetic but inglorious. . . . Wealth and Morality dominated the scene from their granite pedestals, like ponderous Victorian statues: in the shadow of those beneficent powers you grew up miraculously respectable and genteel, like David Copperfield and Oliver Twist. Yet your surroundings sloped sharply down from the demure propriety of home and of the schoolroom (when the teacher was looking) to a tipsy back-alley world of waifs and ne'er-do-wells, where the women (except the young and tender ones) were like Mrs. Gamp, the business men like Mr. Micawber, and the geniuses like Edgar Allan Poe.*

Even in his boyhood America took on in Santayana's eyes, as he glanced around him with a curious mingling of irony and sympathy, those features he was later to delineate as the tokens of the "genteel tradition."

In 1882, almost at the age of nineteen, Santayana entered Harvard College. He found Harvard in the midst of one of its greatest transformations. For thirteen years President Eliot had been in office, and during this time he had done much to remodel the university in accordance with his conception of a scientifically administered liberal education. The underlying change was of course from the uniform curriculum to the elective system. By 1883-84 the only required courses were "Freshman English and German (or French), Sophomore and Junior themes and forensics, and two easy half-year lecture courses, one on Chemistry and one on Physics. Even these could be 'anticipated' or worked off at school by taking extra entrance examinations in those subjects." During Santayana's college years the elective system won unqualified acceptance. Writing in 1894 as an instructor, he looks back on 1884 as the heyday of academic *laissez-faire*.

The reigning feeling was that if a youth passed his examinations and conformed to the other official requirements, it was nobody's business how he spent his time or broke his bones. A student then might make a trip to Cuba or Florida in term time without serious consequences; and I remember that as a sophomore I cut all but two recitations in a course that met once a week throughout the year, and passed by merely taking the examinations, without any warning or sign of disapproval from the authorities.

Although such a situation begot many evils, to Santayana it was stimulating in that it allowed him to follow the dictates of his own

* Reprinted by courtesy of the Boston Latin School Association.

will as to what and when he should study. There was ample time for reading, for friendship, for good talk, for a kind of leisure more often associated with the English universities. In this environment Santayana was able in a way to educate himself, to indulge his instincts and cultivate his tastes without a sense of intellectual confinement or compulsion.

He must have relished, too, the picturesque variety of method, or lack of method, which brought life and color to the routine of the classroom. For the Harvard of Santayana's day was a college of vivid personalities, eccentrics in many ways, but at the same time masterly and inspiring teachers: Palmer, James, and Royce in Philosophy, Child, Briggs, and Wendell in English, Norton in the Fine Arts, to mention only those whose fields touched Santayana's interests. It is true that he did not have all of these men in class; except for the required language courses, he ventured little beyond the department of philosophy. Still they were to be seen on the campus, to be talked about in the dormitories, to be met perhaps at their homes or at whatever social events Cambridge provided. Santayana, for instance, was well acquainted with Charles Eliot Norton, although he took no courses under him.

Santayana's most distinguished work was in philosophy and English. The official catalogues state that he received at graduation Highest Honors in Philosophy and Honorable Mention in English Composition, and that he won in his junior year second prize in the Boylston Elocution contest. His work in the required themes of sophomore year was so memorable that Dean Briggs still recalls the impression it made upon Barrett Wendell, Santayana's instructor, and upon the department in general. Santayana, of course, entered college with a polished style that not many students have achieved at the time of graduation. Still Wendell's insistence upon form was no doubt valuable in checking a certain episodic tendency which has always marked Santayana's writing. He benefited also, he informed the present writer, from Wendell's painstaking correction of mechanical faults.

All of this activity in composition was soon to bear fruit. Early in 1885 the *Harvard Crimson,* then as now a daily undergraduate sheet devoted to campus news, announced a "monthly supplement, to be filled with matter furnished by the English instructors, taken from the best themes and specimens of composition done in the regular college work." As two supplements were issued, enthusiasm grew to a point where plans were made for a new literary magazine. This venture received the backing of the instructors in composition, who declared that the "gentlemen who have this plan in charge possess, as a body, a greater amount and a higher degree of literary ability and promise than any other group of students whom we have known as pupils." These gentlemen were George Santayana, Alanson Bigelow Houghton, subsequently ambassador to Germany and England, George Rice Carpenter, later a distinguished professor of English at Columbia, and T. P. Sanborn, a sensitive, talented youth who committed suicide shortly after graduation. In recalling the plans for the organization of the magazine, William W. Baldwin, who became the first business manager, describes Santayana's part in it thus: "As I recollect it, without any authority except that which we could predicate on his general willingness to oblige, Sanborn and I had already pledged George Santayana's hearty assistance, and when we left Houghton's room, it was to get a ratification of this rather rash promise. . . . Santayana laughed at Sanborn's enthusiasm in a good-natured, Philosophy IV way, but in the end agreed, as we felt sure he would, to make one of the Board." Soon after was the first meeting in Santayana's room. On April 25, 1885, this enterprising group announced the publication of the *Harvard Monthly,* and the next fall a well-known college magazine entered upon its long and notable existence.

The journal prospered and in the first few years, during which time Santayana remained more or less closely in touch with it, the editorial boards contained many members subsequently well known: William Morton Fullerton, George Pierce Baker, Bernhard Berenson, Robert Herrick, H. T. Parker, Norman Hapgood, Robert Morss Lovett, William Vaughn Moody. The standard of poetry was kept high through the contributions of Moody, Bliss Carman, and Santayana. Robert Herrick tried his hand mostly at short stories, and H. T. Parker explored the fields of literary and musical criticism which were later to bring him recognition in the pages of the *Boston Transcript.* There is a happy profusion of talent in the early issues of the magazine, and a catholic spirit withal. "What Is a Sonnet?" rubs shoulders with "Why I Am Not a Republican." And if there is a fair sprinkling of lachrymose ballads to "Sorrow and Stillness" and "Odes to Death," and an occasional story like "A Widow of Appomattox to Her Son," there are bits of criticism and snatches of lyric here and there which show that a genuine literary muse was adding her bounty to the education of the eighties.

Santayana had contributed to the *Crimson Supplement* two themes, "The Problem of the Freedom of the Will in its Relation to Ethics" and "King Lear as a Type of the Gothic Drama." They are well-written discussions rising at times considerably above the level of undergraduate prose. The following excerpt from the first paper forecasts the irony of the later Santayana, with its delight in giving a paradoxical twist to moral truths.

If all the world turned fatalist, we might see our good people face life with a little more calmness and intrepidity; we might expect to find less self-accusation and less of what is called righteous indignation. For if we came to regard wickedness as misfortune and monstrosity rather than sin, we should not find it necessary to be so vehement in our condemnation of wrongdoing, since we should not feel so much secret sympathy with it. Even now, who of us in his heart would not be a rake rather than a hunchback, a villain rather than a fool? In spite of all the moralists, we cannot admire desert or merit as much as the gifts of nature and fortune. There is nothing of which we are so proud as of a good family, a handsome face, a strong body, a ready wit,—of all those things, indeed, for which we are not responsible; but no one is ever proud of trying hard. . . . To be able to do easily what other people do with difficulty, or what they cannot do at all, that is what we are proud of and what we admire.

One cannot but admire the assurance of such a young moralist, and his embarrassing insight into human nature. Santayana's ability to turn a neat definition encompassing in a few words a breadth of generalization is to be found in the "King Lear" theme:

The office of the Gothic drama is not to give us merely the chiseled image of some heroic man agitated by one mighty passion, but rather to display the forces that are struggling in all men; to overawe us with the ghost of our own past and our own future, so that we may truly say: The world is passing in review!

Even the Santayana epigram, barbed in felt, is there. "Closet tragedies are not produced until authors get to be more in love with themselves than with nature."

To the *Monthly* Santayana contributed during his senior year five sonnets, a translation of de Musset's "The May Night," a review of John Fiske's *The Idea of God as Affected by Modern Knowledge*, and an article, "The Ethical Doctrine of Spinoza." The poems were by no means juvenile in conception or execution. Out of the seventy lines of the sonnets only fourteen have been completely changed for later publication, and most of the other changes are substitutions of single words. Forty lines remain absolutely unchanged, and they include all of the most memorable lines of the sonnets. The essay on Spinoza contains passages which exhibit the power of inference and generalization, the grasp of significance which mark Santayana's later criticisms. Though there is a slight stiffness here and there, where the academic gown fits too snugly, there is none of that fumbling for expression which characterizes schoolboy work. Between "President Garfield" and the sonnets, too, a whole philosophy of life has been pondered, and a boy has grown into a man disillusioned beyond his years*

Santayana's other artistic skill, in drawing, found an outlet in the cartoon. He was a member of the *Lampoon* staff during his last three years of college, contributing no articles but furnishing the magazine a steady output of drawings which show at least a facile skill with the pencil. The strokes are bold, the outlines clear, the expressions convincing; the ladies seem more formidable than the men, their protruding chins giving them the appearance of veritable termagants. If one feels that such work is a curious apprenticeship for an embryo philosopher, let him be satisfied that some of the cartoons turn upon nice distinctions and are as philosophic as a humorous magazine's cartoons could well hope to be.†

Santayana was certainly no recluse at Harvard; in fact, for an introspective person, it is surprising how closely he kept in touch with college life and how observant he was of its details. In a much later essay he writes,

In the eighteen-eighties a good deal of old-fashioned shabbiness and jollity lingered about Harvard. Boston and Cambridge in those days resembled in some ways the London of Dickens: the same dismal wealth, the same speechifying, the same anxious respectability, the same sordid back streets, with their air of shiftlessness and decay, the same odd figures and loud humor, and, to add a touch of horror, the monstrous suspicion

---

* For excerpts from the poems and essay, see pages 26–29.
† The following is a characteristic example:
    Lady: Why, Elizabeth! I thought you disapproved of my going to parties.
    Elizabeth (who is a strict Puritan): Oh, no, mum! It isn't like you was a Christian, mum!
    VII (April 25, 1884), 48

that some of the inhabitants might be secretly wicked. Life, for the undergraduates, was full of droll incidents and broad farce; it drifted good-naturedly from one commonplace thing to another. Standing packed in the tinkling horse-car, their coat-collars above their ears and their feet deep in the winter straw, they jogged in a long half-hour to Boston, there to enjoy the delights of female society, the theatre, or a good dinner. And in the summer days, for Class Day and Commencement, feminine and elderly Boston would return the visit, led by the governor of Massachusetts in his hired carriage-and-four, and by the local orators and poets, brimming with jokes and conventional sentiments, and eager not so much to speed the youngsters on their career, as to air their own wit, and warm their hearts with punch and with collective memories of youth.

It is no surprise to us that Santayana's eye was caught by the buildings around him and that he has left interesting impressions of the campus architecture at both Yale and Harvard—Osborn Hall, with its "confused pretentiousness," and the new Yale gymnasium, which "makes one ask whether an athlete or a monarch holds his court at the head of the marble stairs, and whether the *porte-cochère* is meant to give passage to a chariot or to an ambulance." But even athletic contests were not outside the range of Santayana's interest. A good game appeals to the artist in Santayana as well as the philosopher.

A football game is always a fine spectacle, but here upon the broad-backed earth, away from the town, nothing but sky and distant hills about you, where the wind always blows, the struggle has an added beauty. It borrows from the bleak and autumnal landscape something of a pathetic earnestness and natural horror. It seems to embody a primal instinct, to be a symbol of all the prehistoric struggles of our earth-born race. Here the heroic virtues shine in miniature, and the simple joy of the savage world returns as in a dream. The young men stand about absorbed and admiring, commenting like the crowd in Homer upon the prowess of their chiefs. It is an unforgettable sight.

But Santayana was not a mere spectator; in everything he wrote the critical bias is evident, the detachment with which he viewed all the fun and frolic about him. Certainly college was not to be taken too seriously; it was "an idyllic, haphazard, humoristic existence, without fine imagination, without any familiar infusion of scholarship, without articulate religion: a flutter of intelligence in a void, flying into trivial play, in order to drop back, as soon as college days were over, into the drudgery of affairs." Such an attitude was possible because Santayana had within the periphery of his academic and social life at college an inner life unknown to most of his associates, an inner life of unusual solidity. To reconstruct it, one must trace back his religious and philosophical convictions to their Spanish origins and watch their development under the influence of the philosophy he studied at Harvard. It should be said at the outset that Santayana has never made any real distinction between religion and philosophy; both represent a man's honest efforts to solve the riddle of the universe and to live in accordance with his solution; one is as much a way of life, an emotional preference, as the other, and both demand the utmost intellectual integrity.

"By instinct," says Santayana, "all Mediterranean peoples are republican and pagan, not having changed much since antiquity." The Spaniard has more than his share of this heritage, for he represents above all, says Havelock Ellis, "the supreme manifestation of a certain primitive and eternal attitude of the human spirit." In Spain, says Santayana,

> . . . hath mortal life from age to age
> Endured the silent hand that makes and mars,
> And, sighing, taken up its heritage
> Beneath the smiling and inhuman stars.

But with this radical irony the Spaniard has had profound fear of death which has made him cling more fiercely than his Latin brothers to revealed religion. Christianity has been, in Santayana's words, "the only conqueror of Spain indeed," and has burned intensely there, even if the fuel has sometimes been, as George Borrow observes of the Inquisition, national pride rather than spiritual zeal. Thus the Spaniard of the present day, with such a background, is likely, says Santayana, to be either a conservative Catholic or a radical atheist, and the line is sharply drawn between the two. In some earnest thinkers, such as Unamuno, the two strands of national inheritance are both in evidence, producing a spiritual conflict and an emotional unrest. Unamuno's strife, Madariaga maintains, is one between "truth thought" and "truth felt"—"between veracity and sincerity." His heart clings to the faith his mind is unwilling to accept. And the "eternal conflict between faith and reason, between spirit and intellect, between life and thought, between heaven and civilization, is the conflict of Spain herself." Unamuno himself shares this opinion. "The Castilian spirit is either ironic or tragic, sometimes both at once, but it never arrives at a fusion of the irony and the austere tragedy of the human drama."

In Santayana's own family this national drama was enacted in miniature. On the one hand, life in Spain brought him into touch with a kind of Catholicism found only in Catholic countries, rich in associations and vitality, through its very repose and security the better able to avoid the tensions of a religion placed on the defensive, and thus to luxuriate in tenderness and beauty. But he had also been in an atmosphere of free-thinking all his life. Both father and mother, although nominally Catholics, "regarded all religion as a work of human imagination" and felt that "God was too great to take special thought for man: sacrifices, prayers, churches, and tales of immortality were invented by rascally priests in order to dominate the foolish." Santayana agreed with his parents' theology; he differed, however, with his parents in their belief that works of human imagination because they were human were therefore bad.

No, said I to myself even as a boy: they are good, they alone are good; and the rest—the whole real world—is ashes in the mouth. My sympathies were entirely with those other members of my family who were devout believers. I loved the Christian epic, and all those doctrines and observances which bring it down into daily life: I thought how glorious it would have been to be a Dominican friar, preaching that epic eloquently, and solving afresh all the knottiest and sublimest mysteries of theology.

Religion was thus a battleground to Santayana long before he went to Harvard, and having seen the sides so clearly drawn, he was surprised to find how confused the whole issue became in the hands of the Harvard department of philosophy. In the first place, the department encouraged a mild agnosticism in accordance with President Eliot's dictum that "philosophical subjects should be never taught with authority. They are not established sciences." In Professor Palmer's words, there was therefore no "Harvard 'school' of philosophy. . . . We wished . . . our students . . . to study . . . under the guidance of an expert believer and then to have the difficulties . . . presented by an expert opponent." The department thus became a group of original philosophers expounding their respective systems, and refuting each other's arguments in the classroom and out. For many students this mêlée of free philosophical inquiry was valuable instruction, but Santayana's convictions were already formed, and they were remarkably solid, so that the practice of the department neither perplexed him, as it would have done a weaker mind, nor won his admiration. He says,

> As an undergraduate at Harvard, I was already alive to the fundamental questions, and even had a certain dialectical nimbleness, due to familiarity with the fine points of theology: the arguments for and against free will and the proofs of the existence of God were warm and clear in my mind. I accordingly heard James and Royce with more wonder than serious agreement: my scholastic logic would have wished to reduce James at once to a materialist and Royce to a solipsist, and it seemed strangely irrational in them to resist such simplification.

Much more to Santayana's taste was Palmer's genial history of philosophy, unfolding in a brilliant panorama, with the critical spirit of the nineteenth century, successive philosophies, religions, and national epochs.

These picturesque vistas into the past came to fill in circumstantially that geographical and moral vastness to which my imagination was already accustomed. Professor Palmer was especially skilful in bending the mind to a suave and sympathetic participation in the views of all philosophers in turn: were they not all great men, and must not the aspects of things which seemed persuasive to them be really persuasive? Yet [Santayana says] even this form of romanticism, amiable as it is, could not altogether put to sleep my scholastic dogmatism. The historian of philosophy may be as sympathetic and as self-effacing as he likes: the philosopher in him must still ask whether any of those successive views were true, or whether the later ones were necessarily truer than the earlier: he cannot, unless he is a shameless sophist, rest content with a truth *pro tem*.

There is in the Catholic, whether nominal or devout, a love of finality which makes agnosticism deeply repellent. Having once been sure of something, he is not content to see a virtue made of insecurity and ignorance.

But though they differed in almost everything else, Palmer, James, and Royce were all Protestant, in the sense that they believed some harmony was possible between the moral yearnings of mankind and the strict law of a natural universe. This attitude the Catholic in Santayana felt to be a compromise, resulting in a dilemma. One had either to sacrifice the spiritual in man to make him a little more like the orders of nature, or to clothe nature in a moral garment to make it a little more amenable to the wishes of man. The first seemed to him barbarism, the second hypocrisy. As he says, "Nor in Harvard philosophy was it easy for me to understand the Protestant combination of earnestness with waywardness." Most objectionable was the form of idealism worked out by Josiah Royce. At first Royce appealed to Santayana more than did James, for he was "the better dialectician, and traversed subjects in which I was naturally more interested." But his justification for the existence of evil, like that of Hegel, Nietzsche, and Browning, seemed to Santayana a "survival of a sort of forced optimism and pulpit unction, by which a cruel and nasty world, painted by them in the most lurid colours, was nevertheless set up as the model and standard of what ought to be." Such idealism waved a magic wand over the natural world, thinking thereby to have made it good enough to worship.

[But] to *preach* barbarism as the only good, in ignorance or hatred of the possible perfection of every natural thing, was a scandal: a belated Calvinism that remained fanatical after ceasing to be Christian. . . . The duty of an honest moralist would have been rather to distinguish, in this bad or mixed reality, the part, however small, that could be loved and chosen from the remainder, however large, which was to be rejected and renounced.

Worse yet,

. . . this romantic love of evil was not thoroughgoing: wilfulness and disorder were to reign only in spiritual matters; in government and industry, even in natural science, all was to be order and mechanical progress. Thus the absence of a positive religion and of a legislation, like that of the ancients, intended to be rational and final, was very far from liberating the spirit for higher flights: on the contrary, it opened the door to the pervasive tyranny of the world over the soul.

William James, as long as he was a psychologist rather than a philosopher, Santayana followed eagerly. To Santayana he seemed able to feel the very pulse of life, chart the immediacy of sensation in a way that had never been done before. He had a remarkable sense for the "unadulterated, unexplained, instant fact of experience," and a glowing way of putting into words the sensations he had captured. James's studies in abnormal psychology led him to seek the springs of consciousness and conduct in physiological processes. Such a naturalistic psychology served to fortify Santayana's incipient naturalism, and gave to all his thoughts upon psychology what we now have come to call a behavioristic aspect. Ever after, he tried to look behind the mind, and its moral and spiritual ideals, for the physical and material forces which were to him its true matrix, carrying a materialistic interpretation of the universe much further than William James was willing to do. For James believed that consciousness was efficacious, that mind through the energy liberated by attention might move matter, and that the soul of man, working in partnership with God, might rout the forces of evil. This buttressing of religion by means of a free will wrought out of psychological indeterminism seemed to Santayana almost as objectionable as the Protestantism of Royce.

The Harvard department of philosophy offered the student a diversified, comprehensive program, including not only the historical courses of Palmer, James, and Bowen, but also constructive courses in psychology under James, metaphysics under Royce, ethics under Palmer, and philosophy of religion under F. J. Peabody. Special courses were offered by James in the English empiricists, by Palmer in Hegel, and by Royce in Spinoza and Spencer. All of these courses Santayana took, but the greatest impression upon him seems to have been made by the study of Spinoza and the German idealists.

The Germans, particularly Hegel, seemed to Santayana to labor under the same delusion as did Royce, who in many respects put one in mind of them. In one way or another they attempted to soften a relentless nature, cloaking the universe in some sort of absolute or transcendental garment which made it ultimately good and even solicitous of man's welfare. From the first, he says, German philosophy

. . . wore in my eyes a rather questionable shape. Under its obscure and fluctuating tenets I felt something sinister at work, something at once hollow and aggressive. It seemed a forced method of speculation, producing more confusion than it found, and calculated chiefly to enable practical materialists to call themselves idealists and rationalists to remain theologians.*

In spite of the reams of subtle dialectics expended upon it, the philosophy of the German idealists seemed to Santayana a futile, romantic vision.

Not moral life, much less the natural world, but simply the articulation of knowledge occupies them; and yet, by the hocus-pocus of metaphysics,

---

* Cf. the remark of Renan: "There were times when I was sorry that I was not a Protestant, so that I might be a philosopher without ceasing to be a Christian."

they substitute this human experience for the whole universe in which it arises. The universe is to be nothing but a flux of perceptions, or a will positing an object, or a tendency to feign that there is a world.

All their "advances in analysis and in psychological self-knowledge . . . have been neutralized, under the guise of scepticism, by a total intellectual cramp or by a colossal folly." Meanwhile the religion of the Germans

. . . takes the form of piety and affection towards everything homely, imperfect, unstable, and progressive . . . Their idealism is a religion of the actual. It rejects nothing in the daily experience of life, and looks to nothing essentially different beyond. It looks only for more of the same thing, believing in perpetual growth, which is an ambiguous notion.

Subjective in dealing with the external world, materialistic in dealing with the things of the spirit, German philosophy in both instances reverses the insight of the true philosopher. The universe is made over in the image of man not honestly and poetically as in the Christian epic, but with the pretense of scientific or logical validity.

From the transcendentalist's point of view Santayana's criticism is unjust. In the first place, the transcendentalist does not admit an absolute cleavage between the moral and natural orders. With Emerson he feels that they interpenetrate and are part of a larger whole, the Absolute; hence, in establishing their relationship, he is making no compromise, merely expressing a more profound insight into the nature of things. We come here, of course, to a difference in first principles, a Great Divide or watershed in philosophy; both positions are logical given their initial premises, but between these respective premises an insurmountable barrier arises, cutting across the entire field of philosophy. To a strict Catholic impregnated with scholasticism, as to a staunch materialist, transcendentalism is just an impossible point of view. Each considers the other a worthy opponent, but to both the transcendentalist, for that matter the Protestant in general, is merely a man of straw, weakened by concessions and vacillations. So felt Renan in France when he maintained that "outside rigid orthodoxy, there was nothing, so far as I could see, except free thought after the manner of the French school of the eighteenth century." * And from the standpoint of orthodoxy, take Cardinal

---

* Cf. also Charles Eliot Norton in a letter to Carlyle: "To Unitarian Divinity students I conceive there is only one thing possible to say, and that is,—'You can't stay here. You must either go back or go forward.'"

Newman's discussion of the plight of Anglicanism. "It does but occupy the space between contending powers. Catholic Truth and Rationalism. Then indeed will be the stern encounter, when two real and living principles, simple, entire, and consistent, one in the Church, the other out of it, at length rush upon each other, contending not for names and words, or half-views, but for elementary notions and distinctive moral characters."

The impact of this conflict caused Santayana much unhappiness in his youth. For though Catholicism to his way of thinking easily vanquished the sermons of the Unitarian ministers he was taken to hear as a boy, and unsettled the positions of Royce, James, and the Hegelians, when brought up against materialism it was forced to yield ground, at least on the intellectual side. From the earliest he had a deep-seated respect for the claims of materialism. As he has recently stated,

My naturalism or materialism is no academic opinion: . . . it is an everyday conviction which came to me, as it came to my father, from experience and observation of the world at large, and especially of my own feelings and passions. It seems to me that those who are not materialists cannot be good observers of themselves: they may hear themselves thinking, but they cannot have watched themselves acting and feeling; for feeling and action are evidently accidents of matter.

Then, too, Santayana grew up during a period when rationalism and materialism were in the ascendancy. The tide of romanticism had run out, and its conceptions of divinity, the soul, intuition, imagination, were beginning to lose their force and even their meaning. Science was everything; in astronomy, in biology, in archeology, discoveries were constantly being made, unsettling discoveries ruffling the surface of Victorian thought. The scientific method extended in ever widening circles. Buckle showed that national movements were dependent on climate, food, soil. Taine interpreted literary epochs as products of environment. Tylor and Spencer investigated primitive religions, and Francis Newman, Baden Powell, and Bishop Colenso, following the lead of Strauss in Germany, studied the texts of the Bible in the spirit of the higher criticism. Psychology was ridding itself of metaphysics and under the guidance of Bain, Spencer, and the Germans was adopting the methods and gaining the assurance of the physical sciences. It was the aim of John Stuart Mill to carry "into the study of mind and morals, of society and government, the same methods by which the properties of space, the mechanism of the heavens, the composition of matter, and the conditions of animal life had been so successfully unraveled." To integrate the findings of science and to remake philosophy in their light, two systems arose, Comte's positivism and Spencer's synthetic philosophy, both confident in their reliance upon the law of the three stages, that just as metaphysics had succeeded theology, so science would supersede metaphysics.

The decades of the seventies and eighties were the very pinnacle of rationalism and materialism, before the reaction of the nineties set in. They were the decades of Huxley and Leslie Stephen in England, of Taine and Renan in France, of Haeckel and Dühring in Germany, of the *Fortnightly Review,* the *Nineteenth Century,* and the *Revue des Deux Mondes.* At Harvard, Charles Eliot Norton, more than the professors of philosophy, was imbued with this *Zeitgeist.* Secure in his "complete pessimism," he urged G. E. Woodberry "not to be saddened by the imperfection of men and of nature," and took comfort with Leslie Stephen in the thought that they in giving up religion accepted "the irremediable for what it really is," and thus secured "simpler relations with life."

Now Santayana, for all his detachment, kept abreast of the times and could not help absorbing much of this scientific and sceptical spirit. He tells us he read widely in Taine and Matthew Arnold and the *Revue des Deux Mondes* (the last from "cover to cover"). He studied Mill and Spencer in class. Through William James he came in contact with the latest findings of experimental psychology. But perhaps more far-reaching in its influence upon him than anything of the nineteenth century was the work of Spinoza, which he read under Royce with "joy and enthusiasm." It was Spinoza's clear perception of the choice between religious belief and disillusion and his bold choice of the latter which won Santayana's discipleship. Spinoza, like Santayana, believed morality should stand on its own human feet without seeking supernatural support, least of all from a mechanical universe. As Santayana, then a senior, said,

After all, it is a great sacrifice that Spinoza asks us to make when he would have us confess that our approvals and disapprovals are nothing but personal equations; or at most, indications of the needs and interests of the human race. Somehow it gives a man a sense of dignity and self-satisfaction to believe that his interests are those of the universe, and his likes and dislikes those of God; but this faith Spinoza would have us abandon. [For] there is nothing in things to make them better or worse; the difference is in their relation to us . . . all things happen by a uniform law . . . a thing can be understood only by knowing its cause.

And though Santayana felt that Spinoza's ethics were narrow in that they held up intellectual zeal as the only desideratum in life, ignoring the free play of the aesthetic and religious impulses, within the field of philosophical speculation Santayana has always tried to keep out what Spinoza condemns as the personal equation.* There is something poignant in the conclusion of Santayana's essay; it breathes a sad resignation as if the author had faced once and for all grim reality and was not ashamed to accept it on its lowest terms. The mood is partly one of youthful pessimism, but there is a deeper strain too, a sincerity as of a plighted troth. The passage is worth quoting in full, for it explains much that would be otherwise obscure in Santayana's early thought.

I believe that the absolute point of view which Spinoza has so impressively, so overpoweringly enforced cannot be avoided; it is the ocean in which every stream of thought is lost; and for that very reason Spinoza's apparent optimism seems to be deceptive. The final word must always be a contradiction of our ideals, of those ideals which alone make things good or bad. The world becomes one oppressive, tyrannous fact, eternally and inexplicably present. It may be possible to lose one's self in this eternal reality, so as no longer to feel its weight: but why should one wish to do so? It is much easier and much saner to confess once for all what seems to be the truth, and then to go about one's other business, guided by the ideal of one's country and of one's heart.

Five sonnets which appeared in the *Harvard Monthly* during Santayana's senior year reflect his shifting moods before he was able to reach the quiet resignation of the essay on Spinoza. They represent his early philosophy in its most troubled, inchoate state, and reveal the genuine upheavals of spirit he experienced in abandoning the Catholicism of his youth for the naturalism of his ma-

---

* However, a junior forensic of his, entitled "Free Will," shows no such complete acceptance of determinism. In this earlier essay Santayana debates the respective claims of free will and determinism and attempts to reconcile the sense of freedom experienced in the pangs of conscience and in the feeling of responsibility with the determinism implied in the permanence of character. He declares that responsibility is meaningless unless we admit will and intellect as "ultimate elements" rather than assert that they are "swallowed up in mechanical forces of which they are the slowly evolved product." Between the two essays Santayana's point of view seems to have undergone a marked change.

turity. If one thinks of his mature philosophy as marble-like in its rigid purity, one must never forget the inner turbulence these youthful sonnets reveal. There is the mood of defeat, of despair:

> Happy the dumb beast, hungering for food,
> But calling not his suffering his own;
> Blessed the angel, gazing on all good,
> But knowing not he sits upon a throne;
> Wretched the mortal, pondering his mood,
> And doomed to know his aching heart alone.

There is the mood of escape, of forgetfulness:

> I would I had been born in nature's day,
> When man was in the world a wide-eyed boy,
> And clouds of sorrow crossed his sky of joy
> To scatter dewdrops on the buds of May.

There is the mood of doubt, of bewilderment:

> Dreamt I today the dream of yesternight,
> Sleep ever feigning one evolving theme,—
> Of my two lives which should I call the dream?
> Which action vanity? which vision sight?

There is the mood of acceptance, of Stoical piety:

> Love but the formless and eternal Whole
> From whose effulgence one unheeded ray
> Breaks on this prism of dissolving clay
> Into the flickering colours of thy soul.

Stronger than any of these, however, is the mood of loyalty to the "ideal of one's country and of one's heart." In this sonnet the influence of Catholicism is most persistent:

> O world, thou choosest not the better part!
> It is not wisdom to be only wise,
> And on the inward vision close the eyes,
> But it is wisdom to believe the heart.
> Columbus found a world, and had no chart,
> Save one that faith deciphered in the skies;
> To trust the soul's invincible surmise
> Was all his science and his only art.
> Our knowledge is a torch of smoky pine
> That lights the pathway but one step ahead
> Across a void of mystery and dread.

> Bid, then, the tender light of faith to shine
> By which alone the mortal heart is led
> Unto the thinking of the thought divine.

These poems show the cleavage Santayana felt to be between the world of scientific law and the desires of the human heart; and there was cast over him a pessimism not easily dispelled. For a pessimism born of a conflict between one's preferences and one's convictions is deep-seated; neither the intellect nor the heart will yield. Santayana says,

> For my own part, I was quite sure that life was not worth living; for if religion was false everything was worthless, and almost everything, if religion was true. In this youthful pessimism I was hardly more foolish than so many amateur mediaevalists and religious aesthetes of my generation. I saw the same alternative between Catholicism and complete disillusion: but I was never afraid of disillusion, and I have chosen it.

But I believe more than youthful pessimism is to be found in this early work of Santayana's, even though he did steep himself for a time in Schopenhauer and conceive a play whose hero was the grandly melancholy figure of Lucifer. Santayana was experiencing that malady of his age, that nostalgic soul-sickness caused by the retreat of Christianity and the void it had left behind. De Musset and Leopardi, whom he tells us he knew almost by heart, were victims; so were Clough and Matthew Arnold, "wandering between two worlds," with the old "out of date," the new "not yet born." Renan admits that after his renunciation of the faith, "the whole universe seemed to me like an arid and chilly desert. With Christianity untrue everything else appeared to be indifferent, frivolous, and undeserving of interest." Product of a divided heritage and a disillusioned age, Santayana had good grounds for his pessimism, and it was a pessimism founded upon courage and clear vision. But, of course, being a youth, he had "other business" to "go about," his most immediate interest being his graduation from college.

In June 1886 Santayana received his bachelor's degree from Harvard, and put four years of college life behind him, years marked by the transformation of a boy into a man. And though much of his growth and development took place quite independently of his college environment, he was on the whole more closely associated with and more appreciative of the Harvard of his day than his later writings would indicate. The college rather than the graduate and professional schools won Santayana's sympathy, even if he admired Harvard's attempt, as he put it,

> . . . to raise an old-fashioned American college to the level of scholarship, freedom, and decorum which should characterise graduate studies, and at the same time to retain in it, and infuse into a graduate school gathered around it, the corporate traditions, the social life, and the unity of feeling which make the vitality and educational power of the college.

The highest form of education seemed to him "the enlightenment of the pupils through moral discipline." Even in 1920, when his whole point of view in regard to American education had become more cynical, Santayana remembered with some fondness the older type of college which had been the scene of his own education.

It blistered young men's heads for four years and prevented them from practising anything useful; yet at the end they were found able to do most things as well, or twice as well, as their contemporaries who had been all that time apprenticed and chained to a desk. Manhood and sagacity ripen of themselves; it suffices not to repress or distort them. The college liberated the young man from the pursuit of money, from hypocrisy, from the control of women. He could grow for a time according to his nature, and if this growth was not guided by much superior wisdom or deep study, it was not warped by any serious perversion; and if the intellectual world did not permanently entice him, are we so sure that in philosophy, for instance, it had anything to offer that was very solid in itself, or humanly very important? At least he learned that such things existed, and gathered a shrewd notion of what they could do for a man, and what they might make of him.

During the summer vacations Santayana had regularly visited his father in Spain, and as the end of his college course approached, the interest of both turned naturally to the son's choice of an occupation. At first the Spanish army and the Spanish diplomatic service were seriously considered, but the modest influence of Santayana's father commanded few openings, and so these plans were abandoned. The path of least resistance lay in the continuation of study. In the distant future hovered the teaching profession, not the worst of occupations in Santayana's eyes, though it cannot be said to have beckoned him on with any compulsion. For he says,

When I had to choose a profession, the prospect of a quiet academic existence seemed the least of evils. I was fond of reading and observation, and I liked young men; but I have never been a diligent student either of science or art, nor at all ambitious to be learned. . . . Scholarship and learning of any sort seemed to me a means, not an end. I always hated to be a professor.

At any rate, Santayana spent the next three years of his life in graduate study, at the end of which time he received the degree of doctor of philosophy. The first two years he was at the University of Berlin, the concluding year in residence at Harvard.

It was at that time the usual thing for a young scholar to continue his work in Germany. Berlin, in particular, had supplanted Göttingen as the favorite university of those specializing in philosophy, and during the 1880 decade claimed more than a thousand American matriculates. These Americans were treated to an almost unlimited curriculum, library and laboratory facilities beyond any in America, and a roster of world-renowned specialists whom it was possible to know intimately through the seminar system. Yet the intensive study of a German university could not have had great appeal to one who was "not at all ambitious to be learned." Santayana no doubt profited by the advantages of study in Germany, but now as he looks back he likes to remember most what he calls the "life of the wandering student." It is a pleasure to recall the hours spent alone or with good companions in the cafés and beer gardens near his boarding house. Of course, had Santayana been at one of the provincial universities, he would have felt more keenly the local charm of German student life, for, as one commentator remarked,

A student's existence at Berlin is . . . marked by much the same flavourless character as that of a student in the Scotch university towns. Lost in the midst of an ever-increasing population, the Berlin students live on almost unregarded by the surrounding ocean of "philistines" whom they profess to hold in such supreme contempt.

None the less, through his stay in Germany Santayana did come to know the German people, for whom, in spite of their philosophy, he has always had a kindly feeling. "By nature," he later said, "they are simple, honest, kindly, easily pleased. There is no latent irony or disbelief in their souls. The pleasures of sense, plain and copious, they enjoy hugely, long labor does not exasperate them, science fills them with satisfaction, music entrances them. There ought to be no happier or more innocent nation in the world."

Santayana took his graduate study as he had taken his undergraduate, with the same air of gentlemanly leisure. Courses were purely elective; attendance at class was optional; even punctuality was not recognized as a virtue by either lecturer or audience. In short, the academic freedom of the German university was the pattern according to which President Eliot had cut the Harvard cloth. But a graduate student had obligations to his professors back in America when, like Santayana, he expected eventually to receive a degree from them and was at the moment holding a traveling fellowship from Harvard. As time passed, William James, representing his department, began to wonder whether Santayana was spending his time profitably, as became the incumbent of the Walker Fellowship. And with his usual frankness James wrote:

Our fellowships are for helping men to do some definite intellectual thing, and you must expect to have to show next May (if the fellowship is to be continued) that you are on a line of investigation of some sort which is likely to result in something more than a "culture" which to the ordinary committeeman would look vague. I know your ability; and also your way of talking small about yourself. But your ability imposes arduous duties. . . . What you write ought to contain (in addition to the merits of expression and fresh thinking which it certainly will contain) evidence either of considerable research . . . or of original experiment or observation. I can hardly defend your cause in the committee, if on the whole you do not seem pretty definitely working on the lines which lead to philosophical professorships.

But, [wrote Santayana] . . . it is very doubtful that I should ever get a professorship of philosophy anyway, and I hardly care to sacrifice my tastes to that bare possibility . . . what I shall write will certainly not smack so much of a professorship of philosophy as if it were on the normal jerk of the kneepan.

Nevertheless, Santayana claimed to be "quite at ease" about his "duties," stated his intention of asking again for the fellowship, and "by no means" gave himself up as a "bad job." Accordingly, he submitted James a paper, which the latter found "a little too much like a poem," and later offered sufficient evidence of scholarship to win from the committee a renewal of his fellowship.

The upshot of the matter was that Santayana really found very little stimulus in German philosophy or German philosophers. Individual teachers he admired, and a certain empirical approach to philosophy which had succeeded idealism in most of the German universities. Thus he wrote to William James of Professor Gizycki's "vigorous utilitarianism" and his "interesting" lectures on Kant. Hermann Ebbinghaus in psychology he found "an excellent man, very clear and sound"; William James had already familiarized Santayana with the physiological approach to psychology which was at the bottom of Ebbinghaus' investigations. Even more interesting to Santayana was a young *Privatdocent,* Georg Simmel, "sallow and ascetic," who lectured "on pessimism and on contemporary philosophy in its relation with the natural sciences." Simmel was already attacking such formalism as the "catagorical imperative" of Kant, and was looking behind concepts like "duty" to their physical origins in impulse and habit. This materialistic way of interpreting conduct was in keeping with Santayana's own inclination, and was later used by him in formulating the Life of Reason. History, too, Simmel treated in such a way as to rid it of all so-called laws and values: progress, teleology, etc. In general, this relativism of Simmel may have encouraged Santayana to think of ethics, history, religion, and even metaphysics as autonomous creations, constructions of the mind, rather than as revelations of absolute fact. He writes to James,

I confess I do not see why we should be so vehemently curious about the absolute truth, which is not to be made or altered by our discovery of it . . . Philosophy seems to me to be its own reward, and its justification lies in the delight and dignity of the art itself.

But Santayana was not yet ready to bow down before an Unknowable as a desirable or necessary terminus. His dogmatism, both Catholic and naturalistic, was not to be swayed by German any more than by Harvard agnosticism; the authority of science as well as religion might be undermined.

Thus Santayana was out of sympathy with the agnosticism of men like Lange, the materialism of Haeckel and Dühring was only Spinoza more troubled and less pure, and the idealism of Hartmann was but Schopenhauer thinned and secondhand. Santayana did not want to be an investigator in psychology and in time even lost his faith "in psycho-physics, and all the other attempts to discover something very momentous." In desperate tone he writes to James:

My whole experience since I left college and even before, has been a series of disenchantments. . . . What is the use of patience and ingenuity, when the fundamental aim and intention is hopeless and perverse? . . . Indeed, the whole thing has sometimes seemed to me so wrong and futile, that I have suspected that I had made a mistake in taking up philosophy at all, since all the professors of it seemed to be working along so merrily at problems that to me appeared essentially vain.

But there is a ray of consolation.

I have remembered that this very feeling of mine would make as good a ground for a philosophy as any other, if I only had the patience and audacity to work it out.

And so while apparently evading the task which had brought him to Germany, Santayana was all the time laying the foundations for a philosophy which was to be the burden of an entire life and not a mere technical exercise leading to a degree.

And in this larger sense Santayana received the most lasting benefits, not from Ebbinghaus or Simmel or Grimm's "ornamental course . . . on the eighteenth century," but from Friedrich Paulsen. Not that he was in agreement with Paulsen's metaphysics, for the latter believed that mankind was an important part in an "absolute teleological order of things, in a moral world-order, of which the natural order is but an external reflection." That was sheer idealism; what Santayana admired in Paulsen was his ability, much like that of Palmer, to show forth lucidly and sympathetically the character of a whole pageant of civilizations and philosophies. The nineteenth century's penchant for historical reconstruction was evidenced at its finest in Paulsen. In particular, he led Santayana to the fountain of all philosophy, the Greek thinkers, in whom Santayana found a view of life the most permanently satisfying of all he had met.

The Greeks seemed to live without feeling so acutely Santayana's dilemma. Their religion was a gossamer veil thrown over the natural world and over human virtues, both being invested with an allegory whose devices were for the most part transparent. It was a religion which was false neither to man nor to nature, and although it lacked the tragic poignancy and finality of the Catholic epic, it bred a more settled contentment, a happiness of moderation and common sense within the limits of human achievement.

The Greeks in their sanity discovered not only the natural world but the art of living well in it. . . . The Greek naturalists had conceived nature rightly; and their sentiments and maxims, whilst very properly diverse, had all of them a certain noble frankness in the presence of the infinite world, of which they begged no favours.

Nature was essentially understood and honestly described; and . . .

for that very reason, the free mind could disentangle its true good, and could express it in art, in manners, and even in the most refined or the most austere spiritual discipline.

And so we have the paradoxical coincidence that in the country whose philosophy was most distasteful to him, Santayana should have discovered the philosophy to which he could declare his firmest allegiance. "I knew henceforth," he says, "that in the Greeks I should find the natural support and point of attachment for my own philosophy."

In 1888–89 Santayana returned to Harvard to complete his work for the doctorate. He resumed study under William James, "the genial author of *The Principles of Psychology,* chapters of which he read from the manuscript and discussed with a small class of us in 1889." But most of Santayana's time was taken up with work on his dissertation, "Lotze's System of Philosophy." And at the conclusion of the year he was awarded the combined degrees of Doctor of Philosophy and Master of Arts.

Santayana's thesis is a competent piece of critical work, but when viewed in the light of his own philosophy it does not seem particularly important. The keen temper of his irony seems intentionally blunted, for reasons of expediency or kindness it is difficult to say. For with Lotze Santayana had really very little in common. Lotze attempted to square religion with science, and worked out an optimistic compromise which must have seemed to Santayana superficial. But he betrays no impatience with Lotze, and as a result his criticism has a slightly routine, perfunctory character, which is unusual in any writing of Santayana's.

It is easy to see why Santayana chose Lotze as the subject of his thesis. The first sentence of Lotze's *Microcosmos* declares that "between the demands of our emotional nature and the results of human science there is an ancient ever raging strife." This is only saying what Santayana had sadly come to believe since childhood, and what Spinoza had confirmed. Moreover, there was in Lotze a distinctly moral outlook which also won over Santayana just as he was coming under the sway of Greek ethics. There was a recognition of a human standard of worth, of the "significant aims of real, warm-hearted life." Such a life was to be pursued not furtively but frankly.

With Lotze's metaphysics Santayana naturally disagreed. It seemed to him but a patchwork of theism, indeterminism, and teleology.

There were two forces in the universe: God, the principle of order, the beneficent power, and an opposite, capricious agency striving to thwart God and reduce the world to chaos. Much as in William James's philosophy, man was free to ally himself with God and help turn the balance. Eventually all would be well, right would triumph, and man and God would enjoy together the fruits of an enlightened hedonism. This rather childlike philosophy Santayana handles gently indeed. But at the end he asserts what was to become later with him a challenge, almost a creed.

It is unworthy of philosophy to regard affection as evidence, or to contrive a compromise between sentiment and fact. Its business is rather to transform sentiment until it is in harmony with fact, to naturalise the soul in the realm of reality.

How different from William James's opinion of Lotze, "most exquisite of contemporary minds," especially in that he trusts "moral and emotional instincts" as "the best guides to ultimate truth." But, says Santayana,

Had moral impulse in all ages called for the same theories, they surely would have been established and made instinctive long ago, just as belief in other men's consciousness is established and instinctive.

On one count, however, he could exonerate Lotze; unlike most metaphysicians Lotze did not consider this world as yet "the best of possible worlds." He was free from "that sophistry by which some would persuade us that the value of the world does not depend on the good it contains, but that the good itself has value only because it fulfils a necessary function in the universe." Lotze was outside the benevolent monism of traditional German philosophy.

Santayana's thesis was of greatest value to him in affording him an extensive piece of critical work. It served to sharpen his critical faculties, and trained him to grasp a system in its entirety. In point of style the thesis is perhaps one of the best ever written in America. As one turns page after page of the manuscript written out in Santayana's neat, distinguished script, he is constantly distracted from the subtle analysis of ideas by gems of epigram and rolling periods. "The world as an object of experience would be no less picturesque for having a simple explanation." "Those who adore nature in her nakedness should not seek to deck her out in the spoils of an historical deity." "Providence might have had an easier task had Fate been more propitious." Seldom has a piece of routine work been done with so much grace and felicity.

Santayana was admitted to the Harvard department of philosophy in the fall of 1889. He was held to be a young man of extraordinary promise. His grounding in the fundamentals of philosophy had been thorough, his thesis had just been accepted for publication in part by the English philosophical journal, *Mind,* and his power of expression was coming to be recognized in both verse and prose. From his standpoint the career stretching before him at least promised pleasant associations and a quiet academic routine in which he might read and talk and meditate upon the things nearest his heart.

During his years of graduate work Santayana had kept in touch with the *Harvard Monthly,* and a poem of his published in May 1888 and entitled "Two Voices" shows that his outlook on life was becoming clearer and his mood less disturbed. In form a dialogue, it contrasts the fleet footsteps of temporal existence with the permanence of the spiritual and the ideal. One voice is querulous over the past and its relentless encroachment on the present, but the second voice, the more philosophical of the two, challenges, "And who is time to meet us with his measure?"

> The sweet cup I have quaffed is mine forever,
> And mine the bitter draught of precious grief.

Experience does not consist in a vain longing to recall lost moments, but is a treasuring of what the flux of life leaves in its train; bitter or sweet, this residuum is cherished in memory for the growth of the soul. There is something Platonic in such a separation of the permanent from the contingent, and the poem may reflect Santayana's new interest in the Greeks. There is no longer the admonition to "love but the formless and eternal whole." There must be a selection from the whole of only those things which it becomes the human spirit to love. It was as if Santayana saw more distinctly that the only things worth while in life were the pleasures and achievements of the spirit, and that their value was in no sense lessened because their origins were material and their existence transient. A gradual emergence was under way from the pessimism of the sonnets.

In January 1892 the *Harvard Monthly* contained five more sonnets of Santayana in which there is an even more positive affirmation.

Clouds of despair have lifted and the soul begins to discern positive points of attachment in the world about it. The first in the series describes the religious experience Santayana has passed through.

> There was a time when in the teeth of fate
> I flung the challenge of the spirit's right;
> The child, the dreamer of that visioned night,
> Woke, and was humbled unto man's estate.
> A slave I am; on sun and moon I wait,
> Who heed not that I live upon their light.

But resignation, irony, disillusionment are not all. The soul must have some faith to cling to. This it may find to some extent through a confidence in its own intuitions.

> There may be chaos still around the world,
> This little world that in my thinking lies;
> For mine own bosom is the paradise
> Where all my life's fair visions are unfurled.

But even more must its insight into the true status of the natural and the ideal be its support and strength. There is a beauty in the natural world:

> Yet from the seasons hath the earth increase,
> And heaven shines as if the gods were there.
> Had Dian passed there could no deeper peace
> Embalm the purple stretches of the air.

But the ideal world in the true habitation of the emancipated spirit, and the last sonnet is a striking tribute to the Platonism which looks behind appearances for the deeper and inner significance of the ideal.

> Above the battlements of heaven rise
> The glittering domes of the gods' golden dwelling,
> Whence, like a constellation, passion-quelling,
> The truth of all things feeds immortal eyes.
> There all forgotten dreams of paradise
> From the deep caves of memory upwelling,
> All tender joys beyond our dim foretelling
> Are ever bright beneath the flooded skies.
> There we live o'er, amid angelic powers,
> Our lives without remorse, as if not ours,
> And others' lives with love, as if our own;
> For we behold, from those eternal towers,

> The deathless beauty of all winged hours,
> And have our being in their truth alone.

Such an insight shows to the discriminating mind "the high perfection from which nature strays," and Santayana is able to say with a new assurance:

> I loved, and lost my love among mankind;
> But I have found it after many days.
> Oh, trust in God, and banish rash despair,
> That, feigning evil, is itself the curse!
> My angel is come back, more sad and fair,
> And witness to the truth of love I bear,
> With too much rapture for this sacred verse,
> At the exceeding answer to my prayer.

The spiritual experience is complete. No longer is the whole world "ashes in the mouth" if religion is false; the natural world and the realm of spirit conceived rightly may breed a more humble faith, but one all the more satisfying through its very sober disillusionment.

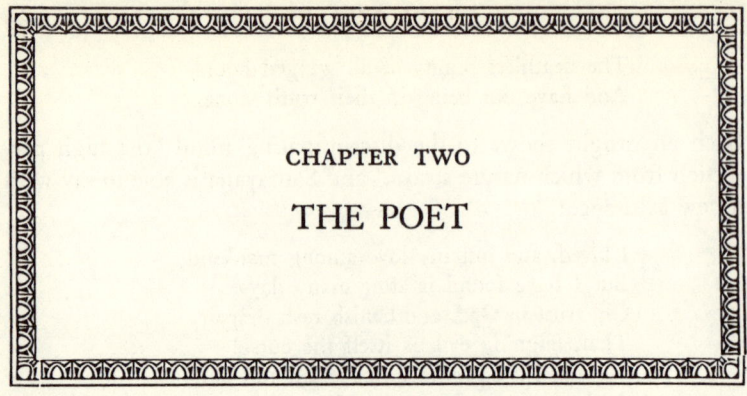

CHAPTER TWO

THE POET

When Santayana began to teach philosophy at Harvard in the fall of 1889, he was entrusted with two well-established courses regularly given by the older members of the department: a course in English philosophy from Hobbes to Hume, given from 1875 to 1882 by Professor Palmer and from 1883 to 1889 by Professor James, and a course in French and German philosophy which Professor Bowen, then retiring, had given for twenty years. These two courses Santayana continued to teach throughout the first decade of his instruction, the latter being entitled, after the first year, "Descartes, Spinoza, Leibniz." They were supplemented, however, in his second year of teaching by another important trust, part of the introductory course in philosophy, which according to a well-defined policy was always given by the best men in the department. Santayana was first assigned (curiously enough in view of his later work, but not in view of his training) the section on psychology; the next year he was shifted to the section on the history of philosophy, which he taught until 1895–96. In his third year of teaching Santayana found an opportunity for more creative work when he was asked to organize a course in aesthetics, a field of philosophy hitherto neglected by the department. In this course "he developed the psychology of taste with reference to the history of aesthetic theories. He presented also the origin and elements of aesthetic judgments and traced the bearing of the more important philosophical theories upon the development of aesthetic feeling." His temperament, his interest in the fine arts, his skill at verse and drawing equipped him admirably for work in aesthetics, and the outcome of the course was his first systematic treatise in philosophy, *The Sense of Beauty,* published in 1896. Meanwhile, in 1893–94 Santayana had conducted his first seminar, in scholasticism, a philosophy with which his Catholic training had long made him familiar. A sabbatical year in 1896–97, which he spent at Cambridge, England, brought to an end the first period of his teaching, a period devoted mainly to aesthetics and the history of philosophy.

But during the nineties Santayana had not yet made his mark as a teacher; he was known rather as a young Spanish poet, mysteriously exotic and more than a little under the spell of *fin de siècle* aestheticism. His life on the campus accentuated this impression. Instead of marrying and settling down to raise a family, Santayana continued to associate with undergraduates who were well born and aesthetically inclined; in fact, his way of life differed not a whit from what it had been when he was an undergraduate. "In student dormitories," Miss Münsterberg tells us, "he made his abode. At first he lived in old Stoughton Hall in the Harvard Yard, and ate his meals at one of the private students' clubs." Later he "had rooms in a made-over private house in Brattle Street, and finally . . . in Prescott Hall, a modest dormitory only a block away from the philosophy building, Emerson Hall, where he gave his lectures." At this time he ate at the "Colonial Club, an old Cambridge house, frequented by professors, some of whom met there regularly at lunch time."

Santayana was a member of Hasty Pudding, Delta Phi fraternity, the English Club, and a French club composed of young men "who met at the members' rooms to read aloud, until the club was disbanded because they could no longer endure one another's French." With the "Harvard Poets" of his day he was particularly intimate, especially with Joseph Stickney. And when Thomas Sanborn, his associate on the original *Monthly* Board, committed suicide, it was Santayana who composed the gracefully touching obituary notice for the magazine. The untimely death of one of his favorite students likewise moved him deeply, and the four sonnets to "W. P." are eloquent testimony to this friendship.

Off the campus Santayana's life was spent largely with his mother and sister, whom he visited with punctual regularity at their home in Brookline. "To them he was devoted, and through continual contact with them he must have kept constantly fresh the spring of his Spanish associations, which otherwise might have dried on Cambridge soil. To his Cambridge friends his Spanish family, who evidently lived in retirement, was wholly unknown," and Santayana seemed to discourage any efforts to penetrate the privacy which surrounded them.

But there were times when he was drawn into certain eddies of Cambridge society, much as he disliked "the small irksome obligations of social life." There was at one time almost a Santayana cult of admiring Cambridge ladies, who considered it fashionable to invite to their salons the young Spanish poet so alien to the reigning Cambridge mode.

When his first slender volume of sonnets appeared, a charming and vivacious Cambridge woman gave the little book a birthday party. The poet requited his hostess and the other guests with graceful little verses in their honor. Occasionally he even entertained them at tea in his bachelor rooms.

Santayana found the Münsterberg home particularly to his liking, for Hugo Münsterberg was exactly his age, a foreigner, and somewhat of a poet and musician. With him Santayana was more intimate than with any other member of the philosophy department. Margaret Münsterberg tells of one evening at her home when Santayana electrified the gathering by reading from his newly completed verse-drama, "Lucifer."

Santayana's life at Harvard was certainly not that of a solitary thinker. However, in spite of these social amenities, there emanated from him an air of mystery which made him seem a strange figure to many, and gave birth to curious rumors and misconceptions. Some of these were childishly silly; others more grave. Miss Münsterberg tells how awestruck she was as a young girl upon hearing that Santayana was reputed to be—of all things—a solipsist, "a man who has the audacity to believe that he is the only soul alive." Philip Littell speaks of how mystified the undergraduates of the nineties were at the occasional appearance of Santayana's sonnets in the *Monthly*. Some reflections from his aesthetic temperament or his aloofness seem even to have cast an unfavorable light upon his chances for professional advancement. When in 1897 the question of appointing Santayana to an assistant professorship arose, President Eliot hesitated to make the necessary recommendation. He said,

The withdrawn, contemplative man who takes no part in the everyday work of the institution, or of the world, seems to me a person of very uncertain value. He does not dig ditches, or lay bricks, or write school-books, his product is not of the ordinary useful, though humble, kind. What will it be? It may be something of the highest utility;

but, on the other hand, it may be something futile, or even harmful because unnatural and untimely.

President Eliot wavered, but James urged the appointment, calling Santayana "a very honest and unworldly character . . . a man . . . of thoroughly wholesome mental atmosphere." Royce, too, and Hugo Münsterberg pleaded Santayana's cause. Münsterberg spoke eloquently of Santayana's work in the department both as a teacher and as an author. He also insisted that his colleague was a "strong and healthy man," a "good, gay, fresh companion." President Eliot finally yielded, though he admitted he could not imagine Santayana a professor at fifty, prophetically enough the very age when Santayana finally renounced his calling.

The root of all rumors and misconceptions was of course Santayana's detachment. As Miss Münsterberg says, "His was the modesty of one who has plenty of humor and few illusions. He was capable of taking a bird's eye view of society, and, without dizziness, seeing his own small place on the map." As a result, "one did not expect to see him in a crowd, at a business meeting, in a hurry to catch a train for an appointment or otherwise going through the motions of a busy man in the whirl of the world's work." And indeed he sedulously kept out of committee work, had no inclination for executive or administrative duties, and apart from his routine teaching delivered only an occasional lecture. "If he was so different a type," says one of his later associates, "it was not so much because he came out of another world as because in a certain sense he resolutely kept living in another world, the world of his taste, his philosophy, and his poetry." Particularly in the last was he able to find the satisfaction such a nature as his demanded.

There was surely more to Santayana's reputation as a writer in the nineties than glamour and mystery. The articles and reviews he was writing for the *Harvard Monthly* and the *New World* were firm and solid. The latter magazine, which had a happy existence from 1892 to 1900, though a commercial publication, was considerably under the Harvard wing. Of its four editors two were professors in the Divinity School—C. C. Everett and Crawford H. Toy—and its contributors and reviewers numbered many distinguished names among the faculty. Among foreign contributors were the biologist Lloyd Morgan, the aesthetician Bernard Bosanquet, the philosophers

F. C. S. Schiller, Lawrence P. Jacks, and Edward Caird, the novelists Mrs. Humphry Ward and May Sinclair. And from other American universities came Morris Jastrow, C. M. Bakewell, John Dewey, and Paul Elmer More. It was thus among distinguished company that Santayana first came to the attention of the public as a capable critic and essayist.

To the *New World* Santayana contributed several book reviews and three articles: "The Present Position of the Roman Catholic Church" (an attack upon modernism in religion), "The Absence of Religion in Shakespeare," and "Greek Religion." The *Harvard Monthly* during the nineties contained essays of Santayana entitled "Walt Whitman: a Dialogue," "What Is a Philistine?" "A Glimpse of Yale," "Philosophy on the Bleachers," "Memories of King's College, Cambridge," and "The Decay of Latin." To the *Educational Review* he also contributed "The Spirit and Ideals of Harvard University," and to the *Atlantic Monthly* an unsigned review of William James's *Psychology*.* These titles alone show the variety of Santayana's interests and the versatility of his pen. The critical pieces are throughout penetrating and candid, as in some of the unfavorable judgments of James, and at times distinctly unorthodox, as in the condemnation of Shakespeare for his lack of a religious and philosophical outlook. The "educational" pieces show keen observation, a pleasant vein of reminiscence, and a style poised and trenchant. There is in all these pieces the graceful irony of the later Santayana.

It is the privilege of Englishmen to live all over the world and to remain everywhere themselves, and they can hardly be expected to carry anything away from Egypt except an added appreciation of the freshness of their own fields and hedgerows, and of the sweet austerity of their own homes.

Even Prussian is not necessarily a term of abuse; anyone except a Frenchman might use it simply to denote a fact of civil allegiance, and to the ears of a corporal or a schoolmaster it might even have a glorious sound.

There is the swift, summarizing epigram. "We have a purified Christianity without authority and a scientific Latin without function." "The Greek world is a realm apart, a realm of quietness, definiteness, and self-contained beauty." "You feel that the inmates [of New Haven] must be worthy people, all the nicer for not having

---

* Santayana pointed out to the present writer that James was quick to identify the author because of the style and the spirited objections to some of James's conclusions.

thriven inordinately and gone to live in New York." There is even the germ of the miniature essay which was to grow into the exquisite "Soliloquies in England."

There is a certain spiritualizing influence in the expanse of waters, which carries the eye and the imagination at once to the clear horizon, and tempts the sailor and merchant beyond it. Voyaging teaches us comparison, and, by revealing the many diversities of life which are possible in this circumnavigable world, breeds a certain noble humility founded upon self-knowledge, and a certain tender and pathetic patriotism, which is not so much a repulsion for the alien as a returning love for the peaceful, comfortable, and familiar. For there are two stages in patriotism as there are two in love. In the first we are proud of our country or our mistress for what we claim her superlative beauties and unrivaled virtues; in the second, we prefer her to all those who outshine her, simply because she is our own.

Santayana in the nineties was beginning to feel his strength as a writer of prose, but he was still inclined to commit to verse his most intimate and important utterances. Between 1894 and 1901 appeared in four small volumes all of the verse he has cared to preserve in book form, so that within the compass of seven years a reader might have read practically the entire poetic output of Santayana. Like Matthew Arnold's, Santayana's poetic spring seemed to dry up in later years under the breath of philosophy and criticism. Perhaps it is more just to say that his creative faculties have been used up in the construction of a system of metaphysics in itself an imaginative flight not unworthy of a great poet. At any rate, he has published only nine poems since 1901.

The themes of Santayana's poetry are neither numerous nor varied. The subject of most of them is, as he says, "simply my philosophy in the making"; all of them, at least the non-dramatic poems, are more or less closely related to the central philosophy which is their inspiration. The most widely known are those sonnets which made up the bulk of his first book, *Sonnets and Other Verses,* a thin volume published in 1894 by the new and enterprising firm of Stone and Kimball, two Harvard men with offices in Cambridge and Chicago. The edition was limited to 450 copies (today it is somewhat of a rarity), with title-page designed by the author. In arranging his sonnets, Santayana took the ten previously published in the *Harvard Monthly,* added ten more, and worked the whole into a loosely woven narrative sequence. The individual sonnets reflect passing moods, however, rather than the orderly progress of a story. Each may be read by and for itself without much thought for its place in the sequence, and to attempt to link each sonnet with an episode in Santayana's life is profitless, if not impossible. The dates 1883-93 appended to the sequence show that the poems were composed over a considerable time and thus do not stand for any transient incident. Rather they pay tribute to the most momentous event of Santayana's whole life, his renunciation of Catholicism in favor of naturalism, and are, as Conrad would have said, the most "anxiously meditated" of all his verse, and probably his finest poetical achievement.

A careful reader will first observe that the sequence falls into four parts.* Sonnets 1, 2, and 20 are explanatory and were written last to form an introduction and conclusion, to frame the picture, as it were. Sonnets 3 to 7 reflect a mood of desperation, when the mantle of the new philosophy is yet to rest gracefully on the shoulders of the poet, and the fabric of the old is still a thing to be longed for. These sonnets are the "dumb misgivings" and "questionings of nature" referred to in sonnet 2, together with some of the "farewell pious looks behind" and "holy echoes" of the "ancient sorrow." The depth of sorrow seems to be reached in sonnet 7, for sonnet 8 is in an entirely different key, and the poet seems chastened and subdued after his complaint of the previous sonnet. Nature is again raised aloft, and the poet, after paying homage to her majesty, points out that sadness and grief are inevitably intertwined with joy, and it is the part of wisdom to take from nature both "dregs and honeyed brim" and to admire her "for sweetening not the draught." No evil is eternal in its duration, and grief itself has the power of cleansing the spirit. Sonnet 10 is even more vehement in its rebuke.

> Doth the sun therefore burn, that I may bask?
> Or do the tired earth and tireless sea,
> That toil not for their pleasure, toil for me?

Calm has supervened upon the poet's anguish, and he is more willing to accept whatever lot nature has in store for him. Despair is suc-

---

* The original arrangement of the sonnets in the *Harvard Monthly* was, according to the final numbering, 7, 5, 6, 3, 4 (1885-1886); 17, 16, 14, 18, 19 (1892). Sonnets 8 to 12 did not appear at all in the *Monthly*, but have a homogeneity of thought and mood which suggests that they were written all at the same time. Interestingly enough, this division of the sequence on the basis of publication coincides with a division on a basis of emotional tone. For the place of the sonnets in relation to the evolution of Santayana's thought see above, pp. 27-29.

ceeded by resignation, and by sonnet 11 the poet has discovered his lot and fixed his attitude toward life.

> For some are born to be beatified
> By anguish, and by grievous penance done;
> And some, to furnish forth the age's pride,
> And to be praised of men beneath the sun;
> And some are born to stand perplexed aside
> From so much sorrow—of whom I am one.

With this discovery the burden is lifted and the poet cries out,

> Farewell, my burden! No more will I bear
> The foolish load of my fond faith's despair,
> But trip the idle race with careless feet.

This note of affirmation is joyfully carried on to the conclusion of the sequence. Sonnets 14 and 15 are tributes to the integrity of the inner life, "this little world that in my thinking lies"; these sonnets have a peculiar winsomeness, a beauty all their own. The remaining sonnets celebrate the abiding satisfaction Santayana finds in his new love.

Such beauty is not to be scorned because of its natural origin, for

> . . . heaven shines as if the gods were there.
> Had Dian passed there could no deeper peace
> Embalm the purple stretches of the air.

After all,

> The soul is not on earth an alien thing
> That hath her life's rich sources otherwhere;
> She is a parcel of the sacred air.

There have been few finer tributes to naturalism, ordinarily an unpoetic philosophy, than this sonnet sequence of Santayana's. Of course, the love of beauty and of the ideal is Platonic, but it is able to stand firm on its natural foundations and yet call forth that pure zeal, that devotion more often evoked by the supernatural and the mystical.

Several other poems in Santayana's first volume strike much the same note as that of the sonnet sequence. A beautiful sonnet, "Gabriel," reveals again the conflict over religion between the poet's mind and heart. In "Easter Hymn" and "Good Friday Hymn" the same theme is treated. These three poems of all Santayana's verse are the most Catholic in imagery and allusion.

> I love the pious candle-light,
> The boys' fresh voices, void of thought,
> The woman's eager, inward sight
> Of what in vain her heart had sought.
>
> . . . .
>
> I love the Virgin's flowering shrine,
> Her golden crown, her jewelled stole,
> The seven dolorous swords that shine
> Around her heart, an aureole.
>
> . . . .
>
> Perchance when Carnival is done,
> And sun and moon go out for me,
> Christ will be God, and I the one
> That in my youth I used to be.

And yet the poet is not sure.

> Sing softly, choristers; ye sing
> Not faith alone, but doubt and dread.
> Ring wildly, Easter bells; ye ring
> For Christ arisen, and hope dead.

The other hymn is more resigned and suggests the solution arrived at in the sonnet sequence.

> My soul's Lord, too, paid life with death,
> And empty was her wide abode;
> She saw her child yield up his breath,
> She knew the passing of her God.
>
> And she said: Lord, since thou art gone,
> Thou canst my love no farther prove;
> But while I live each flower and stone
> Shall bear thy name and prove my love.

These three poems were never reprinted after the 1896 edition of Santayana's verse, but, together with some of the sonnets, they bring us very close to the fountain-head of Santayana's religion, to a time when his opinions were still unsettled and he lacked the calm assurance of middle age.

But Santayana in this early volume looked not only inward but outward, and his vision found much in the world to plunge the soul into despair. A vehement dissatisfaction with modern civilization is found in the five "Sapphic" odes of Santayana. The first longs for "a chamber in an eastern tower," where amid the color and pageantry of the Orient the poet may dream awhile and

> . . . ease a little
> The soul long stifled and the straitened spirit,
> Tasting new pleasures in a far off country
> Sacred to beauty.

The reason for this wish is clear from the next ode:

> My heart rebels against my generation,
> That talks of freedom and is slave to riches,
> And, toiling 'neath each day's ignoble burden,
> Boasts of the morrow.
>
> No space for noonday rest or midnight watches,
> No purest joy of breathing under heaven!
> Wretched themselves, they heap, to make them happy,
> Many possessions.

This is a theme often found in Santayana's prose, especially in the early essays, "Philosophy on the Bleachers" and "What Is a Philistine?" and it is repeated in ode 3, with a lengthy preamble delineating the history of America. Contrasted with the money-mad Philistine is the simple ploughman (the subject of the shortest and possibly the most beautiful ode) whose "patience is good for man and beast," whose humble life is a lesson to the wisest philosophers. Ode 5 is a lengthy and elaborate panegyric, addressed to that queen of seas, the Mediterranean. If even the Northman was moved to love thee, says Santayana,

> The more should I, O fatal sea, before thee
> Of alien words make echoes to thy music;
> For I was born where first the rills of Tagus
> Turn to the westward,
>
> And wandering long, alas! have need of drinking
> Deep of the patience of thy perfect sadness,
> O thou that constant through the change of ages,
> Beautiful ever,
>
> Never wast wholly young and void of sorrows,
> Nor ever canst be old, while yet the morning

> Kindles thy ripples, or the golden evening
>   Dyes thee in purple.

There is a marked pessimism in these odes, more far-reaching and desperate than in the sonnets, since the sensitive soul of the poet is bruised more by the outer world than in its own communings. The height of this pessimism is reached in ode 3. The poet believes that future generations, if they still remember this present "spawn of ant-like creatures,"

> Our wisdom and our travail and our sorrow,
> They never can be happy, with that burden
>   Heavy upon them.
>
> Knowing the hideous past, the blood, the famine,
> The ancestral hate, the eager faith's disaster,
> All ending in their little lives, and vulgar
>   Circle of troubles.
>
> But if they have forgot us, and the shifting
> Of sands has buried deep our thousand cities,
> Fell superstition then will seize upon them;
>   Protean error,
>
> Will fill their panting heart with sickly phantoms
> Of sudden blinding good and monstrous evil;
> There will be miracles again, and torment,
>   Dungeon, and fagot,—

There is no escape

> Until the patient earth, made dry and barren,
> Sheds all her herbage in a final winter,
> And the gods turn their eyes to some far distant
>   Bright constellation.

The wise man will soak himself in beauty (ode 1), or pause to watch quiet, patient labor (ode 4), or contemplate the calm majesty of nature (ode 5), or, better yet, search for what is eternal among the fleeting moments of temporal existence (ode 2).

> What better comfort have we, or what other
>   Profit in living,

> Than to feed, sobered by the truth of Nature,
> Awhile upon her bounty and her beauty,
> And hand her torch of gladness to the ages
>   Following after?
>
> She hath not made us, like her other children,
> Merely for peopling of her spacious kingdoms,
> Beasts of the wild, or insects of the summer,
>   Breeding and dying,
>
> But also that we might, half knowing, worship
> The deathless beauty of her guiding vision,
> And learn to love, in all things mortal, only
>   What is eternal.

If Santayana should ever devise a testament to humanity, no lines could sum up its burden more eloquently than the Platonic conclusion of the second ode.

The first volume of Santayana's contained also several miscellaneous sonnets on art and philosophy and the four sonnets written upon the death of a favorite student. The latter reveal a genuine sorrow, although they are burdened with much conventional figure and rhetoric.

The few reviews of *Sonnets and Other Verses* were for the most part favorable and encouraging. The *Literary World* of Boston found the poems "profoundly true," "finely expressed," with little of the joy that comes "with wider vision," but with a "serious calm," in its way "a thing as good." The *Atlantic Monthly* considered them "somewhat lacking root in homely earth," but found the plane on which they moved "high and pure." Their peculiar brand of pessimism, however, gave rise to some regrets on the part of the reviewers. The *Literary World* sighed for a "clear, final strain that might signify a buoyant acceptance of conditions, or even a daring challenge to the unknown and the unseen." The *Harvard Graduates' Magazine* felt that the "sin and wretchedness and incompleteness of life offend" the author's "taste rather than his moral nature," and thought that he suffered from a mild case of "Walter Paterism." Santayana's pessimism, however, was not a pose but the result of a sensitiveness which, if youthful, was at least sincere. And was it not better that the poet, as the *Literary World* pointed out, "should remain true to himself than that he should utter the word of a conventionalized hope."

Santayana was thus accepted by Boston—if with reservations. To the rest of the country he was still unknown, and the fact that his first sheaf of poems brought so little critical recognition outside of Boston was really no fault of his own. His début was made in a harvest of poetic plenty. At about the same time appeared Thomas Bailey Aldrich's *Unguarded Gates,* William Watson's *Odes and Minor Poems,* Gilder's *Five Books of Song,* Yeats's *Land of Heart's Desire,* Tabb's *Poems,* and Hayne's *Sylvan Lyrics.*

As we look back now upon Santayana's first book of verse, we see that for all his individuality and detachment not a little of his age has crept into his poetry; not every impulse came to him from within or from afar. His was too sensitive a nature not to be touched by the aesthetic movement of the eighties and nineties. It is true that the full force of this movement was not felt across the Atlantic; not only the Anthony Comstocks and the Frances Willards, but a cultivated gentleman like Charles Eliot Norton would go out of his way to avoid meeting Oscar Wilde, and would write to his daughter of the "wretched" Yellow Book ". . . vile place for a manly, hearty genuine-English poem." New England was still basking in the afterglow of the Golden Day and hardly had eyes for any moon rising out over the Atlantic. Even many of the younger generation thought the Symbolists and their followers in England decadent and effete, and were willing with Richard Hovey to "let the age be damned." None the less, in their own way the young Harvard poets were distinctly a product of the age, and Santayana, with his foreign residence and his intimate knowledge of French literature, was of all of them the most cosmopolitan and open to influence from abroad. In him there were no Puritan inhibitions to be overcome, no robust Americanisms fighting for mastery. He was a Latin, a poet, an aesthete.

He expresses his age in the first place by adding his voice to that insistent protest on the part of the emancipated against the material things of an increasingly material civilization. Falling back upon Matthew Arnold's definition of culture, these rebels fought resolutely against the popular worship of the instruments rather than the ends of civilization.* "Philistine" became their battle cry, a piercing word

---

* Santayana's attitude toward wealth, industry, athletics, in general, the whole machinery of life, is anticipated in Matthew Arnold, at times in very similar language: Culture "places human perfection in an *internal* condition." "The human spirit is wider than the most priceless of the forces which bear it onward." "Human life in the hands of Hellenism is invested with a kind of aerial ease, clearness, and radiancy; . . . the beauty and rationalness of the ideal have all our thoughts."

intended to dichotomize once and for all the cosmos. In America, where felt at all, the issue was all the more sharply drawn. Norton could say, "Nowhere in the civilized world are the practical concerns of life more engrossing; nowhere are the conditions of life more prosaic; nowhere is the poetic spirit less diffused." So, too, Santayana wrote "What Is a Philistine?" attacking conventionality and spiritual indifference. "Avila" and the second Sapphic ode, "My heart rebels against my generation," say the same thing in verse. But Santayana did not extend his protest as far or as indiscriminately as did many of the rebels of his generation. Certainly the naturalist in Santayana could not follow Villiers de l'Isle Adam in condemning science, nor could the future author of a Life of Reason say with Arthur Symons that our only chance of happiness lies "in shutting the eyes of the mind." The eighties and nineties were trying to rid themselves of the Victorian obsession with intellectuality as well as with morality, but Santayana had no Victorian roots to pull up, and his main stalk of naturalism was too deeply planted to be loosened by the sensationalism of the age.

However, in turning his back upon the world, Santayana did hunt out those places of refuge sought by the fleeing aesthetes of his time. One such haven was beauty. Under the impetus of Ruskin and Pater, beauty was cultivated in a way new to England and America. There was in the eighties an amazing revival of interest in the art and literature of the Italian Renaissance, and a poet like Shelley became, says one commentator, the idol of the generation, "more than a literary taste . . . almost a religion." Even cynics like Anatole France could admonish, "Since all is illusion and truth escapes us, let us pursue beauty." Thus, when Santayana does homage to "subtle Beauty, sweet persuasive worth . . . Thirsting for thee, we die in thy great dearth," he is echoing the cry of his generation. Most typically *fin de siècle* of all his poems are "Sybaris," with its Eastern pageantry, and his first Sapphic ode, which begins,

> What god will choose me from this labouring nation
> To worship him afar, with inward gladness,
> At sunset and at sunrise, in some Persian
>   Garden of roses;
>
> Or under the full moon, in rapturous silence,
> Charmed by the trickling fountain, and the moaning
> Of the death-hallowed cypress, and the myrtle
>   Hallowed by Venus?

> O for a chamber in an eastern tower,
> Spacious and empty, roofed in odorous cedar,
> A silken soft divan, a woven carpet
>   Rich, many-coloured . . .

But a great deal of his verse in imagery and mood reveals what the Harvard critic aptly termed a mild case of Paterism.

Santayana, however, kept close to the more restrained aestheticism of Ruskin and Pater and avoided the exotic extremes of both his French and English contemporaries. The bizarre was to him merely romantic barbarism, amiable at best but trifling always. The abnormal and the immoral were likewise outside the province of art as he was defining it in *The Sense of Beauty*. He did not believe, as did many men of his age, that everything was to be sacrificed before the claims of feeling, that gem-like flames were to be fanned in every corner for the world to see. Thus, placed beside the work of the French Symbolists or their English followers, Santayana's work seems singularly chaste and austere. He wrote of love, but he could hardly say with Verlaine, "J'ai la fureur d'aimer." Like many of his contemporaries, for Catholicism was suddenly fashionable, he wrote of the Church and her mysteries and symbols. But there is no intense feeling in Santayana's religious verse comparable to Verlaine's "My God, thou hast wounded me with love," or Francis Thompson's "I fled Him, down the nights and down the days." He might echo Huysmans' words, "Lord, have pity of the Christian who doubts, of the sceptic who would fain believe," but he could not rush to embrace in a surge of mysticism the very faith his mind rejected.

In general, Santayana shared his age's enthusiasms for beauty, for the Catholic Church, for medievalism, but he shared them with restraint and sobriety. And though like most of his contemporaries he was searching for the ideal, he expected the imaginative power of the mind itself to dissociate the ideal from the actual without recourse to elaborate sensuous symbols or overwrought mystical raptures. The thought in some of his poems is abstruse, but he is rarely guilty of what Symons called "over-subtilizing refinement upon refinement." He is most like certain quieter eddies outside the main current of the age, the more reflective moments of Ernest Dowson or Lionel Johnson, when the former is celebrating the institutions of the Church or the latter is recording in verse his fondness for the classics.* Lionel Johnson was indeed a friend of Santayana's and his tender rebuff to Santayana's naturalism may well stand as the rebuke of his age.

> Exiled in America
> From thine own Castilia,
> Son of holy Avila!
> Leave thine endless tangled lore,
> As in childhood to implore
> Her, whose pleading evermore
> Pleads for her own Avila.
> . . . .
> Leave the false light, leave the vain:
> Lose thyself in Night again,
> Night divine of perfect pain.
> Lose thyself, and find thy God.

It is clear, then, that Santayana was of his age, and yet in every respect with certain reservations. Perhaps it is more just to say that the latter years of the nineteenth century furnished an environment particularly conducive to poetry such as Santayana's, but that for the most part Santayana expressed his age more in his long Spanish cloak, his fondness for pictures of the saints, and his attendance at *salons* than in what he actually put on paper. With all the manner-

---

* Certain stanzas actually suggest Santayana in imagery and phrasing, for instance, the opening lines of Ernest Dowson's "Carthusians":
> "Through what long heaviness, assayed in what strange fire,
> Have these white monks been brought into the way of peace,
> Despising the world's wisdom and the world's desire,
> Which from the body of this death bring no release?
>
> "Within their austere walls no voices penetrate;
> A sacred silence only, as of death, obtains;
> Nothing finds entry here of loud or passionate;
> This quiet is the exceeding profit of their pains."

Or Lionel Johnson's "Lucretius," which anticipates Santayana's treatment of Lucifer:
> "Visions, to sear with flame his worn and haunted eyes,
> Throng him: and fears unknown invest the black night hours
> His royal reason fights with undefeated Powers,
> Armies of mad desires, legions of wanton lies;
> His ears are full of pain, because of their fierce cries:
> Nor from his tended thoughts, for all their fruits and flowers,
> Comes solace: for Philosophy within her bowers
> Falls faint, and sick to death. Therefore Lucretius dies."

isms of the aesthete, Santayana had a sterner side, a stability, which kept his life and his verse from the extravagances of the decadents.

Yet I should not maintain, as some critics have done, that Santayana's verse could have been written in any age or country, that it is universal and timeless. It seems to me to presuppose a long literary tradition and particularly a period of changing ideals and sober disillusionment such as marked the nineteenth century. His, says Santayana, is the hand of "an apprentice in a great school." "A Muse—not exactly an English Muse—actually visited me in my isolation; the same, or a ghost of the same, that visited Boethius or Alfred de Musset or Leopardi." It is of course easy to press these parallels too far, for Santayana is not a slavish imitator of any one, but he shows his usual discernment in selecting his literary forbears. Boethius' disillusionment, unlike Santayana's, represents a turning away from fame and riches; still he achieves peace through the true wisdom philosophy brings. Boethius has been a companion to all those who have sought to ease a troubled soul in contemplation. But De Musset and Leopardi are nearer to Santayana; in their disillusionment the scepticism of their age, the loosening hold of religion, plays a large part. De Musset, says Santayana, best represents a whole group of French Catholics who express "regret and tenderness for a faith . . . entirely lost. He has expressed more perfectly than perhaps any one else the attitude common among men of intelligence and feeling in Catholic countries toward their church—an attitude of estrangement not unmixed with self-accusation and discouragement." This is unmistakably Santayana's attitude, and he belongs with these men rather than with the positivists and agnostics outside the church. How well these lines of De Musset express what Santayana himself felt so bitterly:

> I am not one, O Christ, who dwells within thy fold;
> Too late have I set foot within a world too old.
> The earth has long outgrown her superstitious youth,
> And sought and found the things of a material truth,
> And 'mid the ruined temples of long-vanished days
> The phantoms of her Faith in veiled silence stays.

But Leopardi is even nearer to Santayana; there is in both the same note of quiet melancholy, the same sceptical questioning, for Leopardi, like Santayana, felt a profound spiritual estrangement from the life and the religion of his fellow countrymen. Unlike Santayana, he was driven further into himself by the tyranny of an excessively pious father. His birthplace came to seem provincial, his boyhood faith suspect, and the larger world, particularly Rome, corrupt and frivolous. There is thus in his poetry an otherworldliness and a sad resignation akin to the prevailing mood of Santayana's first sonnet sequence. But Santayana never felt the intense emotion or gave way to the tragic pessimism of Leopardi:

>   this earth
> Deserveth not a sigh! Bitter is life
> And wearisome, nought else;
> The world's defiled!
> Despair for the last time and then be still!
> Fate made us at our birth no gift save death.

The optimism of the Greeks, the idealism of Plato and of the Catholic church, made such a view of life untenable for Santayana beyond a momentary impulse.

These brightening influences are felt even more in his next poetical venture, which turned for inspiration to an age far removed from both Boston and the modern world. Santayana had long been interested in the Italian poets of the Renaissance and the Platonic love expressed in their lives and work, and in 1895 and 1896 this interest seems to have claimed most of his creative energy. He lectured on the subject before a slightly shocked audience of women in Buffalo, then published in a Founders' number of the *Harvard Monthly* (October 1895) ten sonnets in the Italian manner. Finally, in 1896 appeared a reprint of *Sonnets and Other Verses,* with an additional sequence of thirty love sonnets, including the ten from the *Monthly.*

The story beneath these sonnets is rather elusive.* Sonnets 34 to 37 are clearly autobiographical and point to a particular young woman as the immediate source of inspiration. Who she was will probably remain a secret, and for an appreciation of the poems the fact of her existence is enough. Santayana, now looking back upon the experience, admits that his mind if not his heart was touched, but also declares that the sequence was somewhat of a literary exercise, an

---

* Like the first sequence, this one in its original publication followed an arrangement different from that later adopted. Of the thirty sonnets in the final arrangement, the following appeared in the *Monthly* in this order: 21, 22, 23, 25, 30, 28, 33, 47, 46, 50. (Santayana carries the numbering of the first sequence over into the second, so that the second begins with sonnet 21, not sonnet 1). These ten sonnets present all the moods of the sequence, but they are not the more autobiographical and explanatory poems.

attempt to emulate the love poets of the Italian Renaissance. Before reading Santayana's love poems, then, one should read his essay on "Platonic Love in Some Italian Poets" (The Buffalo lecture, later reprinted in *Interpretations of Poetry and Religion,* 1900) and possibly the sonnet sequences of Dante and Michelangelo.

Platonic love Santayana describes as the

> ... transformation of the appreciation of beautiful things into the worship of an ideal beauty and the transformation of the love of particular persons into the love of God.... As the senses that perceive, in the act of perceiving assert an absolute reality in their object, as the mind that looks before and after believes in the existence of a past and a future which cannot now be experienced, so the imagination and the heart behold, when they are left free to expand and express themselves, an absolute beauty and a perfect love. Intense contemplation disentangles the ideal from the idol of sense, and a purified will rests in it as in the true object of worship.

There are three elements in all truly Platonic love poetry: the philosophical, which stems from Plato himself; the religious, which is a product of medieval mysticism; and the sensuous, which is an outgrowth of chivalry. Not that the lover need be aware of the tradition behind his passion; much Platonism is naïve and instinctive, as at the time of the Renaissance. But Santayana was a scholar and familiar with the whole Platonic tradition, so that he quite consciously makes love of woman a stepping-stone to love of beauty, love of God, love of a universal whole. In these broader vistas the second sonnet sequence at times touches the first and seems to imply the larger spiritual experience contained there.

The sequence is most intelligible if the underlying narrative is taken to consist of three parts: an early experience of a more physical passion, unsatisfying on this account, a period of disillusionment and resignation, and a later experience more spiritual and Platonic, with its envisagement of ideal beauty. Whereas sonnet 24 suggests a consummation of love ("Though our lips meet, and clasp thee as I list ... And we said we were happy, you and I"), in sonnet 36 the poet admits that his lady is not even aware of the love he holds for her. The evidence then seems to point to two ladies as well as two experiences, but one should not press literality too far in Platonic love poetry.

Like the first sequence, this one breaks up into groups of sonnets linked by a similarity of emotional tone, and the emotional progression is the same as in the first series. Sonnets 21 to 26 reveal the poet in a state of despair; he has found love of a sort, but it is a love without spiritual dimensions. He calls it in sonnet 23 only "hunger for love, while love is yet to learn." Sonnet 22 seems to be outside the prevailing mood of the others, but its paean of praise to a universal love

> . . . that moveth the celestial spheres
> In endless yearning for the Changeless One,

may be taken to be the poet's sad contrast with his own "hunger for love" in the next sonnet. Sonnet 24 sketches in the details of the experience which leaves the poet unsatisfied,

> Although I decked a chamber for my bride,
> And found a moonlit garden for the tryst
> Wherein all flowers looked happy as we kissed,
> Hath the deep heart of me been satisfied?
> The chasm 'twixt our spirits yawns as wide
> Though our lips meet, and clasp thee as I list,
> The something perfect that I love is missed,
> And my warm worship freezes into pride.

and in sonnet 25 he attempts to escape his sorrow through the carefree thoughts of youth (compare sonnet 4), only to be awakened and "to find despair before us, vanity behind." As in the first sequence, just before dawn is the darkest hour; sonnet 26 plumbs the depths of the poet's sorrow.

> For what sin, Heaven, must I thus atone?
> Was it a sin to love what seemed so fair?
> If thou deny me hope, why give me care?
> I have not lived, and die alone, alone.
>
> . . . .
>
> I know, strong Fate, the trodden way I go.
> Joy lies behind me. Be the journey brief.

Sonnets 27 to 29 show a change of mood. Despair has given way to a quiet resignation, which brings with it a greater insight into the nature of love and happiness. A beautiful sonnet (27) marks the transition:

> Sleep hath composed the anguish of my brain,
> And ere the dawn I will arise and pray.
> Strengthen me, Heaven, and attune my lay

Unto my better angel's clear refrain.
For I can hear him in the night again,
The breathless night, snow-smothered, happy, grey,
With premonition of the jocund day,
Singing a quiet carol to my pain.
Slowly, saith he, the April buds are growing
In the chill core of twigs all leafless now;
Gently, beneath the weight of last night's snowing,
Patient of winter's hand, the branches bow.
Each buried seed lacks light as much as thou.
Wait for the spring, brave heart; there is no knowing.

And in sonnet 28 the poet's rendering of some lines of Petrarch sets the key for the remainder of the sequence:

"Hence comes the understanding of love's scope,
That, seeking thee, to perfect good aspires,
Accounting little what all flesh desires;
And hence the spirit's happy pinions ope
In flight impetuous to the heaven's choirs:
Wherefore I walk already proud in hope."

With sonnet 30 we seem to be in the presence of a new love. The poet tries out his mettle in the fashion of the courtly sonneteers (sonnets 30 to 33), with assertions of the character and strength of his love, and the power his mistress exerts over him. This delineation of the poet's love is, however, interrupted by four sonnets (34 to 37) which relate more specifically the circumstances underlying his love. He and his lady were

. . . far divided in our birth
By nature's gifts and half the planet's girth,
And speech, and faith, and blood, and ancient wars.

Moreover,

We needs must be divided in the tomb,
For I would die among the hills of Spain,
And o'er the treeless melancholy plain
Await the coming of the final gloom.
But thou—O pitiful!—wilt find scant room
Among thy kindred by the northern main,
And fade into the drifting mist again,
The hemlocks' shadow, or the pines' perfume.

Once the poet longed to tell his lady of his love,

> How drop by silent drop my bosom bled,

but when he had read her the verses he had composed, she merely replied, "I like the verses; they are written well."

> And I was silent. Now you do not know,
> But read these very words with vacant eyes,
> And, as you turn the page, peruse the skies,
> And I go by you as a cloud might go.
> You are not cruel, though you dealt the blow,
> And I am happy, though I miss the prize;
> For, when God tells you, you will not despise
> The love I bore you. It is better so.
> My soul is just, and thine without a stain.
> Why should not life divide us, whose division
> Is frail and passing, as its union vain?
> All things 'neath other planets will grow plain
> When, as we wander through the fields Elysian,
> Eternal echoes haunt us of this pain.

The remaining sonnets return to the exposition of the poet's love. Many changes are rung on this one underlying theme, the eternal satisfaction such a love brings its possessor. In some poems the imagery is Christian and the poet visualizes his loved one in Heaven, or recounts the heavenly joys her radiant image brings him. In others the thought is more Platonic, and the poet is led by his beloved to the discernment of eternal truth and beauty. In still others the beauty of his loved one seems to pervade all nature, so that

> For thee the garlands of the wood are wet,
> For thee the daisies up the meadow's sweep
> Stir in the sidelong light, and for thee weep
> The drooping ferns above the violet.

Finally, he is able to say,

> Heaven it is to be at peace with things;
> Come chaos now, and in a whirlwind's rings
> Engulf the planets. I have seen the best.

Santayana's second volume of verse, because it was mainly a reprint of his first volume, and because he was still little known outside of Cambridge, received scant recognition from the press. But in recent years these Platonic love poems have been more and more admired; in the opinion of some competent critics (Jessie Rittenhouse and William Archer, for instance) they are Santayana's best poetical work. Personally I prefer the first sequence. The experience there revealed cuts deeper into Santayana's character; his whole future life is built upon the philosophical and religious convictions these sonnets show in the process of formation. Beside this momentous experience the incident of the second sequence seems a transient "brain storm," to quote his own remark in the course of a conversation with the present writer. Of course, events, no matter how significant, are hardly a criterion of great poetry, nor will they always give rise to it. But it does seem that Santayana's sequence of love sonnets is studded with much conventional rhetoric, despite the unquestioned beauty of some of the individual poems and their generally skilful workmanship. The poems are less original, too. Others have written more happily of love before, even of the Platonic love Santayana celebrates, but no one else sounds quite the same note as his in the first series. These poems are really unique as a contribution to sonnet literature.

Santayana's love sonnets are of course less an imitation of any particular poet than a fully original work in which there is a large infiltration of the Platonic tradition. By the time he was a young instructor Santayana was sufficiently familiar with the Italian poetry of the Renaissance to review books on the subject, and his lecture on Platonic love in 1896 was not only authoritative, but revealed a keen appreciation of certain poets who must have influenced him deeply. Of these Michelangelo was foremost, because he represents the finest flowering of late Renaissance Platonism.

We find in Michael Angelo's poems [says Santayana] the varied expression of a single half aesthetic, half religious creed. The soul, he tells us in effect, is by nature made for God and for the enjoyment of divine beauty. All true beauty leads to the idea of perfection; the effort toward perfection is the burden of all art, which labours, therefore, with a superhuman and insoluble problem. All love, also, that does not lead to the love of God and merge into that love, is a long and hopeless torment.

Love which is merely of the senses is not love, but, in the words of Michelangelo, "lawlessness accurst." The reader will see from the following sonnet how close Michelangelo's conception is to Santayana's.

> From thy fair face I learn, O my loved lord,
> That which no mortal tongue can rightly say;
> The soul, imprisoned in her house of clay,
> Holpen by thee to God hath often soared:
> And though the vulgar, vain, malignant horde
> Attribute what their grosser wills obey,
> Yet shall this fervent homage that I pay,
> This love, this faith, pure joys for us afford.
> Lo, all the lovely things we find on earth,
> Resemble for the soul that rightly sees,
> That source of bliss divine which gave us birth:
> Nor have we first-fruits or remembrances
> Of heaven elsewhere. Thus, loving loyally,
> I rise to God and make death sweet by thee.

Santayana did not paraphrase Michelangelo, but he did respond to a stimulus the counterpart of that which moved the great sculptor. And like Michelangelo, he wrote with a full consciousness that he was composing Platonic love poetry; there was in both men the same detachment, the same quality of idealization.

Yet at times, particularly in the more Catholic passages, Santayana suggests the religious tone of Dante. The immaterial Platonic idea is replaced by the figures of the Trinity, and the Platonic realm of pure being becomes Heaven. Santayana here echoes the Catholicism of his youth, but he does so in a way which reveals that he has read Dante carefully. Santayana's loved one, like Dante's, "before the angels fell,"

> . . . didst follow the celestial seven
> Threading in file the meads of asphodel.

And now she seems

> . . . shade of Him
> Who only liveth, giveth, and is fair.

Moreover, the loved one has the power to lead the lover to Paradise. This note, which is the theme of the *Paradiso,* is struck in several of Santayana's sonnets, particularly where the lady's kiss is said to

> . . . help me on to paradise
> As if I kissed the consecrated bread
> In which the buried soul of Jesus lies.

It is the privilege of the beloved to confer upon the lover grace, a state of blessedness. This bestowal of grace (Ital. *merzede*) is the culmination of love in both Dante and Guido Cavalcanti. And Santayana, following the tradition, speaks thus of his loved one:

> In her unspotted heart is steadfast faith
> Fed on high thoughts, and in her beauteous face
> The fountain of the love that conquers death;
> And as I see her in her kneeling-place,
> A Gabriel comes, and with inaudible breath
> Whispers within me: Hail, thou full of grace.*

Petrarch, Santayana says,

> ... is musical, ingenious, learned, and passionate, but he is weak. His art is greater than his thought. In the quality of his mind there is nothing truly distinguished. The discipline of his long and hopeless love brings him little wisdom, little consolation.

Nevertheless, when Santayana wants a passage to set as the keystone in the arch of his sonnet sequence, he goes to Petrarch. The reason is that Petrarch set the style for all later Platonic love poetry, especially in England, with his elaborate celebration of the person and features of the beloved. Santayana is more austere than Petrarch, less sentimental, less luscious, less ornamental. Still in lines such as the following he is in the Petrarch tradition:

> And might I kiss her once, asleep or dead,
> Upon the forehead or the globed eyes,
> Or where the gold is parted on her head,
>
> And, limner, the soft lips and lashes heed,
> And set her in the midst, my love indeed,
> The sweet eyes tender, and the broad brow cold.
>
> Let my lips touch thy lips, and my desire
> Contagious fever be, to set aglow
> The blood beneath thy whiter breast than snow.

Santayana has paid his debt to his literary masters in a number of translations which catch the spirit of the originals with remarkable fidelity. They are clearly the result of long study and sincere devotion. But neither are they mere paraphrases or literal translations; each is a finely wrought poem in its own right, and might easily in idiom and figure be mistaken for an original poem of Santayana's.

---

* For parallel passages from Dante and the other Italian poets, see Appendix.

The following translation of Michelangelo's "Gli occhi miei delle cose belle" is a characteristic example:

> Ravished by all that to the eyes is fair,
> Yet hungry for the joys that truly bless,
> My soul can find no stair
> To mount to heaven, save earth's loveliness.
> For from the stars above
> Descends a glorious light
> That lifts our longing to their highest height
> And bears the name of love.
> Nor is there aught can move
> A gentle heart, or purge or make it wise,
> But beauty and the starlight of her eyes.

Santayana's original poems are not, however, merely exercises in the Italian manner. Other notes creep in here and there. There is occasionally a reminiscence of Plato himself, as in the line "Their risen selves with the eternal blend," or the conclusion of sonnet 43, suggesting as it does the *Phaedrus*. Sonnet 32, the only one of Santayana's referring to a scornful mistress, seems to hark back, perhaps through Petrarch, to the troubadours. The figure in the conclusion of the octave is a familiar one in Provençal poetry, as is the suggestion at the end that the "wagging tongue of men" helps keep apart the poet and his loved one. Santayana handles the theme with originality and his remark,

> If I am poor, in death how rich and brave
> Will seem my spirit with the love it gave;

would have seemed to most of the troubadours a remote and belated compensation for the pains of unrequited love. The sonnet quoted on page 60 is again different from the prevailing tone of the sequence, having about it a fresh earthiness which seems traditionally English. In fact, many literary traditions and impulses blend in the sonnets, sometimes throughout the length of a sonnet, sometimes even in a single line. Thus, when Santayana says that love "chained the whirling earth to Phoebus' throne," he is drawing his main idea from the middle ages, but he is basing his astronomical figure on modern, not Ptolemaic science, with a reference to Greek mythology in the bargain. Sonnet 39, for another example, is Platonic in its octave, with a suggestion of Michelangelo, but its sestet after a description of the beloved in the Petrarchan manner passes to a consummation of love which is strongly Catholic, suggesting Dante in its idea if not in its imagery. And so one may dissect the poems and admire the reading and scholarship behind them, but to do so is perhaps to miss their intrinsic charm and poetic worth, for they are the work of a poet first and of a scholar only second.

In the fall of 1896 Santayana took advantage of a sabbatical leave of absence to renew his acquaintance with England, which he had first visited in the course of a mid-term holiday while he was studying at the University of Berlin. He says,

I wished . . . to fill some of the more obvious gaps in my reading, and no place seemed more appropriate to that end than the University of Cambridge, which had opportunely opened its doors to graduates of foreign universities who might wish to study there, with such academic status as their age and position might justify. My application (not unaccompanied by various documents and affidavits) was accepted first by King's College and then by the University. The College very courteously gave me most of the privileges of their own Masters, with a seat at high table in Hall, a key to the Fellows' Garden, and the use of the Senior Combination room, the smoking and sitting rooms used by the Dons in common. My lodgings were at first in the town, but later I was able to move into a friend's room in Gibbs or (as it is called) the Fellows' Building, where my windows on one side dominated the great lawn cut by the narrow channel of the Cam and hedged in beyond by the giant trees of the Backs and the beautiful façade of Clare.

Here Santayana first came to love the country in which some of his happiest days were to be spent.

I was not mistaken in surmising that in England I should find a *tertium quid,* something soberer and juster than anything I yet knew, and at the same time greener and richer. I felt at once that here was a distinctive society, a way of living fundamentally foreign to me, but deeply attractive. At first all gates seemed shut and bristling with incommunication; but soon in some embowered corner I found the stile I might climb over, and the ancient right of way.

It was inevitable that such an experience should call for poetic expression, and five poems were the immediate result: "King's College Chapel," "In Grantchester Meadows," and three sonnets entitled "Before a Statue of Achilles." These were first published in the *Harvard Monthly,* and were later included in a group of poems published in *A Hermit of Carmel and Other Poems,* 1901. This group of some half-dozen poems is one of Santayana's finest achievements and contains some of his most seasoned reflections upon life. Throughout the poems runs a mood of spiritual estrangement or exile. "King's College Chapel" commemorates one of the occasions in England when Santayana was overpowered by a spiritual loneliness. The college gathers for vespers; there is beauty and mystery in the blaze of "gorgeous windows," the courtly prayer "answered still by hymn and organ-groan," the "long rows of tapers," the "floating voices" of the choristers, "measured music, subtle, sweet, and strong." But the Catholic in Santayana feels a hollowness in the ceremony, misses the significance which should ennoble it and deepen its pathos. He asks, "Feel ye the inmost reason of your singing? Know ye the ancient burden of your song?" and in sadness he goes "forth into the open wold" to "make me forget the exile that I am."

> Exile not only from the wind-swept moor
> Where Guadarrama lifts his purple crest,
> But from the spirit's realm, celestial, sure
> Goal of all hope and vision of the best."

But Santayana was not only a stranger, a Latin, and a Catholic in Protestant, Saxon England; neither could he find solace in the country or the religion of his childhood. In "Avila," Santayana's only serious poem with a Spanish background, the ruins of the "purple uplands of Castile" remind the poet of the devout, suffering generations who have gone before, and make him regret the greedy generations of the present—in terms suggesting the Sapphic odes. The poet can only exclaim,

> Abroad a tumult, and a ruin here;
> Nor world nor desert hath a home for thee.

The implicit faith of the past can never be recaptured and the modern world seems fatally out of joint. What is then left for the poet? One recourse is escape, to view the world as a dream or a creation of the poet's disordered brain.

> For whence but from my soul should all things borrow
> So deep a tinge of woe?

"Solipsism" reflects this mood:

> I keep the secret doubt within my breast
> To be the gods' defence,
> To ease the heart by too much ruth oppressed
> And drive the horror hence.

But such a mood brings scant consolation:

> For that is part of me
> That feels the piercing pang of grief and love
> And doubts eternally.

Another avenue of escape is beauty, and the poet may trance himself with the storied charms of yesterday. "Sybaris," with its ornate diction and imagery, is the result. But these moods cannot be prolonged. Life must be faced even on its lowest terms. "In Grantchester Meadows" and "Midnight" come to the profound conclusion that sorrow and humanity are inseparable, that man can no longer spend his birthright in the "idle catches" of youth, in the pure joy of the skylark:

> Too late thou biddest me escape the earth,
> In ignorance of wrong
> To spin a little slender thread of song;
> On yet unwearied wing
> To rise and soar and sing,
> Not knowing death or birth
> Or any true unhappy human thing.
>
> To dwell 'twixt field and cloud,
> By river-willow and the murmurous sedge,
> By thy sweet privilege,
> To thee and to thy happy lords allowed.
> My native valley higher mountains hedge
> 'Neath starlit skies and proud,
> And sadder music in my soul is loud.

Or in "Midnight":

> But how should reptiles pine for wings
> Or a parched desert know its dearth?
> Immortal is the soul that sings
> The sorrow of her mortal birth.
> O cruel beauty of the earth!
> O love's unutterable stings!

Human suffering brings in its train its own recompense: knowledge and understanding and deep human sympathy.

These two poems show a profound appreciation of the tragedy involved in the nature of existence itself. More than "bric-a-brac" sentiment lies beneath them. Later in *Soliloquies in England* the same countryside and the same "tragic sense of life" were to inspire many of Santayana's most heartfelt utterances. Of the two poems, "In Grantchester Meadows" is more mellow, more of one piece, more charming in its intricate pattern suggesting a fragment of an ode. But "Midnight" has lines of vigor and strength. It is strident, insistent, beating out aphorisms as if an oracle were in pain. Both poems may be compared with a later "soliloquy in England," "At Heaven's Gate," itself a poem in prose. And so Santayana is able to conclude that quatrain of "Avila" which sounds his deepest pessimism with lines which ring with consolation and hope.

> Out of the sorrows of the barren year
> Build thou thy dwelling in eternity.

With this insight there is much that the spirit may hold fast to. It may listen for "the muffled syllables that Nature speaks," intimations

> . . . that from the depths of being
> Exhales an infinite, a perfect good.

"Premonition" is one of Santayana's most elusively beautiful poems, a poem that may mean many things to many people, whatever of truth and beauty the soul may perceive when it is most closely attuned to Nature, a harmony however that is at best fleeting and inadequate.

> Our heart strings are too coarse for Nature's fingers
> Deftly to quicken as she pulses on,
> And the harsh tremor that among them lingers
> Will into sweeter silence die anon.
>
> We catch the broken prelude and suggestion
> Of things unuttered, needing to be sung;
> We know the burden of them, and their question
> Lies heavy on the heart, nor finds a tongue.
> . . . .
>
> Though the heart wear the garment of its sorrow
> And be not happy like a naked star,
> Yet from the thought of peace some peace we borrow,
> Some rapture from the rapture felt afar.

And if this lofty idealism is too difficult, there are

> The little pleasures that to catch the sun
> Bubble a moment up from being's deep,
> The glittering sands of passion as they run,
> The merry laughter and the happy sleep,—
>
> These are the gems that, like the stars on fire,
> Encrust with glory all our heaven's zones;
> Each shining atom, in itself entire,
> Brightens the galaxy of sister stones.

There is art, too, in which the ideal may be imprisoned. The best of the many poems Santayana has devoted to art are the three sonnets, "Before a Statue of Achilles." These sonnets are graceful tributes to the manly perfection of Achilles, and the Greeks in general, though there is also a neatly turned compliment for the English universities, which are to be commended for keeping Achilles' "laurels fresh." The keynote of the sonnets is the concluding line, "The perfect body is itself the soul." "On an Unfinished Statue by Michael Angelo in the Bargello, Called an Apollo or a David" also is worth mention. It is a series of quatrains pondering the relation of art to life and the difference between matter and the form which gives it meaning. This form-giving power of art, however, is nowhere in Santayana more aptly and concisely expressed than in the sonnet, "The Power of Art," published in 1894 and 1896, but never reprinted.

> Not human art, but living gods alone
> Can fashion beauties that by changing live,—
> Her buds to spring, his fruits to autumn give,
> To earth her fountain in her heart of stone;
> But these in their begetting are o'erthrown,
> Nor may the sentenced minutes find reprieve;
> And summer in the blush of joy must grieve
> To shed his flaunting crown of petals blown.
> We to our works may not impart our breath,
> Nor them with shifting light of life array;
> We show but what one happy moment saith;
> Yet may our hands immortalize the day
> When life was sweet, and save from utter death
> The sacred past that should not pass away.

The title poem of *A Hermit of Carmel* and its companion piece, "The Knight's Return," are lesser things, in my judgment, than the shorter poems. In spite of stage directions and *dramatis personae* they are hardly dramatic at all. They go on in their quiet way, not without arousing in the reader a mild sort of interest less in what will happen next than in the dignity of the thought and in the polished phrasing. A knight kneeling before a cross on Mount Carmel is spied by a hermit, who detects a familiar note in the knight's voice. They engage in conversation and it turns out that the hermit is the knight's long-lost brother, who was captured in childhood by a band of marauders, and sold to a Jew. Later he took on the ways of his evil masters and led a life of riotous dissipation, for which he is at the moment doing penance. Abject as he is, he does not reveal his identity to his brother, who goes on his way after hearing the hermit's tale, told as of a friend. "The Knight's Return," a sequel, has less of a story. Palmerin, the Knight, returns to find Lady Flerida harassed by Sir Ulric, in whose care he had left his lady. Very little happens except the reunion of the lovers and the pardon of Ulric after he has been rebuked and admonished at sufficient length for the good of his soul. There are some well-written love lyrics and some interesting bits of dialogue, but Palmerin's habit of discoursing interminably at the slightest provocation destroys the interest of the tale. Santayana creates a Shakespearean nurse in the opening scene, but her garrulousness and her fair-weather philosophy have been better done before. These playlets have something to repay the effort of reading, but they are not things one returns to again and again with increased pleasure.

A Hermit of Carmel contained also a sheaf of convivial and occasional poems, not riotously mirthful but at least indicative of a side of the poet never seen in his more serious work. They attest to the jolly sociability of their author when congenial company beckoned him out of seculsion. In them the philosopher generally lurks behind the comic mask, and is at his best when he can be satiric, as in "Six Wise Fools," "The Poetic Medium," and "Young Sammy's First Wild Oats." "Six Wise Fools" is a symposium in which scholar, sport, critic, pessimist, lover, and the poet himself, relate the stories of their lives or expound their chosen philosophies. "The Poetic Medium," in the manner of the eighteenth-century wits, permits Santayana, through a Sibyl called Mrs. Fakir, to pay his respects to the poetasters, and some of the poets, too, who happen to arouse his wrath. But the cleverest of these pieces is "Young Sammy's First Wild Oats." Ostensibly a dialogue between two old deacons, the poem attacks the policy of the United States in annexing Puerto Rico and the Philippines after the Spanish-American War. The allegory is cleverly maintained, as in this passage:

> Cousin Sammy's gone a-tooting
>   To the Creole County fair,
> Where the very sun's polluting
>   And there's fever in the air.
> He has picked up three young lasses,
>   Three mulattoes on the mart,
> Who have offered him free passes
>   To their fortune and their heart.
> One young woman he respected,
>   Vowed he only came to woo.
> But his word may be neglected
>   Since he ravished the other two.
>   .   .   .   .   .   .
> He's not Uncle Sam, the father,
>   That prim, pompous, pious man,
> Yankee or Virginian, rather:
>   Sammy's an American—
> Lavish, clever, loud, and pushing,
>   Loving bargains, loving strife,
> Kindly, fearless-eyed, unblushing,
>   Not yet settled down in life.
> Send him forth; the world will mellow
>   His bluff youth, or nothing can.
> Nature made the hearty fellow,
>   Life will make the gentleman.

It is a far cry from the buffoonery of "Young Sammy" to the grave dignity of *Lucifer,* a poetical drama Santayana had brought out two years before, in 1899. The appearance of a short preliminary sketch with the same title in the 1894 poems, together with Santayana's reference in "Brief History of My Opinions" to the play as an example of his sympathy with heroic agonies and romantic sentiment, stamp its conception as quite early. It represents the stage of disillusionment when Christianity embraced all that Santayana held dear, whereas naturalism (personified by Lucifer) stood for all that Santayana held true. The tone of the play suggests the melancholy of the early sonnets. Great issues stalk its pages, nothing less than the expulsion of Satan, the mission of Christ, and the respective claims of naturalism, classicism, and Christianity as ways of life. There are three sets of characters: Christ, Michael, and St. Peter; Lucifer, Mephistopheles, Azazel, Belial, and Turel; and Zeus, Hermes, Ares, Hera, Athena, and Aphrodite. Most of the characters are self-explanatory, but Lucifer himself needs clarification. "He represents," says an early reviewer, "at once the rebellion from God, the love of paganism, the love of truth and the Byronic desire for solitary unhappiness and importance." He stands for the stark honesty of naturalism and the sublime conceit of romantic pessimism; there is in him not a little of the youthful Santayana. He dominates the play as do none of the other characters, a metaphysical sort of devil, unhappy because he sees the folly of all desire and yet cannot stop desiring. On the score of truth and intellect he conquers Christ, but is forced to bow where love is concerned, for an arrow has pierced his own heart in his affection for Hermes.

The limitations of the play as drama were early pointed out. Only the longer speeches count. The business of moving people about is clumsily handled; the events and transitions "are without movement, and as knitting together a story, have only a vague outline interest. There seems to be little a-doing in the play, which is yet concerned with the most gigantic of all subjects." There is no need to recount the plot; in fact, one forgets it before one has finished the book. There are, however, some effective scenes, not as drama, but as the poetical expression of profound contrasts of thought. There is intellectual liveliness in the contest for supremacy between Christ and Lucifer, Act IV, Scene 2, and the play is not without humor of a sort, when St. Peter denies Hermes admission to Heaven but willingly admits Lucifer, and when Zeus, upon Christ's declaration that he is the Father, thinks old Kronos has returned to be avenged.

The charm of the book is, as Hutchins Hapgood said, "the style, the contemplative, impersonal spirit, the cool reflection, the chaste and elevated phrase." The book is the result of "long pondering on a few great subjects." "The nature of Paganism, the nature of Christianity, the nature of the Devil are conceived with clearness and distinction. The book breathes a daily interest in the sensuous beauty of innocent form, the mystic redemption of an old world, and the proud consciousness of personal and therefore devilish superiority."

Lucifer cannot be dismissed without mention of the very interesting and just review of the play written anonymously for the *Harvard Monthly* by the author himself.

Although a certain strangeness may remain in the notion, so novel and audacious, of bringing the divinities of various religions into the presence of one another, we soon perceive that sensationalism is quite foreign to the spirit of the author. He has evidently not sought out this collocation of characters to obtain a *succès de scandale*. He found them lying together in his mind, as they lie in the mind of every man whose education has made him heir of both the Christian and Pagan tradition. . . . In confronting the spirit of revelation with the spirit of nature and the spirit of abstract doubt, the author leaves us to draw our own conclusions; for while we may judge that his temperament is rather expressed by "Lucifer" than by the other characters, his judgment seems by no means to lean to that side. Even the persuasive sadness of the verses is instinct with too much piety and with too positive an appreciation of the beautiful to be called pessimism.

He concludes by wondering whether readers will be found for "poetry of this sort, sprung from the soil of scholarship and critical philosophy, and demanding great imaginative sympathy." *

By 1902 Santayana's reputation as a poet had grown considerably. By this time his discussions of poetry in *The Sense of Beauty,* 1896, and *Interpretations of Poetry and Religion,* 1900, were coming to be better known and were helping to create an interest in his verse. In 1901 William Archer introduced his work, with favorable comment, to the English readers of *Poetry of the Younger Generation*. And in 1904 Jessie Rittenhouse included Santayana among the most significant younger American poets in her book entitled *Younger American Poets*. However, critical opinion was by no means undivided as to the merit of the poems. Though the *Dial* welcomed Santayana as one of the three or four leading poets of the younger generation, and the *Harvard Graduates' Magazine* found him an antidote to the "tumty-tum balladry" of the "marine and bellicose bards," the *Nation* felt that verse, even of a serious character, was not his strong point, and the *Academy* found in him "little of that rich and lyric humanity which is the life-blood of song." The *Independent's* judgment may be taken as fairly representative of the impression Santayana made upon the reading public of the turn of the century.

---

* "The editors having confessed that they could find no one to do it, I said: 'I will write it myself, but it will be complimentary. People will expect that, seeing I am one of the founders of the paper.' " From a letter of Santayana's to the present writer.

On the whole, then, we cannot conscientiously rate the poet in Mr. Santayana so high as the critic. . . . His verse written in the best traditions leaves us cold; aspiring to a classical severity it often succeeds in being only austere; while sometimes, it is to be feared, it flats to a note very like that French commonplace or matter of fact, which is the poetic view of the prose virtue of lucidity or common sense, the result of the transportation of the critical faculty into poetry.

Among lovers of a quiet, reflective poetry his reputation was unquestionably greater.

But just as Santayana was coming to be recognized as a poet, he abandoned his Muse completely, or at least withdrew it from the public eye. In the first few years of the twentieth century he published in the *Harvard Monthly* three dramatic fragments somewhat in the style of *Lucifer*. One deals with the sorrow of Castor, immortal, yet bound to earth by a mortal love for his brother; one is a rousing invective on the part of Helen of Troy against family and country; and the third is a philosophical colloquy of four Greeks: Plato, Aristippus, Antichthonus, and Antisthenes. The first two poems have a calm, almost plastic beauty, but like the knight's tale have no really dramatic force, since they are so brief and have no real obstacle for their characters to overcome. The third exhibits Santayana's first interest in the "imaginary conversation," a form in which he was later to excel in the prose *Dialogues in Limbo*. Since these three pieces Santayana has published a "Minuet upon Reaching the Age of Fifty," a sonnet in tribute to Shakespeare, an "Imitation of Calderón," and three sonnets written during the War and published in *Soliloquies in England*. There is also a hitherto unpublished sonnet of Santayana's in the recent limited Triton edition of his *Three Philosophical Poets*. The Shakespeare sonnet is somewhat perfunctory and made to order, but the others show no diminution of power. A few poems in thirty years, however, are clear evidence that Santayana's heart is elsewhere than in poetic creation.

And I fear his conversion to prose is absolute and final. He says,

Sometimes it seems to me that I resemble my countryman Don Quixote, when in his airy flights he was merely perched on a high horse and a wooden Pegasus; and I ask myself if I ever had anything to say in verse that might not have been said better in prose. And yet, in reality, there was no such alternative. What I felt when I composed those verses could not have been rendered in any other form. Their sincerity is absolute, not only in respect to the thought which might be abstracted from them and expressed in prose, but also in respect to the aura of literary and religious associations which envelops them. . . . In one sense I think that my verses, mental and thin as their texture may be, represent a true inspiration, a true docility. . . . When that compulsion ceased, I ceased to write verses. My emotion—for there was genuine emotion—faded into a sense that my lesson was learned and my troth plighted; there was no longer any occasion for this sort of breathlessness and unction.

It is true that Santayana the poet could never have reached the level of the great poet conceived by Santayana the critic. Santayana's poet was to be a painter with the cosmos for his canvas, a prophet and maker in the olden style; beside this ideal Santayana's own Muse must have seemed personal and thin. But there is room on Parnassus for many varieties of art, and if Santayana's niche is small, it is finely carved and commands a wide prospect. And despite his own modest opinion of his poetic talent, he saw fit to publish in 1923 a collected edition of his verse, chosen on the whole with unerring discrimination. Although only one poem was new, the 1923 volume was welcomed far more widely and far more enthusiastically than the same poems had been when originally published. Many discovered for the first time that a well-known philosopher had once been a promising young poet; in a way the prose versions of Santayana's philosophy had prepared the way for a better understanding and a wider appreciation of the poetic. But Santayana's poetry was felt to be able to stand on its own feet regardless of the prose. The *London Times* declared, "His verse would be worth reading and we should, we believe, find it remarkable if we had never read any of his prose." The *New Republic* felt that Santayana's own estimate of his poetry expressed in the delightfully candid preface was unnecessarily modest and disarming, and the *Freeman* wondered whether "English verse" had "ever been written as excellently as Mr. Santayana has written it, by any one else to whom the English language was not native."

Now as we look back across the years, Santayana's poetry interests us first because it expresses most of his ideas in a personal and emotional setting which has been later removed. The negative and positive poles of his philosophy are clearly marked out: on the one hand, his aversion to the civilization of his day and, more profoundly, his estrangement from his religion and his country ("abroad a tumult and a ruin here"); on the other hand, his recognition of the necessity of sorrow ("unhappy human things"), his acknowledgment of an inevitable naturalism ("the soul is not on earth an alien thing"), his envisagement of the ideal ("the deathless beauty of all winged hours"), and his sympathy with all human interests that are honest and within sight of the ideal: love, beauty, religion, art, even work where it is a quiet, patient sort. Santayana's universe is the universe of physical science, depressing and unpoetical as that may be, but his naturalism is tempered by a Catholicism which expresses itself not only in Christian symbol and allusion but also in a glowing tribute to faith, the "soul's invincible surmise," and a warm human sympathy. There is Hellenism, too, in the occasional buoyant acceptance of life and in the fondness for earthly beauty which breathes through some of his lines. The great philosophical traditions which have molded Santayana's thought are all reflected in his poetry. In *Lucifer,* particularly, they confront each other, sharply defined. Truth must be tempered by love; love must be founded on truth; youth and joy and beauty must be cherished, but within the inexorable demands of reality and with the consummate understanding of love. Perhaps in this way conflicting ideals may be harmonized. *Lucifer* explicitly does not go thus far; Santayana has not yet woven his strands of thought into the consistent pattern of later years. In *Lucifer* he has not yet fully felt the solvent power of Platonism. In the second sonnet sequence, in "Avila," in "Premonition," however, Platonism is already to be reckoned with, a Platonism which is Catholic and Renaissance as well as Greek. Perhaps there is something Platonic in that isolation of soul, that timelessness of outlook that marks the man Santayana. Spain, America, the modern world, are painted backdrops to an inner life that is saddened by the world in which it finds itself, but rises at times completely above its surroundings to glimpse the changeless and eternal. The seeds of *The Realm of Essence* are already sown in the Platonism of Santayana the poet. True, this Platonism is still troubled and incomplete, thus the surge of emotion, the melancholy that runs through the poems. But with calm and serenity there will no longer be the need for verse, for that "breathlessness and unction" Santayana speaks of in his poetry.

For I believe Santayana's poetry is genuine poetry, that it is something more than a mere repository of philosophical and literary traditions. Of course, to many readers it seems that there is never in Santayana's Muse any abandon, any welling up and flooding over the careful patterns of formal structure. Even the admiring Jessie Rittenhouse says that Santayana's work is "faultily faultless"; the poems are "so finished that one would welcome a false note now and then, that suggested a choke in the voice, or a heartbeat out of time." Whether or not false notes are desirable in poetry, however completely the heartbeat may be out of time, at any rate no one is more frank than Santayana in admitting the lack of intense feeling in his verse.

Of impassioned tenderness or Dionysiac frenzy I have nothing, nor even of that magic and pregnancy of phrase—really the creation of a fresh idiom—which marks the high lights of poetry. Even if my temperament had been naturally warmer, the fact that the English language (and I can write no other with assurance) was not my mother-tongue would of itself preclude any inspired use of it on my part: its roots do not quite reach to my centre. I never drank in in childhood the homely cadences and ditties which in pure spontaneous poetry set the essential key. I know no words redolent of the wonder-world, the fairy-tale, or the cradle.

Santayana's diction, as Miss Rittenhouse says, lacks "the creative flexibility, the quick, warm ductile adaptability, that a much less accomplished poet may give to his words." In spite of the trenchant phrase, the lovely image, the simple ease of some of his lines, Santayana's poetic diction has not the masterly assurance of his prose at its best. For one thing, it shows too close an acquaintance with the major English poets, too conscious an attempt to phrase in the traditional manner of English reflective poetry. There are echoes of Shakespeare (the dramas rather than the sonnets) and of Milton, and a keen ear will even detect Wordsworth, Tennyson, and Shelley now and then in Santayana's lines. Santayana does not actually borrow, but he has retained from his reading a kind of distillation of the language of English poetry. But this acknowledgment is not to brand Santayana's verse as a "careful complication of trite similes; hackneyed verbal associations." The poems that "creak and totter on the stilts of rhetoric" are fewer than many readers suppose. Beside lines like

> Your ship lies anchored in the peaceful bight
> Until a kinder wind unfurl her sail;

or portions of "Athletic Ode," which tries to make poetry out of a football game and a track meet, or "Spain in America," the grandiloquence of its Spenserian stanzas groaning under a heavy ballast of history and geography, may be placed many more lines testifying to their author's ability to speak eloquently in verse as well as in prose.

> It is not wisdom to be only wise,
> And on the inward vision close the eyes,
> But it is wisdom to believe the heart.

> But whose life is his choice?
> And he who chooseth not hath chosen best.

> Living you made it goodlier to live,
> Dead you will make it easier to die.

> Immortal is the soul that sings
> The sorrow of her mortal birth.

Santayana says, "The verses of a philosopher will be essentially epigrams, like those which the Greek Sages composed"; and the remark is true of a great part of his work. The best of these epigrammatic lines have a finality which makes the memory of them linger.

> Feel ye the inmost reason of your singing?
> Know ye the ancient burden of your song?

> Not knowing death or birth
> Or any true unhappy human thing.

> The perfect body is itself the soul.

> Had he seen God, to write so much of him?

> Truth is a dream, unless my dream is true.

The simplicity of these lines is part of their strength and charm. And the best of Santayana's lines are invariably simple and to the point. His verse is much less luxuriant than his prose. Moreover, it has melody and rhythm as well as precision; Santayana is not always insensitive to the sound value of his verse, mental as the content may be. The following lines stand out because of the harmonious blending of vowel and consonant tone-colors.

> Mingling the love, the laughter, and the groan
> In the large hollow of the heaven's bowl,

> The mountains sleep behind thee, and the main
> Awaits thee, lulling an eternal pain
>
> In peace the slow tides pulse from shore to shore,
> And ancient quiet broods from pole to pole.
>
> O subtle beauty, sweet persuasive worth.
>
> The breathless night, snow-smothered, happy, grey,
>
> Out of the dust the queen of roses springs;
> The brackish depths of the blown waters bear
> Blossoms of foam;

In the sestet of a sonnet entitled "Cathedrals by the Sea" Santayana really succeeds in giving us a kind of strange sea music through his choice of melodious words:

> Then the wild winds through organ-pipes descended
> To utter what they meant eternally,
> And not in vain the moon devoutly mended
> Her wasted taper, lighting Calvary,
> While with a psalmody of angels blended
> The sullen diapason of the sea.

Santayana's melodies are subdued, like quiet organ reveries, but they are to be listened for especially in the sonnets. Of course, his verse is restrained and formal, he would be the last to deny it; Santayana makes no bid for originality in either imagery or thought, but though he is always a careful technician, he is not a virtuoso intent only on the skilful handling of his instrument.

Neither is he formal to the point of monotony. There is more variety, more experimentation in his verse than is generally supposed. The bulk of Santayana's serious work is to be found in traditional forms, for, he says, "like the orders of Greek architecture, the sonnet of the couplet or the quatrain are better than anything else that has been devised to serve the same function; and the innate freedom of poets to hazard new forms does not abolish the freedom of all men to adopt the old ones." Nevertheless, Santayana has experimented with various unusual stanzaic patterns, to such an extent indeed that the average person will be surprised at the number of different stanzas to be found in his work. Most he abandoned after a single attempt, but the fact of their existence at all will dispel the widespread illusion that Santayana wrote nothing but sonnets, a few odes, an occasional quatrain, and one or two specimens of blank verse.

The metrical experimentation is to be found chiefly in the lyrics which accompany Santayana's dramatic verse. Here one finds the free and graceful movement characteristic of the English song. Take the song of the witches and devils, Act III, *Lucifer,* with its magical triads and its longer last line as if to indicate the conclusion of a round,

> I hear the great bell
> And I sniff the smell
> That I love full well
> Of a roast on the roaring hearth.

Or the songs of the angels, Act IV, written curiously enough in the stanza of the Shakespearean "Phoenix and Turtle."

> As the grass-blade in the sod
> Turns to heaven from the clod,
> I from nothingness to God.
>
> As a little star on fire
> Twinkles in thy silent choir,
> My heart sings with joy entire.
>
> As the snow-flake in the sky
> Willeth with the storm to fly
> Living in thy life I die.

If these are not entirely effective, the reason is to be found less in the lack of melody or rhythm than in the absence of that whimsical, faëry imagery which always accompanies such lines in English verse. Invention is present, but not the genuine mood of fantasy.

Santayana's convivial and occasional verses, though negligible as poetry, are also interesting as experiments in metrical forms he never chose to employ in serious stanzas. There alone one finds the ballad stanza and the heroic couplet and a number of stanzas of intricate rime scheme and line length. But interesting as are these experiments, Santayana's mastery of versification is displayed more convincingly in the familiar forms. The famous quatrain, or "heroic stanza" of Gray and Dryden, is Santayana's favorite for a short, serious poem, appearing in "Premonition," "Avila," "King's College Chapel," and

"On an Unfinished Statue." The solemn movement of the lines expresses admirably the musings of the philosopher. Next to the sonnet and possibly the irregular ode, Santayana handles this form with the greatest skill, and from its hallowed measures evokes music of real beauty.

Of even greater interest to the student of poetry are Santayana's Sapphic odes. These are not strict Sapphics, since Santayana makes no effort, as did Sidney and Swinburne, to adhere to the rather difficult pattern of the true Sapphic. Instead, he allows the verse to follow the normal five-stress pattern of the English line. The result is pleasing, introducing a stanza into English which seems indigenous rather than an awkward imitation of the classics. When Santayana begins his lines with the stress on the first syllable, he most closely approximates the true Sapphic, as in the stanzas of the fourth ode:

> Slowly the black earth gains upon the yellow,
> And the caked hill-side is ribbed soft with furrows.
> Turn now again, with voice and staff, my ploughman,
>   Guiding thy oxen.
>
> Lift the great ploughshare, clear the stones and brambles,
> Plant it the deeper, with thy foot upon it,
> Uprooting all the flowering weeds that bring not
>   Food to thy children.
>
> Patience is good for man and beast, and labour
> Hardens to sorrow and the frost of winter.
> Turn then again, in the brave hope of harvest,
>   Singing to heaven.

But an even greater favorite with Santayana is the irregular, or Cowleyan, ode. The variable line length and what Patmore called "the license to rime at indefinite intervals" are utilized by Santayana in such a way that they seem to conform to a rhetorical pattern. There is a pleasing variety to the meter, yet the lattice of interwoven rime is always a unifying device and gives a measured stateliness to the lines. "In Grantchester Meadows" is the finest of these odes, but all are polished, dignified, and skilfully constructed. In "A Minuet on Reaching the Age of Fifty" the rhythm set up by the variable line length actually suggests the poised steps and graceful turns of the minuet.

However, despite the excellence of the odes, Santayana's finest poetical achievement is in the sonnet, which because of its interrelated parts he calls in *The Sense of Beauty* the "most classic of modern poetical forms." The variety possible within its unity, the possible blending of melody and meaning, appeal strongly to Santayana, and within its narrow bounds he has found his greatest poetical inspiration. In every instance there seems to be a reason why he has chosen the sonnet form rather than one more loose and lengthy, and to acknowledge that is perhaps to make the finest compliment that can be paid a sonneteer. A mood, a doubt, a conviction are imprisoned neatly within fourteen lines. Distinguished sonnets do not need floods of emotion; they spring into being out of the very intellectual, reflective subsoil of such a nature as Santayana's. In them a man of letters may versify successfully without being a great poet, as Santayana says, of "Dionysiac frenzy." The student of the sonnet will admire Santayana's subtle uses of rime and rhythm to bring out meaning, will feel that Santayana deserves a place beside the craftsmen of the past. But any lover of poetry without even a sense for metrics must acknowledge the beauty and the thoughtfulness of Santayana's sonnets, must admit that in his hands philosophy is truly wedded to art.

In all long poems Santayana gives up strophic arrangement for continuous meter, and in view of his attitude toward rime it is not surprising that he has put so few of his longer poems into blank verse: only "A Hermit of Carmel," "The Knight's Return," and "Philosophers at Court." As he says in *The Sense of Beauty,* rime is "much more classic in spirit than blank verse, which lacks almost entirely the power of synthesizing the phrase, and making the unexpected seem the inevitable." Even the two narrative poems do not seem to demand blank verse; in fact, rime would give them a kind of ornamentation in keeping with their medieval setting. "Philosophers at Court" is a fragment of philosophical dialogue, where the subtleties of thought are quite appropriately couched in blank verse. Santayana's blank verse is smooth and capable, but I do not feel that it has the distinction or originality of his rimed verse. Below is one of the finest passages:

> Long I questioned fate.
> No answer came from heaven to my doubts;
> But with the Spring and the reviving note
> Of thrush and swallow, and the ploughman's song
> Heard from the fields, I somewhat calmed my griefs,

> And my heart took new counsel. Though a wave
> Mirror a star and sink into the sea,
> It cannot suffer; though the summer fade
> It shivers not at autumn; though the spheres
> Crash back to chaos they lament it not.
> Never the blasted deserts of the moon
> Mourned their lost verdure or implored reprieve.
> But my loud heart-beats, self-contemplative,
> Note their own weariness, and death foreknown
> Makes life a grim and halting agony.
> Yet something in me rides on circumstance
> And swims the tide of change.

It is significant that Santayana chose for his most ambitious dramatic piece not blank verse but rime. Two other poems, "The Dioscuri" and "The Flight of Helen," dialogue renditions of classical story, also show that Santayana felt rime to be more appropriate for anything hallowed by antiquity. The continuous pattern of rimed verse he employs is essentially his irregular ode without stanzaic grouping and with a larger proportion of five-stress lines. There will be entire pages, especially in the weightier portions, without a single short line, but in the more lyrical passages and in the rapid interplay of conversation the shorter lines are more abundant. Rimes are picked up and balanced in the form of couplets, quatrains, and occasionally more intricate combinations as happens to suit the author's fancy and the exigencies of the meaning. The effect is of a tapestry where certain figures form and blend with other figures so that the eye discerns here and there a pattern, here and there a recurring figure, but no intelligible total design. It is as if a fugue were bound by no clearly discernible fugal laws. The meter would result in slovenliness in some hands, but Santayana's instinct for form molds of it a thing of beauty, capable of many nuances of expression.*

From this résumé it is apparent that Santayana's most distinguished poetical work is in the more traditional forms, but it is equally apparent that he handles these forms with freshness and originality. Even in the individual line Santayana is more than a mere formalist. True he seldom indulges in irregularities; one can count syllables in Santayana's verse and almost always come out right; but to read his verse thus with the regularity of doggerel is to

---

* For a more detailed discussion of Santayana's technique of versification, see Appendix.

miss much of the subtle inflection and the indubitable music it contains. Santayana writes English verse not as a foreigner, but with an awareness of those peculiarities which have given it individuality ever since the time of the Anglo-Saxons. When all is said and done, he is more than a conscientious versifier; he is a true poet.

One must of course be attuned to the sensitiveness of such a temperament as Santayana's to detect the emotion which the sonnets and certain of the other more personal verses reveal. One must share his aesthetic responsiveness, his sincere deference in the presence of beauty, his delight in quiet contemplation, his high seriousness. Santayana's Muse asks no plaudits of the crowd, desires no throng of admirers or followers. His poetry is personal and aloof, the discourse of a man with his soul, a soliloquy hardly more than a whisper, or perhaps a prayer.

One man cannot be all things. And if Santayana's mansion has few windows for the world and its multiform life, at least it is spacious within, firmly grounded upon solid earth, and open above in illimitable vistas to the sky—or to heaven, as he would prefer to say. Certainly his wide view of art and its place in life is an assurance against decadence. There is even a certain strength in Santayana's verse. As Archibald MacLeish says, Santayana's manner is the "manner of swordsmanship, and the blade, though daintily raised, bites in." There is at times "desperate courage in the stab of a phrase." When Santayana espouses the cause of art or beauty or the view of life which is his own, there is nothing weak or halting in his attack; his words for all their decorum strike fire.

What will be the judgment of posterity? Santayana himself is very modest where the merit of his verse is concerned. He says, "I think the discerning reader will probably prefer the later prose versions of my philosophy: I prefer them myself, as being more broadly based, saner, more humorous." Santayana is, as we shall see, a critic of discrimination; and, I think, here his judgment is sound. The later prose versions, in my own opinion at least, sound a more mature philosophy and some of them, the dialogues and soliloquies for instance, are artistically finer than the poems. To say this is not to deny the unquestionable excellence of much of the poetry and its permanent appeal to a class of readers not overly large but of taste and discrimination. Santayana is mainly, says Miss Rittenhouse, "for those who are deeply subjective, . . . He is for the meditative hours when we are sounding the depths of ourselves and come back to the surface of things, bringing with us the unsatisfied pain of being." And I believe his verse will always find an audience in those, as he says, "whose ear it may strike sympathetically and who, crossing the same dark wood on their own errands, may pause for a moment to listen gladly."

CHAPTER THREE

THE MORAL PHILOSOPHER

In 1900 Santayana was known to his reading public as a young poet who dabbled in philosophy; in 1910 he was a moral philosopher who had once been a poet. This change of front was brought about, figuratively over night, and in the middle of the decade, by the publication of *The Life of Reason*. The five volumes comprising this work cover the entire range of Santayana's early philosophical speculation, and even today are considered by many critics his most important contribution to human knowledge. *The Realms of Being,* now in the process of completion, alone approaches *The Life of Reason* in magnitude, and even this monumental work, because of its restriction to technical metaphysics, has less range and considerably less appeal to the general reader.

The period of the Life of Reason is a unique one in the history of Santayana's thought. Neither before nor after did he search so systematically for the bases of rational living, or try so zealously to determine for mankind its chances of achieving happiness. Heretofore he had looked inward, sought his own happiness, achieved his own peace with nature. And later in life he was to look past man to nature herself in an effort to spy her innermost secrets. But through his early middle life he was the moral philosopher, looking outward upon his fellow men in the full flush of his interest in the Greeks and with something of the Greeks' confidence that reason and knowledge will make an orderly world and a harmonious way of life.

The Life of Reason, though it took Santayana's readers somewhat by surprise, was really the result of a long preparation. He traces the first suggestion of such a work back to his student days, when he was reading Hegel's *Phaenomenologie des Geistes.*

It had seemed to me that myth and sophistry there spoilt a very fine subject. The subject was the history of human ideas: the sophistry was imposed on Hegel by his ambition to show that the episodes he happened to review formed a dialectical chain: and the myth sprang from the constant suggestion that this history of human ideas made up the whole of cosmic evolution, and that those episodes were the scattered syllables of a single eternal oracle. It occurred to me that a more honest criticism of progress might be based on tracing the distracted efforts of man to satisfy his natural impulses in his natural environment. Yet if these impulses were infinitely wayward and variable, and if the environment itself was inconstant or undiscoverable, what criterion of progress could it be possible to set up?

In short, was there any basis in naturalism for a construction of the ideal? "The suggestion of such a work accordingly lay dormant in my mind for years." However, a fresh approach to the problem came to Santayana in his study of the Greek thinkers under Henry Jackson at Cambridge, England.

Maturity, aided by Platonic studies, supplied me with a fresh point of departure, and enabled me to conceive the whole subject in a way that seemed to rescue it at once from pretension and from futility. All that was needed was to know oneself. No unnatural constancy need be imposed on human nature at large: it sufficed that the critic himself should have a determinate character and a sane capacity for happiness. He was not likely to be so original that, if he was sincere, nobody else would be found to share and approve his judgments.

There is thus a curious blend of modesty and egotism in the requirements Santayana sets up for the author of a Life of Reason; modesty in his brushing aside so lightly his own preparation for the task, egotism in his assumption that it can be brushed aside so lightly. The Life of Reason, as Santayana conceived it, was to be spun from within; like the poems and the later soliloquies, it was to be the product of introspection—or meditation, if you will. And in a certain sense the book is just that. Outwardly it avoids quotations, references, footnotes; more vitally, it reflects much of the temperament and reveals most of the attachments and disavowals of its author. It is like a vast soliloquy.

Yet a man cannot, unless he is a fool or a parrot, soliloquize throughout five volumes without levying upon the store of other minds. As in his poems, Santayana borrows richly of the past, disclaiming originality as his aim or his accomplishment. Indeed, the philosophical systems of the past were already taking on in Santayana's eyes the alignment that he described vividly in a much later essay entitled "The Progress of Philosophy":

> Suppose I arrange the works of the essential philosophers—leaving out secondary and transitional systems—in a bookcase of four shelves; on the top shelf (out of reach, since I can't read the language) I will place the Indians; on the next the Greek naturalists; and to remedy the unfortunate paucity of their remains, I will add here those free inquirers of the renaissance, leading to Spinoza, who after two thousand years picked up the thread of scientific speculation; and besides, all modern science: so that this shelf will run over into a whole library of what is not ordinarily called philosophy. On the third shelf I will put Platonism, including Aristotle, the Fathers, the Scholastics, and all honestly Christian theology; and on the last, modern or subjective philosophy in its entirety.

The last shelf was never to influence Santayana to any extent, and the influence of the first shelf was to come much later, but the two middle shelves, marking out as they do the realms of fact and value respectively, were the opposite poles of Santayana's early philosophy.

Platonism tended to justify a moral order based upon values rather than upon facts, whereas naturalism with its mechanical explanation of the universe looked upon values as ephemeral and dependent upon the facts which brought them into being. Feeling that the relation between these two points of view must be established permanently before one could hope to be a moral philosopher, Santayana attacked the problem as early as 1890 in a dialogue entitled "Walt Whitman." One of the speakers, Van Tender, pays tribute to the romantic impulse in literature, expansive, all-embracing in its conquest of new forms and new material. Van Tender pleads for freshness, originality, and the suitability of all facts for poetic treatment. Breadth and novelty are his criteria. But McStout replies,

> It seems to me that the illusion is what is poetic, and the fact is so only when in fancy we assimilate it to the fiction . . . The reason why Walt Whitman is ridiculous is that he talks of real objects as if they could enter into poetry at all. It isn't art to point to objects, nor poetry to turn out "chants of Ohio, Indiana, Illinois, Wisconsin, Iowa, and Minnesota."

Here is a challenge to Van Tender, a definition of the sphere and scope of poetry, restrictive and classical in its impulse. There is such a thing as value inherent in the material of poetry, and such a faculty as selection among the true gifts of the creative artist, a selection which springs from the just appraisal of value.

We have thus in this dialogue Santayana's first attempt to come to grips with a vital problem of literary criticism. But the issue at stake underlies much more than literary criticism, for, as Santayana rightly insists, the critical standards of an age are a reflection of its *mores*. McStout contends that "the times are favorable" to Whitman's "vague pantheism, his formlessness, his confusion of values, his substitution of emotion for thought, his trust in impulse rather than in experience." Whitman stands for "a kind of profound piety that recognizes the life of everything in nature . . . and worships its intrinsic worth." Such an attitude is only the rudiment of morality, however genuine and necessary it may be in its place. A mature ethics will consider it immoral merely to "treat life as a masquerade, as a magic pantomime in which acts have no consequences and happiness and misery don't exist."

Van Tender and McStout in this dialogue represent diametrically opposite points of view. The tender or soft one is passive, tolerant, humble, reverent, contemplative. With this attitude Santayana's own temperament finds much in common, and his naturalism by reducing everything to its physical origins is always a force tending to justify whatever exists. On the other hand, the attitude fostered by Catholicism and Platonism is a stout or hard one, unyielding, selective, judicial. It posits standards and fights for their acceptance. It defends human ideals against any encroachment on the part of the physical and natural. It sternly draws the line between right and wrong, good and bad, actual and ideal. In 1890, Santayana seems to side with McStout, who in a parting diatribe declares, "The trouble with your contemplation and impartiality is that it unnerves a man and makes him incapable of indignation or enthusiasm." The tender attitude gives up something very human and very precious, about which all man's loyalties are spun.

"Walt Whitman: a Dialogue" is thus an important landmark in the evolution of Santayana's thought. On the side of literary criticism it forecasts the cardinal principles of *Interpretations of Poetry and Religion;* its ethical stand anticipates that of *The Life of Reason,* and its dialogue form is Santayana's first essay in a style which was to become his favorite for the give-and-take of philosophical controversy. Above all, it is perhaps the first real indication in Santayana of what Dickinson Miller so aptly calls the "adamant underneath—the absolute refusals that fortified his life . . . the inner instinct and demand of his nature . . . in a degree unknown to most men, imperiously definite." The early Santayana was more McStout than Van Tender.

If a moral order is justified in "Walt Whitman," in "What Is a Philistine?", 1892, another significant essay, its general nature is marked out. The philistine mind, says Santayana, harbors an aversion to art, true religion, or anything of the spirit. It scorns the saint and the voluptuary alike, both being indifferent to practical achievement. It is blind to the "elemental and immediate," ignorant of the "supreme and ultimate." Its essence is worldliness, a subordination of the spirit to the instruments of living. On the other hand, "to be unworldly is to look upon the judgment of society, its prizes and its pleasures, with the serenity and sadness of one whose treasure is elsewhere and whose eyes have beheld the vision of better things. . . . It is to live in the sight of the ideal." This assertion of the claim of the ideal will become in 1905 the keystone of *The Life of Reason*. The renunciation of philistinism and all that goes with it is one of the chief "absolute refusals" that man must make if he wants to grow in moral stature.

It may be worth while pointing out that Santayana gives his idealism an unusual turn that removes from it the conventional antithesis of the flesh and the spirit. He even prefers the sensualist, with his absorption in the delights of the flesh, to the worldly Puritan who scorns the flesh but heaps up the materials of life with no clearer spiritual goal than to accumulate goods and wealth or to expend energy. "We have forgotten," he says, "that there is nothing valuable or worthy in the motion, however rapid, of masses, however great, nor in the accumulation of objects, however numerous and complicated, nor in the organization of societies, however great and powerful, unless the inward happiness of men is thereby increased or their misery diminished." In view of the many similar attacks upon an industrial civilization, particularly that of America, which have appeared in the last decade, it is interesting to find the matter presented with such a clear insight into its ethical implications in a college magazine back in the nineties.*

---

* Passages in "What Is a Philistine?" forecast the attack upon wealth and industrialism in Volume II, *The Life of Reason* and the brilliant apology for the practical man is repeated almost verbatim. The distinction between two kinds of patriotism is also the basis of the chapter devoted to patriotism in Volume II, *The Life of Reason*.

These two essays together advocate a point of view which is in the classical, humanistic tradition. They represent respectively the Socratic and Platonic strands in Santayana's ethics. Morality as an absolute end is justified in "Walt Whitman," but morality must be built upon a basis of spirituality for it to be a truly liberating force. As Santayana the poet had said,

> . . . learn to love, in all things mortal, only
> What is eternal.

The foundations were thus laid for the Life of Reason, but the entire edifice was not yet to be built. Santayana's approach to his great task was gradual and thorough; he picked first for investigation that field in which his own creative talent lay—art. In *The Sense of Beauty,* 1896, he undertook a general formulation of aesthetic theory, and in *Interpretations of Poetry and Religion,* 1900, applied this theory to the solution of certain problems of literary criticism. *The Sense of Beauty* was very largely a writing out of his lectures in aesthetics at Harvard. There was some delay in finding a publisher, but the book was finally accepted by Scribner's, who have published Santayana's major work ever since.

In *The Sense of Beauty* Santayana first attempts to lay his foundations by drawing upon the materials of psychological research. He wants to discuss "why, when, and how beauty appears, what conditions an object must fulfil to be beautiful, what elements of our nature make us sensible of beauty, and what the relation is between the constitution of the object and the excitement of our susceptibility." He finds that beauty is a "value, that is, it is not a perception of a matter of fact or of a relation: it is an emotion, an affection of our volitional and appreciative nature." This value is "positive, intrinsic, and objectified." Beauty, contrary to morality, has no negative side; "it is the sense of the presence of something good, or (in the case of ugliness) of its absence. It is never the perception of a positive evil." It is enjoyed in and for itself, again contrary to morality, without any thought of remote utility. The third character of beauty is more difficult for the layman to grasp, because, according to our author, the layman is not sufficiently a psychologist to perceive the illusion inherent in all beauty. Being pleased by a lovely painting or sunset, he naïvely thinks that some quality of beauty in the painting or sunset awakes in him an emotional response, an irresistible gladdening of the heart. What in reality happens is that his pleasure casts over the object such a glamour that he mistakes his own rapture for an authentic voice of nature. To a psychologist this phenomenon by which an element of sensation is transformed into a quality of a thing is all too common; even the attentive layman observes that the colors, the sounds, and the odors he finds in things are not properties of matter.

Santayana goes on to determine what agencies produce the peculiar kind of pleasure objectified as beauty. Within the body certain vital functions such as the sexual are unquestionably instrumental. The traditional five senses, especially the eye and ear, by their ability to capture pure sensation, furnish the materials of beauty, and there is simple aesthetic pleasure in recognizing pure color and tones, the sheen of velvet and the vibration of a violin string. More complex, though not necessarily finer, is the aesthetic pleasure derived from form, the harmonious or symmetrical arrangement of sense materials, the design or pattern into which objects fall. Still a third kind of beauty is the beauty of expressiveness, in which the given object pleases not through its material or form but through the memories or associations it arouses in the beholder. To material, to form, and to expression Santayana devotes separate chapters; under expression he also considers the sublime, the comic, and the grotesque, and is thus able by way of conclusion to formulate a philosophy of art.

The moral justification of art is in its creation of the beautiful. Whether that beauty be perfection of form, or an expression of other kinds of perfection, such as nobility of character, it is a partial realization of the "harmony between our nature and our experience." It is a tribute to the idealizing power at the very center of human nature. "A pledge of the possible conformity between the soul and nature," it is "a ground of faith in the supremacy of the good."

This brief synopsis will show the difficult undertaking Santayana has embarked upon: to account for beauty on the ground of psychological determinism, and at the same time to justify its manifestations on moral and ideal grounds. His naturalism will explain beauty as a peculiarly subjective phenomenon, while his Platonism will insist upon its absolute validity in the world of moral values. The first position, like all explanations of fact in aesthetics, is the more open to objection.

Most debatable is the thesis that beauty is pleasure objectified. Such a subjective explanation of beauty is objectionable not because it is necessarily erroneous on the ground of physiological fact but because its terms are unable to do justice to the experience they aim to describe. The physical substratum of the sense of beauty is treated as if it were the entire phenomenon. Moreover, what is to distinguish beauty from other objectified pleasures such as humor? I think Santayana, too, underestimates the intellectual faculty involved in the judgment of value and ignores the form or content which inspires such judgment. However much of a pathetic fallacy may enter into the appreciation of the beautiful, the appreciation in itself is of some objective fact or relationship, which is perceived and comprehended by the mind at the same time as it stimulates the emotions.

Curiously enough, after the first chapter Santayana himself pays just tribute to all the objective manifestations of beauty. The fault lies largely in his method of definition. What in the first chapter is but tentative is treated as if it were final and authoritative. But there is this to be said for his definition. By insisting upon the pleasure underlying the perception of beauty, it demands more than lip service to beauty and makes the asethetic experience a genuinely emotional one.

There is much that is fine in Santayana's discussion of the beauty of material, form, and expression. The first element particularly is neglected by some writers in aesthetics and often scorned by the common man as trivial and by the dilettante as barbarous. Thus Santayana's admiration of pure sensuous beauty is as ingenuous as it is profound.

There is no effect of form which an effect of material could not enhance, and this effect of material, underlying that of form, raises the latter to a higher power and gives the beauty of the object a certain poignancy, thoroughness, and infinity which it otherwise would have lacked.

On the subject of form a man of Santayana's temperament and with his classical inclinations will be bound to speak soundly. His discussions of symmetry and multiplicity in uniformity, the latter containing the fine illustration of the starry heavens, are in his best vein. And the exemplification of the formal principle in the construction of character is well brought out, although I feel that more of the beauty of the typical character is due to its expressiveness than Santayana here admits.

The most interesting portion of the chapter on form, in the light of Santayana's later work, is his treatment of what he calls "indeterminate organization." He means by this "the vague, the incoherent, the suggestive, the variously interpretable." Many admirers of this kind of beauty and the art in which it finds expression think to have found a profundity, a glimpse of infinite perfection which the more ordered beauty denies. But the defects of indeterminate art are vagueness and poverty. Since it offers so little that is concrete and well defined, each man brings to it his own store of experience and his own imagination and carries away with him an interpretation vastly different from that of his neighbor. Although its imaginative stimulus is fascinating, such art adds nothing new to a person's experience.

Nor is Santayana's attack on general principles alone. He applies his thesis trenchantly to the modern love of landscape, and to modern painting and literature with their exploitation of the formless. Our art is "disorganized, sporadic, whimsical, and experimental. The crudity we are too distracted to refine, we accept as originality, and the vagueness we are too pretentious to make accurate, we pass off as sublimity." "Sentimentalism in the observer and romanticism in the artist are examples of this aesthetic incapacity. Whenever beauty is really seen and loved, it has a definite embodiment: the eye has precision, the work has style, and the object has perfection." This is largely the ground of Santayana's later attack upon the romantic temper, an attack which colors most of his early criticism.

A just estimate of Santayana's position is difficult because the critic's judgment is molded by his own classical or romantic affinities. It seems to me that Santayana's attack cuts through to first principles and shatters much art that is inchoate and slipshod; its effect however is too damaging, for there is a genuine beauty in the imaginatively suggestive, even where the outlines are not well defined, in the chiaroscuro of fantasy, in the half-lights of the Celtic otherworld. The emotional effect of music and of the musical element in poetry affords an approach to a theory of art different from that taken by Santayana, whose sympathies are more with the plastic arts and in literature with the epic and the drama.

In respect to beauty of expression, Santayana maintains that early art confined itself to things inherently beautiful or good.

The whole Homeric world is clean, clear, beautiful, and providential, and no small part of the perennial charm of the poet is that he thus immerses us in an atmosphere of beauty; a beauty not concentrated and reserved for some extraordinary sentiment, action, or person, but permeating the whole and colouring the common world of soldiers and sailors, war and craft, with a marvelous freshness and inward glow . . . [and] if our consciousness were exclusively aesthetic, this kind of expression would be the only one allowed in art or prized in nature.

But the press of life is too great.

The accumulation of values too exclusively aesthetic produces in our minds an effect of closeness and artificiality. . . . We are more thankful for this presentation of the unlovely truth in a lovely form, than for the like presentation of an abstract beauty. . . . Thoughts of labour, ambition, lust, anger, confusion, sorrow, and death must needs mix with our contemplation and lend their various expressions to the objects with which in experience they are so closely allied.

Thus Santayana admits the claim of the real to artistic expression, and seems on the way to working out an aesthetic which will weigh in the balance the respective claims of truth and beauty and perhaps incorporate both in a philosophy of art. But his admission of the claim of realism is somewhat grudging and the concession is made on moral rather than aesthetic grounds. Thus one of the chief functions he assigns to art is that of sweetening an otherwise unpalatable reality. "Art does not seek out the pathetic, the tragic, and the absurd; it is life that has imposed them upon our attention, and enlisted art in their service, to make the contemplation of them, since it is inevitable, at least as tolerable as possible." Thus tragedy must assuage its horrors with beauty of sensuous material and formal presentation, and a "continual suggestion of beautiful and happy things." There is some truth in this statement, but the conclusion drawn seems extravagant.

The description or suggestion of suffering may have a worth as science or discipline, but can never in itself enhance any beauty. Tragedy and comedy please in spite of this expressiveness and not by virtue of it; and except for the pleasures they give, they have no place among the fine arts.

Of course, Santayana is ready to admit, "Our practical and intellectual nature is deeply interested in truth. What describes fact appeals to us for that reason; it has an inalienable interest." Our pleasure of recognition is "one of the keenest we have," so that

> ... many people, in whom the pursuit of knowledge and the indulgence in sentiment have left no room for the cultivation of the aesthetic sense, look in art rather for this expression of fact or of passion than for the revelation of beauty. ... If, on the other hand, the primary interest is really in beauty, and only the confusion of a moral revolution has obscured for a while the vision of the ideal, then as the mind regains its mastery over the world, and digests its new experience, the imagination will again be liberated and create its forms by its inward affinities, leaving all the weary burden, archeological, psychological, and ethical, to those whose business is not to delight.

In this decisive subordination of truth to beauty, Santayana is consistently following the principle he has set up in his book, that beauty is a value, a matter for the affections rather than the intellect, first and foremost an agreeable sensation, a pleasure. And as long as he is speaking of beauty, the only objection one might make is that some natures do experience an exaltation closely akin to the aesthetic in not mere recognition of fact, but in that insight which transmutes fact into truth; Keats's identification is to them not mere rhetoric. But in reality Santayana is writing not only a psychology of aesthetics but also a philosophy of art, and while the two are not incompatible, in *The Sense of Beauty* they are more or less tacitly assumed to be identical. Whereas few would object to Santayana's statement that "nothing but the good of life enters into the texture of the beautiful," they would not consider it a corollary that nothing but the good of life enters into the texture of art. The Gordian knot of the relation of truth to beauty cannot be so easily sundered.

However, Santayana's identification of the artistic with the beautiful, premature as perhaps it is, is indeed a challenge to those today who make art merely a pulpit for "the blind instinct of self-expression," or a laboratory for the dissection of monstrosities. And the fact that he runs against the current is no deterrent to Santayana. Throughout the whole modern period creative effort, to his mind, has run amuck and by its glorification of the ugly and the formless has left upon the Muses a lasting stain.

The Sense of Beauty was generally well received by the press. The *Nation* called it "one of the best contributions ever made to the subject," and *Mind* chided the author for his unwarranted modesty in disclaiming originality. And though Grant Allen and H. R. Marshall had previously written on aesthetics from the standpoint of psychological research, Santayana's was the first book by an American to treat the whole subject systematically from this point of view. Moreover, Santayana, more than Allen and Marshall, dealt with the broader philosophical implications of beauty and art. Beside his book, earlier American works like those of Bascom and Day seem mere popular compendiums or textbooks. The chief objection of contemporary critics, both philosophical and literary, was to Santayana's defining beauty as an "objectification of pleasure." As the *Academy* put it, "We are certainly unwilling to accept without protest the tendency shown throughout this book to treat the sensations or judgments of beauty as merely concomitants of more naturalistically explicable states of consciousness." The *Philosophical Review* and the *New World* took the same point of view. Not that a naturalistic approach to aesthetics was new. That beauty was merely a subjective phenomenon had been assumed in the works of Marshall and Allen, in the "inner imitation" theory of Groos, and in less technical studies such as *Florentine Painters of the Renaissance* by Bernhard Berenson, a former associate of Santayana's on the original *Monthly* board. But there was something bald and point-blank about Santayana's definition, so much so that it has always stuck in the minds of later aestheticians as his unique contribution to aesthetics.

The real difficulty with Santayana's position, as I see it, was not that he renounced, as do some of our modern behaviorists, the significance of man's spiritual gifts because of their physical origins. A later statement of his stand in this matter may be taken almost as a lifelong creed.

While the existence of things must be understood by referring them to their causes, which are mechanical, their functions can only be explained by what is interesting in their results, in other words, by their relation to human nature and to human happiness.

But whereas this cleavage between the natural origins of things and their human significance seems to many a fundamental rift of nature, to the early Santayana it seemed that if philosophy could show that the natural origins of things, their mechanical causes, lead directly and automatically to values conducive to human happiness, and that man's sorrows are the result of a perversion rather than an evolution of natural forces, then a sublime consistency would be achieved, a simplification which is the goal of almost every philosopher. Thus in *The Sense of Beauty* Santayana must show that a recognition of form is not only an example of man's power of idealization, a glimpse of perfection as it were, but also an accommodation of the eye muscle; that the beauty of expressiveness, besides being a mark of all that is excellent in life, is a manifestation of the ease of association of ideas; that the sublime is not only a liberation of self, a mystical scaling of heaven, but a "sensation of deep or arrested respiration" in the throat and lungs. Thus Santayana is able to conceive of the sense of beauty as a real harmony between our innermost nature and the farthest reaches of our experience.

When our senses and imagination find what they crave, when the world so shapes itself or so moulds the mind that the correspondence between them is perfect, then perception is pleasure, and existence needs no apology.

One admires Santayana for his effort and his faith, but one wonders somehow whether the simplification is achieved at the expense of ignoring some of the more refractory elements of nature, of art, and of mankind.

Though one may pick flaws and note inconsistencies in *The Sense of Beauty,* the book by and large is greater than the argument abstracted from it would indicate. The range and variety of topics treated is amazing. "He who tarries may here read why the stars are beautiful; why 'home' is a concept of happiness; why the obligation to enjoy oneself is absurd; why nothing is objectively impressive; why criticism and idealisation involve each other; why a gay prison and a prison-like church fail to appeal; why we smile when Punch beats Judy in the puppet show; why beauties are incompatible; why a sense of form is Heaven's last gift to a creative mind." There is a thickness, a richness to the book as remarkable as the genuine love of beauty which pervades it. In reading it one has constantly the feeling that the author writes as one who has himself created beauty and enjoyed it from others. The insights and appreciations are the work of a remarkably sensitive and gifted nature. At all times Santayana's style and manner are generally so pleasing that one may, as the reviewer of the *Bookman* puts it, enjoy the "flower besprent crevices" in the "craggy ridge of the author's argument." Professionally *The Sense of Beauty* established Santayana as an original thinker and as a writer of distinction in a field which, as far as America was concerned, he had largely to himself.

Interpretations of Poetry and Religion, 1900, was made up of previously published essays on Greek religion, Shakespeare, and Platonic love, additional essays on Christianity, Emerson, Whitman, and Browning, and an introduction and conclusion in which Santayana developed his general thesis regarding the nature of religion and poetry and their relationship. His position can best be presented in his own words. "Religion and poetry are identical in essence, and differ merely in the way in which they are attached to practical affairs. Poetry is called religion when it intervenes in life, and religion, when it merely supervenes upon life, is seen to be nothing but poetry."

There are for Santayana three levels of poetry. The lowest level is sheer virtuosity in the handling of words and rhythms, absorption in the sensuous materials of verse.

Long passages in Shelley's "Revolt of Islam" and Keats' "Endymion" are poetical in this sense; the reader gathers, probably, no definite meaning, but is conscious of a poetic medium. . . . It bears that relation to great poems which scales and aimless warblings bear to great singing— they test the essential endowment and fineness of the organ which is to be employed in the art.

At a higher level is the play of fancy in which the poet indulges, capturing the brilliant hues of the surrounding world and the phantasmagoria of emotions which are neglected by prose. Prose must be quick, exact, uniform; but poetry dares to linger over the visible forms of things and to play over the feelings they arouse in men. The poet "dips into the chaos that underlies the rational shell of the world . . . he paints in again into the landscape the tints which the intellect has allowed to fade from it." In this way the poet is more true than is the scientist to the richness of the garb in which experience comes clad. But he has a still higher function. On the third level the poet through his creative imagination remolds experience into a form more intelligible to man; through a higher synthesis of the elements of experience he has decomposed on the second level, he is enabled to construct new forms and find new significances with an authority we recognize as vision.

But the "intermediate sphere" has not that logical finality which a philosopher is looking for. Of all the provinces of poetry it is the one most fraught with peril. It is dangerous to revert to the world of fancy, of impulse, of passion. This world of immediacy reason has left behind in its zeal for truth, a world all the more dangerous for being so pleasing and congenial to the mind. Such "recovery of sensuous and imaginative freedom," had poetry no higher function, would be at best but a relaxation without spiritual discipline. At worst there would be a positive evil. Part of the charm of poetry lies in the way it drapes over nature webs of feeling which are spun in the poet's own soul. Such a false personification, harmless enough on the surface, becomes an evil when nature herself is held to be the author of the graces so gratuitously bestowed upon her and is made a source of religious or moral inspiration. "We dye the world of our own colour; by a pathetic fallacy, by a false projection of sentiment, we soak Nature with our own feeling, and then celebrate her tender sympathy with our moral being."

Inability to rise above the second level of poetry and ignorance of the true function of the imagination have led to the poetry of barbarism, so loudly condemned by Santayana as the vice of the modern era.

The comparatively barbarous ages had a poetry of the ideal; they had visions of beauty, order, and perfection. This age of material elaboration has no sense for those things. Its fancy is retrospective, whimsical, and flickering; its ideals, when it has any, are negative and partial; its moral strength is a blind and miscellaneous vehemence. Its poetry, in a word, is the poetry of barbarism.

Browning and Whitman represent two levels of this poetry; even Shakespeare is not free from its blemish. "There is more or less rubbish in his greatest works." "Homer, the first of poets, was also the best and the most poetical." "The poetry of barbarism is not without its charm. It can play with sense and passion the more readily and freely in that it does not aspire to subordinate them to a clear thought or a tenable attitude of the will." But it has serious defects: "lack of distinction, absence of beauty, confusion of ideas, incapacity permanently to please."

The expression of emotion should be rationalized by derivation from character and by reference to the real objects that arouse it—to Nature, to history, and to the universe of truth; . . . In this way alone can poetry become an interpretation of life and not merely an irrelevant excursion into the realm of fancy, multiplying our images without purpose, and distracting us from our business without spiritual gain.

Santayana's conception of poetry derives logically from the concluding portions of *The Sense of Beauty,* where the true function of beauty is held to be the idealization of nature and life, pointing toward perfection. The emphasis is placed here more strongly on the ethical implications of art and the need of its relevance to life. "The highest poetry . . . is not that of the versifiers, but that of the prophets, or of such poets as interpret verbally the visions which the prophets have rendered in action and sentiment rather than in adequate words." And "the highest example of this kind of poetry is religion." "Poetry raised to its highest power is then identical with religion grasped in its inmost truth."

This view of poetry was attacked, as was only natural, by many critics of the day. They felt that Santayana's objections to Browning and Whitman robbed poetry of much of its contact with vital passions, with the pulse and throb of life itself; that response to a poet's own inner impulse was an adequate test of poetry; to demand that poetry be a criticism of life was sheer pedantry. Santayana seemed to them in love with bloodless abstractions, Platonic ideas, Utopian fancies, which might never be realized on this planet.*

There is some weight to these objections. If the third level of poetry is assumed to be the only poetry worthy of the name (and Santayana does so assume in many of his individual judgments), his critique excludes much that lovers of poetry have always held dear. There would seem to be no place for Poe or Burns or Swinburne or the Elizabethan songsters. If *The Sense of Beauty* went to one extreme in slighting the importance of truth in literature, *Interpretations of Poetry and Religion* seems to go to the other in ruling out of poetry all beauty which is not dependent upon truth. It must be remembered, however, that Santayana is undertaking to define the essential character of the greatest poetry, and somehow the judgment of the ages in that respect has not differed so widely from Santayana's. Homer, Dante, Milton, Shakespeare—these are the poets who have been immortalized and because of the very qualities Santayana sets forth as the marks of great poetry. Even the distaste he has for the poetry of barbarism is due to a clear and steady visualization of the best and a resolution to be satisfied with nothing but the best. Such an attitude will lead to intolerance, and narrowness if you

---

* A typical example is Hutchins Hapgood's review in the *Bookman*. The critic says that Santayana "cares only for the Platonic qualities of things, not for the things themselves," has a "philosophic hatred of the passionate and the irrational," is "endowed with rare gifts of philosophy and expression," but "lacking in warmth, in humanity, and in robust, intellectual impulse."

will, but it is a narrowness with height and perspective and a sense of unlimited excellence.

The more devout critics, who felt that poetry was ennobled by being identified with religion, were in turn shocked and alienated when they found that there were two sides to this identification, religion being reduced to the level of poetry. And there was no gainsaying the author's clear pronouncement of his position. The supernatural basis of religion was to be but a myth, without substantial reality.

Santayana fortifies his position by a brief survey of the history of the Greek and Christian religions. He admires the transparency of early Greek mythology. Lightly veiled by delightful personification and fantasy, the forces of nature and the ideals of man shone through the more clearly. And in Aristotle's theology, the culmination of Greek religion, we find a "true idealism, I mean an idealism itself purely ideal, which establishes the authority of human demands, ethical and logical, without impugning the existence or efficacy of that material universe which it endows with a meaning and a standard." But mankind was not ready for such an austere theology as would establish a "dualism between the actual and the ideal against which the human mind easily rebels." So paganism was succeeded by Christianity, which undertook a new reconciliation of the physical and moral, building historically in time instead of cosmically in space. Christianity united the creation of the world with the history of a chosen people and set its moral drama of the life of Christ in the perspective of this historical background. The very cosmos it constructed, "vast, massive, steadfast," furnished a habitat in which its moral precepts might be illustrated free from their confusions in the world of nature.

Christian fictions were at least significant; they beguiled the intellect, no doubt, and were mistaken for accounts of external fact; but they enlightened the imagination; they made man understand, as never before or since, the pathos and nobility of his life, the necessity of discipline, the possibility of sanctity, the transcendence and the humanity of the divine.

But Christianity, too, is likely to be destroyed by

... entangling itself with a particular account of matters of fact, matters irrelevant to its ideal significance, and further by intrenching itself, by virtue of that entanglement, in an inadequate regimen or a too narrow imaginative development, thus putting its ideal authority in jeopardy by opposing it to other intuitions and practices no less religious than its own. . . . The greatest calamity, however, would be that which seems, alas! not unlikely to befall our immediate posterity, namely, that while Christianity should be discredited, no other religion, more disillusioned and not less inspired, should come to take its place.

How strangely prophetic have thirty years made these words.

Until the imagination should have time to recover and to reassert its legitimate and kindly power, the European races would then be reduced to confessing that while they had mastered the mechanical forces of Nature, both by science and by the arts, they had become incapable of mastering or understanding themselves, and that, bewildered like the beasts by the revolutions of the heavens and by their own irrational passions, they could find no way of uttering the ideal meaning of their life.

The only hope Santayana holds out is in the form of a poetry-religion based upon myth and fancy, a religion which will be stimulating to the imagination and authoritative for the conscience. Such a "religion of disillusion" might well be the salvation of the modern world; yet its acceptance would be beset with practical difficulties. One may seriously question whether a mythical and poetical religion, however sage in its counsels, would ever be received with the authority of religion by the rank and file of human beings if they fully realized it to be but a creation of human imagination. In the words of Ernest Albee, "The faith which is essential in all religions must, for the believer himself, be something very different from mere poetic appreciation or even moral approbation." * And there is always the wonder whether reason could not accomplish as much as a religion of this sort.

In reality, Santayana in 1900 has already adopted the rationalistic point of view of *The Life of Reason,* with the understanding set up as the sole criterion of truth. The function of the imagination is to embroider and weave patterns out of the material supplied by the senses. "Those conceptions which, after they have spontaneously arisen, prove serviceable in practice, and capable of verification in sense, we call ideas of the understanding. The others remain ideas of

---

* Santayana himself admits, "Had Christianity or any other religion had its basis in literary or philosophical allegories, it would never have become a religion, because the poetry of it would never have been interwoven with the figures and events of real life."

the imagination." Santayana is thus in opposition to the whole German school of idealism, with its distinction between imagination and fancy, reason and understanding, two levels of truth, of which the higher one is attainable only through a sort of post-rational intuition.

It is true the imagination has "a noble rôle to play in the life of man." It blazes a trail far in advance of the more plodding understanding; by its quick access to the emotions, it makes articulate "national and family spirit, so useful for moral organization and discipline"; it expresses "the universal self, the common and contagious element in all individuals, that rudimentary potency which they all share." The understanding, with its more laborious method of trial and error, would take centuries to substantiate what the imagination can disclose in a moment's flash. Still it is a dangerous force.

While its inspirations coincide with what would be the dictates of reason, were reason audible in the world, all is well, and the progress of man is accelerated by his visions; but being a principle *a priori* the imagination is an irresponsible principle; its rightness is an inward rightness, and everything in the real world may turn out to be disposed otherwise than as it would wish. . . . The too hasty organization of our thoughts becomes the cause of their more prolonged disorganization, for to the natural obscurity of things and the difficulty of making them fit together among themselves, we add the cross lights of our prejudices and the impossibility of fitting reality into the frame we have made for it in our ignorance of its constitution and extent.

Its effects are most disastrous when it is intensely cultivated in the form of mysticism.

The ideal of mysticism is accordingly exactly contrary to the ideal of reason; instead of perfecting human nature it seeks to abolish it; instead of building a better world, it would undermine the foundations even of the world we have built already; instead of developing our mind to greater scope and precision, it would return to the condition of protoplasm—to the blessed consciousness of an Unutterable Reality.

It is true "a partial mysticism often serves to bring out with wonderful intensity those underlying strata of experience which it has not yet decomposed," and "moderately indulged in and duly inhibited by a residuum of conventional sanity," it illuminates such legitimate abstractions as the divine, the absolute, the universal, the one. But although it suggests superhuman gifts, "it is not, however, in the least superhuman." "Nothing is more normal than abstraction," and "the better side of mysticism is an aesthetic interest in large unities and cosmic laws." "It serves to keep alive the conviction, which a confused experience might obscure, that perfection is essentially possible; it reminds us, like music, that there are worlds far removed from the actual which are yet living and very near to the heart." The danger from its abuse arises when the mystic mistakes his visions for the existence of an actual world and claims for his raptures the "only way of life."

A theory of knowledge is the last court of appeal in philosophy. One cannot go beyond a philosophic dictum as to what constitutes truth and how it is attained. Whether one accepts or rejects a theory of knowledge will determine one's approval or disapproval of a philosopher's entire system. And so if one objects to Santayana's choice of the understanding as the avenue to truth, he may as well expect to find himself at odds with everything Santayana has written. Between mysticism and rationalism there is no halfway ground.

Santayana's naturalism, however, does not involve the confinement of soul and barrenness of outlook which some might expect of it. On a purely naturalistic basis the world still offers much to a man in quest of either knowledge or pleasure. "Science and history are not exhausted" and the imagination kept in its rightful place can create at will the "true realm of man's infinity, where novelty may exist without falsity and perpetual diversity without contradiction."

If we renounced mysticism altogether and kept imagination in its place, should we not live in a clearer and safer world, as well as in a truer? Nay, are we sure that this gradually unfolding, intelligible, and real world would not turn out to be more congenial and beautiful than any wilful fiction, since it would be the product of a universal human labour and the scene of the accumulated sufferings and triumphs of mankind?

There is thus ample room for what Bertrand Russell called "a free man's worship."

These quotations from *Interpretations of Poetry and Religion* show that the Life of Reason is almost at hand. And the prospect it opens out before one should not discourage anyone willing to accept nature and the universe as they are.

As has been stated above, the book was not cordially received by the critics. The religious press, where it deigned to notice at all, denounced its philosophy as pagan, one reviewer going so far as to sound "Paul's warning to the Colossians against philosophy and vain deceit, after the rudiments of the world." Even the *Spectator* declared that there was more religion in Shakespeare's oaths than in "all our author's sanctimonious negations." In general, the book came as a distinct and rather unpleasant shock to the reading public of 1900.

Not that its religious stand was new or strange. The *New World* pointed out that there was much "agnostic orthodoxy" in the air, and that a similar point of view was to be found in the Ritschlian theology, in Lange's *History of Materialism,* and in Coubertin's *History of the French Republic.* And had not Mill and Arnold anticipated Santayana's remarks about the relation of religion to poetry? Religion is "but morality touched by emotion"; in the best Greek art, religion and poetry are one. "Religion and poetry address themselves . . . to the same part of the human constitution: they both supply the same want, that of ideal conceptions grander and more beautiful than we see realized in the prose of human life." Nor was Santayana's position unexpected if one had followed his previous writings. It had been at least implied in the poems and more explicitly stated in *The Sense of Beauty*. The novelty of *Interpretations of Poetry and Religion* was in the thoroughgoing identification of poetry and religion and the plain, unvarnished manner in which this was done. The book did not voice any change of opinion or new conviction of its author, but it did place squarely before the public Santayana's critical position. One might read the poems and, guided by their conventional diction, interpret them according to the dictates of one's own heart. One might dismiss *The Sense of Beauty* as a philosophical treatise or a textbook on aesthetics. But there was no mistaking the plain prose of *Interpretations of Poetry and Religion,* with its informality and its human interest. Even those who were repelled by the theory were often constrained to acknowledge the strength of argument, to admire the independent judgment throughout, and to delight in the beauty of style. Upon reading the book, William James wrote immediately to George Herbert Palmer, "Although I absolutely reject the Platonism of it, I have literally squealed with delight at the imperturbable perfection with which the position is laid down on page after page. It is refreshing to see a representative of moribund Latinity rise up and administer such reproof to us barbarians in the hour of our triumph."

Nor were the barbarians to be let off with a single reproof. As if to consolidate his gains, Santayana immediately turned his attention to formulating the Life of Reason. Yet he did find time between 1900 and 1905 for a few magazine articles in the *International Monthly* (later *Quarterly*), by this time the chief outlet for occasional articles by members of the Harvard faculty. "The Search for the True Plato" dealt with Lutoslawski's attempt in *The Logic of Plato* to solve the problem of the chronology of Plato's works. "The Two Idealisms" voiced for the first time Santayana's lifelong hatred of German idealism and thus prepared the way for *Egotism in German Philosophy,* 1916.

A more important article, "What Is Aesthetics?" Santayana contributed to the *Philosophical Review* in May 1904. It carries certain implications of *The Sense of Beauty* to their logical conclusions, and in so doing forecasts his position in *Reason in Art,* Volume IV of *The Life of Reason.* Santayana's general thesis is that there is no distinct science of aesthetics. On the one hand, beauty is by no means a servant to art alone; on the other, art itself is linked inseparably with the other interests of life. "What Is Aesthetics?" shows less sympathy with the psychological method than did *The Sense of Beauty.*

To reduce everything to the experience which discloses it is doubtless the mission of psychology . . . so that the subject-matter of aesthetics, however various in itself, may be swallowed up in the psychological vortex, together with everything else that exists.

Moreover, there is a firmer conception of the relation of beauty to art than was evidenced in *The Sense of Beauty.*

What exists in the ideal region in lieu of an aesthetic science is the art and function of criticism . . . an intelligent critic must look impartially to beauty, propriety, difficulty, originality, truth, and moral significance in the work he judges.

Finally in 1905 appeared, two volumes at a time, *The Life of Reason* itself. Santayana explains the purpose of his work thus:

Starting with the immediate flux, in which all objects and impulses are given, to describe the Life of Reason; that is, to note what facts and purposes seem to be primary, to show how the conception of nature and life gathers around them, and to point to the ideals of thought and action which are approached by this gradual mastering of experience by reason.

Reason itself is

... vital impulse ... when it is modified by reflection and veers in sympathy with judgments pronounced on the past. ... Man's rational life consists in those moments in which reflection not only occurs but proves efficacious. ... The Life of Reason is the happy marriage of two elements—impulse and ideation—which if wholly divorced would reduce man to a brute or to a maniac. The rational animal is generated by the union of these two monsters. He is constituted by ideas which have ceased to be visionary and actions which have ceased to be vain. [Again,] The *Life of Reason* will then be a name for that part of experience which perceives and pursues ideals—all conduct so controlled and all sense so interpreted as to perfect natural happiness. ... Though this be an ideal, yet everyone gives it from time to time a partial embodiment when he practises useful arts, when his passions happily lead him to enlightenment, or when his fancy breeds visions pertinent to his ultimate good. Everyone leads the Life of Reason in so far as he finds a steady light behind the world's glitter and a clear residuum of joy beneath pleasure or success.

In all these definitions two important attributes of reason are stressed: its natural basis in instinct and its ideal significance in determining goals of conduct. Santayana tries throughout his book to lay equal stress upon these two aspects of a rational life, and, wherever possible, to reconcile their claims.

Volume I of *The Life of Reason* is the most important in its metaphysical implications. It proceeds to trace the gradual evolution of man from vegetative consciousness to the rational life. At some momentous period in prehistoric times the physical structure of the body became so highly coördinated and complex that a special sense was developed which might survey the body's needs and assist in its preservation. This sense was rudimentary reason. By reflecting on certain animal impulses, it endeavored to promote and prolong pleasure and comfort and to avoid pain. Gradually it came to distinguish natural objects as apart from man himself, and so in a vague way achieved a separation of self and other. In time these natural objects were unified in an external world, from which was gradually pared away the integument of animism. The external world, thus relieved, shrank and solidified, the domain of mind became enlarged and set apart from that of external nature, and so another important distinction was achieved by reason. Fellow minds were discovered by what Santayana terms the "transposition of tertiary qualities": i. e., emotions such as pleasure, fear, anger were attributed to those beings who were felt to produce such emotions in the person affected, and where there happened to be a coincidence of emotion, as in the battle, the chase, or the festival, a great step was made in the direction of sympathetic understanding and rudimentary psychology. Thus bit by bit man came to understand the world in which he found himself, myth gradually giving way to science as the rational faculty increased in strength and extended its dominion.

Santayana is then in a position to state explicitly the relation of man to nature as he had poetically implied it in the sonnets.

Mind is the body's entelechy, a value which accrues to the body when it has reached a certain perfection, of which it would be a pity, so to speak, that it should remain unconscious; so that while the body feeds the mind, the mind protects the body, lifting it and all its natural relations and impulses into the moral world, into the sphere of interests and ideas.

This conception of the relation of mind to matter occurs constantly throughout Santayana's entire work and is the basis of his apparently paradoxical stand as an idealistic materialist. Mind owes its origin, growth, and development to matter, but the strange child repays his parent a hundredfold with the riches he pours in her lap. Nature gives birth to consciousness; consciousness gives value to nature.

Some readers may feel that Santayana's thesis concerning the dependence of mind on body is somewhat arbitrary and dogmatic in the face of the evidence he offers, even if such dogmatism enables him to march boldly and consistently through an undergrowth of metaphysics which might entrap the more circumspect philosopher. In reality, Santayana's belief in the dependence of mind on body follows directly from his conception of nature as mechanism. Mind cannot produce the marvelous effects of consciousness but can only enjoy and express them. The old notion of the freedom of the will, though true in a broad poetic sense, is utterly false if by it is meant that consciousness enters the arena of force and matter and imposes upon nerve and tissue its imperious mandates. Nature is throughout mechanical, and mind is only a part of nature. And if it seems to you that nature has been pointing toward the glory of man from time immemorial, that there is in the universe a sublime teleology, a "final cause" in the Aristotelian sense, remember that

... the process by which an arrangement which is essentially unstable gradually shifts cannot be said to aim at every stage which at any moment it involves. For the process passes beyond. It presently abolishes all the forms which may have arrested attention and generated love; its initial energy defeats every purpose which we may fondly attribute to it ... the process, taken in the gross, does not, even by mechanical necessity, support the value which is supposed to guide it. That value is realised for a moment only; so that if we impute to Cronos any intent to beget his children we must also impute to him an intent to devour them.

Man cannot hide optimistically behind the specious claims of teleology. Teleology is, of course, not incompatible with determinism; from the beginning of time there is predestined for some Christians a glorious, heavenly future, for some Hegelians a glorious, earthly present. Even mechanism as a mere logical principle does not preclude teleology. But teleology withers beside the evidence of natural science. The later stages of any evolution are bound to show a descending curve hostile, perhaps fatal, to man and all his aspirations. Though men may flourish, man is eventually doomed. Santayana's faith is, as always, in naturalism, not as a logical *sine qua non,* but as the only possible interpretation of experience. He holds to the postulates of Victorian science, with its vision, as he says in one of his poems, of the "patient earth, made dry and barren," shedding "all her herbage in a final winter." Though modern science is not sure whether the universe is really running down or winding up again at the same time, whether its construction is mechanical or mathematical, or simply forever impossible to determine, Santayana has not once swerved from his lifelong conviction, and it underlies the entire metaphysical structure of *The Life of Reason.*

But a practical difficulty immediately occurs to some readers of *The Life of Reason.* If mind is but an entelechy, asks one critic, how can "vital impulse" be "modified by reflection," how can thought become "practical," how can "conduct" be "controlled"? If there were no freedom of the will to choose the rational in preference to the irrational, there would be little need for anyone's writing a Life of Reason and no need for anyone's reading one. Predetermined instinct would map out the course of one's life, and moral advice would be wasted effort, unless by accident it might come in the way of character already susceptible to its influence. Here it would seem as if Santayana, the naturalist and the pragmatist, standing firm for the physical origin and basis of consciousness, and Santayana, the Platonist and the perfectionist, believing in the possibility of a Life of Reason and in the pursuit and attainment of ends of conduct, had at last met in mortal combat. But Santayana, the entire man, entertained no such thought.

He replied that his critics considered reason in two different senses, confused the physiological fact of consciousness with the moral concept of rationality, and attempted to identify something mechanical with something figurative and ideal. Santayana's reply illuminates his own position, but it still does not satisfactorily solve the problem of whether moral initiative can be accounted for on grounds of determinism. This is one of the thorniest problems of ethics, one which has troubled all philosophers from the Greeks down who have attempted to build an idealism upon the foundations of naturalism.

Santayana's discussion of the evolution of reason is equal in simplification to his treatment of mind and body. Reason is a simple, unitary phenomenon throughout its many stages of development. The principle of continuity is the recognition of identity in the flux, whether the flux be of sensation, or on a higher level, of passion, or still higher, of conflicting aims. The first step consciousness makes is "association by similarity," which gives rise to ideas of simple qualities. Following this, qualities allocated together in space are conceived as ideas of simple things. "Sensuous experience is solidified into logical terms, these into ideas of things, and these, recast and smelted again in imagination, into forms of spirit." The same innate preference of the mind for order is reflected in the simplest concretion and in the choice of the most sublime ideal. Idealism is native to thought in all its stages of development. If one agrees with Santayana's assertion, a remarkable consistency is achieved. A logical hierarchy has been created with the Idea of the Good, the ultimate preference, at the top. And such a hierarchy the Greeks created, crowned by Aristotle's conception of God. But, from Santayana's point of view, the logical hierarchy is at the same time an evolutionary process, spread out seriatim throughout history at the same time as it is concentrated in its entirety in the mental phenomena of a mature human being.

But the plain man may not glimpse the genesis of reason so clearly, or see how ideas shade so easily into ideals, may sense a simplification beyond what his experience reveals to him. He will maintain that any inquiry into the origin of reason must deal with conditions admittedly unscientific. There are three avenues of approach: the anthropological attempts to trace the dawn of reason in mankind, the biological searches for it by analogy in the animal kingdom, the psychological watches it in the development of the infant mind. Santayana utilizes all three approaches; but he scrupulously avoids the scientific method of presenting evidence, and thus leaves one often in doubt which avenue he is taking or sometimes whether he is following any at all. The treatment is largely imaginative and Reason stalks the pages like the protagonist of a drama, with the world and mankind for a vague backdrop. Indeed it seems as if Santayana carried out to the letter his statement that in writing *The Life of Reason* "all that was needed was to know oneself."

In regard to the survival of ideals, the pathway by which concretions ascend into the realm of moral values seems in Santayana's treatment beset with fewer dangers than is true of this real world of ours. Other instincts, the possessive, the combative, fear, seem just as natural and as fundamental as the rational faculty. Moreover, is reason, once developed, coterminous with virtue; what assurance is there that the clearest of concretions may not be used for malevolent purposes? Mephistopheles had a clearer vision than Faust; and Lucifer, in Santayana's version, is the personification of reason without faith. Moreover, there are many men who glimpse the ideal but have not moral strength to pursue it. Santayana has apparently forgotten William James's varieties of the obstructed will. There is at times in Santayana a strain suggesting Rousseau rather than the Greeks. "Nature is innocent, and so are all her impulses and moods when taken in isolation; it is only on meeting that they blush." There seems to Santayana a joyful serenity about the lark poised in flight, the otter basking in the sunlight, the cat curled upon the hearth. Animal bliss is rudimentary idealism; it exhibits a state of equilibrium in which all bodily functions contribute to pure sensual enjoyment. But one wonders whether this state is really as fundamental to animal life as are the more utilitarian instincts of self-preservation and reproduction. One wonders also whether "impulses and moods" can ever be maintained "in isolation" since animal life is throughout gregarious. A second amœba in an aquarium would forever prohibit such a natural Utopia. One wonders, finally, what connection this biological hedonism really has with the idealism of human beings. All of these considerations suggest that the rational and the moral have a more complex relationship than Santayana admits. The Socratic maxim which Santayana accepts, that knowledge is virtue, requires a simplification of human nature and a faith in its inherent nobility as scientifically debatable as it is ethically praiseworthy.

Later in the third volume Santayana himself admits:

> When we have skimmed from life its incidental successes, when we have harvested the moments in which existence justifies itself, its profound depths remain below in their obscure commotion, depths that breed indeed a rational efflorescence, but which are far from exhausted in producing it, and continually threaten, on the contrary, to engulf it.

In view of this admission, one wonders why Santayana in *The Life of Reason* has not investigated more the internal constitution of the mind. This omission is partly intentional, for Santayana is more concerned pragmatically with the operation of reason than transcendentally with its nature; he hopes thus to avoid the pitfalls of German metaphysics. But the matter cannot be so easily dismissed; one looks for more illumination of the shadowy region where reflection supervenes upon impulse, where the rational lapses into the irrational, where the conscious springs from the unconscious. Reason is too often treated as if it were in a vacuum. What William James called the fringe of consciousness, that realm of dream shapes and forgotten memories, when considered at all, is viewed with a sort of horror as a remnant of the vegetative consciousness, the limbo in which nature slumbers but from which man has risen to the clear vision of thought. Every philosophy has its devil to exercise, and subliminal consciousness seems to be Santayana's.

There may well be intense consciousness in the total absence of rationality. Such consciousness is suggested in dreams, in madness, and may be found, for all we know, in the depths of universal nature. Minds peopled only by desultory visions and lusts would not have the dignity of human souls even if they seemed to pursue certain objects unerringly; for that pursuit would not be illumined by any vision of its goal.

Though *The Life of Reason's* metaphysics is open to the objections I have enumerated, its ethical position is wholly admirable. All the parts which seem to fly asunder when considered as explanations of fact fit neatly in place when viewed as ideals of conduct. Thus the natural basis of all ideals, which can with difficulty be made to account for the moral stamina ideals possess, is an excellent check against their becoming thin and visionary. Santayana's morality is always fixed to this earth no matter how high it may soar.

The keystone of Santayana's ethics is of course the ideal, and much of *The Life of Reason* is a careful examination of the conditions under which idealism is possible. In the first place, an ideal must spring from natural impulses; "it must be a resultant or synthesis of impulses already afoot." Moreover, it must be particular and concrete. To place the strength of an ideal in its vagueness and "in an elasticity which makes it wholly indeterminate and inconsistent" is a gross error of barbarism and unbridled romanticism. The ideal must be a form-giver; it must resolve the cross purposes and conflicting aims of one's life. To consider life as a perpetual round of warring impulses, to devour experience as a glutton would gorge himself with food is the height of unreason. To Santayana the feverish pursuit of the unattainable, as in Goethe's *Faust,* seems futile and sad and spells for him the madness of the modern world. As he pointed out in *Interpretations of Poetry and Religion,* there must be discipline in life, self-imposed it is true, but none the less vigorous and authoritative.

Such control over impulse must, however, be wise and tolerant. To deny the initial right of any impulse is not morality but fanaticism. However determined may be the prohibition which reason opposes to some wild instinct, that prohibition is never reckless; it is never inconsiderate of the very impulse which it suppresses. . . . The texture of the natural world, the conflict of interests in the soul and in society, all of which cannot be satisfied together, is accordingly the ground for moral restrictions and compromises. Whatever the upshot of the struggle may be, whatever the verdict pronounced by reason, the parties to the suit must in justice all be heard, and heard sympathetically.

If reason is what Paul Elmer More calls an "inner check," it is so on the ground of efficacy, and it is ever ready to reconstruct "worn conventions" if need be with "a fresh sense for the universal need and cry of human souls." Santayana's ethics does no lip-service to tradition and conventionality, though it recognizes a permanent core of human nature which tends to maintain uniformity in moral values.

Moral codes imposed from without seem to Santayana subversive of true morality. The individual alone is judge of what shall be his ideal, for he alone feels the impulses which his ideal is to direct and harmonize. There is a staunch individualism in Santayana's ethics which suggests Emerson. But lest such an individualism run toward moral license and anarchy, Santayana has imposed upon it certain checks and balances. Not only must a person's entire life be considered, the sum total of his wants and aspirations, in the construction of an ideal, but "a harmony and coöperation of impulses should be conceived, leading to the maximum satisfaction possible in the whole community of spirits affected by our action." If Santayana's morality is self-centered, its breadth renders this self-interest innocuous in practice. And the naturalness of self-love and self-interest may indeed make such an ethics more practical than the lofty altruism of such a system as the Christian one.

It is often objected that Santayana's ethics is weakened by a separation of the ideal from the real. And in one sense such an objection carries weight. By definition, the ideal cannot be the real, the existent, the material. But all thought to Santayana is representative; ideas are not felt in the way one experiences the brute fact of living. Ideas and ideals are real in the sense that they alone are intelligible. And if one is disillusioned because he cannot clasp them to him as he would a living creature, there is compensation in a settled "satisfaction which the coveted prize, could it have been attained, would hardly have secured." This is Platonism if one's beliefs must have a badge, but it by no means implies that one must feel sorrowful or estranged in the presence of ideals, which are the true companions of the spirit. And in a figurative sense there is no untruth in saying that one achieves his ideal.

The ideal requires, then, that opportunities should be offered for realising it through action, and that transition should be possible to it from a given state of things. One form of such transition is art, where the ideal is a possible and more excellent form to be given to some external substance or medium. . . . Matter . . . is therefore a necessary condition for realising an ideal at all.

The imposition of form upon matter, upon character, upon life itself is the attainment of an ideal. Such an idealism is in the truly classical tradition.

We are now in a position to inquire what is the ultimate desideratum of the good life? Santayana's answer is brief—happiness. "Happiness is the only sanction of life; where happiness fails, existence remains a mad and lamentable experiment." There is nothing shameful to him in acknowledging pleasure as a criterion of moral worth. Santayana's philosophy is a frank hedonism. "The more pleasure a universe can yield, other things being equal, the more beneficent and generous is its general nature; the more pains its constitution involves, the darker and more malign is its total temper. ... To deny that pleasure is a good and pain an evil is a grotesque affection." It will be noticed, however, that the pursuit of pleasure is not to be a mere selfish enterprise. The ideal is lost sight of "when a man cultivates his garden-plot of private pleasures, leaving it to chance and barbarian fury to govern the state and quicken the world's passions." The happiness of the greatest number must be striven for. "Any system that, for some sinister reason, should absolve itself from good-will toward all creatures, and make it somehow a duty to secure their misery, would be clearly disloyal to reason, humanity, and justice."

But pure Hedonism is likely to lead to a life which is merely passive and contemplative, one in which there is little opportunity for creative activity. Lest he seem to advocate such a way of life, Santayana wrote the volumes on art, science, and society, which give ample opportunity for the expression of the creative impulse. As Santayana says in *Reason in Art,*

A creature like man, whose mode of being is a life or experience and not a congealed ideality, such as eternal truth might show, must accordingly find something to do; he must operate in an environment in which everything is not already what he is presently to make it.

Thus the Life of Reason urges that man cultivate ideal interests because they afford him not only passive enjoyment but also purposeful activity.

The application of Santayana's idealism to society, religion, art, and science can be treated more briefly. In *Reason in Society,* Santayana makes his only excursion into the field of social science, discussing such matters as love; the family; industry, government, and war; the aristocratic and democratic ideals; patriotism; and free and ideal society. The treatment is not as abstract or as abstruse as one would expect at the hands of a philosopher; in fact, the book is more readable than many portions of *Reason in Common Sense.*

Santayana begins with love, viewing it as the strongest impulse among the animal passions and the loftiest ideal in the realm of moral values. In fact, the latter is the result of the former's being so deeply grounded in the experience of the race and issuing from the very instinct to perpetuate the species. Santayana is more frank than most philosophers in his emphasis upon the natural basis of love in the sexual instincts and functions, for he believes "there can be no philosophic interest in disguising the animal basis of love, or in denying its spiritual sublimations, since all life is animal in its origin and all spiritual in its possible fruits." "Popular feeling . . . makes the origin of love divine and its object natural: which is the exact opposite of the truth." Santayana thus wisely condemns an unnatural suppression of sexual instincts. He feels, with perhaps a tinge of the sentiment we observed in *Reason in Common Sense,* that the complexity of man's interests has muddied over the clear stream of primitive passion, with the result that love becomes morbid or erotic.

Having paid his respects to the natural basis of love, Santayana turns to a discussion of the idealization of love, which suggests the earlier essay on the Italian love-poets. The treatment is decidedly Platonic. Set afire by a spark of animal instinct, love burns brightly until its blaze may kindle the noblest aspirations of man, yearnings for beauty, goodness, truth. But these ideals are never completely actualized in the world of material things and human beings. There is always an underside of disillusionment to love.

There is indeed no idol ever identified with the ideal which honest experience, even without cynicism, will not some day unmask and discredit. Every real object must cease to be what it seemed, and none could ever be what the whole soul desired. Yet what the soul desires is nothing arbitrary. Life is no objectless dream, but continually embodies, with varying success, the potentialities it contains and that prompt desire. Everything that satisfies at all, even if partially and for an instant, justifies aspiration and rewards it. . . . The ideal is accordingly significant, perpetual, and as constant as the nature it expresses; but it can never itself exist, nor can its particular embodiments endure.

But to have loved is something.

Love is a true natural religion; it has a visible cult, it is kindled by natural beauties and bows to the best symbol it may find for its hope; it sanctifies a natural mystery; and, finally, when understood, it recognises that what it worshipped under a figure was truly the principle of all good.

What has Reason to say of this strange, irrational Eros? Well, reason can but admit that the "lover knows much more about absolute good and universal beauty than any logician or theologian, unless the latter, too, be lovers in disguise." But even the lover can accept counsel in the direction of happy rational living. "A man who has truly loved, though he may come to recognise the thousand incidental illusions into which love may have led him, will not recant its essential faith. He will keep his sense for the ideal and his power to worship." To many this view of love seems to ignore the simple human affections, the love of flesh and blood and the warm glow of personality; to others it does not seem inevitable that the pursuit of the ideal must needs be accompanied by dissatisfaction with the actual; and there are even those who deny any such cleavage between ideal and actual, believing the one to reside in the other. To such men the Platonism of Santayana is repugnant; to the first it seems unreal; to the second, unnecessary; to the third, untrue. Whatever one believes himself, however, he must admit that Santayana has paid eloquent tribute to the love which animated Dante and Michelangelo and which has given rise to some of the noblest conceptions of poetry and religion; that he has consistently interpreted love in terms of his naturalism and his idealism; that he has accounted for much of the joy and much of the sorrow we see in the world about us; and that he has offered a rational way of life which would save many an unwary lover from spiritual shipwreck.

"Love is but a prelude to life, an overture in which the theme of the impending work is exquisitely hinted at, but which remains nevertheless only a symbol and a promise." Communal life has imposed upon man certain institutions such as the family and the state partly as a means of protection, partly as a means of harmonious coöperation.

The family is one of nature's masterpieces. It would be hard to conceive a system of instincts more nicely adjusted, where the constituents should represent or support one another better. The husband has an interest in protecting the wife, she in serving the husband. . . . Parents lend children their experience and a vicarious memory; children endow their parents with a vicarious immortality.

The force of the reproductive instinct and the length of childhood with its need for protection and education seem to make some sort of family life imperative, both naturally and ideally, so that "no suggested substitute for the family is in the least satisfactory."

Yet conditions are expedient rather than ideal. The family has assumed "offices which might have been allotted to some other agency, had not the family preëmpted them, profiting by its established authority and annexing them to its domain." The family imposes an arbitrary paternalism upon its members, it needlessly confines the free spirit, which might find more kindred associations elsewhere, and it

... perpetuates accidental social differences, exaggerating and making them hereditary. ... Young men escape as soon as they can, at least in fancy, into the wide world; all prophets are homeless and all inspired artists; philosophers think out some communism or other, and monks put it in practice. ... Family life, as Western nations possess it, is still regulated in a very bungling, painful, and unstable manner. Hence ... prostitution, adultery, divorce ... genius and religion thwarted by family ties, single lives empty, wedded lives constrained, a shallow gallantry, and a dull virtue.

The task of the Life of Reason is to "combine the maximum of spiritual freedom with the maximum of moral cohesion," but as yet it can only suggest the directions improvements would take.

They would reform and perfect the function of reproduction without discarding it; they would maintain the family unless they could devise some institution that combined intrinsic and representative values better than does that natural artifice, and they would recast either the instincts or the laws concerned, or both simultaneously, until the family ceased to clash seriously with any of these three things: natural affection, rational nurture, and moral freedom.

Just how reproduction would be altered (as if it could be discarded) and how these basic instincts could be recast, Santayana does not tell us. But in spite of this negligence, and a treatment of woman that suggests not only a man but also a bachelor, these remarks on the family are well considered, and if a bit academic on the surface, are at heart genuinely concerned for the best interests of humankind.

Santayana's treatment of the state is much similar to that of the family. The state like the family has evolved naturally, we have it on our hands, but the fact should not prevent an honest inquiry into its utility and its rationality. The civilized state secures three chief advantages: "greater wealth, greater safety, and greater variety of experience." These are indubitable goods, but they are means rather than ends. They are opportunities, one might almost say requisites, for a spiritual life, but they are not in themselves spiritual at all. For instance, "wealth must justify itself in happiness. Someone must live better for having produced or enjoyed these possessions." Irrational industry too often "has put into rich men's hands facilities and luxuries which they trifle with without achieving any dignity or true magnificence in living, while the poor, if physically more comfortable than formerly, are not meantime notably wiser or merrier."

No one who has watched the economic development of this country can deny the justice of Santayana's arraignment. It is one of the most forceful passages in *Reason in Society*. And the emphasis is placed correctly, on the false value of quantity set up as an ideal.

The highest building, the largest steamer, the fastest train, the book reaching the widest circulation have, in America, a clear title to respect. When the just functions of things are as yet not discriminated, the superlative in any direction seems naturally admirable.

I suppose quantity is a legitimate end, for grandeur and sublimity are sources of genuine aesthetic experiences; moreover quantity has a function in prolonging quality. But to worship quantity indiscriminately, to blot from one's vision anything but material size, is unreason, barbarism. This whole discussion is the logical outcome of Santayana's early essay, "What Is a Philistine?" and, as in the early essay, there is no mincing of words in Santayana's condemnation.

Santayana is just as trenchant in condemning war. Though pugnacity is a human instinct, it may be curbed and diverted into competitive sport. War is utterly irrational. To insure safety, however, there must be some political organization; Santayana weighs both aristocracy and democracy in the balance and casts his lot for a timocracy—a government by men of merit. The aristocratic ideal is true to man's inherent inequality and it fosters culture and civilization, without which life would revert to barbarism. Beside it an ideal of social democracy reduces everything and everybody to a dead level of mediocrity. Aristocracies, however, seemingly have no way of stamping out the injustice, the humiliation, and the suffering which arise from political inequality. "Democratic theory seems to be right . . . about the actual failure of theocracies, monarchies, and oligarchies to remain representative and to secure the general good." What then of timocracy?

[It] would differ from the social aristocracy that now exists only by the removal of hereditary advantages. People would be born equal, but they would grow unequal, and the only equality subsisting would be equality of opportunity. If power remained in the people's hand, the government would be democratic; but a full development of timocracy would allow the proved leader to gain great ascendancy. The better security the law offered that the men at the top should be excellent, the less restraint would it need to put upon them when once in their places . . . it would be just and open to every man, but it would not depress humanity nor wish to cast everybody in a common mould.

This is the Life of Reason's political ideal, an ideal quite in keeping with the recent exaltation of the leader even in democratic countries, but Santayana has to confess that it is largely Utopian. There is no way in the present state of things to assure equal privilege, no way of finding just the right spot on this planet for a man's spiritual development. Society would have to be extremely mobile, and the conditions of birth more accidental than they are at present. Moreover, it would require nothing short of a transformation of human nature for the masses to accept knowingly what is considered their due.

The remainder of *Reason in Society* is devoted chiefly to the conflicting claims of the local and the universal upon a human life. Patriotism in its broadest sense is the claim of the first, loyalty to family, to community, to country; friendship in its broadest sense is the claim of the second, the free association of kindred souls unrestricted by the barriers of birth or condition. Both claims must be listened to; patriotism sums up man's natural allegiances, and no soul can afford to pull up its roots in mother nature; but friendship transcends the exigencies of nationality and finds spiritual affinities which are outside space and time altogether. Nationality like her parent nature is a principle of differentiation, of variety, but in the universal man finds a uniformity and a permanence which are even more priceless possessions.

Many critics have found *Reason in Society* inferior to the more metaphysical portions of *The Life of Reason,* have felt the philosopher to be blinded by the glare of the forum and the market-place. I cannot share this opinion. Although space limitations permit Santayana only a brief survey of the institutions he discusses, so that he is, unable to solve all the problems his remarks suggest, I feel that he applies judiciously his ethical principles to the practical affairs of social, economic, and political organization, and although he refrains from offering detailed plans for reform, he indicates the direction reforms must take and he is well aware of the difficulties they will encounter. For Santayana never loses sight of the material core at the heart of society; he never forces upon society a pattern in any way contrary to nature. Yet he never loses sight of the ideal harmonies inherent in social intercourse, harmonies which a better organization might bring out, to make living a thing of joy and beauty rather than the compound of tyranny and suspicion it has so often been in the past.

Reason in Religion adds nothing new to Santayana's treatment of religion. His diatribe against supernaturalism is repeated. In the history of the several religions, the poetry has tended "to arrogate to itself literal truth and moral authority, neither of which it possesses," to give unsubstantiated information about experience and reality in another world, "to offer imaginary remedies for mortal ills, some of which are incurable essentially, while others might have been really cured by well-directed effort." In short, religion has no foundation in physics or metaphysics. Nevertheless, religion has a vital place in the Life of Reason. "It makes absolute moral decisions. It sanctions, unifies, and transforms ethics. Religion thus exercises a function of the Life of Reason. And a further function which is common to both is that of emancipating man from his personal limitations." The particular virtues religion promotes—piety, charity, and spirituality—are among the finest expressions of the Life of Reason. Religion is thus a great humanizing force.

Reason in Religion differs from *Interpretations of Poetry and Religion* in its more systematic inquiry into the origin and development of religion and in its more thorough appraisal of the ideals religion fosters. It is to be expected that Santayana would stress the cradling of religion in primitive want and fear. But he deals fairly with the superstition underlying religion, and his treatment of mythology shows, as usual, sympathy and insight. Mythology has carried religion "over from superstition into wisdom, from an excuse and apology for magic into an ideal representation of moral goods." Santayana's survey of religious history is penetrating, too, despite its brevity. Particularly suggestive are his interpretations of Hebrew and Protestant ethics, especially his conception of Protestantism as a reflorescence of the national religion of the Teutons asserting itself energetically in behalf of the individual conscience. His statement that Protestantism is "a religion of pure spontaneity, of emotional freedom, deeply respecting itself but scarcely deciphering its purposes," is bound to be provocative, but it at least challenges denial. On the other hand, Santayana's treatment of the conquest of the western world by Christianity has neither the charm nor the adequacy of the similar treatment in *Interpretations of Poetry and Reli-*

gion. The reasons given for the spread of Christianity are not so fully and so convincingly presented as in the earlier book. Santayana's discussion of eclecticism in the perfected Christian theology is, however, painstaking and sound.

But all this historical matter, interesting as it is, serves merely as background for a consideration of the virtues bred by religion and the place it occupies in a Life of Reason. Considered historically, religion had a most important function in the early stages of civilization.

We must not blame religion for preventing the development of a moral and natural science which at any rate would seldom have appeared; we must rather thank it for the sensibility, the reverence, the speculative insight which it has introduced into the world.

But what of the present and future? Here Santayana is less convincing, but evidently he feels deeply that what good religion can do in the establishment of ideals overbalances what error it may give rise to in the mistaking of these for actual facts. For, as he says,

. . . this struggling and changing force of religion seems to direct man toward something eternal. It seems to make for an ultimate harmony within the soul and for an ultimate harmony between the soul and all the soul depends upon. So that religion, in its intent, is a more conscious and direct pursuit of the Life of Reason than is society, science, or art.

And there is infinite hope for refinement in religion, making it less and less literal and factual, and more and more symbolical and moral.

Reason's reconstruction of religion does overturn two of humanity's most cherished beliefs, in the efficacy of prayer and in personal immortality. Prayer is rational in that it clarifies the ideal, reconciles man to the inevitable, promotes discipline and spirituality. But that prayer is at all supernatural is both unbelievable and unworthy of belief. Such a conception reduces the spiritual to the mechanical, to the level of telepathy. Likewise, to Santayana a belief in immortality is not merely absurd but ignoble. It is an evidence of fear or selfishness or vanity, untenable on physical grounds and undesirable on moral. An existence in the future unlike this one on earth is inconceivable, and one similar to this (what most people unconsciously desire), ridiculous in its duplication.

But one cannot help wondering, if reason demolishes most of the foundations on which religion exists, how can religion continue to perform its function as a necessary part of the Life of Reason? As I have pointed out above, the main objection to Santayana's conception of religion is that it seems crowded out of the Life of Reason by the very process of rationalization. It is almost impossible to conceive of religious attitudes at all without their full mystical and supernatural implications. They merely wither and become something else in the cold blast of reason.

And yet what seems to be a destruction of religion in Santayana's hands may turn out to be a purgation. Religion may emerge finer, quintessential, a thing of pure spirituality within the limits of the genuinely natural. Take, for instance, Santayana's conception of ideal immortality, the very pinnacle of his idealism.

Since the ideal has this perpetual pertinence to moral struggles, he who lives in the ideal and leaves it expressed in society or in art enjoys a double immortality. The eternal has absorbed him while he lived, and when he is dead his influence brings others to the same absorption, making them, through that ideal identity with the best in him, reincarnations and perennial seats of all in him which he could rationally hope to rescue from destruction.... By becoming the spectator and confessor of his own death and of universal mutation, he will have identified himself with what is spiritual in all spirits and masterful in all apprehension; and so conceiving himself, he may truly feel and know that he is eternal.

This passage may be compared with the thought of "Avila" and "Midnight" in the way it links man's mortality with his spirituality and his essential humanity. "That was a heroic and divine oracle which, in informing us of our decay, made us partners of the gods' eternity, and by giving us knowledge poured into us, to that extent, the serenity and balm of truth." And, even on a purely material plane, "every attainment of perfection in an art—as for instance in government—makes a return to perfection easier for posterity, since there remains an enlightening example, together with faculties predisposed by discipline to recover their ancient virtue." Santayana here for the first time evokes the deep undertones of comfort and faith in the face of death and destruction which swell so nobly from *Soliloquies in England.*

Reason in Art, like *Reason in Religion,* is largely an expansion of earlier material, its premises being stated in *The Sense of Beauty* and restated in *Interpretations of Poetry and Religion.* The birth of art, like that of reason itself, is spontaneous and automatic. The values it later achieves can by no means account for its origin. Such a view, as is usual with Santayana, tends to throw over the advent of art, like that of reason itself, something of the accidental and the miraculous. If man "happens, by a twist of the hand, to turn a flowering branch into a wreath, thereby making it more interesting, he will have discovered a decorative art and initiated himself auspiciously into the practice of it." Or, in the case of music, "that the way in which idle sounds run together should matter so much is a mystery of the same order as the spirit's concern to keep a particular body alive, or to propagate its life." In such a way does Santayana attempt to avoid the slightest suggestion of teleology in his explanations. From the point of view of the artist art is just as spontaneous and automatic. Instruction and practice make artistic expression to a certain degree habitual and predictable, since skill is mechanical, but uncertainty and indirection never entirely disappear, so that an artist's creation may come limping forth to his dismay, or may be a Pegasus to carry him to the skies.

A happy balance of two opposing forces has resulted in the perpetuation of art.

On the one side is purely spontaneous fancy, which would never foresee its own works and scarcely recognise or value them after they had been created; and on the other side is pure utility, which would deprive the work of all inherent ideality, and render it inexpressive of anything in man save his necessities. . . . The meanest arts are those which lie near the limit either of utility or of automatic self-expression. They become nobler and more rational as their utility is rendered spontaneous or their spontaneity beneficent.

But "any operation which . . . humanises and rationalises objects is called art." In the first place, art cannot be confined to what we customarily think of as the fine arts.

Art has accordingly two stages: one mechanical or industrial, in which untoward matter is better prepared, or impeding media are overcome; the other liberal, in which perfectly fit matter is appropriated to ideal uses and endowed with a direct spiritual function. . . . All industry contains an element of fine art and all fine art an element of industry.

In the second place, since art is widened to include most of man's creative effort, it follows that art cannot be independent of the moral values which govern life and promote happiness.

To criticise art on moral grounds is to pay it a high compliment by assuming that it aims to be adequate, and is addressed to a comprehensive mind. The only way in which art could disallow such criticism would be to protest its irresponsible infancy, and admit that it was a more or less amiable blatancy in individuals, and not *art* at all. If an artist's inspiration has been happy, it has been so because his work can sweeten or ennoble the mind and because its total effect will be beneficent. Art being a part of life, the criticism of art is a part of morals.

Modern art is marred, Santayana believes, by its failure to insist upon this intimacy between art and life. As a result, art resembles "an opiate or a stimulant." It is but "some little closed circle in experience, some dream in which we lose ourselves by ignoring most of our interests, and from which we awake into a world in which that lost episode plays no further part and leaves no heirs."

Having defined the function and sphere of art, Santayana proceeds to survey the several fine arts, tracing out their origins and estimating their place in the Life of Reason. The discussion of poetry and prose repeats much that was said in *Interpretations of Poetry and Religion,* but the treatment of the plastic arts is more expansive than was possible in *The Sense of Beauty,* and the chapter on music is entirely new. Of this last art Santayana is more appreciative than might be supposed, since his approach to art is usually through literature or the plastic arts. In fact, he pays great tribute to pure music, with its ideal world of forms, forms as intricate as those in mathematics and more vital in their emotional content. Music, through the emotional response it so easily awakens, gives "form to what is naturally inarticulate," and expresses "those depths of human nature which can speak no language current in the world."

Santayana assigns to art a very high place in the Life of Reason. In art there seems to be the greatest opportunity for the subordination of matter to mind. "Art, in establishing instruments for human life beyond the human body, and moulding outer things into sympathy with inner values, establishes a ground whence values may continually spring up." Art has thus a twofold significance in promoting a rational life. "The value of art lies in making people happy, first in practising the art and then in possessing its product." In another sense its value is twofold.

It prepares the world in some sense to receive the soul, and the soul to master the world; it disentangles those threads in each that can be woven into the other. . . . Art springs so completely from the heart of man that it makes everything speak to him in his own language; it reaches, nevertheless, so truly to the heart of nature that it coöperates with her, becomes a parcel of her creative material energy, and builds by her instinctive hand.

There is indeed some justification for calling art "the best instrument of happiness."

Santayana's conception of art, as I have said before, is objectionable to all those who advocate art for art's rather than life's sake, and who consider art a separable sphere of human activity. And is he entirely just in condemning all art which escapes life and creates realms of beauty fancy-free? The appreciation of the most remote beauty and the contemplation of the most irrelevant truth are conducive to happiness, and though life is urgent, the soul may be better prepared to face it after such experiences. These objections, however, seem negligible when one considers the worth of Santayana's effort to free art of bloodless preciosity and to make it more organically a part of the sum total of life.

Reason in Art in one respect is the most satisfying of all the volumes of *The Life of Reason*. In it the illustrative material is most familiar to Santayana. He is on firm ground when he speaks of literature and painting, and his treatment has a concreteness frequently lacking in the other volumes. And even where the philosopher may become confused, the taste of the artist remains fine and genuine, filling the book with appreciations and interpretations well worth reading for their charm, their sanity, and their justness.

Reason in Science fittingly comes last. It is the culmination of *The Life of Reason*. Nowhere else does Santayana give a present human activity such wholehearted support. With much in present-day society, art, and religion he is out of sympathy; but modern science seems to him the crowning achievement of the age. It is true his faith in science is somewhat accounted for by his liberal interpretation of the term. By science he does not mean any particular method of experiment or research, but the general notion of systematized and ordered knowledge. Thus, to doubt certain findings of science because of their inadequacy or even error does not constitute a sceptical indictment of science itself; it may be rather confidence that the science of the future will correct and augment that of the present. In one sense, "science is always its own best critic." After all, science is only common sense extended through experiment to those regions where sense perception is inadequate.

But Santayana sees the limitations of science as well as its potentialities. There may well be recesses in nature into which human knowledge cannot penetrate, gaps left in the network of the many related sciences. Nature at heart may be a surd. "Science is a great disciplinarian, and misses much of the sport which the absolute is free to indulge in." Yet within its realm, and its realm is ever growing wider, it is a sovereign power gradually annihilating the forces of myth and superstition which have too long garrisoned the citadel of human nature.

Santayana divides all science roughly into two parts, physics and dialectics, whose matter differs but whose methods are essentially the same. The physicist as well as the logician looks for recurrence and identity; he employs formulas and hypotheses and constructs laws; test-tube and syllogism perform the same function in the ordering of experience. Physics looks for and finds in nature a dialectical principle—mechanism, based on the orderly interrelation of natural phenomena. It is this principle which enables science to predict and reduce chaos to order. The laws governing mechanism which science discovers are not facts of existence at all, however, but pure essences revealed to dialectic because they are of the same stuff. Mechanism pervades all nature and probably all mind, but there is nothing intimidatingly materialistic about this notion; in fact, our distinction between mind and matter needs renovation. Both submit to rationalization and order, but both have an irrational core beyond the reach of knowledge.

The sciences surveyed in *Reason in Science* are history, psychology, physics, and logic, and though there is little detailed discussion of their methods and terms, there is a lucid interpretation of the principles upon which they are based. The most frequent objection to the book is that it ignores particular scientists, their discoveries, and the general progress of science in the concrete. One will look in vain for Copernicus and Newton, for the conservation of energy or the laws of thermodynamics. As a result, there is not the richness of illustration which is to be found in *Reason in Religion* and *Reason in Art*. On the other hand, Santayana's aim is to write a philosophy of science rather than a history of the special sciences; and perhaps a first-hand knowledge of science such as a scientist possesses would reveal to Santayana so much that is tentative and insecure in its methods and findings that its clear-cut outlines would be blurred. In *Reason in Science* Santayana's faith in science reaches its peak.

It is impossible to base science on a deeper foundation or to override it by a higher knowledge. What is called metaphysics, if not an anticipation of natural science, is a confusion of it with dialectic or a mixture of it with myths. . . . To live by science requires intelligence and faith, but not to live by it is folly. . . . If science thus contains the sum total of our rational convictions and gives us the only picture of reality on which we should care to dwell, we have but to consult the sciences in detail to ascertain, as far as that is possible, what sort of a universe we live in. The result is as yet far from satisfactory. The sciences have not joined hands and made their results coherent, showing nature to be, as it doubtless is, all of one piece. The moral sciences especially are a mass of confusion. . . . Yet exactly the same habits and principles that have secured our present knowledge are still active within us, and promise further discoveries. It is more desirable to clarify our knowledge within these bounds than to extend it beyond them. For while the reward of action is contemplation or, in more modern phrase, experience and consciousness, there is nothing stable or interesting to contemplate except objects relevant to action—the natural world and the mind's ideals.

The reception of *The Life of Reason* by the reading public was extremely varied. At one extreme the *Academy* praised Santayana as the "Elder Brother" who makes men "realize the charm of divine philosophy," and the *Journal of Philosophy, Psychology, and Scientific Methods* affirmed that "nowhere has the essentially *vital* character of reason been more clearly, forcefully, and gracefully stated." At the other extreme the *Athenaeum* doubted "whether the course of contemporary thought will be seriously modified by the present contribution," and a critic of the *International Journal of Ethics* declared the work so "wanting in clearness of thought that I doubt whether it can be of much use to anyone." Philosophers themselves disagreed over its value. William James termed its philosophy "irrational," "supercilious"; John Dewey thought it a "work nobly conceived and adequately executed." For the most part, the literary magazines valued *The Life of Reason* more highly than did the philosophical journals, whose critics confessed themselves puzzled by Santayana's intention and his treatment of his subject.

This attitude of bewilderment marked so many reviews of Santayana's work that we must try in some way to account for it. In the first place, Santayana's style as a vehicle for philosophical writing bothered professional philosophers considerably; the philosophical reviews felt the expression to be hazy, inaccurate, and too figurative for the subject matter. As G. E. Moore in the *International Journal of Ethics* said, "Santayana usually expresses his views in words which convey at the same time several different propositions, some of which may be true while others are false." A certain technical vocabulary has grown up in the interest of scientific exactness, and where a philosopher departs from that vocabulary it is generally only to substitute a more specialized set of symbols of his own making. Now Santayana dispenses for the most part with the tools of his trade and uses instead the vocabulary of life and letters, the old familiar words freighted with centuries of varied associations. God, matter, spirit, soul, throng his pages even if they are not the God, matter, spirit, soul, of popular tradition. For philosophical purposes this method results in a lack of precision, but for the general reader the gain in literary worth is indeed a compensation.

The other charge of the philosophers is more serious. The fault lies less in Santayana's style than in his method of treatment, which in turn comes from his intention. Desiring an unobstructed presentation of his ideas, he does away for the most part with all documentation and ignores all controversy. A gain in simplicity results and sometimes in clarity, but as the *Hibbert Journal* says, "When a system is shattered in an epigram, or an important controversy dismissed in an allusion, our craving for explicitness is sometimes left unsated." By ignoring other thinkers past and present Santayana imparts to his work a certain freshness, but it is a surface freshness, rippling over turbid waters of controversy below. In volumes I and V this tendency is most objectionable.

The Life of Reason gathers together all the individual strands of Santayana's early philosophy and weaves them into a finely knit garment of thought. In *The Life of Reason* all his trenchant comments on morals, on art, on literature, on metaphysics are brought within the focus of a point of view materialistic in regard to origins, pragmatic in regard to effects, and Platonic in regard to ultimate values. Toward *The Life of Reason* were pointing the poetic naturalism of the sonnets, the justification of art on aesthetic grounds in *The Sense of Beauty* and on moral grounds in *Poetry and Religion,* the reconstruction of religion in the latter book, the respect for science in the early essay on Spinoza, and the definition of the ideal in the two early *Harvard Monthly* essays. In *The Life of Reason* is felt particularly the stern side of Santayana, the absolute refusals that are the source of his strength. Nor has he ever again reached such a peak of confidence in reason, such an assurance that reason will make for mankind a better world as fear and ignorance are gradually dispersed. This Socratic assurance of Santayana is well illustrated by a few remarks at the conclusion of the work.

Could a better system prevail in our lives a better order would establish itself in our thinking. It has not been for want of keen senses, or personal genius, or a constant order in the outer world, that mankind have fallen back repeatedly into barbarism and superstition. It has been for want of good character, good example, and good government. There is a pathetic capacity in men to live nobly, if only they would give one another the chance. The ideal of political perfection, vague and remote as it yet seems, is certainly approachable, for it is as definite and constant as human nature. The knowledge of all relevant truth would be involved in that ideal, and no intellectual dissatisfaction would be felt with a system of ideas that should express and illumine a perfect life.

The Life of Reason of course brought Santayana a much wider reputation as a philosopher. Constable published the book in England, and notices there were more frequent and full than in the case of Santayana's previous work. The better foreign philosophical journals, such as the *Philosophisches Jahrbuch* and the *Archiv für Systematische Philosophie,* mentioned the book in their lists, although, as far as I can discover, none gave it an extended criticism. At a time when philosophical treatises were becoming technical and specialized, *The Life of Reason* had the distinction of being a work in the older manner, general in its scope, ranging throughout the broad area of human activity. It was in no sense a complete cosmology, however, omitting all considerations of nature and the universe outside of their influence upon human nature, which was in truth the protagonist of the book.

Viewed now in historical perspective, *The Life of Reason* seems to be but the culmination of nineteenth-century rationalism, and we must not today overstate the originality of many of Santayana's individual judgments. His debt to the nineteenth century has been overlooked by both himself and his critics. In particular, the naturalistic basis of *The Life of Reason* was hardly novel in the light of what had come to be, after the retreat of romanticism, a fairly prevalent conception of the threefold relationship of God, man, and nature. Far from being the quiet benefactor to man, as Wordsworth felt, nature to Mill

... impales men, breaks them as if on the wheel, casts them to be devoured by wild beasts, burns them to death, crushes them with stones like the first Christian martyr, starves them with hunger, freezes them with cold, poisons them by the quick or slow venom of her exhalations ... all this ... with the most supercilious disregard both of mercy and of justice. ... The scheme of Nature regarded in its whole extent, cannot have had, for its sole or even principal object, the good of human or other sentient beings.

As for man, he "has no power to do anything else than follow nature; all his actions are done through, and in obedience to, some one or many of nature's physical or mental laws." The same point of view was expressed poetically by Matthew Arnold.

> Man errs not that he dreams
> His welfare his true aim,
> He errs because he dreams
> The world does but exist that welfare to bestow.
> The world is what it is for all our dust and din.

Even Newman, looking out upon the world, found little evidence of comfort or hope there.

To consider the world in its length and breadth ... the tokens so faint and broken, of a superintending design, the blind evolution of what turn out to be great powers or truths, the progress of things, as if from unreasoning elements, not towards final causes ... the defeat of good, the success of evil, ... the prevalence and intensity of sin, the pervading idolatries, the corruptions, the dreary hopeless irreligion ... all this is a vision to dizzy and appall.

And if one thought of taking refuge in the mind or soul, Comte was ready to declare that "a scientific account of the mental life must be expressed in terms of the physiology of the nervous system," and Spencer looked upon mind as no more than "a particular aspect of life, the vital function which has to bring the activities of living beings into harmony with their environment." There is little room for God, too, in a universe where, says Huxley, "the further science advances, the more extensively and consistently will all the phenomena of Nature be represented by materialistic formulae and symbols." "The physiologist finds life to be as dependent for its manifestation on particular molecular arrangements as any physical or chemical phenomenon."

No, Santayana's conception of the universe, could not have struck the thinking world as a bombshell. Nor was his advocacy of reason unanticipated. Wundt had demonstrated that thought might be reduced to the single fact of inference, and Huxley justified the use of the understanding as a guide to happiness by maintaining that "natural knowledge, seeking to satisfy natural wants, has found the ideas which can alone still spiritual cravings," and "lay the foundations of a new morality." Nor was reason thus conceived the Reason of the Germans, a special intuitional moral sense; it was merely the light of consciousness playing over the turbid waters of instinct below. Physiological psychology was constantly demonstrating that, in Wundt's words, "the unconscious is the theatre of the most important mental phenomena. The conscious is always conditioned upon the unconscious." Not only the Spencerians and the Positivists but over a century earlier Hume had marked out, in words curiously anticipating Santayana's, the relation of intelligence to instinct. "Reason, being cool and disengaged, is no motive to action, and directs only the impulse received from appetite or inclination, by showing us the means of attaining happiness or avoiding misery." Even Paulsen, who was by no means a materialist in fundamentals, was moved by his age to affirm that "the processes of consciousness are based on an unconscious or, if we choose, sub-conscious psychical life which bears them, from which they rise, and by which their action is determined." As a result, ethical concepts such as duty were coming to be considered what Simmel called bundles of habits, the more binding the less their origins were known. The sense of freedom we feel in carrying out the dictates of our conscience, Simmel concluded to be an illusion, a mere "name which we give to our ignorance of psychological causality." Morality, like everything else, had to bend the knee before the empirical spirit of the age.

There had been attempts, too, very much like Santayana's, to salvage religion from the flux. The general effect of Arnold's writings, says T. S. Eliot, was to "affirm that the emotions of Christianity can and must be preserved without the belief." Mill, too, felt that religion and poetry "supply the same want," and wondered whether "the idealization of our earthly life" would not supply "a poetry, and, in the best sense of the word, a religion, equally fitted to exalt the feelings, and . . . still better calculated to ennoble the conduct, than any belief respecting the unseen powers." How near this is to Santayana's "religion of disillusion" in *Interpretations of Poetry and Religion!* Comte and Mill called such a religion a "religion of humanity," and believed that those who zealously practised it would not only attain spiritual satisfaction in this life, but would also "live ideally in the life of those who are to follow them." Which is tantamount to Santayana's "ideal immortality." *

And so one could go on and on. In general, Santayana's naturalism in its uncompromising severity follows the course of French rather than English naturalism, for most Englishmen retained an ounce of traditional dogma in their pound of rationalism: Spencer teleology, Mill theism, Arnold a "power that makes for righteousness." And the English were less likely than Santayana to allow speculative freedom in ethics to overturn conventional habits and practices. But the chief difference between the Life of Reason and the materialistic ethics of the day, both French and English, was not in the foundations, but in the spires and turrets of the edifice, in the ultimate demarcation of the good life.

The Positivists, says Santayana,

. . . may furnish a theatre and properties for our drama; but they offer no hint of its plot and meaning. . . . If they combine with physical speculation some elements of morals, these are usually purely formal, to the effect that happiness is to be pursued (probably, alas! because to do so is a psychological law); but what happiness consists in we gather only from casual observations or by putting together their national prejudices and party saws.

Worst of all is the tendency of utilitarians to lump together indiscriminately all pleasures according to a quantitative measure of happiness. The Life of Reason is hedonistic and utilitarian, but with a richness of content lacking in positivism and British utilitarianism. Mill, "deeper and sweeter" to Santayana "than his critics," tried to preserve from the leveling of utilitarianism what he called man's "sense of dignity," but the modern world was too much for even him. What can be expected of modern ethics when, says Santayana, "one half the learned world is amused in tinkering obsolete armour . . . deputing it, after a series of catastrophes, to be at last sound and invulnerable," while "the other half, the naturalists who have studied psychology and evolution, look at life from the outside, and the processes of Nature make them forget her uses." The Life of Reason must turn elsewhere for its inspiration. The positive content of its

---

* See also Lecky: *A History of Rationalism in Europe*, I, 268–269, and *The Prose Remains of Arthur Hugh Clough*, pp. 415–419, for similar tributes to the aesthetic and moral power of a disillusioned and purified religion.

morality is drawn from the ancient Greeks, with here and there a trace of the Catholic and Spanish inheritances which suffuse all of Santayana's thought and literary work.

Spain gave Santayana a certain touchstone of actuality, a racial mother wit which keeps the eyes of Spanish philosophers on man and nature rather than on the infinite and the abstract. The Spaniard's chief concern has always been with what Unamuno calls the "man of flesh and bone." "Spain's genius," says Madariaga, "is homocentric." It "considers man as a whole, in his struggle and dealings with the great elementary powers: Evil, Death and Love." And so when Santayana turned to construct a Life of Reason, it was perhaps the blood in his veins that kept his ethics from being either visionary or fanatical.

With the Spaniard, as with the ancient Greeks, morality is not a distinguishable phase of life, but is life itself; it is less a restraint than a sense of freedom, goodness pursued aesthetically. There is never in the Spaniard, as so often in the Anglo-Saxon, a tendency to split passions into respectable and animal ones, and to clamp a tight lid over the latter. This legacy of Puritanism is absent from Santayana's ethics; he never identifies the natural with the evil. Like the true Spaniard that he is, Santayana makes an art of life, so that morality never loses in his hands a certain aesthetic persuasiveness just as art has no need to be set apart from or opposed to morality.

The life of the perfected individual, a Spaniard believes, will be reposeful and gracious; his impulses will be harmonized and his ideals clarified. Such an individual will be little concerned to dictate morality to others. Everyone will be sole judge of those standards to which he will subscribe. And so the Life of Reason requires only that he have standards and an end in view. To many Anglo-Saxons this individualism seems "moral anarchy."

In moral philosophy [says Santayana] (which is my chosen subject) I find my unsophisticated readers, as I found my pupils formerly, delightfully appreciative, warmly sympathetic, and altogether friends of mine in the spirit . . . But the other philosophers, and those whose religion is of the anxious and intolerant sort, are not at all pleased. They think my morality very loose: I am a friend of publicans and sinners, not (as they are) in zeal to reform them, but because I like them as they are; and indeed I am a pagan and a moral sceptic in my naturalism. On the other hand (and this seems a contradiction to them), my moral philosophy looks strangely negative and narrow; a philosophy of abstention and distaste for life. What a horrible combination, they say to themselves, of moral license with moral poverty! They do not see that it is because I love life that I wish to keep it sweet, so as to be able to love it altogether: and that all I wish for others, or dare to recommend to them, is that they should keep their lives sweet also, not after my fashion, but each man in his own way.

Such a view of morality is to the Spaniard the only one possible; and I believe it is essentially Spanish, perhaps Latin, rather than Christian or ancient Greek. Classic and Christian liberty, as Santayana was later to point out, restricted the freedom of the individual beyond a certain point by imposing upon him an accepted, authoritative moral code. One was free and privileged to be a good Greek or a good Christian. In Spain, however, a strong group consciousness is lacking; the Spaniard acknowledges few moral ties outside of family and friends. As a result, political and social anarchy flourishes beside a strong cultivation of the individual personality. Morality is a private matter to be settled according to *el honor*.

However, Santayana is not only a Spaniard but also a Catholic, and he has always admired Christianity for teaching that "moral distinctions are absolute," and for denying that whatever is "regular or necessary or universal is therefore right and good." Santayana's insistence that there must be morality, however variable, and that for the individual his own moral code is necessary and authoritative forms a kind of Catholic core at the center of all his naturalistic individualism. Even later years of disillusionment have not entirely worn away this "adamant underneath."

It is the sterner rather than the gentler side of Christianity that finds expression in Santayana's work. Although one chapter of *Reason in Religion* is devoted to charity, and several passages emphasize the welfare and happiness of humanity in general, Santayana's concrete proposals for a rational life are pointed at individual self-expression rather than social harmony. Even *Reason in Society* is written from the standpoint of individual happiness. The Christian virtues of humility and benevolence receive scant notice in *The Life of Reason*. Nor is there much of the sentimental Christian in Santayana's temperament; he is keenly sensitive to suffering and tolerant of sin, not because his heart goes out to humanity in the lump but because he cannot stand unhappiness or ugliness in his perfected individual. If Christianity may be said to have two sides, Santayana represents the humanistic rather than the humanitarian.

And here is one of his many affinities with Hellenism, for at least until the time of the Stoics the Greek world did not recognize a brotherhood of man. Greek ethics, like Santayana's, was perfectionist, not utilitarian. It is no wonder, then, that Santayana found most of the materials for the Life of Reason in Greek ethical teaching; the essential framework of Santayana's ethics is there intact. Even the materialistic foundation, in principle, needs only a compound of Democritus and Heraclitus. Nature as mechanism, nature as flux: what more honest description of nature, says Santayana, can there be? "All later observation, down to our own day, has done nothing but fill out and confirm" their philosophies. "We owe to Democritus this ideal of practical intelligibility," whereas Heraclitus remains for all time "the honest prophet of immediacy." A morality based upon observation and inference, a rationalistic ethics, was the aim of every Greek from Heraclitus to the late Stoics. Truly the original authors of a Life of Reason were the Greeks.

But Santayana received from the Greeks more than a foundation and an incentive. He appropriated, first of all, two of the most prevalent axioms of Greek morality, that virtue is knowledge and that right is a mean between two extremes. The Greeks, unlike many moderns, did not feel that some natural impulses were ignoble in themselves; vice consisted in excess and presumption of all kinds. Moreover, morality was not a conquest of the victorious will over evil instincts; it consisted in understanding the limitations and possibilities of human nature and then acting in accordance with such insight. Knowledge would automatically lead to virtue.

As a result of these borrowings Santayana's ethics has a certain wholeness and spontaneity like that of the Greeks. But it sometimes achieves unity and simplicity by ignoring the many dilemmas that time has woven into the woof of modern ethics. Take for instance the initial equation that virtue equals knowledge. It would never have occurred to a Greek that a man, once he possessed knowledge of right and wrong, would act otherwise than in accordance with his best judgment. But the pages of history and the findings of psychology have accumulated such evidence to the contrary that a modern moralist can hardly accept so naïvely the Greek axiom. The Greeks, too, did not separate self and other as we have come to do; egotism and altruism were not so sharply differentiated as opposite poles of conduct. In a small city-state self-interest was closely linked with the general good. As Sidgwick says,

In Platonism and Stoicism, and in Greek moral philosophy generally, but one regulative and governing faculty is recognized under the name of Reason—in the modern ethical view, when it has worked itself clear, there are found to be two,—Universal Reason and Egoistic Reason, or Conscience and Self-love.

Santayana is here again aligned with the Greeks rather than with the moderns. The difficulty of reconciling self-love with benevolence, which disturbed the whole course of English utilitarianism, especially Butler and Bentham, simply does not seem to have entered Santayana's head at all. He is just as little bothered by the correlated antithesis of spirit and flesh, the soul and the world, intimated by Plato and driven into modern consciousness by centuries of Neo-Platonism and Christianity. As for squaring virtue with happiness, Santayana is less perplexed by this problem than were Plato and Aristotle (cf the *Gorgias*); enjoyment seems to him, as it seemed to Socrates, the natural concomitant of virtue.

By avoiding the quandaries of modern ethics, Santayana achieves a fresh, simplified point of view which is at once aesthetic and moral. In doing so he only reveals once more how devoted a lover he is of the Greeks. Whether his allegiance is more to Plato or more to Aristotle is a moot point. In the first place, the two Greek philosophers had more in common than is sometimes realized, and many of the things they shared are the very things Santayana drew from them. Plato was not only a mystic but also a practical moralist intent upon formulating rules of conduct, just as Aristotle's body of practical advice was to be carried out in sight of an ideal goal. Thus it is making a facile distinction to say that the idealism of the Life of Reason is Platonic, and the design of living Aristotelian. Perhaps the problem can be solved by observing what Santayana did not appropriate of either philosopher. Santayana did not follow the mystical, ascetic side of Plato, the Plato who wished to reduce ethics to rigid, inviolable standards, as if it were mathematics. Plato, says Santayana, "outran at times the limits of the Hellenic and the rational. . . . If as a work of imagination his philosophy holds first place, Aristotle's has the decisive advantage of being the unalloyed expression of reason." In his frank acknowledgment of the claims of natural impulse, in his willingness to submit all moral criteria to empirical test, in his treatment of reason itself as a kind of inductive process, Santayana follows Aristotle rather than Plato. But he will have nothing of Aristotle's "final cause," which attributes "dynamic function" to ideals and "obliges them to inhabit some fabulous extension to the physical world," a perversion of truth more subtly dangerous than Plato's frank allegories, an error which "condemned thought to confusion for two thousand years." More of a temptation to Santayana might be expected in Aristotle's exaltation of intellectuality as the *summum bonum,* but Santayana resists the temptation and keeps his idealism in its highest reaches tempered by the emotional and the aesthetic. In this respect he avoids a certain aridity in Aristotle and keeps nearer to the fluid, comprehensive idealism of Plato. Yet the underlying systematic treatment, the classification of rational activities, is rather Aristotelian.

If Plato and Aristotle together have adequately marked out the course of the rational life, what need, the reader may ask, for a modern philosopher to write a Life of Reason at all? Wherein is Santayana original? First, I should say, in an almost unprecedented attempt to reconstruct ethics in accordance with Greek concepts. To recall to the modern world something of the freshness and simplicity of the ancient world is no mean feat of originality in itself. Grant that the effort is not wholly successful, that the waters of thought have been too long muddied to be cleared instantly by an influx of even the purest spring, that time has accumulated problems and dilemmas that Santayana, being a modern man, has no right to ignore—grant all this, yet the Life of Reason remains not only a *tour de force* of ingenuity but also a genuine inspiration to saner and happier living. And of course, the outlines of a Life of Reason are all the Greeks can contribute. The whole must be filled in from the later march of civilization, although in keeping with Greek principles. Modern science, for instance, can correct "the lamentable misunderstanding" brought about by Aristotle's "final cause," and so restore the physical basis of morality to what it was in Democritus and Lucretius. This Santayana has tried to do, utilizing whatever findings of psychology, physics, or anthropology he comes across to account for mind or beauty or art or religion. Moreover, times change, and ethical principles themselves need illustration from the plenitude of recent history and modern society. Thus, in spite of Platonic love and Aristotelian friendship and a governing body curiously reminiscent of the elect in the *Republic,* Santayana in the main fits his ethical pattern to the cloth of the modern world. Certainly the strong infusion of individualism in *The Life of Reason* is modern Spanish or eighteeenth-century republican rather than classical Greek.

Just here, too, may be the weakness of *The Life of Reason*. It makes too little of the social, economic, and political pressure which the increasingly gregarious habits of mankind have generated and which, like an incubus, has come back to plague its maker. It is essentially a way of life for an individual whose place in the world is as secure and fortunate as that of an Athenian aristocrat at Pericles' court. But this objection in no way invalidates the Life of Reason in its proper sphere. Religion, art, friendship, love, ideal immortality, even scientific achievement, are personal satisfactions, and in making his claim for a perfected individual, Santayana is content to be deeply humanistic rather than broadly humanitarian.

CHAPTER FOUR

THE CRITIC AND ESSAYIST

In *Interpretations of Poetry and Religion* Santayana had set out to define and judge poetry by what were to become the standards of the Life of Reason. He had divided poetry into three kinds, reserving for the name of great poetry only that which exhibited a power of idealization and found in the discrete material of life a comprehensive unity. Great poetry was, then, to be formal in the genuinely classical sense, noble in theme, clear in outline, broad in scope. If form was the essence of great poetry, poor poetry would be identical with formlessness. It would be the poetry of barbarism, incoherent, its vision distorted, its range narrow. It would worship passion rather than reason, intensity rather than repose, vagueness rather than clarity. In the modern world its name, said Santayana, is romanticism.

Santayana, then, began his critical career as a staunch classicist bitterly opposed to everything romanticism stands for. And the form he sought in art is at the service of reason, is equivalent to order, harmony, synthesis, the principle of design applied to life and the world as well as to literary technique. Since art is at bottom moral, moral values, significance to humanity, will be the keystone of the greatest poetry. But this will be achieved at no sacrifice of beauty, for not only are the good and true ultimately beautiful, but the means of attaining them can only be clarity of outline and serenity of mood. The texture of Homer is as beautiful as the vision, and one matches the other.

Santayana's definition of great poetry excludes three kinds of poetry: (1) the indeterminate, because it can never *inform* the mind, lacking as it does definiteness and precision; (2) the irrational, no matter how intense or rapturous, since it shuts off reason, the one avenue to order; and (3) the short-winded, no matter how perfect in miniature, because all other things being equal, value increases with dimension. Now Santayana's judgment falls heavily upon romanticism because the latter encourages vague suggestiveness, passionate or mystical intensity, and ecstatic short-windedness. To Poe a great poem could not be long; to Santayana it cannot be short. A true romanticist would insist, too, that the "deeper, innate cravings of the mind" are not rational at all, but emotional and mystical, and are best satisfied by what is elusive, by "indeterminate art." There is, of course, between him and Santayana a conflict in first principles; they disagree over the nature of knowledge and the nature of the universe itself. There can be no compromise between the romantic and classical points of view, consistently and honestly held. We shall see McStout battling Van Tender throughout Santayana's literary criticism, for the issues and sides were clearly drawn back in that early dialogue, "Walt Whitman." Is art an imitation of life or an interpretation of it; does art reproduce the instinctive, passionate flux of existence, or does it, following the footsteps of consciousness itself, subject this lazy vitality to the integrating power of thought, to the discipline of the ideal?

Starting from the classical position, Santayana naturally finds himself at odds with the whole body of romantic poetry, and the whole clan of romantic readers and critics will rise to challenge his final judgment upon any romantic author. But Santayana is not a man of fierce and narrow prejudices. His analysis of poetry is careful and discriminating, even of those elements in it he dislikes, and the very decisiveness of his judgment has a way of illuminating the whole field of artistic creation, so that its problems stand out with the clarity of fundamental issues. In *Interpretations of Poetry and Religion* the most brilliant critical pieces are the four studies of romanticism as exemplified in Whitman, Browning, Emerson, and Shakespeare.

Whitman and Browning represent the poetry of barbarism, Whitman at a lower level than that of Browning.

The dissolution has progressed much farther in Whitman than in Browning, doubtless because Whitman began at a much lower stage of moral and intellectual organisation; for the good will to be radical was present in both. The elements to which Browning reduces experience are still passions, characters, persons; Whitman carries the disintegration further and knows nothing but moods and particular images. The world of Browning is a world of history with civilisation for its setting and with the conventional passions for its motive forces. The world of

Whitman is innocent of these things and contains only far simpler and more chaotic elements. . . . The order of his words, the procession of his images, reproduce the method of a rich, spontaneous, absolutely lazy fancy. . . . We find the swarms of men and objects rendered as they might strike the retina in a sort of waking dream. It is the most sincere possible confession of the lowest—I mean the most primitive—type of perception. . . . Walt Whitman has gone back to the innocent style of Adam, when the animals filed before him one by one and he called each of them by its name. . . . He has approached common life without bringing in his mind any higher standard by which to criticise it; he has seen it, not in contrast with an ideal, but as the expression of forces more indeterminate and elementary than itself; and the vulgar, in this cosmic setting, has appeared to him sublime.

Browning's strength, too, is in his vivid representation of the immediate flux of life; "the pulse of the emotion, the bobbing up of the thought, the streaming of the reverie—these he can note down with picturesque force or imagine with admirable fecundity." What is admirable in Browning is "pregnancy of phrase, vividness of passion and sentiment, heaped-up scraps of observation, occasional flashes of light, occasional beauties of versification,—all like

> the quick sharp scratch
> And blue spurt of a lighted match."

But for all his show of metaphysics, Browning's philosophy is amorphous and grotesque.

He remained in the phenomenal sphere: he was a lover of experience; the ideal did not exist for him. No conception could be farther from his thought than the essential conception of any rational philosophy, namely, that feeling is to be treated as raw material for thought, and that the destiny of emotion is to pass into objects which shall contain all its value while losing all its formlessness. This transformation of sense and emotion into objects agreeable to the intellect, into clear ideas and beautiful things, is the natural work of reason; when it has been accomplished very imperfectly, or not at all, we have a barbarous mind, a mind full of chaotic sensations, objectless passions, and undigested ideas. Such a mind Browning's was, to a degree remarkable in one with so rich a heritage of civilisation.

Santayana traces this indifference to perfection in the turgid style, the undramatic presentation of dramatic material, the fragmentary characterization, as well as in the underlying thought.

To speak of Whitman and Browning in the same breath was heresy to the literary circles of 1900. Whitman was still an outcast from polite society, but Browning was the subject of study programs and the reigning hero of innumerable women's clubs. To address a Browning society with the bold assertion that one did not care for Browning, as Santayana dared to do, was to be branded as unintelligent and queer. None the less, Santayana spoke out his convictions, and proceeded to show, with a vigor and clarity seldom equaled, the limitations of both Browning and Whitman. Defenders of either poet will not find their task easy unless they merely accept Santayana's analysis without admitting that it in any way invalidates poetic worth. If one believes it is the task of poetry to reflect the kaleidoscopic quality of existence, beautiful and ugly alike, and to embrace it the more readily by abandoning reason for a kind of intuitive sympathy, then Whitman is a great poet; he has "accomplished by the sacrifice of almost every other good quality something never so well done before." Likewise if one agrees with G. K. Chesterton that Santayana's definition of barbarism "is an excellent and perfect definition of the poet," that Santayana, having discovered the "root virtue of Browning's poetry," proceeds to call it "a vice," then there is no further need for argument. One accepts Santayana's analysis but not his judgment; one sides with Van Tender against McStout.

But most admirers of Browning and Whitman would have these authors prophets as well as poets; all the learned commentaries, all the encomiums on Browning particularly had not been merely for the sake of establishing him as a man of letters; he was to the generation of the nineties a spiritual guide, a bulwark against materialism and pessimism. So, too, has Whitman been looked up to by later generations as a prophet of liberty or democracy or transcendentalism.

Now there is undoubtedly a side of Browning that is all Santayana says of him. Browning himself would have been the last to deny his love of an active, strenuous moral life, with its emphasis upon will and energy rather than upon intellect and composure. I am not sure that he would have even rejected the term "barbarian"; better to be a barbarian, he would have thought, than a hollow conformist. One must live life to the hilt, for better if possible, but rather for worse than not at all. Better to aspire yet never attain than to stagnate on the star Rephan. Perfection itself would cloy, there must be struggle, resistance: wrongs to be righted, sufferings to be endured, victories to be won. Now all this seems to Santayana but "muscular Christianity," a love of effort rather than of accomplishment.

To the irrational man, to the boy, it is no unpleasant idea to have an infinite number of days to live through, an infinite number of dinners to eat, with an infinity of fresh fights and new love-affairs, and no end of last rides together. But it is a mere euphemism to call this perpetual vagrancy a development of the soul. . . . Browning has no idea of an intelligible good which the phases of life might approach and with reference to which they might constitute a progress. . . . That life is an adventure, not a discipline; that the exercise of energy is the absolute good, irrespective of motives or of consequences. These are the maxims of a frank barbarism.

With such a philosophy Browning often prefers this life to a hypothetically perfect other life,

> . . . others may need new life in Heaven—
> . . . .
> Let earth's old life once more enmesh us,

and even prefers life to art, which to a disciplined mind clarifies and ennobles life, but to Browning is a kind of mechanical dexterity, like that of Del Sarto, which cramps and confines vitality.

Indeed, Browning is hardly a philosopher at all. He accepts implicitly certain articles of Christianity, believes in the reality of love, faith, and salvation, and is sure that ultimately the universe will be on the side of man. But Browning is not particularly concerned to remove the contradictions his theology bristles with, or even to reconcile the unworldliness of radical Christianity with his own bustling, worldly temperament. It is enough to have "found God . . . his visible power; yet felt . . . his love . . . too, was the nobler dower."

Browning's method, says Santayana, is "to penetrate by sympathy rather than portray by intelligence," and such a method does not lead to coherent philosophies or even to a detachment which surveys human character in its true relation to the world and to its own destiny. It is true that Browning did not reach "the intellectual plane of such contemporary poets as Tennyson and Matthew Arnold, who, whatever may be thought of their powers, did not study consciousness for itself, but for the sake of its meaning and of the objects which it revealed."

In some ways Whitman is more genuinely a philosopher than Browning; his eye is fixed more constantly on nature and the universe, and on human nature in the aggregate. And he has woven the strands of his thought into something approaching unity, however vaguely and subjectively he has conceived the cosmos. Santayana pays tribute to Whitman's transcendentalism, his pantheism, and his mysticism as far as a rationalist can do so. "When the intellect is in abeyance . . . when we are weary of conscience and of ambition, and would yield ourselves for a while to the dream of sense, Walt Whitman is a welcome companion." But it is doubtful if either transcendentalism or mysticism can long satisfy an active mind on such a low, sprawling level; it is extremely doubtful whether there was enough intellectual grasp in Whitman for him to view the universe other than in relation to himself, a dangerous expedient for one who aspires to be a philosopher. Both Whitman and Browning represent the "soliloquizing soul," ruminating "on its own accidental emotions." But "the best things that come into a man's consciousness are the things that take him out of it—the rational things that are independent of his personal perception and of his personal existence."

I believe the justification of Whitman and Browning as prophets is to be sought for on the moral rather than the intellectual plane. There is in Whitman a warm, if indiscriminate, sympathy with humanity everywhere which seems as Christian as his hearty celebration of the body seems pagan and Greek. Both of these sides of Whitman receive Santayana's notice. Santayana admits that Whitman's "tolerance of moral weakness" and "genuine admiration for bodily health and strength, made him bubble over with affection for the generic human creature." But I think Santayana underestimates the moral value of both, for there is in each at least a claim to that preëminent third level which Santayana reserves for great poetry. To envisage a universal fraternity and charity and to sweeten and ennoble the physical and natural are accomplishments in the moral world; and it is surprising that Santayana does not acknowledge the Hellenism of the latter even if the humanitarianism of the former is foreign to his own ethics. But perhaps Santayana sees too clearly Whitman's limitations as moralist. Here, too, Whitman is all sensibility and no judgment. "Whitman's insight into man did not go beyond a sensuous sympathy; it consisted in a vicarious satisfaction in their pleasures, and in instinctive love of their persons. It never approached a scientific or imaginative knowledge of their hearts." In a remarkable passage Santayana shows truly why Longfellow is the poet of the masses, while Whitman appeals not "to those whom he describes, but rather to the *dilettanti* he despises. He is regarded as representative chiefly by foreigners, who look for some grotesque expression of the genius of so young and prodigious a people."

Browning has Whitman's humanitarianism on a more highly cultivated level, a humanitarian feeling for individual personality rather than mere gregariousness. This trait of Browning is perhaps his most genuinely Christian; his heart goes out to sinner and sinned against; even his concern with the forgotten rather than the renowned men of history, the piddling grammarians and worldly bishops, is not mere romantic delight in paradox; it is part of Christianity's search for the ounce of good in the pound of evil. One takes from Browning a greater respect for the integrity and the importance of the individual; even Emerson was no more of a staunch individualist, and Emerson would not have soiled his hands with the "religious slumming" which Santayana found so distasteful in William James as well as in Browning and Whitman.

There is in Browning an idealization of love which Santayana underestimates because Browning romantically ties love to the actual instead of keeping it Platonically sundered. Santayana recognizes Browning's preoccupation with love, and correctly defines the quality of Browning's emotion. "It never sinks into sensuality; in spite of its frequent extreme crudeness, it is always, in Browning's hands, a passion of the imagination, it is always love." But it seems also to Santayana that Browning's love "never rises into contemplation: mingled as it may be with friendship, with religion, or with various forms of natural tenderness, it always remains a passion; it always remains a personal impulse, a hypnotisation, with another person for its object or its cause." True, Browning's lovers are blinded by the intensity of their passion, and to Santayana such lovers, like those of Dante in Hell, are standing "among the ruins" of their own love, for emotion cannot perpetuate beyond a moment its own blaze. Love's eternity is ideal and directed outward upon life, not inward upon itself. For all this, Browning is not a mere sensualist, an amative Epicurean. His lovers, especially the rejected ones, find their whole lives transformed by love; to have loved is to be reborn. And though some long for nothing more than an eternal last ride together, others like David in "Saul" and Caponsacchi in "The Ring and the Book" have felt a universal benevolence and humility which has somehow made them better men for the experience. Browning's lovers are not contemplative and their love is closely linked with the person of their loved one, but their lives are most certainly *reformed,* not merely energized, which would be on the level of barbarism, but reshaped and redirected. I do not believe one can deny here a variety of idealization, however un-Platonic it may be.

But stimulating as Browning is as a moralist, there is a grave threat to morality itself in some of his teachings. And the danger lurks in that very characteristic of Browning which endears him to many readers, his optimism. I refer not only to his naive pantheism, which blinds itself to the evil in the world (serious enough error on an intellectual plane), but also to a certain obfuscation of right and wrong which, like Whitman, he reveals on a moral plane. Browning's love of the paradoxical sometimes leads him to see not only good in evil but also evil in good. It is hard to defend morally Porphyria's lover, or the lady in "The Glove," or Browning's advice to the heroine of "The Statue and the Bust."

> Oh—a crime will do
> As well, I reply, to serve for a test,
> As a virtue golden through and through.

Courage is the rudiment of all morality, but moral acts are not mere counters to be staked as tests as if they had no inherent worth of their own. Browning never gave wrong or evil its just place in the world, never really looked upon the inscrutable sadness beneath existence; his temperament forbade it. And herein, though he is a stimulating guide and prophet, he is not always trustworthy or permanently satisfying. Browning viewed life too readily from the vantage point of his own irrepressible buoyancy; the pathetic fallacy is strong in him for all his show of profundity.

Emerson and Shakespeare escape being "barbarians" in Santayana's judgment because the world in which they move is less than Browning's a creation of the private imagination and more conformable to historical reality; nevertheless, each suffers in his way from an excess of the romantic spirit and is consequently not quite satisfying to the disciplined mind of the classicist. Emerson was, of course, not a consistent metaphysician; even those who uphold transcendentalism admit that he allowed incongruities to blur his vision and never took pains to systematize his thought. Professional philosophers generally patronize Emerson because he was so unphilosophic; the originality of Santayana's criticism lies in his admiration of what has generally been considered Emerson's chief weakness. Santayana herein is not being paradoxical or playing truant to his principles. He merely feels that transcendentalism being an untenable delusion, a romantic folly, Emerson did wisely not to stifle his inspiration in its strait-jacket.

He never tried to seek out and defend the universal implications of his ideas, and never wrote the book he had once planned on the law of compensation, foreseeing, we may well believe, the sophistries in which he would have been directly involved. . . . The faculty of idealisation was itself what he valued. Philosophy for him was rather a moral energy flowering into sprightliness of thought than a body of serious and defensible doctrines. In practising transcendental speculation only in this poetic and sporadic fashion, Emerson retained its true value and avoided its greatest danger.

Emerson then is peculiarly the prophet of the imagination, and his vision is less distorted than Browning's, and soars far beyond that of Whitman. He belongs among the true mystics; yet even here his native common sense keeps one foot on earth, so that he has a respect for history and science not often found among his brothers. There was a sweetness and sanity about Emerson that endeared him to those who could not hope to understand or to agree with some of his doctrines. The man was always greater than the work; his audiences

. . . flocked to him and listened to his word, not so much for the sake of its absolute meaning as for the atmosphere of candour, purity, and serenity that hung about it, as about a sort of sacred music. They felt themselves in the presence of a rare and beautiful spirit, who was in communion with a higher world. [And in reality] his heart was fixed on eternal things, and he was in no sense a prophet for his age or country. He belonged by nature to that mystical company of devout souls that recognise no particular home and are dispersed throughout history, although not without intercommunication. He felt his affinity to the Hindoos and the Persians, to the Platonists and the Stoics. Like them he remains "a friend and aider of those who would live in the spirit."

Santayana thus explains accurately and sympathetically Emerson's moral nature and the secret of his influence. Yet Santayana's admiration is bound to be tempered by the fundamental conflict between his own philosophy and Emerson's. Emerson's scorn of tradition, the mark of an undisciplined mind, is but symptomatic of his whole tendency to elevate the imagination at the expense of the understanding. "All nature is an embodiment of our native fancy, all history a drama in which the innate possibilities of the spirit are enacted and realized." This conception is a tribute to the constructive power of the imagination, but in matters of fact the intellect is the truer guide. Emerson, like most mystics, disregards evil or explains it by false analogies, and substitutes for laws of nature spiritual and moral "harmonies" which simply do not exist and by their presence becloud the genuine moral horizon. The limpid humility of the Orient, Emerson's best side, is too often agitated by a certain draught of egotism that betrays its origin in German metaphysics. Emerson at heart belongs with the romantics; his office is to stimulate rather than to teach, and he will be treasured by the heart longer than by the mind.

Now Santayana's criticism of Emerson, admirable as it is in exposing certain deficiencies of its subject, neglects certain other qualities which might go far to redeem Emerson even in the eyes of a staunch classicist. Emerson is a treacherous subject anyhow for criticism; the temptation to over-simplify, to find in him just what you are looking for is encouraged by his own lack of system and talent for improvisation. Recent scholarship has done much to balance Emerson's transcendentalism by bringing into the foreground his Platonic and humanistic tendencies. Beside the benevolent monism which Emerson inherited from German metaphysics there is to be found in his writings a sharply defined dualism, Platonic and Christian in outline, which sets off the world against the spirit, opinion against truth, matter against mind. "Law for man, and law for thing"; and Emerson at times does not minimize the power of the latter. Nature has for him a sternness as well as a mildness; it is discipline as well as comfort. And there is, especially in his off-hand moments, a Yankee respect for the real quite at odds with his more official mysticism and idealism. "Allston's pictures are . . . serene but unreal"; "American geniuses . . . all lack nerve and dagger"; Brook Farm is but "arithmetic and comfort." Santayana's criticism of Emerson is one-sided in ignoring all of these attributes which by rights should receive his approval. And yet Santayana, like Emerson in this respect, is inclined to base judgment upon predominant and ultimate impressions, and herein the individualism, transcendentalism, and romantic exuberance of Emerson perhaps outweigh his occasional classicism and realism. Certainly the devices by which he reads a moral and divine purpose into nature, his law of compensation, his oversoul, his evolutionary meliorism all to Santayana smack of the legerdemain of German metaphysics and are enough to damn Emerson in his eyes. So he chooses to dwell fondly upon the personal and poetical charm of Emerson, and condemns his philosophy and religion.

Santayana's essay on Shakespeare is the most debatable of the four studies of romanticism. Not that his attack is inconsistent with that of the other essays, but there is a slight shifting of emphasis among the criteria which go to make up the classical standard. Design, moral significance, idealization give way to the criterion of breadth or wholeness. It is true that, compared with Shakespeare, "no other poet has given so many-sided an expression to human nature, or rendered so many passions and moods with such an appropriate variety of style, sentiment, and accent." In Shakespeare's works "we recognize the truest portrait and best memorial of man." Yet Shakespeare's record of human activity is incomplete—there is no place for religion, no cosmic outlook. Neither characters nor creator recognize the very human desire to seek and establish oneself in relation to the ultimate which we call religion. The absence of religion in Shakespeare's characters is undramatic and in himself unphilosophic. For

. . . the human race hitherto, whenever it has reached a phase of comparatively high development and freedom, has formed a conception of its place in Nature, no less than of the contents of its life; and . . . this conception has been the occasion of religious sentiments and practices; and further, . . . every art, whether literary or plastic, has drawn its favourite themes from this religious sphere. The poetic imagination has not commonly stopped short of the philosophical in representing a superhuman environment of man. . . . Shakespeare, however, is remarkable among the greater poets for being without a philosophy and without a religion.

Santayana supports his contention with abundant evidence from the works of Shakespeare, but even devout Shakespeareans would not be inclined to challenge something so apparent. Santayana goes on to account correctly, I believe, for Shakespeare's indifference to religion. The Reformation, perhaps the Renaissance too, saw a divorce of religion from art. Literature abandoned "the serious and sacred things of life," and religion turned away from the delightful and beautiful. As a result,

. . . those of us . . . who think that both human reason and human imagination require a certain totality in our views, and who feel that the most important thing in life is the lesson of it, and its relation to its own ideal,—we can hardly find in Shakespeare all that the highest poet could give.

We have here one of the most spirited and confident attacks ever made upon the reputation of the great dramatist. And Santayana's judgment is consistent with strict classicism, as if Homer, Lucretius, and Dante were guiding his aim. And yet one is not sure that Shakespeare is quite dislodged from the pedestal upon which millions of readers have placed him.

In the first place, is there really no sense in which Shakespeare has a view of life in its totality? Is he perhaps by the very negation of religion a philosopher—an early agnostic or positivist? No, says Santayana, even "the Pagan" in Shakespeare seems not to "have spoken frankly." "The material forces of Nature" do not stand solidly "behind his heroes." Nor is he so philosophically minded as to shape his incidents in a "larger drama" to which they have "at least some symbolic relation." But is Santayana here quite right? True, Shakespeare's is not the exploring or philosophic mind, but his dramas, for all their variety, unite in what seems to be a premeditated indifference to the supernatural. Neglect of cosmic implications is in Shakespeare almost tantamount to denial of them. On the contrary, human life is everything to human beings. The human world is a plane, but as such it includes everything relevant to human nature. Is then Shakespeare's work consonant with a sound humanism?

Before this question can be answered, it is perhaps pertinent to ask whether totality as a criterion of literary worth is so important and obligatory outside the human scale, whether a full rendition of human nature, honest and morally sound, is not perhaps worth more in the long run than a cosmic range which may outrun the confines of both truth and human interest. Is literature to be measured by the same stick as philosophy? Is the ordering of experience which is the function of the highest poetry to be measured by quality or size? The issue is important because Santayana's position is vulnerable not only to the attack of the romanticist, but to that of the humanist as well. It is true that Shakespeare's method is to deal with the "successive empirical appearance of things," but it is not true that he leaves us, as Whitman does, with a mere impression of their successiveness. And there emerges from Shakespeare's world a moral pattern, a demarcation of good and evil, of the heights and depths of human nature that is unique in a writer at the same time filled with romantic exuberance. Santayana's critique of Shakespeare is valuable in that it shows from what quarter of the critical compass the great dramatist is open to attack, but it raises the question of whether that quarter is quite the same as the more generally humanistic one in the attack upon Whitman, Browning, and Emerson.

In presenting Santayana's treatment of the romantic movement, I have tried to proceed in accordance with his own assumptions, and have offered objections only when it seemed to me that he neglected or obscured certain characteristics of his subjects which entitled them to greater recognition even according to his standard of judgment. I have thus accepted his dictum that the greatest poetry is equivalent to prophecy, that it must interpret and idealize life, and that the poet's vision must be bounded by reality and sobered by reason. Many lovers of poetry, I know, contend that Santayana neglects in his judgment of poetry that element which seems most poetic to them—the imaginative. Certainly he pays slight attention to the magic, the wonder which in Whitman and Emerson lights upon the most common materials and makes them glow with the fire of true poetry. It is an achievement of no mean order to give the familiar old world a new charm and pregnancy. And it does seem as if reason in Santayana's hands threatens to blight and wither something very warm and human in Browning and Shakespeare. In Santayana's defense, however, let it be said that he is not insensitive to imagination in poetry, nor to passion and melody and rhythm. He feels that these are ingredients of poetry without which poetry ceases to exist; at the same time they alone do not lift poetry to that level where it becomes a sounding-board for the finest overtones of the human spirit. And somehow the verdict of the ages has been with Santayana that glorious and stirring as poetry may be in the hands of Keats, or Schiller, or Catullus, it is to Homer and Virgil and Dante that we look for the finest flowering of the art of letters.

'The emphasis upon totality which marked the Shakespeare essay has become the dominant theme in Santayana's criticism by 1910. In *Three Philosophical Poets* Santayana decrees that poetry "is not poetical for being short-winded or incidental, but, on the contrary, for being comprehensive and having range." Thus, Lucretius and Dante were truly great poets who sought to embrace the world, to find in their poetry a place for everything within heaven and earth. Lucretius "sees the world to be one great edifice, one great machine, all its parts reacting upon one another, and growing out of one another in obedience to a general pervasive process or life." Likewise Dante's poetry "covers the whole field from which poetry may be fetched, and to which poetry may be applied, from the inmost recesses of the heart to the uttermost bounds of nature and destiny."

Yet totality alone does not determine great literature; in the critical scales with it must be placed other criteria; truth and fullness must be considered as well as range; wholeness must not be an illusion of empty grandeur. Dante did not escape this weakness; he was a child of his age, and in some matters his age was purblind.

There is an attenuated texture and imagery in the *Divine Comedy* . . . a thin boy-treble . . . The reason is that the intellect has been hypnotised by a legendary and verbal philosophy. It has been unmanned, curiously enough, by an excess of humanism; by the fond delusion that man and his moral nature are at the centre of the universe.

In matters of scientific fact Lucretius was nearer the truth. His wisdom rests on an understanding "of things, so that what happiness remains to us does not deceive us, and we can possess it in dignity and peace. Knowledge of what is possible is the beginning of happiness." But Lucretius, too, has the limitations of his age.

There is a great deal, a very great deal, in Goethe that Lucretius does not know of. Not knowing of it, Lucretius cannot carry this fund of experience up to the intellectual and naturalistic level; he cannot transmute this abundant substance of Goethe's by his higher insight and clearer faith; he has not woven so much into his poem. So that while to see nature, as Lucretius sees it, is a greater feat than merely to live hard in a romantic fashion, and produces a purer and more exalted poem than Goethe's magical medley, yet this medley is full of images, passions, memories, and introspective wisdom that Lucretius could not have dreamed of. The intellect of Lucretius rises, but rises comparatively empty; his vision sees things as a whole, and in their right places, but sees very little of them; he is quite deaf to their intricacy, to their birdlike multiform little souls. These Goethe knows admirably; with these he makes a natural concert, all the more natural for being sometimes discordant, sometimes overloaded and dull. It is necessary to revert from Lucretius to Goethe to get at the volume of life.

In turn Goethe is not to be trusted too far, for volume is not synonymous with value.

A poet who merely swam out into the sea of sensibility, and tried to picture all possible things, real or unreal, human or inhuman, would bring materials only to the workshop of art; he would not be an artist. To the genius of Goethe he must add that of Lucretius and Dante.

Great poetry is then a difficult, an intricate thing to measure, but its boundaries become clearer to Santayana as he studies its representation in Lucretius, Dante, and Goethe. It must strive for a comprehensive unity, but its range must not be attained at the expense of either truth or volume. In reality, the perfect poet has not yet appeared in this imperfect world. He should "live in the continual presence of all experience, and respect it; he should at the same time understand nature, the ground of that experience; and he should also have a delicate sense for the ideal echoes of his own passions, and for all the colours of his possible happiness." In short, his genius should contain and transcend the genius of Goethe, Lucretius, and Dante. The ideal philosophical poet would

... make us see how beautiful, how satisfying, is the art of being observant, economical, and sincere ... He would have a taste for the world in which he lived, and a clean view of it. [But] there remains a second form of rational art, that of expressing the ideal towards which we would move under these improved conditions. ... The outer life is for the sake of the inner; discipline is for the sake of freedom, and conquest for the sake of self-possession. ... To the art of working well a civilized race would add the art of playing well. To play with nature and make it decorative, to play with the overtones of life and make them delightful, is a sort of art. It is the ultimate, the most artistic sort of art, but it will never be practised successfully so long as the other sort of art is in a backward state; for if we do not know our environment, we shall mistake our dreams for a part of it, and so spoil our science by making it fantastic, and our dreams by making them obligatory. The art and the religion of the past, as we see conspicuously in Dante, have fallen into this error. To correct it would be to establish a new religion and a new art, based on moral liberty and on moral courage.

Santayana's vision of the poetry of the future returns to the lofty aestheticism of *The Sense of Beauty*. In a clearer and brighter world than even that of ancient Greece poetry can leave all the care and sorrow and perplexity which this world has saddled it with, and abandon the pathos of tragedy for a beauty of sheer loveliness, "the most artistic sort of art." But not before reason has made such a world possible and such an art significant.

This is Santayana's final word on the nature of poetry; and it is one of the finest attempts of rationalism to penetrate a mystery which by its very nature is partially veiled to reason. The criteria of great poetry are weighed and adjusted in a delicate balance which may be applied to the poetry of the future as well as to that of the past. It would almost seem as if nothing further could be said on poetry from the standpoint of the Life of Reason. But *Three Philosophical Poets* is valuable for its individual studies as well as for its general theory. Nowhere else has Santayana given us criticism of such breadth or of such painstaking scholarship. The essays on Lucretius, Dante, and Goethe, though their author humbly offers them as "impressions of an amateur . . . an ordinary reader," are really the product of an exact knowledge and of years of study and meditation.

One is inclined to dismiss with fewer words the studies of Lucretius and Dante, perhaps because they coincide more with conventional opinion than does the study of Goethe; but they are fine pieces of criticism permeated by a wholehearted appreciation which, of course, Santayana is unable to give the romantic movement. There is in them a careful appraisal of the poets' age, philosophic background, and mental habits; in fact, the book is really a study of men as the mouthpieces of civilizations.

Thus the strength of Lucretius is shown to be his clear-cut expression of that Greek naturalism which in Democritus set out to examine nature as nature and not as the figment of the hypothesizing soul; his weakness is shown to arise from the Epicurean abstention from life which cramped moral enthusiasm and bred a crabbed cynicism in respect to religion which is not the temper of the impartial and sympathetic observer. "Lucretius studies superstition, but only as an enemy; and the naturalistic poet should be the enemy of nothing." There is a trace of the Puritan in Lucretius, of the zealous reformer; "he should have unbent now and then and shown us in some detail what those pleasures of life may be which are without care and fear." Even friendship, which Epicurus found considerable place for, is given scant notice by Lucretius. But what Lucretius set out to do, he did well. "Lucretius, more than any other man, is the poet of nature . . . he is a poet of the source of landscape, a poet of matter." He, therefore, "studied everything in its truth. Even moral life, though he felt it much more narrowly and coldly than Wordsworth did, was better understood and better sung by him for being seen in its natural setting."

Dante is correspondingly shown to be not only the exemplar of the Middle Ages, but the supreme exponent of Platonism wherever found, of that geocentric point of view which regards "moral values" as "forces working in nature," of an idealism "taken as a view of the central and universal power in the world." Santayana shows how Christianity took over Platonism, to which it had real affinity, and how both received their fullest expression, cosmological and moral, in *The Divine Comedy*. Santayana is especially penetrating in his study of Dante's moral hierarchy, both of saints and sinners, in its relation to Aristotelian and Christian ethics. The tortures and penances of Dante are shown to have genuine moral appropriateness, and his heaven is shown to embrace the more worldly virtues as well as the purest of aspirations. The length and breadth of life have never been surveyed by so discriminating and sound a moralist. But Santayana does not gloze over Dante's faults. Quite apart from limitations which he shared with his age, Dante at times marred the serenity of his vision by fierce hatreds and violent prejudices which must have carried over from his life of intrigue and exile. "The Bonifaces and the Ugolinos," though "powerful and vehement," are not the "truly deep, the truly lovely figures of the *Divine Comedy*," but rather the "vulgarities." "A casual personal sentiment towards them, however passionate, cannot take the place of the sympathetic insight that comprehends and the wide experience that judges." There is something at times offensive, too, in the very obtrusiveness of Dante's personality, whether meek or vindictive; he never leaves the stage to his actors. "One may tire sometimes of his perpetual tremblings and tears, of his fainting fits and his intricate doubts." There is about him, too, that perverse righteousness of the Puritan which not only hates evil but also enjoys the punishment it entails. "The damned" to Dante "are damned for the glory of God," through a moral perversion which is perhaps less the result of Dante's nature than "the folly of an egotistic or anthropocentric philosophy," "desperate at heart." And so it is not through neglect of Dante's faults that Santayana is able to pronounce Dante a great poet; his faults, serious as they are, dwindle beside his achievement, which was, "with the tenderest sense of colour, and the firmest art of design," to "put his whole world into his canvas. Seen there, that world becomes complete, clear, beautiful, and tragic. It is vivid and truthful in its detail, sublime in its march and in its harmony." "Dante fulfilled this task, of course under special conditions and limitations, personal and social; but he fulfilled it, and he thereby fulfilled the conditions of supreme poetry."

Santayana is, up to a point, not only in agreement with most critics of *Faust* but also beyond them in a sympathetic understanding of the poem. He traces the earlier history of the Faust legend and shows why it appealed particularly to the exuberant, youthful Goethe. He analyzes the layers of growth of Goethe's Faust in terms of Goethe's interests and activities. Turning to the story itself, he follows scene by scene in a vivid narrative that somehow penetrates to the inner meaning of each situation. Santayana particularly insists upon what seems to him Goethe's wisdom, a rationalism, almost classical, which reveals Faust's romantic excesses as the folly they most certainly are. Thus, Faust's inability to encompass the Earth-Spirit, though a hard lesson to one who aspires to the infinite, is only a sage reminder "that the life possible and good for man is the life of reason, not the life of nature." The unfortunate experience with Margaret, too, leads him to see that man's proper sphere is public life rather than the private world of indeterminate imagination. "Let us turn our backs upon the sun," thinks Faust, "upon infinite force and infinite existence. Fitter for our eyes the waterfall over against it, the torrent of human affairs, broken into a myriad rills. Upon the mists that rise from it the sunlight paints a rainbow, always vanishing, but always restored. This is the true image of rational human achievement." To Santayana this scene is Goethe's summit of wisdom in *Faust,* though Goethe again is sound in refusing to countenance the marriage of Faust and Helena and in making the offspring of an artificially stimulated classicism wildly romantic and thoroughly futile. Santayana shows, too, that Faust's building of dykes is less a public service than an outlet of his indomitable energy and his craving for mastery. Certainly, from a perfectionist point of view, the results of Faust's long struggle to dominate nature and achieve self-satisfaction are puny and trifling. "After Greece, Faust has a vision of Holland." And even on a humanitarian basis, says Santayana, what "some simple-minded commentators dignify with the name of altruism and of living for others, has no steady purpose or standard about it."

So far, Santayana's interpretation of *Faust,* I believe, is faithful to the intention of Goethe. But I am not so sure Goethe would have accepted Santayana's explanation of Faust's salvation or his summary of what he calls the poem's "official" philosophy. Is it true that "Faust seen under the form of eternity, shows forth his salvation? . . . The blots on that life were helpful and necessary blots; the passions of it were necessary and creative passions. To have felt such perpetual dissatisfaction is truly satisfactory; such desire for universal experience is the right experience." Is the official moral of Faust that "the worth of life lies in pursuit, not in attainment; therefore, everything is worth pursuing, and nothing brings satisfaction—save this endless destiny itself"? Goethe, I believe, intended Faust to be saved in the sight of eternity; but, I also believe, he indicated a transformation or evolution of the Faust nature before such salvation was possible. I am not so sure critics like Kuno Francke, George Henry Lewes, and Bayard Taylor are being merely simple- or tender-minded in attributing humanitarianism and altruism to Faust and Goethe. Faust believes, too, that he has created and perfected something in his last project of a race of happy burghers; he has achieved what Santayana and the Greeks call "ideal immortality." Moreover, there is in the concluding scene a tribute to Catholic Christianity which is more than "sentimental landscape-painting" and "vague mysticism." The final redemption of Faust must proceed from a grace quite outside his own nature and achievements. To represent Faust as changeless and intractable seems to me to miss the point of Goethe's whole conception. Goethe himself in a remark to Eckermann stated that " 'The key to Faust's rescue may be found' in 'an ever higher and purer form of activity to the end, and the eternal Love coming down to his aid from above.' "

Santayana is too Latin and perhaps too logical to see that a Protestant German romanticist finds no inconsistency between the worth of pursuit and the worth of attainment. The eventual self-effacement and self-realization of Faust justify the very striving and erring which made them possible, but the latter would be worthless without the former. To Santayana, however, the original Faust legend seems more morally sound than Goethe's drama. There was a wilful perversity about Goethe's Faust from the beginning; a seasoned and rational mind would have needed no such immersion in experience to discern the eternal difference between good and evil. There is about Goethe that compromising temper which throughout German philosophy is only too ready to accept evil and pronounce it good. Like Faust, Goethe left in his train wrecks of heartbreak and sorrow, and chalked them up in his moral score to experience or to good intentions. He, no doubt, felt that he too was saved in the sight of eternity and that a ripe wisdom in old age not only expunged the waywardness of youth but also could not have existed without it.

Thus, I believe Santayana misreads the "official moral" of *Faust*, but is true to the deeper spirit of both the poem and the poet. That "the worth of life lies in pursuit, not in attainment" is not the "official" philosophy of the poem, nor merely "an afterthought"; it is the essence of the romantic temper which shines through Faust and Goethe, even when the latter is trying most vigorously to give his creation a classical or Christian coloring. The "official" intention of a poem is often annulled by the deeper instincts of both the poet and his age. And when one analyzes Faust's achievements, they are seen to be, as Santayana quite rightly points out, mere embodiments of his own temper. True, he has given himself to the creation of a happy people, but wherein are they to be happy? Only by the perpetuation of Faust's own romantic struggle.

What satisfies Faust is merely the consciousness that this will to will is to be maintained, and that neither he, nor the colonists he has brought into being, will ever lick the dust, and take comfort, without any further aspiration, in the chance pleasures of the moment. Faust has maintained his enthusiasm for a stormy, difficult, and endless life. He has been true to his romantic philosophy.

Even Faust's colonists must battle for their existence lest their ideals grow rusty and they succumb to Mephistopheles' lure. And like most romantic reformers, Faust "calls the thing he wants for others good, because he now wants to bestow it on them, not because they naturally want it for themselves." Faust has not the temperament to plan a happy life for mankind on rational principles. "Incapable of sympathy, he has a momentary pleasure in policy; and in the last and 'highest' expression of his will, in his statesmanship and supposed public spirit, he remains romantic and, if need be, aggressive and criminal." And would Faust himself ever be satisfied with his creation? Emphatically no, says Santayana. "The career of Faust himself had been far more free and active than that of his industrious burghers could ever hope to be." As for his heavenly profession of teaching wisdom to the souls of those who died young, Faust could never abide the duties of schoolmaster on earth, let alone pass the rest of his days in such resigned apathy.

The truth is that Goethe created a personage who was too powerful and too logically indivisible to be contained by the reconciliations and compromises which satisfied his creator. Faust is more than a literary creation of one man; he is the supreme manifestation of an eternal attitude of the human spirit, which once evoked cannot be stilled by all the Helenas and Hollands. And yet there is a certain wisdom in romanticism which Santayana does not deny.

The great merit of the romantic attitude in poetry, and of the transcendental method in philosophy, is that they put us back at the beginning of our experience. They disintegrate convention, which is often cumbrous and confused, and restore us to ourselves, to immediate perception and primordial will. . . . Herein we may see the radical and inalienable excellence of romanticism; its sincerity, freedom, richness, and infinity. [But] herein, too, we may see its limitations, in that it cannot fix or trust any of its ideals, and blindly believes the universe to be as wayward as itself, so that nature and art are always slipping through its fingers. It is obstinately empirical, and will never learn anything from experience.

Goethe almost grasped the disillusionment as well as the glory of romanticism, but he was too much of a romantic himself to maintain throughout Faust the necessary critical detachment to do so. Santayana's criticism has carried through what Goethe only intimated, and stands out as one of the most penetrating studies of romanticism yet undertaken.

Santayana's *Three Philosophical Poets* was on the whole well received. The *Academy* called it a "literary work which should give him high place among the thinkers and philosophers with whom he must be associated," and remarked that "Professor Santayana has a grace of style, a serenity of argument, and a steadfastness of outlook that are really striking." Especially admired was the essay on Goethe, which Jefferson Fletcher in the *Journal of Philosophy, Psychology and Scientific Method* called "audaciously unorthodox" and a "justification of the saying that true criticism of literature is itself creative literature."

Three Philosophical Poets is the high-water mark of Santayana's classicism and his most ambitious undertaking in literary criticism. Hereafter, philosophies and cultural movements occupied him more than did men of letters; the problems of literature were merged with the larger problems of life itself. But before finally turning away from literature, Santayana included among essays published in 1913 and

1922 two studies which conclude the chapter of his literary criticism and are individually among his finest work in the field. In both essays the strict classicism of 1900–10 is sufficiently relaxed to enable Santayana to treat sympathetically authors who would be crushed by the rigorous demands of the perfect philosophical poet. Yet Santayana does not alter his central philosophical attitudes; he merely makes room for authors who, without being of first magnitude, are nevertheless sound and wholesome within their spheres of influence. In both papers Santayana rises to defend authors unjustly censured, and his tone is therefore more enthusiastic and less ironic than in the various studies of romanticism. His defense, too, is so unorthodox and brilliant that these studies of Shelley and Dickens are perhaps his most unexpected and yet most generally admired critical pieces. The romanticism of Shelley and Dickens seems to Santayana less perverse and barbarous than that of Browning, Whitman, and Goethe. It does not paint an ugly world in glowing colors; it does not flatter with rosy visions the finite spirit of man. Dickens is content with the humble world of actuality, touching the familiar and the commonplace with a romantic glow, flooding it with highlights of sentiment and sympathy, but not distorting its contours or its moral chiaroscuro. Shelley, far from being an "ineffectual angel, beating his wings in luminous void," as Matthew Arnold supposed, is not trying to describe this world at all, but is singing of an ideal world wherein the promptings of the spirit may find a sympathetic ear and a just reward. Any estimate of Shelley, says Santayana, raises the whole question of the "poetic value of revolutionary principles." Now the "classical principle of criticism" has always

... asserted that substance, sanity, and even a sort of pervasive wisdom are requisite for supreme works of art. On the other hand—who can honestly doubt it?—the rebels and individualists are the men of direct insight and vital hope. The poetry of Shelley in particular is typically poetical. It is poetry divinely inspired; and Shelley himself is perhaps no more ineffectual or more lacking in humour than an angel properly should be. Nor is his greatness all a matter of aesthetic abstraction and wild music.

If one looks closely, says Santayana, one will find that Shelley does indeed express an idealism, a true Platonic idealism. "He looked on the types and ideals of things as on eternal realities that subsist, beautiful and untarnished, when the glimmerings that reveal them to our senses have died away." He saw clearly the distinction between evil and goodness and envisioned the "ideal goals of life, the ultimate joys of experience."

Of course, Shelley's poetry in one sense is an illusion and has no solidity; "it is a series of landscapes, passions, and cataclysms such as never were on earth, and never will be." He is a romantic in believing that matter and nature can be brushed aside so easily. But "his obtuseness to things dynamic—to the material order—leaves his whole mind free to develop things aesthetic after their own kind; his abstraction permits purity, his playfulness makes room for creative freedom, his ethereal quality is only humanity having its way." The idealism of Shelley is sound and penetrating, man's moral impulse at its fullest and highest, only romantic and impractical in its Utopian character, in its neglect of the fact of man's natural endowment. And indeed must all poetry be, as Matthew Arnold says, a "criticism of life"?

Is life, we may ask, the same thing as the circumstances of life on earth? Is the spirit of life, that marks and judges those circumstances, itself nothing? Music is surely no description of the circumstances of life; yet it is relevant to life unmistakably, for it stimulates by means of a torrent of abstract movements and images the formal and emotional possibilities of living which lie in the spirit. By so doing music becomes a part of life, a congruous addition, a parallel life, as it were, to the vulgar one. I see no reason, in the analogies of the natural world, for supposing that the circumstances of human life are the only circumstances in which the spirit of life can disport itself.

"The future, too, even among men, may contain, as Shelley puts it, many 'arts, though unimagined, yet to be.'" There is even a scientific interest in Shelley's poetry.

It opens to us emotionally what is a serious scientific probability; namely, that human life is not all life, nor the landscape of earth the only admired landscape in the universe; that the ancients who believed in gods and spirits were nearer the virtual truth (however anthropomorphically they may have expressed themselves) than any philosophy or religion that makes human affairs the centre and aim of the world.

In the concluding remarks Santayana almost abandons the humanistic point of view of his earlier criticism, and perhaps in attempting to justify Shelley, leans almost too far away from his former criterion of relevancy to human life. But this very extension of poetry to include the imaginative and lyrical broadens the range of Santayana's criticism and shows on his part a hitherto unsuspected sympathy with "pure poetry." There is perhaps a forecast in this essay of the much later Santayana whose preoccupation with "pure spirit" has seemed to many readers Oriental as well as Platonic.

The study of Dickens is a masterpiece in appreciation. Through some artistic alchemy the vitality and color of Dickens' panorama is reflected in Santayana's criticism. The very wealth of illustration, as well as the sympathetic insight, aids in producing this effect. No one but a man steeped in Dickens could have written the essay; yet a mere idolator could never have achieved the measured judgment of Dickens' strength and weakness. The world of Dickens is perfectly marked off.

In his novels we may almost say there is no army, no navy, no church, no sport, no distant travel, no daring adventure, no feeling for the watery wastes and the motley nations of the planet, and—luckily, with his notion of them—no lords and ladies. Even love of the traditional sort is hardly in Dickens's sphere—I mean the soldierly passion in which a rather rakish gallantry was sobered by devotion, and loyalty rested on pride.

But in spite of these exclusions "almost everything is left, almost everything that counts in the daily life of mankind, or that by its presence or absence can determine whether life shall be worth living or not." There is

. . . the charm of humble things, the nobleness of humble people, the horror of crime, the ghastliness of vice, the deft hand and shining face of virtue passing through the midst of it all; and finally a fresh wind of indifference and change blowing across our troubles and clearing the most lurid sky.

And the place of Dickens himself as spectator of his creation is just right.

Walt Whitman, in his comprehensive democratic vistas, could never see the trees for the wood, and remained incapable, for all his diffuse love of the human herd, of ever painting a character or telling a story; the very things in which Dickens was a master.

Even what we call his caricature is a self-deception on our part.

We profess that it is very coarse and inartistic of Dickens to undo our life's work for us in an instant, and remind us of what we are. And as to other people, though we may allow that considered superficially they are often absurd, we do not wish to dwell on their eccentricities, nor to mimic them.

We like the delicacy, the restraint of humor. But "pure comedy is scornful, merciless, devastating, holding no door open to anything beyond."

What displeases us in Dickens is that he does not spare us; he mimics things to the full; he dilates and exhausts and repeats; he wallows. He is too intent on the passing experience to look over his shoulder, and consider whether we have not already understood, and had enough.

Yet Dickens is a consummate comedian. "The most grotesque creatures of Dickens are not exaggerations or mockeries of something other than themselves; they arise because nature generates them, like toadstools; they exist because they can't help it, as we all do." His "comic genius . . . carried him beyond the gentle humour which most Englishmen possess to the absolute grotesque reality." Dickens was a true moralist, too. Not that his ethics were radical or even far-sighted. "He denounced scandals without exposing shams and conformed willingly and scrupulously to the proprieties." He was middle class in sympathies and limitations. He "had more genius than taste, a warm fancy not aided by a thorough understanding of complex characters. He worked under pressure, for money and applause, and often had to cheapen in execution what his inspiration had so vividly conceived." Nevertheless, within his sphere he distilled "with the perfection of comedy, the perfection of morals."

He put the distinction between good and evil in the right place, and . . . he felt this distinction intensely. . . . Love of the good of others is something that shines in every page of Dickens with a truly celestial splendour. How entirely limpid is his sympathy with life—a sympathy uncontaminated by dogma or pedantry or snobbery or bias of any kind! How generous is this keen, light spirit, how pure this open heart! And yet, in spite of this extreme sensibility, not the least wobbling; no deviation from a just severity of judgement, from an uncompromising distinction between white and black.

Santayana's essay is perhaps too sparing of Dickens' inadequacies; the author of *Three Philosophical Poets* should almost be bound to find Dickens lacking in grasp of plot, in integrating power, in sensitiveness to the subtleties of human character. But, for the moment, Santayana is accepting the romantic author's privilege of bounding his vision. Dickens' range is limited, but unlike most romanticists, to Santayana he seems true to the segment of life he selects. He is perhaps true to the surface of all life, which is comic.

And there is no countenancing of evil in either Dickens or Shelley. Both allow goodness to overcome evil with greater ease than is possible in this real world of ours, but evil in being conquered is acknowledged and forced to show its true colors; it does not change its spots and pose as "experience" or "negation" or "error." In overpowering evil, they do not even, like Dante, count upon the support of the supernatural. Whatever good man achieves is the product of his own will and a sign of the perfectibility of his own nature.

It will be seen from this résumé that Santayana's criticism is philosophical criticism (but what criticism worthy of the name is not at bottom?), that it is more concerned with content than with form or expression, that its impulse is classical and ethical, that it avoids purely technical and literary problems for the graver ones of ultimate worth and significance, and that it is not dismayed by figures of first magnitude. The individual studies are but reflections of a central, luminous literary theory, which in turn is frankly Santayana's general philosophy. Perhaps his greatest service as a critic is to bring within a single focus, rationalistic and formal and ethical, authors as widely varied as Lucretius and Goethe, Whitman and Dante, Dickens and Shakespeare. Consistency in criticism clears the air, and Santayana is remarkably consistent for a literary critic. Equally outstanding is his power of sympathy, his ability to see from even a stranger's or an enemy's point of view, and to present that point of view faithfully. But this absorption of critic in subject is accomplished with no loss of independence or irony. Santayana is always judge, never merely expositor, and his criticism is basically a challenge to the romantic point of view, a challenge that is deeply grounded and cuts through, as true criticism should do, to first principles.

While he was composing *The Life of Reason* and the volumes of criticism, Santayana continued to teach philosophy at Harvard. His course in aesthetics and a new course in Greek philosophy made up the greater part of his teaching, but he also gave two courses in ethics, "Kant and Socrates" in 1895-96 and "Origins and Forms of Moral Life" in 1899-1900, and in the academic years of 1903-04, 1909-10, and 1911-12 worked out a systematic course in metaphysics entitled "The Order of Knowledge and the Order of Nature." Two popular courses of Santayana on the borderland of philosophy were

"The Philosophy of History," which he taught continually from 1902 to 1910, and "Three Philosophical Poets," the nucleus of his book by that name, which he gave from 1907 to 1910. Santayana also conducted seminaries in "Scholasticism," 1894-95, 1897-98, 1898-99, "The Metaphysics of Aristotle," 1899-1900, 1900-01, "Aesthetics," 1900-01, "Ancient Philosophy," 1901-02, 1902-03, and "Philosophy of History," 1906-07.

In 1904-05 Santayana was granted his second sabbatical leave, and the following year he was exchange professor at the Sorbonne. He admired there the "intellectual *room*. . . You can say what is *really true*. You needn't remember that you are in Cambridge, or are addressing the youth entrusted to your paternal charge." However, despite this feeling of compulsion Santayana managed to impart to the youth in his care something of his own independence. As one of his students put it, "Mr. Santayana facing a class at Harvard was always the same composed, smooth-browed, frictionless being, contemplating the subject at his leisure and having no motive or temptation to do aught but report exactly what he saw. . . He spoke rather deliberately, choosing the true word with conscience, and there was a characteristic smile now and again . . . the smile of one who shares the pleasure of some fine insight with any listeners who may catch it—with a little wistful question in the eyes whether you really did catch it and sympathize. . . . The value of his teaching lay less in the order and balance of exposition than in the greatness of single thoughts and of the spirit and intellectual attitude throughout."

It is the opinion of Professor Ralph B. Perry of Harvard that on the whole Santayana's undergraduate teaching was more notable than his graduate teaching. His influence over candidates for higher degrees was not comparable to that of James and Royce. He largely avoided the time-worn, controversial problems of philosophy, and he never relished what he felt appealed to Royce, "the degustation and savour of difficulties." He did, however, profoundly influence a few graduate students, notably Horace Kallen and B. A. G. Fuller, both of whom have since established themselves as prominent teachers and authors. Among his undergraduate courses Professor Perry says that the most successful were "Greek Philosophy" and "Three Philosophical Poets," and one can well see why this should have been true, since both courses dealt with his favorite subjects, his intellectual companions, and both brought philosophy close to art and letters. Professor Palmer says that he was particularly successful in lecturing on the history of philosophy and by the time of his resignation was one of the department's most brilliant lecturers.* Undeniable it is that he won for himself a place among the greatest collection of teachers that have ever graced the Harvard department of philosophy.

In general, it may be said that Santayana's courses paralleled the subjects of his books. Also one cannot help noticing that they tended gradually away from the center of philosophy to the outskirts where philosophy borders on life and letters. This movement was only natural in that Santayana hardly considered himself a philosopher at all, and was really more interested in viewing all life at a philosophical angle than in formulating or defending an original system of metaphysics.

Teaching, too, no matter how successful, was with Santayana hardly more than an avocation, and his writing began to take an increasing toll of his time and energy. Thus, when Harvard reopened for the first term of 1911-12, Santayana proposed that he be allowed to teach one semester of the academic year and devote the other to writing. President Lowell reluctantly granted Santayana's request, but before the arrangement could go beyond one term, the death of Santayana's mother severed his final ties with America, and his gradually increasing income gave him the freedom and leisure he desired. So came to a close Santayana's connections with Harvard, not as has been frequently supposed, with strained feelings on either side, beyond the growing conviction on Santayana's part that the teacher must make way for the critic and philosopher. In January 1912 he left America, never, it would seem, to return.

After leaving Harvard, Santayana was drawn by the ties of blood and childhood to Spain, where he spent two winters in the picturesque city of Seville. But Spain held little attraction for him. In the summer he traveled, or established himself in Paris with his friend, Professor C. A. Strong. The World War put an end temporarily to this untrammeled existence; residence in Paris was for the time being out of the question; rather must one quietly settle down in England and await this new and frightful aberration from the Life of Reason, whose impact was to be felt by even the most secluded of philosophers. And so for five years Santayana remained in England,

---

* Santayana said, much later, "I liked to regard all systems as alternative illusions . . . vistas for the imagination. . . I have not lost nor do I wish to lose, a certain facility and pleasure in taking those points of view at will, and speaking those philosophical languages."

meditating and writing, with only the occasional whir of an airplane to break the quiet of the countryside.

He had signalized his departure from Harvard and America by an unusual book, *Winds of Doctrine,* issued in 1913, on the eve of conflict, as it were. Somehow it suggests the pulling up of old roots in the author's life, the burning of bridges which have been crossed, the emergence from the academic cloister of a man of the larger, outer world. There is something prophetic, too, about the mission of the book; it looks out upon waters of philosophy muddied and troubled; it sees something ominous in the air, which the weather eye of the careful observer is able to detect. It is the critic's business to chart the cross-currents, the gales and gusts of doctrine which are buffeting a storm-tossed world.

In the rôle of such an observer Santayana finds much to his distaste. The world seems far removed from a Life of Reason. German idealism is still entrenched in high places; pragmatism is still resolved to turn appearance into reality. Philistinism is still rampant.

Those who speak most of progress measure it by quantity and not by quality; how many people read and write, or how many people there are, or what is the annual value of their trade; whereas true progress would rather lie in reading or writing fewer and better things, and being fewer and better men, and enjoying life more.

Newer attempts at the Life of Reason, vitalism in philosophy and liberalism in theology, seem abortive because they are not at bottom rational at all. Moreover, in the flaunting of a tight, militant nationalism, unreason threatens to disturb the peace and perhaps destroy the very existence of mankind.

Nationalism has become of late an omnivorous all-permeating passion. Local parliaments must be everywhere established, extinct or provincial dialects must be galvanised into national languages, philosophy must be made racial, religion must be fostered where it emphasises nationality and denounced where it transcends it.

Written in 1913, these words seem almost an augury of the next quarter century.

In 1905 Santayana had remarked that "the darkest spots are in man himself, in his fitful, irrational disposition"; the animal still "barks in the midst of human discourse." But there was hope that a better order of thinking and living might supervene if reason were allowed its rightful place in the life of mankind. "There is a pathetic capacity in men to live nobly, if only they would give one another the chance." In *Winds of Doctrine,* however, Santayana seems even less sure that reason will prevail. It is too much to expect the old Adam to become bright Athena overnight. In these times

... the intellect, the judgment are in abeyance. Life is running turbid and full; and it is no marvel that reason, after vainly supposing that it ruled the world, should abdicate as gracefully as possible, when the world is so obviously the sport of cruder powers—vested interests, tribal passions, stock sentiments, and chance majorities. Having no responsibility laid upon it, reason has become irresponsible.

Such a quandary would be expected to cast a rationalist into irremediable gloom; but Santayana himself in the meantime has changed. Less optimistic than in 1905, he sees, however, a new spirit arising, a new promise of hope.

The civilisation characteristic of Christendom has not disappeared, yet another civilisation has begun to take its place. We still understand the value of religious faith; we still appreciate the pompous arts of our forefathers; we are brought up on academic architecture, sculpture, painting, poetry, and music. We still love monarchy and aristocracy, together with that picturesque and dutiful order which rested on local institutions, class privileges, and the authority of the family. We may even feel an organic need for all these things, cling to them tenaciously, and dream of rejuvenating them. On the other hand the shell of Christendom is broken. The unconquerable mind of the East, the pagan past, the industrial socialistic future confront it with their equal authority. Our whole life and mind is saturated with the slow upward filtration of a new spirit—that of an emancipated, atheistic, international democracy.

Such a spirit may be called the "intellectual temper of the age." And what shall the philosopher do in its presence? Well, after all, there is nothing he can do.

These epithets may make us shudder; but what they describe is something positive and self-justified, something deeply rooted in our animal nature and inspiring to our hearts, something which, like every vital impulse, is pregnant with a morality of its own. In vain do we deprecate it; it has possession of us already through our propensities, fashions, and language.

The philosopher may if he chooses rail at the times, but his voice, shrill and unheard, will be drowned by the Babel he attempts to dispel. And perhaps this spirit is

... amiable as well as disquieting, liberating as well as barbaric; and a philosopher in our day, conscious both of the old life and of the new, might repeat what Goethe said of his successive love affairs,—that it is sweet to see the moon rise while the sun is still mildly shining.

It is not difficult for the reader with keen ears to detect here a different note from the authoritative voice of the Life of Reason. He will observe on the part of Santayana an extension of interest and sympathy to activities which seem outside the pale of reason, though of course this may merely mean that reason is to be rediscovered through fresh impulses and new avenues of approach.

Not that all these winds of doctrine are to be admired. The observer must distinguish fair weather from foul, must see which tendencies lead to enlightenment and which still wear the black garb of barbarism. The nineteenth century bequeathed the present century a belief in the efficiency of reform, but Santayana reminds us that not all attempts at reform do re-form, do reconstruct a better order out of that which has been laid aside. Some changes seem to indicate reform which is "integrating and creative."

The veering of the advanced political parties from liberalism to socialism would seem to be a clear indication of this new tendency. It is manifest also in the love of nature, in athletics, in the new woman, and in a friendly medical attitude toward all the passions.

There is encouragement here; "in the fine arts, however, and in religion and philosophy, we are still in full career towards disintegration. ... Artists have no less talent than ever; their taste, their vision, their sentiment are often interesting; they are mighty in their independence and feeble only in their works." As for philosophy,

... besides the survival of all the official and endowed systems, there has been of late a very interesting fresh movement, largely among the professors themselves, which in its various hues may be called irrationalism, vitalism, pragmatism, or pure empiricism. But this movement, far from being a reawakening of any organising instinct, is simply an extreme expression of romantic anarchy. It is in essence but a franker confession of the principle upon which modern philosophy has been building—or unbuilding—for these three hundred years, I mean the principle of subjectivity.

This movement is best illustrated by the vitalism of Henri Bergson, a philosophical error Santayana deems of sufficient importance to devote an entire chapter to. So with a brief thrust at Bergson he concludes "The Intellectual Temper of the Age," a chapter of stock-taking which in its importance suggests in a different day and age Carlyle's "Characteristics" or "Signs of the Times."

The remainder of *Winds of Doctrine* contains a paper on Bertrand Russell reprinted from the *Journal of Philosophy,* a lecture delivered in 1911 on "The Genteel Tradition in American Philosophy," a chapter on Bergson, a chapter on "Modernism and Christianity," and the essay on "Shelley: or the Poetic Value of Revolutionary Principles." The discussion of Bergson is somewhat technical and perhaps therefore of little interest to the general reader. The gist of Santayana's analysis is summed up at the conclusion of the chapter. Bergson's doctrine is "indeed alluring."

Instead of telling us, as a stern and contrite philosophy would, that the truth is remote, difficult, and almost undiscoverable by human efforts, that the universe is vast and unfathomable, yet that the knowledge of its ways is precious to our better selves, if we would not live befooled, this philosophy rather tells us that nothing is truer or more precious than our rudimentary consciousness, with its vague instincts and premonitions, that everything ideal is fictitious, and that the universe, at heart, is as palpitating and irrational as ourselves. Why then strain the inquiry? Why seek to dominate passion by understanding it? Rather live on; work, it matters little at what, and grow, it matters nothing in what direction. Exert your instinctive powers of vegetation and emotion; let your philosophy itself be a frank expression of this flux, the roar of the ocean in your little sea-shell, a momentary posture of your living soul, not a stark adoration of things reputed eternal.

Since Bergson and Santayana clash over the nature and source of knowledge, Bergson relying on what he calls *élan vital,* the subliminal springs of consciousness, the pulse of primordial, vegetative existence, and Santayana holding firmly to intelligence and reason and a representative knowledge, the clash is in first principles and admits no compromise. One will take sides in accordance with his own philosophy. To Santayana at least, Bergson's philosophy is a "confession of a certain mystical rebellion and atavism in the contemporary mind," a symptom of the times.

This is not an age of mastery; it is confused with too much business; it has no brave simplicity. The mind has forgotten its proper function, which is to crown life by quickening it into intelligence, and thinks if it could only prove that it accelerated life, that might perhaps justify its existence; like a philosopher at sea who, to make himself useful, should blow into the sail.

Much more sane and wholesome is Bertrand Russell, who with his associate G. E. Moore seems to give assurance that "reason and faith in reason are not left without advocates." Their philosophy has a logical precision reminiscent of the scholastics; in fact, Santayana calls it "a new scholasticism" and thinks of it as a tonic in an age of loose, emotionalized thinking.

He admires Russell's attack upon the pragmatists. Like the idealists they are keen psychologists, but, again like the idealists, they turn the vivid panorama of experience their method reveals into the only possible reality. Bertrand Russell, realist that he is, recognizes not only the external world as independent of the mind, but also a realm of truth whose ideal relationships, like mathematical rules, are forever true even if no human mind should happen to stumble upon them. This construction of a realm of eternal forms seems particularly happy to Santayana, for his own metaphysics has been leading him more and more in that direction.

Winds of Doctrine is an important book. On the surface it seems not only unduly controversial but vague and inconsistent, without any central thesis. But though each essay almost advocates a different point of view and champions a different cause, all unite in indicating in Santayana a growing breadth and tolerance, an unwillingness to measure everything by the yardstick of a single formula. Now he argues in behalf of atheistic democracy, now strict clericalism; in one breath he champions Shelley and in the next Walt Whitman; William James and Bertrand Russell, as wide as the poles, both receive his enthusiastic support. But what on the surface seems an inconsistent and indiscriminate taking of sides is underneath perhaps only the relish of the ironic spectator content to see the "moon rise while the sun is still mildly shining." When gusts of doctrine are blowing, it is the privilege of the true spectator to "feel that the sphere of what happens to exist is too alien and accidental to absorb all the play of a free mind, whose function, after it has come to clearness and made its peace with things, is to touch them with its own moral and intellectual light, and to exist for its own sake. This in view of the inner life of Santayana is the most significant statement of the book, and it defines his attitude for the next twenty-five years. He has never outlived the lines of an early sonnet:

> It is my crown to mock the runner's heat
> With gentle wonder and with laughter sweet.

And with this deepening feeling that he is a spectator has come a growing tolerance, an unbending of the stern Santayana with his "absolute refusals." The age breeds "a certain contrite openness of mind," though perhaps with some less of central, animating purpose.

Like most volumes of controversy, *Winds of Doctrine* was variously received. Most enthusiastic was the *Athenaeum,* declaring that its "downright manner and robust sense make the book fresh and lively, almost frolicsome in parts. But it should be taken seriously, for its high spirits are the natural result of that feeling of enhanced power which accompanies the exercise of keen critical faculties." On the other hand, the *Nation* felt that Santayana's attitude was rather "that of the conscious possessor of the truth who, with Puck, delights to note what fools these mortals be," and his "espousal of the materialistic philosophy" an "example of the modern tendency to 'burrow downwards toward the primitive.'" The discussion of modernism in religion the *Hibbert Journal* felt to be "singularly inept and unwarranted," but the *Catholic World* urged that it be "carefully studied by Catholic apologists." The essay on Shelley was generally admired, and was considered by a number of critics the finest thing in the book. Perhaps the variety of opinion called forth by *Winds of Doctrine* was better proof than anything else could have been of the truth implied in its title.

The years 1914 to 1918 Santayana spent in England, chiefly at Oxford, although frequent rambles took him through a large part of the picturesque countryside in the center and south of England. In Oxford "he led a quite isolated life, and had few or no relations with members of the University. With Robert Bridges he was, however, fairly well acquainted, and used to go up to Boar's Head sometimes to see him." During this whole period Santayana was actively engaged in writing, and his work falls into two large divisions. First to appear in print were a series of articles which came out in the *New Republic* at intervals from November 1914 to January 1916. These articles were topical and were directly inspired by the war. Some considered the common enemy, Germany, but others looked back upon the United States, which Santayana had not forgotten even if he had left its shores. At the same time Santayana was composing his famous *Soliloquies in England,* which seem less touched by the war and reveal more of the inner thoughts and life of their author. They later appeared in part in the *Athenaeum* throughout 1919 and 1920. The World War thus saw the germination of three of Santayana's books: *Egotism in German Philosophy,* 1916, *Character and Opinion in the United States,* 1920, and *Soliloquies in England,* 1922.

The *New Republic* articles show Santayana's attention directed outwards at public affairs. At no other time has he written so much about national character, international relationships, and the underlying problems of political economy. It seems as if once out of the academy, Santayana is resolved to become a citizen of the world.

He inquires in "The Logic of Fanaticism" how the Germans can be at the same time barbarian and possessed of the "highest *Kultur.*" He finds an explanation in their mad desire to impose *Kultur* upon the world at large, a *Kultur* which would be foreign and detrimental to the ethos of other nations. In "Heathenism" Santayana accuses the Germans of a primitive exaltation of will above reason, although he admits there is something basic about the heathen point of view. It is after all a "revulsion against the difficult and confused undertakings of reason . . . a retreat into immediate experience and animal faith. Man used to be called a rational animal, but his rationality is something eventual and ideal, whereas his animality is actual and profound. Heathenism, if we consider life at large, is the primal and universal religion." No longer does Santayana hope for any universal acceptance of the Life of Reason.

"Spanish Opinion on the War" is an interesting analysis of two trends of thought in Spain, one aristocratic and conservative favoring the German cause, the other liberal and democratic favoring that of the Allies. The first point of view is held by the clergy and by "that high-principled, austere, believing minority of the upper classes which feels itself to be the healthy part of the nation." The other is the view of the "laboring classes and the talking and bustling public that sits in cafés and reads the newspapers." With prophetic vision Santayana has marked out the alignment leading to the present civil war in Spain. This is no chance alignment in the eyes of Santayana, but a division which cuts through to first principles. The conservatives, including the clergy, prefer Germany because she represents an established order, a definite regimen which, in spite of being Protestant and Nordic, is to be preferred to an anarchic liberalism intent upon loosening the bonds of traditional morality, religion, and politics. For the liberals at heart "wish to reorganize Christian society on a pagan basis. The conservatives wish to prevent that reorganization and to restore, in a modern form, the old moral integrity of Christian nations."

The philosophic dilemma suggested by the situation in Spain seems to have laid firm hold upon Santayana's mind; in four ensuing articles he considers the problem and ponders long over the possibility of a solution. The most pressing need in political economy is to reconcile the claims of society and the individual. In "The Indomitable Individual," a sketch for a proposed volume on political economy which Santayana never got around to writing, he presents vigorously the claim of the individual. "Those who frame political or religious or aesthetic systems ought not to expect that they should be long carried out or widely accepted in the spirit in which their authors conceived them. They must reckon with their host, with the unaccountable, ever young, irrepressible individual. . . . Society exists by a conspiracy of psychological, physiological forces; however rigid you may make its machinery, its breath of life must come from the willing connivance of a myriad fleeting, inconstant, half-rational human souls."

In modern times a political philosophy has arisen which aims to give free play and full voice to this demand of the individual. Liberalism is its name. It limits the "prescriptions of the law to a few points, for the most part negative, leaving it to the initiative and conscience of individuals to order their life and conversation as they like, provided only they do not interfere with the same freedom in others."

Unfortunately, however, the problem cannot be solved so simply. If individualism is an instinctive trait of human nature, there lies almost as deep, perhaps deeper, man's gregariousness, his desire to share others' opinions and to have others share his, his craving to lead and willingness to be led. A liberal government or church will always mean a flourishing of smaller private organizations which in their more insidious way exert a pressure of public opinion and exact a uniformity quite as much as do state religions and autocracies.

In a society honeycombed by private societies a man finds his life supervised, his opportunities preëmpted, his conscience intimidated, and his pocket drained. Every one he meets informs him of a new duty and presents him with a new subscription list. At every turn he must choose between being incorporated or being ostracized.

Moreover, the desire of many liberals to convert others to their one formula, or to force into the fold of liberalism those who are quite content to be regimented, is a fact that must be reckoned with. Such is the irony of liberalism.

Nor is it just to assume that only those in a liberal environment feel free. The sense of freedom is subjective and relative. To the ancient mind liberty meant something far different from what liberalism stands for in this day and age.

Perhaps the deepest assumption of classic philosophy is that nature and the gods on the one hand and man on the other, both have a fixed character; that there is consequently a necessary piety, a true philosophy, a standard happiness, a normal art. The Greeks believed, not without reason, that they had grasped these permanent principles better than other peoples. They had largely dispelled superstition, experimented in government, and turned life into a rational art. Therefore when they defended their liberty what they defended was not merely freedom to live. It was freedom to live well, to live as other nations did not, in the public experimental study of the world and of human nature.

The Christian church took over this classic conception of liberty; it felt its mission was to free man from sin and the world by indoctrinating him in a "corporate scientific discipline" closely bound up with an institution. To the church the wild waywardness of modern liberalism would have been a reversion to heathenism; "to waver in the pursuit of the orthodox ideal could only betray frivolity and want of self-knowledge."

Strangely enough, German *Kultur* is the modern representative of classic liberty. It "resembles the polity of ancient cities and of the Christian church in that it constitutes a definite, authoritative, earnest discipline, a training which is practical and is thought to be urgent and momentous. It is a system to be propagated and to be imposed. It is all-inclusive and demands entire devotion from everybody." In fact, the very word "Kultur" is the symbol of classic liberty as the word "culture" is of modern liberalism.

Every nation has certain characteristic institutions, certain representative writers and statesmen, past and present, certain forms of art and industry, a certain type of policy and moral inspiration. These are its *Kultur,* its national tradition and equipment. . . . *Kultur* is transmitted by systematic education. It is not, like culture, a matter of miscellaneous private attainments and refined tastes, but, rather, participation in a national purpose and in the means of executing it.

On the other hand,

. . . culture came into the modern world with the renaissance, when personal humours and remote inspiration broke in upon the consecrated mediaeval mind. . . . Culture is a triumph of the individual over society. It is his way of profiting intellectually by a world he has not helped to make. . . . Culture requires liberalism for its foundation, and liberalism requires culture for its crown. It is culture that integrates in imagination the activities which liberalism so dangerously disperses in practice.

Kultur is homogeneous and spontaneous; it fosters the creative impulse; ages of *Kultur* produce the great masterworks of art. Culture is diversified and sophisticated; it cultivates the critical and appreciative faculties; ages of culture enjoy and classify the masterworks of their predecessors.

What then shall the ideal spectator say of these contradictory claims, both grounded in natural instinct, both promising freedom of a sort, one confident in a common human nature, the other humble before the multiple variations of individual men and women? A judgment here is one of the hardest a philosopher is ever called upon to make. One will look in vain in Santayana's articles for a neat, facile solution; in fact, it is not always possible to see just where Santayana stands in respect to the two sides of the case, for he feels deeply the strength of either position. Nor is he interested in a weak, tentative compromise. In fact, he seems unwilling to attempt even a systematic formulation of the problem; he prefers to illuminate now one aspect, now another with the dispassionate light of common sense, allowing the reader to come to his own conclusion after he has clearly seen the grounds of his choice. Thus the articles taken individually seem perhaps inconsistent and contradictory, but considered as a whole they piece together the complex parts of this ethical puzzle. "The Indomitable Individual" is balanced by "Liberalism and Culture"; "Classic Liberty" sets off "German Freedom." The following passages seem to indicate Santayana's own convictions and his recommendations for a more harmonious way of life. On the side of individualism the philosopher must always remember that "the aim of life is some way of living, as flexible and gentle as human nature; so that ambition may stoop to kindness, and philosophy to candor and to humor. Neither prosperity nor empire nor heaven can be worth winning at the price of a virulent temper, bloody hands, an anguished spirit, and a vain hatred of the rest of the world." German *Kultur,* and the classical and Christian systems for that matter, must recognize the fact that "the pursuit of any single end, ravishing and incomparable as it may seem to the enthusiast, strains and impoverishes human nature, and sometimes, by detaching it too much from common and humble feelings, actually debauches it." The classic and Christian systems grew out of a greater homogeneity of human interest than seems to obtain in the modern world with its multiplication of national and racial *mores.*

Yet if culture rather than *Kultur* is to be the watchword of the present,

. . . it is in the subsoil of uniformity, of tradition, of dire necessity that human welfare is rooted, together with wisdom and unaffected art, and the flowers of culture that do not draw their sap from that soil are only paper flowers. . . . After all, antiquity must have been right in thinking that reasonable self-direction must rest on having a determinate character and knowing what it is, and that only the truth about God and happiness, if we somehow found it, could make us free. But the truth is not to be found by guessing at it, as religious prophets and men of genius have done, and then damning every one who does not agree. Human nature, for all its substantial fixity, is a living thing with many varieties and variations. All diversity of opinion is therefore not founded on ignorance; it may express a legitimate change of habit or interest. The classic and Christian synthesis from which we have broken loose was certainly premature, even if the only issue of our liberal experiments should be to lead us back to some such equilibrium. Let us hope at least that the new morality, when it comes, may be more broadly based than the old on knowledge of the world, not so absolute, not so meticulous, and not chanted so much in the monotone of an abstracted sage.

This seems to be Santayana's final pronouncement in the matter, the closest he comes to a reconciliation of individualism with authority, of liberalism with classic liberty, of *Kultur* with culture.

The reason why a settlement of this kind is so difficult for Santayana is the same reason that he sees both sides of the case so clearly. Both points of view are represented in his own nature and the cultural heritages from which he has drawn sustenance. Temperamentally he loves the free leisure which liberalism permits and which in turn promotes culture. His remarks about human nature being flexible and gentle, about ambition stooping to kindness and philosophy to candor and humor, about the man of culture sometimes smiling a little at his own culture, seem to be reflected from the clear mirror of Santayana's own life. He says later in *Soliloquies in England,*

I have no wish to propagate any particular character, least of all my own; my conceit does not take that form. I wish individuals, and races, and nations to be themselves, and to multiply the forms of perfection and happiness, as nature prompts them. . . . The good, as I conceive it, is happiness, happiness for each man after his own heart, and for each hour according to its inspiration.

Here we have the reason why Santayana has not followed up *The Life of Reason* with a more specific ethics, pleading a definite system of conduct. Temperamentally the moralist and the reformer ill become him; he is ever the spectator, essaying but a comment here, a judgment there. It is significant that the essays on political economy end on the note of irony, that state of mind most congenial to the spectator.

On the other hand, Santayana was brought up under Catholic influence and came to know and love the Greek philosophers and poets. Thus he not only has a warm spot in his heart for traditional and institutional morality, but derives a great deal of the cast of his thought, particularly in matters of ethics and aesthetics, from these two systems. He has a respect for law, order, and tradition which is foreign to most liberals; he admires in art harmony, form, and wholeness with a passion as strong as the radical's mania for impressionism and license. He has a certain pious reverence for what is established, whether it be a man's religion or his nationality, an attitude served by the deterministic cast of his philosophy. Spirit does not attempt to move matter; it accepts its material bonds since it knows its nature is such that it can always take wing and escape to a more congenial realm. Thus Santayana can say truthfully, "I should not be afraid of the future domination, whatever it may be. One has to live in some age, under some fashion; I have found, in different times and places, the liberal, the Catholic, and the German air quite possible to breathe." This statement is not meant to be inconsistent with the previous desire for "human nature flexible and gentle," but perhaps a sentimental illusion lurks in it. Santayana's love of the Greeks and the Christian church is a cultural attachment, flourishing through a kind of remoteness which is only possible in a world strongly tinctured by liberalism. His happiness is dependent upon inherited monuments rather than a life "in compulsory unison." "Primitive, dragooned, unanimous ages," he says himself, "cannot possess culture"; they result in *Kultur*. And they would soon curb, if their prevailing temper were otherwise (as it would certainly be), his materialistic atheism, or perhaps his aesthetic morality, or even his playful irony. *Kultur* can do without spectators; one must put oneself to the plow or have the plow run over him.

In these discussions we are reminded once more of McStout and Van Tender, for the ethical problem these gentlemen debated in a literary talkfest is the same one extended here over the fields of religion, morality, and government. Van Tender is beginning to hold his own, and the contest looks more like a stalemate. Perhaps the odds are with Van Tender, for McStout shows the tender attitude of accepting and enjoying tradition and discipline rather than the aggressive one of extending their dominion and cementing their authority.

Instead of a book on political economy or even a treatise on the principles of ethics, which might have been expected from the philosophical turn of Santayana's later articles in the *New Republic,* he gave his reading public in 1916 *Egotism in German Philosophy*. For once he gave his public exactly what in the frenzy of wartime it wanted.

Not that *Egotism in German Philosophy* is hastily contrived, or a mere essay in propaganda. It is, as Santayana points out, "the fruit of a long gestation," the result of twenty years' teaching and reading, as well as an honest effort to be "clear and just" about German philosophy, "more clear and just, indeed, than it ever was about itself." Whatever injustice the book contains is due to Santayana's lifelong hatred of German philosophy rather than to anything as transient as the World War. It was, however, timed to appear just when sober, unbiased thinking was at a low ebb, and no doubt it fomented its share of unpleasant misunderstanding. Certainly its timeliness accounts for the fact that for many years it was the only work of

Santayana's to be translated into foreign languages.* At the outset, Santayana makes clear that the phenomenon he is describing is neither the religion of the Germans, which is traditional Catholic or old-fashioned Protestant, nor the irreligion, which is modern scientific materialism. "The foreign religion and the foreign irreligion of Germany are both incompatible with German philosophy." German philosophy is the subjective transcendentalism which is native to the German people and which underlies their national character and explains their shortcomings as well as their accomplishments. Santayana's thesis is that the subjectivity inherent in German idealism did not remain theoretical and academic, but was a dangerous principle which led to wilfulness in conduct, and in time found an inevitable outlet in international war. He thereupon traces a steady progression of German thought through Luther, Goethe, Kant, Fichte, Hegel, Schopenhauer, and Nietzsche, up to Kaiser Wilhelm. Hints of egotism in Goethe become seeds of egotism in Kant; so far egotism remains gentle in a literary or philosophical way. But Fichte and Hegel, while maintaining lip-service to Christianity, mix with their pure metaphysics a belief in the divinely appointed superiority of the Prussian state. In Schopenhauer and Nietzsche the mask of Christianity is dropped once and for all, and Will, which has been persistently gaining ground in German philosophy, is at last enthroned king and given physical embodiment in the superman. From the superman to *der Tag* is just a matter of sufficient accumulation of pent-up energy together with the invention of sufficient apparatus of war for this energy to make use of.

Santayana's book is witty, clever, and at times convincing. Nor does it lack a show of logical reasoning. In fact, that is the book's chief fault; finding certain parallels throughout the history of German thought, Santayana forces them into a steady progression which seems to do injustice to the complexity of the facts. Hints and seeds of egotism did exist, no doubt, in early German thought, and there is a possibility that they developed as Santayana says they did, but one could find many other hints and seeds that do not lead so directly to the temper which plunged Germany into war. In a sense German egotism is like Walt Whitman's, self-obliterating, the individual absorbed by the cosmic whole. Self-love should be made in-

* *L'erreur de la philosophie allemande*, Paris, 1917; *L'io nella filosofia germanica*, Lanciano, 1920.

nocuous in a true transcendentalism. And if by some perversion idealism becomes distraught and militant, how can the same formula which explains this phenomenon account for "such glaring traits of the German as his capacity for patient research and for organization, his pedantry, his dull sentimentality, his honesty, and law-abidingness"? Moreover, working back from effect to cause, if Germany's belligerence is due to her philosophical egotism, how explain the belligerence of the other combatants? As one critic says pertinently, "Other nations also are in urgent need of a drastic reconstruction of their present conception of nationalism." And if one's ears hear correctly, there is more than a little saber-rattling today in Santayana's adopted Italy. What has happened is that again Santayana has been led to a simplification by his remarkable feeling for analogy, a simplification which, as in *The Sense of Beauty* and *Reason in Common Sense,* does violence to the intricacy of brute fact. Here again, the barrier so easily leaped is the transition from theoretical metaphysics to practical conduct, from "subjectivity in thought" to "wilfulness in morals." In general, the more temperate critics felt that Santayana had overstepped the mark of fairness and truthfulness. Horace Kallen, a former pupil of Santayana's, said, "The work is really too sketchy and too abstract and its tone too biting and passionate to carry the conviction that is due the truths it expresses," and Professor Perry spoke of its "omissions and exaggerations . . . so obvious as to suggest caricature rather than criticism."

And yet, in spite of its hasty generalizations and its personal animus, *Egotism in German Philosophy* cannot be dismissed lightly. Something about its central thesis returns to haunt the reader, and make him wonder, especially in the light of modern Nazism, whether this clear-headed Latin has not glimpsed through all the fog of German metaphysics a very deep-rooted and mischievous moral principle which may extend unbroken from Alaric to Hitler. In all of its stages German philosophy represents the protestant spirit, the subjection of tradition to individual judgment, the refusal to accept without continual criticism, the setting up of the self over against authority. Now all this is necessary up to a certain point, and it is one of the genuinely worthwhile legacies of early Protestantism. But the Germans, like Emerson, become so enamored of protest that they entertain scant respect for religion or science or any discipline imposed from without by the external world or by the civilized past. With the lively insouciance of youth, they trust themselves sooner than the world, and their very metaphysics by reducing nature to idea rationalizes as it plays into the hands of this temperamental subjectivism. Of course, in Luther and Leibniz and Kant Christian orthodoxy is still a restraining force. Yet Kant for all his piety, perhaps because he wished to preserve his piety from the disintegrating effect of his agnostic metaphysics, voiced a principle which in the hands of his successors became the most deadly of all ethical weapons. The famous "categorical imperative" at the same time as it justified duty, a worth-while aim in itself, made duty independent of everything but the mandate of the individual conscience. The moral law was to be a God-given intimation of a higher sphere outside the realm of nature and history altogether. Reason was to be abdicated in favor of intuition, and through intuition the whole moral order was to be reintroduced, the very order which the understanding seemed unable to justify in the world of nature. Now Kant formulated his "categorical imperative" in order to preserve nothing more dangerous than God, heaven, and free-will, the postulates of orthodox Christianity. However, he established duty as an irresponsible yet obligatory function which later moralists might fill out with their own private enthusiasms. And Fichte and Hegel were ready to substitute for Kant's abstract formula the concrete Prussian state, made mandatory and apparently sanctioned by a false reading of history as an evolutionary process. Santayana, then, shows the tragic futility of erecting morality upon the basis of duty alone, without reference to experience or utility. Duty will shortly be made the handmaiden of personal or national ideals, and because her voice is authoritative and divine, these ideals will be forced upon the world at large. Santayana shows that even devout Fichte conceived of a "normal people," the ideal and pattern of the human race, who were at the same time the Germans, or at least their Nordic archetype we hear so much of today. In a final invective against the egotism of such a morality, Santayana gives us one of his most eloquent testimonies to the need of tolerance and humility and respect for fact in the framing of a system of ethics.

The whole transcendental philosophy, if made ultimate, is false, and nothing but a private perspective. The will is absolute neither in the individual nor in humanity. Nature is not a product of the mind, but on the contrary there is an external world, ages prior to any idea of it, which the mind recognises and feeds upon. There is a steady human nature within us, which our moods and passions may wrong but cannot annul. There is no categorical imperative but only the operation of instincts and interests more or less subject to discipline and mutual adjustment. Our whole life is a compromise, an incipient loose harmony between the passions of the soul and the forces of nature, forces which likewise generate and protect the souls of other creatures, endowing them with powers of expression and self-assertion comparable with our own, and with aims no less sweet and worthy in their own eyes; so that the quick and honest mind cannot but practise courtesy in the universe, exercising its will without vehemence or forced assurance, judging with serenity, and in everything discarding the word absolute as the most false and the most odious of words.

What Santayana has done is to attack moral absolutism everywhere, and in this larger sense his book has a wider application than merely to wartime Germany. Perhaps the German people are particularly youthful, "have not taken the trouble to decipher human nature, which is an *endowment,* something many-sided, unconscious, with a margin of variation, and have started instead with the will, which is only an *attitude,* something casual, conscious, and narrowly absolute." John Dewey had summed up the situation similarly in *German Philosophy and Politics,* 1915, a book which is less ambitious than Santayana's, more restrained and simply plausible.

Having disposed of Germany in two hundred pages, Santayana next turned his attention to America. In fact, before he left the United States, Santayana had begun his now well-known analysis of the "genteel tradition" in a lecture delivered in 1911 before the Philosophical Union of California. Up to this time Santayana had condemned practical, money-crazed America; perhaps he had been too thoroughly immersed in New England culture to be able to stand off and view it objectively, as he was to do in this lecture. At any rate, his audience must have received a shock at the unexpected vehemence of his attack upon American philosophy from Jonathan Edwards to William James.

The "genteel tradition," according to Santayana, is that attitude toward life, escape from life he would say, which has always characterized polite society and academic circles in New England or in other regions distinctly under New England influence. The foundation of this philosophy Santayana believes to be a diluted Puritanism, softened still further by transcendentalism and centuries of New England culture. The "genteel tradition" is humane, urbane, mildly dogmatic, and intensely conservative. Calvinism and transcendentalism were of course once "living fountains; but to keep them alive they required, one an agonised conscience, and the other a radical subjective criticism of knowledge." The former was impossible after the colonial period, and the latter was too philosophical to survive long in a pure, healthy state. Thus it became conventionalized and, then, the property of the academic cloister "for want of anything equally academic to take its place." Meanwhile in the mart of business and in daily life an entirely different but generally unacknowledged philosophy of life was taking root, something instinctive, pragmatic, expressive of the "gush and go" of the aggressive American spirit. Thus America may be said to be a country

> ... with two mentalities, one a survival of the beliefs and standards of the fathers, the other an expression of the instincts, practice, and discoveries of the younger generations. In all the higher things of the mind—in religion, in literature, in the moral emotions—it is the hereditary spirit that still prevails, so much so that Mr. Bernard Shaw finds that America is a hundred years behind the times. The truth is that one-half of the American mind, that not occupied intensely in practical affairs, has remained, I will not say high-and-dry, but slightly becalmed; it has floated gently in the back-water, while, alongside, in invention and industry and social organisation, the other half of the mind was leaping down a sort of Niagara Rapids. This division may be found symbolised in American architecture: a neat reproduction of the colonial mansion—with some modern comforts introduced surreptitiously—stands beside the sky-scraper. The American Will inhabits the sky-scraper; the American Intellect inhabits the colonial mansion. The one is the sphere of the American man; the other, at least predominantly, of the American woman. The one is all aggressive enterprise; the other is all genteel tradition.

This is an excellent piece of analysis, and the whole lecture strikes fire from the flint of truth. Nevertheless, many readers, though they admit the truth of this genealogy which Santayana gives the "genteel tradition," will feel in their hearts that Santayana misses the spirit animating such a tradition. In particular he colors the "genteel tradition" emotionally with a reflection of his own personal distaste for it. It seems to him starved and impoverished, and he constantly assumes that everyone within its ranks will be affected likewise. "The genius of Poe and Hawthorne, and even of Emerson," seems to him "employed on a sort of inner play, or digestion of vacancy ... in danger of being morbid, or tinkling, or self-indulgent"; yet I am sure none of these authors felt thus enervated or devitalized.

Santayana's lecture closes with two examples of men, one a poet, the other a philosopher, who dared to challenge the "genteel tradition" and express a more spontaneous, native point of view. The impact of Walt Whitman and William James is one from which the "genteel tradition" will find it hard to recover. "The academic mind . . . has had its flanks turned. On the one side came the revolt of the Bohemian temperament, with its poetry of crude naturalism; on the other side came an impassioned empiricism, welcoming popular religious witnesses to the unseen, reducing science to an instrument of success in action, and declaring the universe to be wild and young, and not be harnessed by the logic of any school."

Santayana continued his studies of America in the *New Republic* with "Genteel American Poetry," an expansion of the latter part of the California lecture, "The Alleged Catholic Danger," and "Shakespeare Made in America." But more important than these was a lecture Santayana gave in England in 1918 entitled "Philosophical Opinion in America." In reality this lecture was a continuation of "The Genteel Tradition in American Philosophy," carrying the thread from William James on to the new realists. It revealed on Santayana's part even more of a feeling that the "genteel tradition" was on the wane, that vital, democratic America had made its presence felt even in the academy, that behind these recent philosophers was a hard-headed, courageous, frontal attack upon the facts of nature which the "genteel tradition" would have feared to make. The new professor of philosophy, for instance, seemed to Santayana no longer an apologist for a particular sect, or a vague, troubled idealist; some of the systematic hardness of the business world had crept into his manner, and some of the business man's worship of fact into his thought. It is true, technicians have found their way into philosophy as into other departments of learning; and instead of benign incumbents of such spacious chairs as the Professorship of Natural Religion and Moral Polity, we find specialists in logic, in psychology, in epistemology and ontology, sometimes retaining with a kind of fatuous innocence those sweeping titles (and their pecuniary rewards) which their predecessors have bequeathed to them. The new professor of philosophy "is less eloquent and apostolic than the older generation of philosophers, very professional in tone and conscious of his *Fach*."

But most characteristic of the American philosophical soil is the vigor with which it nourishes the new realism. These new realists are descendants of the idealists and the pragmatists, but the disintegration of philosophy, which began by denying the external world in favor of consciousness, goes on to its paradoxical conclusion in the denial of consciousness in favor of the external world. This is swinging the pendulum too far to the other extreme, but in such a frank recognition of real objects, in this homage paid to sense and to science, there is hope for the future. There is, at least in intellectual matters, "a sort of happy watchfulness and insecurity. Never was the human mind master of so many facts and sure of so few principles."

"Materialism and Idealism in American Life," an article written for the *Landmark*, is of even greater interest to the general reader; it is perhaps Santayana's most significant criticism of American life. The essay poses the query whether materialism or idealism is more fundamental to the American character. America, with an inheritance of adventurous pioneer blood, with the need of clearing a continent for a constantly expanding population, with no monuments of indigenous culture to gaze upon, has naturally adopted a materialistic point of view. Its founders were men who had broken with tradition, and though tradition continued to color what official religion and philosophy these men and their followers retained, there was a new spirit in the air of physical conquest, of the practical control of material forces. American materialism Santayana correctly defines as a worship not of wealth but of quantity, a desire to have the biggest buildings, the biggest industries, even the biggest churches. A worship of quantity implies an indifference to quality; and there is a kind of idealism the American as yet knows nothing of: "to be poor in order to be simple, to produce less in order that the product may be more choice and beautiful, and may leave us less burdened with unnecessary duties and useless possessions."

Yet the American has an idealism of a sort, an idealism the more staunch because its ends can be easily achieved.

He is an idealist working on matter. . . . His imagination is practical and the future it forecasts is immediate. . . . When a poor boy, perhaps, he dreams of an education, and presently he gets an education, or at least a degree; he dreams of growing rich, and he grows rich— only more slowly and modestly, perhaps, than he expected; he dreams of marrying his Rebecca and, even if he marries a Leah instead, he ultimately finds in Leah his Rebecca after all. He dreams of helping to carry on and to accelerate the movement of a vast, seething, progressive society, and he actually does so. Ideals clinging so close to nature are almost sure of fulfilment; the American beams with a certain self-confidence and sense of mastery; he feels that God and nature are working with him.

Whether such an idealism will ever shake off its materialistic trappings, whether the imagination of the American will be sobered and refined, time and a great spiritual crisis will tell. For the American is still young; his faults, like his intense vitality, are signs of adolescence.

The American is wonderfully alive; and his vitality, not having often found a suitable outlet, makes him appear agitated on the surface; he is always letting off an unnecessarily loud blast of incidental steam. Yet his vitality is not superficial; it is inwardly prompted, and as sensitive and quick as a magnetic needle.

His youthful optimism must at some time be bruised; but

... if serious and irremediable tribulation ever overtook him ... it is then that we should be able to discover whether materialism or idealism lies at the base of his character. Meantime his working mind is not without its holiday. He spreads humour pretty thick and even over the surface of conversation, and humour is one form of moral emancipation. He loves landscape, he loves mankind, and he loves knowledge; and in music at least he finds an art which he unfeignedly enjoys. In music and landscape, in humour and kindness, he touches the ideal more truly, perhaps, than in his ponderous academic idealisms and busy religions.

The future for America is not dark.

When the senses are sharp, as they are in the American, they are already half liberated, already a joy in themselves; and when the heart is warm, like his, and eager to be just, its ideal destiny can hardly be doubtful. It will not be always pumping and working; time and its own pulses will lend it wings.

In 1920, when *Character and Opinion in the United States* was published, the two essays just discussed appeared as two of the most important chapters of the book. The opening chapter, "The Moral Background," is a rewriting in a more popular form of "The Genteel Tradition in American Philosophy." "The Academic Environment" is a description of Harvard and its surroundings as Santayana knew them from having studied and taught there, and two chapters on

CRITIC AND ESSAYIST 191

James and Royce respectively survey American philosophy as revealed in two of its most impressive representatives.

These two studies have been the source of much heated controversy. Santayana's somewhat patronizing air, his faint praise and vigorous damning of his former colleagues, have been naturally resented and attacked by pupils and admirers of James and Royce. And when philosophies are as radically different as are those of James, Royce, and Santayana, it is difficult for one philosopher to deal fairly with either of the others. It will be remembered William James called Santayana's philosophy "fantastic," "a perfection of rottenness." However, Santayana is, with allowance for the difference in point of view, eminently fair in dealing with the opinions of James and Royce; it seems to me he oversteps the mark of fairness only in his analysis of the motives underlying these opinions, in attributing to both men prejudice or evasion or ulterior purpose. Santayana is right to link philosophy with life, but before he condemns he should be more sure that a philosopher's motives are really what they seem to be to an opponent. For instance, he says that James held no firm convictions at all, was at heart an agnostic. In spite of his apparent theism, "he did not really believe; he merely believed in the right of believing that you might be right if you believed." There was in him an instinctive distrust of orthodoxy; the faiths he investigated in *The Varieties of Religious Experience* he did not expect to be "discoveries of absolute fact, which everybody else might be constrained to recognize ... not ... that it was *impossible* that such an orthodoxy should be true, but with a firm conviction that it was to be feared and distrusted ... I think it would have depressed him if he had had to confess that any important question was finally settled." Now the results of James's empiricism may be agnostic, but to say that James delighted in or strove to insure agnosticism is to read his character through the lenses of Santayana's irony. He was puzzled and distressed by the problem of evil; he was at times hesitant, even inconsistent; but I agree with Professor Perry that he was essentially "a man of convictions, who found it necessary to believe, and lived what he believed; who felt that he had the truth, and endeavored to propagate it." What James really distrusted was dogmatism. He refused to judge until the evidence was all in, and he sought in byways and corners for anything that might contribute to the truth. And he offered the same privilege to others, not because he delighted in error or ignorance, but because he felt truth was so difficult of attainment.

Likewise, Santayana mars a remarkably acute interpretation of Josiah Royce by maintaining that his reasoning was "not pure logic or pure observation," but "always secretly enthusiastic or malicious," with its results already "presupposed." "He resembled some great-hearted medieval peasant visited by mystical promptings.... His was a gothic and scholastic spirit, intent on devising and solving puzzles, and honoring God in systematic works.... In his heart there was no clearness." This portrait may be Royce in the sight of Santayana or even of eternity, but it is not the man his pupils knew, and perhaps Dickinson Miller is justified in calling it a "caricature ... both acrid and feeble" based on "general malperception" and even "false details of fact."

I think Santayana in many respects understood neither James nor Royce. A certain troubled earnestness and moral restlessness, frequently the possession of the Protestant mind, seemed to the Catholic Santayana confused and wayward. It seemed to him that James and "the people about him" and "modern philosophers anywhere" had no knowledge of the "good life." "They had standards of character and right conduct; but as to what might render human existence good, excellent, beautiful, happy, and worth having as a whole, their notions were utterly thin and barbarous. They had forgotten the Greeks, or never known them." They were bound, being Puritans, to "smell of brimstone." But to cry shrilly that whatever displeases one is barbarism is neither to understand it nor to do it justice. And Professor Perry rightly reminds Santayana that

James and Royce and others of the lingering brimstone age in American philosophy, did not regard duty as a stage of angelic perfection, but as being a relatively tolerable state of mind *in a world in which evil abounds.* Moralism is, it is true, unbeautiful; it is strained, harsh, distraught. But what, the state of the world being such as it is, shall we say of the philosophers whom Mr. Santayana describes as concentrating their lives as much as possible in pure intelligence in order that *they may be led by it into the way of peace?* There is a point of view from which a peace so purchased is hard, complacent, inhumane, and frivolous.

Outside the universities the portraits of James and Royce were more generally admired. Harold Stearns in the *Freeman* predicted that they will go down in history as the "classic essays" on the two philosophers, "critical estimates that are, at the same time, most engaging and revealing personal portraits." And there is in Santayana's essays just as much kindliness for the persons of both James and Royce as there is unfriendliness toward their philosophies. Speaking of James, Santayana says,

> In person he was short rather than tall, erect, brisk, bearded, intensely masculine. While he shone in expression and would have wished his style to be noble if it could also be strong, he preferred in the end to be spontaneous, and to leave it at that. . . . The rough, homely, picturesque phrase, whatever was graphic and racy, recommended itself to him. . . . Everybody liked him, and delighted in him for his generous, gullible nature and brilliant sallies. He was a sort of Irishman among the Brahmins, and seemed hardly imposing enough for a great man. . . . I think he was glad when the bell rang, and he could be himself again until the next day. But in the midst of this routine of the class-room the spirit would sometimes come upon him, and, leaning his head on his hand, he would let fall golden words, picturesque, fresh from the heart, full of the knowledge of good and evil. Incidentally there would crop up some humorous characterisation, some candid confession of doubt or of instinctive preference, some pungent scrap of learning; radicalisms plunging sometimes into the sub-soil of all human philosophies; and, on occasion, thoughts of simple wisdom and wistful piety, the most unfeigned and manly that anybody ever had.

The pleasant intimacy of these character sketches makes us wish Santayana had done more in this vein; their passages of reminiscence are among the most engaging parts of his criticism.

In general, *Character and Opinion in the United States* was admired by the press, the consensus of critical opinion being that Santayana's generalizations were as accurate as any could hope to be. Although in any selection of characteristics such as Santayana makes there are bound to be omissions which disturb the fine balance of national character, Santayana's collection of American traits will be immediately recognized as American by anyone who has ever let his eyes roam over the American scene. J. Middleton Murry, writing in the English *Nation,* warns his readers that there is a lesson for them too in the book.

We are implicitly condemned by the standards against which America is measured. . . . Under a light so searching England will not look appreciably better than America. . . . Indeed throughout this book we are conscious that American character and opinion is merely a piece of the general texture of modern life in which the pattern happens to be more conspicuous.

This wider application of Santayana's book gives it a depth and importance denied most casual observations of America from the pen of foreigners. Not merely America but modern civilization as a whole is brought before the bar of a judgment as rigid as it is sympathetic. And it is Santayana's heartfelt wish that

Heaven . . . make the new world a better world than the old! In the classical and romantic tradition of Europe, love, of which there was very little, was supposed to be kindled by beauty, of which there was a great deal: perhaps moral chemistry may be able to reverse this operation, and in the future and in America it may breed beauty out of love.

It remained, however, for England to draw from Santayana his most mellow reflections upon human life and character. What five years' leisure and meditation in England had really meant to Santayana was not revealed until 1919, when the first "Soliloquies in England" began to appear. While his attention all this time had been apparently turned outward toward Germany and America, inwardly he had been deeply moved by the war, by the English nation, and by the English countryside. A certain settling of character had taken place, a broadening of sympathy, and a loss of faith in political and philosophical panaceas.

The composition of the soliloquies Santayana describes in a prologue he wrote when the essays were later collected in 1922 and published as *Soliloquies in England and Later Soliloquies*.

During those five years, in rambles to Iffley and Sandford, to Godstow and Wytham, to the hospitable eminence of Chilswell, to Wood Eaton or Nuneham or Abingdon or Stanton Harcourt . . . these Soliloquies were composed, or the notes scribbled from which they have been expanded. Often over Port Meadow the whirr of aeroplanes sent an iron tremor through these reveries, and the daily casualty list, the constant sight of the wounded, the cadets strangely replacing the undergraduates, made the foreground to these distances. Yet nature and solitude continued to envelop me in their gentleness, and seemed to remain nearer to me than all that was so near. They muffled the importunity of the hour; perhaps its very bitterness and incubus of horror drove my thoughts deeper than they would otherwise have ventured into the maze of reflection and of dreams.

These soliloquies, like the earlier sonnets, reflect many moods; they are intimate broodings over nature, over mankind, over the meaning of life itself. They are utterly unsystematic, some placed in juxtaposition seem even inconsistent, but they are faithful records of an intense earnestness and a desire to think honestly and clearly. Aside from their literary excellence they are invaluable in forecasting the whole direction of Santayana's later thought. Considerately he provides us not only with his finished systems but with the blocks from which they are built.

Although many points of view are represented in the soliloquies, it is not difficult to trace certain definite strands of thought. First of all, the meager faith of Santayana in human progress is shattered. The first essay, "Atmosphere," is an ironic commentary on befogged mankind, unable and unwilling to see the stars. The note is repeated with more bitterness and irony in "Tipperary," addressed to disillusioned soldiers upon their return from the front. It is not a rosy picture that the philosopher paints.

This war has given you your first glimpse of the ancient, fundamental, normal state of the world, your first taste of reality. It should teach you to dismiss all your philosophies of progress or of a governing reason as a babble of dreamers who walk through one world mentally beholding another. . . . Each generation breaks its egg-shell with the same haste and assurance as the last, pecks at the same indigestible pebbles, dreams the same dreams, or others just as absurd, and if it hears anything of what former men have learned by experience, it corrects their maxims by its first impressions, and rushes down any untrodden path which it finds alluring, to die in its own way, or become wise too late and to no purpose.

The utopia of a Life of Reason has faded far into the distance.

Yet whereas man in the abstract has fallen so low in Santayana's estimation, the flesh-and-blood animal has taken on a new significance. Santayana has grown more tolerant of the irrational instincts and longings which are the "atmosphere of the inner man," "the weather in his soul." The quiet pleasantness of the English countryside, the humble contentment of its inhabitants, the daily routine of market-place, hearth, church, and village green have left their mark on Santayana in a greater understanding of human life. No one acknowledges their influence more than Santayana himself when he speaks admiringly of the English.

Their aspect, their habits, their invincible likes and dislikes seemed like an anchor to me in the currents of this turbid age. They were a gift of the gods, like the sunshine or the fresh air or the memory of the Greeks; they were superior beings, and yet more animal than the rest of us, calmer, with a different scale of consciousness and a slower pace of thought. . . . These self-sufficing Englishmen, in their reserve and decision, seemed to me truly men, creatures of fixed rational habit, people in whose somewhat inarticulate society one might feel safe and at home.

And so Santayana goes on, not to a completed portrait, but with a series of masterstrokes in which the Englishman stands before us, his vitality, his humor, his slow, stubborn persistence absolutely unimpaired. Santayana's countryman, Salvador da Madariaga, has recently revealed the Englishman in much the same light, but he has substituted for the fluidity of Santayana's treatment a rigid formula which somehow dries up the warm humanity of the Briton. Not that Santayana merely presents us with disconnected impressions of the Englishman either. His main effort is by synthesis to determine just what sort of man all the varied traits and habits of the Englishman add up to, even to account for them if he can as outward manifestations of a certain innate disposition, a "humour" in the Elizabethan sense. And he is remarkably successful; the prologue, "Distinction in Englishmen," and "The British Character" are criticism of a high order. Santayana succeeds particularly in stripping the native English trunk of all its acquired foliage. "When he ceases to be sensual and national, adventurous and steady, reticent and religious, the Englishman is a mad ghost." The Englishmen Santayana met "when they were very exquisite or subtle" seemed "like cut flowers; the finer they were the frailer, and the cleverer the more wrong-headed. Delicacy did not come to them, as to Latin minds, as an added ornament, a finer means of being passionate. . . . It impoverished their sympathies, it severed them from their national roots, it turned to affectation or fanaticism, it rendered them acrid and fussy and eccentric and sad." No, the distinction of Englishmen is of another sort.

The Englishman does in a distinguished way the simple things that other men might slur over as unimportant or essentially gross or irremediable; he is distinguished—he is disciplined, skilful, and calm—in eating, in sport, in public gatherings, in hardship, in danger, in extremities. It is in physical and rudimentary behavior that the Englishman is an artist; he is the ideal sailor, the ideal explorer, the ideal comrade in a tight place; he knows how to be clean without fussiness, well-dressed without show, and pleasure-loving without loudness.

And the Englishman is right, he is wise. "Refinement, like charity, should begin at home." The body should first be put in order, then "speech and manners" and the habits of social life.

The mind of the Englishman, starting in this proud and humble and profound way from the inner man, pierces very often, in single directions, to the limit of human faculty. [However,] he is at his best when free impulse or familiar habit takes an unquestioned lead, and when the mind, not being expected to intervene, beats in easy unison with the scene and the occasion. . . . Then grace returns to him, so angular often in his forced acts and his express tenets; the smile comes unaffectedly, and the blithe quick words flow as they should; arm is linked spontaneously in arm, laughter points the bull's-eye of truth, the whole world and its mysteries, not being pressed, become amiable, and the soul shines happy, and beautiful, and absolute mistress in her comely house. Nothing in him then is gross; all is harmonised, all is touched with natural life. His simplicity becomes wholeness, and he no longer seems dull in any direction, but in all things sound, sensitive, tender, watchful, and brave.

The Englishman is at a disadvantage where the reason is concerned; his religion, his philosophy, his politics are irrational though comfortable compromises.

What governs the Englishman is his inner atmosphere, the weather in his soul. It is nothing particularly spiritual or mysterious. When he has taken his exercise and is drinking his tea or his beer and lighting his pipe . . . when, well-washed and well-brushed, he resolutely turns in church to the East and recites the Creed (with genuflexions, if he likes genuflexions) without in the least implying that he believes one word of it . . . when he adopts a party or a sweetheart . . . when he is choosing his clothes or his profession—never is it a precise reason, or purpose, or outer fact that determines him; it is always the atmosphere of his inner man. [Yet] never since the heroic days of Greece has the world had such a sweet, just, boyish master. It will be a black day for the human race when scientific blackguards, conspirators, churls, and fanatics manage to supplant him.*

* Cf. Emerson's remarks on the Englishman: "Their habits and instincts cleave to nature. They are of the earth, earthy; and of the sea, as the sea-kinds, attached to it for what it yields them, and not from any sentiment. They are full of coarse strength, rude exercise, butcher's meat and sound sleep; and suspect any poetic insinuation or any hint for the conduct of life which reflects on this animal existence. . . . They stoutly carry into every nook and corner of the earth their turbulent sense; leaving no lie uncontradicted; no pretension unexamined. . . . Here exists the best stock in the world, broad-fronted, broad-bottomed, best for depth, range and equability."

Santayana's portrait of the Englishman is his finest sketch of national character, and one of the shrewdest descriptions of the subject ever penned by an American. Emerson's *English Traits* may plumb deeper to the roots of British greatness, may give us the Briton nearer to his infinite variety, but Santayana's Englishman, if more of a type, is justly representative and remarkably vivid.

Turning next from man to nature, Santayana feels more keenly than ever before the vastness and complexity of the external world and man's inevitable humility in its presence. Existence seems to Santayana more and more a flux; cloud castles, ever building and dissolving, are a fit symbol of nature everywhere. Impermanence is beneath all form and measure. Heraclitus, not Parmenides, was right in his vision of perpetual change. There is a human scale, a scale of intelligibility, of reason, but the human scale is not nature's scale, and man had best recognize his limitation. The clemency of English climate cannot blind us to "parched deserts, hard mountains, night with its overwhelming moon . . . Here the human scale is altogether transgressed; nature is cruel, alien, excessive, to be fled from with a veiled face." It is striking that in an island where Nature seems most mild and amenable to human wishes, Santayana should have discerned most clearly the stern indifference beneath her pleasant mask.

But having paid homage to the natural scale, "it is sweet and necessary that the works of man should respect the human scale when everything in nature so infinitely transcends it." And there is a lesson in those very cloud castles which reveal everywhere restlessness and insecurity.

Even cloud castles . . . have a double lien on permanence. A flash of lightning is soon over, yet so long as the earth is wrapped in its present atmosphere, flashes will recur from time to time so very like this one that the mind will make the same comment upon them, and its pronouncements on its past experience will remain applicable to its experience to come. Fleeting things in this way, when they are repeated, survive and are united in the wisdom which they teach us in common. At the same time they inwardly contain something positively eternal, since the essences they manifest are immutable in character, and from their platonic heaven laugh at this inconstant world, into which they peep for a moment, when a chance collocation of atoms suggests one or another of them to our minds. To these essences mind is constitutionally addressed, and into them it likes to sink in its self-forgetfulness.

It is only our poor mother Psyche, being justly afraid of growing old, who must grudge the exchange of one vision for another.

It seems in these soliloquies as if Santayana penetrated to a spiritual dimension hitherto closed to him, as if a more sober wisdom descended upon him and left in its train a largeness of vision and an abiding peace. Then his morality, without changing its essential properties, becomes softened and alembicated. In these soliloquies life takes on many hues, depending on the perspective in which it is viewed. It is perhaps like a carnival with both tragic and comic masks. After several essays developing either of these themes, Santayana brings his thoughts within a single focus in the remarkable essay "Carnival," which is the crux of his whole philosophy of life.

All facts and objects in nature can take on opposite moral tints. When abstracted from our own presence and interests, everything that can be found or imagined is reduced to a mere essence, an ideal theme picked out of the infinite, something harmless, marvellous, and pure, like a musical rhythm or geometrical design. The whole world then becomes a labyrinth of forms and motions, a castle in the clouds built without labour and dissolved without tears. The moment the animal will reawakes, however, these same things acquire a new dimension; they become substantial, not to be created without effort nor rent without resistance; at the same time they become objects of desire and fear; we are so engrossed in existence that every phenomenon becomes questionable and ominous, and not so much a free gift and manifestation of its own nature as a piece of good or bad news. . . . We are caught in the meshes of time and place and care; and as the things we have set our heart on, whatever they may be, must pass away in the end, either suddenly or by a gentle transformation, we cannot take a long view without finding life sad, and all things tragic. This aspect of vanity and self-annihilation, which existence wears when we consider its destiny, is not to be denied or explained away, as is sometimes attempted in cowardly and mincing philosophies. It is a true aspect of existence in one relation and on a certain view; but to take this long view of existence, and look down the avenues of time from the station and with the emotions of some particular moment, is by no means inevitable, nor is it a fair and sympathetic way of viewing existence. Things when they are actual do not lie in that sort of sentimental perspective, but each is centred in itself; and in this intrinsic aspect existence is nothing tragic or sad, but rather something joyful, hearty, and merry. A buoyant and full-blooded soul has quick senses and miscellaneous sympathies: it changes with the changing world; and when not too much starved or thwarted by circumstances, it finds all things vivid and comic. Life is free play fundamentally and would like to be free play altogether. In youth anything is pleasant to see or to do, so long as it is spontaneous, and if the conjunction of these things is ridiculous, so much the better: to be ridiculous is part of the fun.

Humor and pathos are products of the press of life, but it is the spirit's privilege at times to return to the first attitude, the most spiritual of the three.

Contemplation, when it frees itself from animal anxiety about existence, ceases to question and castigate its visions, as if they were mere signals of alarm or hints of hidden treasures; and then it cannot help seeing what treasures these visions hold within themselves, each framing some luminous and divine essence, as a telescope frames a star; and something of their inalienable distinction and firmness seems to linger in our minds, though in the exigencies of our hurried life we must turn away from each of them and forget them.

Santayana is thus able to combine these three points of view in a brilliant generalization, one of the most significant truths he has ever uttered. "Everything in nature is lyrical in its ideal essence, tragic in its fate, and comic in its existence." Man's duty is to face courageously his natural limitations, but it is his privilege, too, to relish the humor of the pageant of existence, and to glory in the imperishability of the things of the spirit, far above the accidents of the flesh.

All in all, *Soliloquies in England* was the most generally admired book which had so far come from Santayana's pen. The urbanity of his philosophic musings, the flavor and quality of his style, the sensitiveness of his temperament, were all acknowledged in the reviews. The appreciation of the English national genius was felt to be remarkably keen and accurate, although Bertrand Russell reminded the readers of the *Dial* that Santayana's England was "rapidly disappearing, and being replaced by things which no contemplative spirit can admire," that Santayana's England after all was the England "fashioned in the time of Queen Anne—a land of leisure and beauty, of aristocratic culture, of tolerance and good humor." It was felt in some quarters that Santayana's aristocratic detachment neglected the lot of the common man, that he was out of touch and sympathy with the problems of the new industrial democracy, that his stoicism and fatalism in regard to the war was small comfort to "some young soldiers" who "were still moody and silent, even when the Armistice was signed." These charges were neither unfounded nor particularly new; Santayana's point of view had always been recognized as individualistic rather than social or humanitarian. It is not true, however, that the war affected him lightly, or that he was insensitive to its horror and its futility. Lest he seem "to have been piping soliloquies whilst Rome was burning," he added to the preface to *Soliloquies in England* three sonnets, "desperate verses extorted from me by events" during the war years. These verses, in spite of their conventional phrasing, show a spirit deeply moved by grief and suffering. And of course many of the soliloquies at farther remove show traces of where the war has etched itself on Santayana's consciousness.

Soliloquies in England established Santayana as an essayist of marked power and distinction. Tributes ranged from Bertrand Russell's modest comment, "It is superfluous to praise the style of Mr. Santayana, which must delight every lover of good English," to extravagant assertions that finer English never had been and never would be written than Santayana's. In fact, Santayana's fame among men of letters and his recognition by the general reading public were growing by leaps and bounds. Never, except perhaps now, has he been so much before the public eye as in the period from 1920 to 1923. The years 1920, 1922, and 1923 saw each the publication of one new book and one revision or reissue: 1920, *Character and Opinion in the United States* and *Little Essays from the Works of George Santayana;* 1922, *Soliloquies in England* and *The Life of Reason* (reissued); and 1923, *Scepticism and Animal Faith* and *Poems* (selected and revised). Thus within three years appeared the whole range of Santayana's work, from the earliest poems and the earliest treatises (in excerpts) through *The Life of Reason* and *Soliloquies in England* to his new system expounded in *Scepticism and Animal Faith.* One at that time might have surveyed the evolution of Santayana's entire philosophy without digging into the archives of the past. No less than thirteen articles, exclusive of book reviews, dealing with Santayana either as philosopher or as man of letters appeared from 1920 to 1924. And sections were devoted to Santayana in such general surveys of the literary scene as J. B. Priestley's *Figures in Modern Literature,* 1924, and Carl Van Doren's *Many Minds,* 1924.

Letters were written to the magazines, especially liberal journals like the *Freeman* and the *New Republic,* vigorously condemning or praising Santayana.

Out of all this mêlée, however, was arising a clear conception of Santayana's place in the world of letters, and a just appraisal of his peculiar gifts and what they might offer the modern man. No better short definition of Santayana's sphere appeared than that of Harold Stearns in a review written for the *Freeman.*

None have written before—and few perhaps will write again—of metaphysical problems with the worldly shrewdness, the rather Roman touch of austere detachment, the aesthetic graciousness, the verbal felicity, the non-technical aptness of phrase, in brief, with the distinction that has been Mr. Santayana's most constant quality.

And Santayana's mission (if one could speak of Santayana in such evangelistic terms) was felt to be twofold. Through his personal detachment and the aesthetic bias in his writings, he was instrumental in keeping aloft, above the welter and sordidness of everyday living and thinking, a clear ideal of beauty, serenity, and repose, so much so that the *Freeman* called him "Beauty's Servant-Cavalier." But directed outwards, the keenness of his mind challenged artificiality and incoherence everywhere they raised their heads; his own sanity and balance gave him the equipoise of a great critic. In this rôle he was admired by many who felt repelled by his philosophy or even his worship of beauty. The *Nation and Athenaeum,* with perhaps a grain of hyperbole, said,

We believe, for instance, that he is the best literary critic of our time. It seems as if he can only exhibit his true powers when he is dealing with what other men have thought about life. Provided life comes to him at one remove he is magnificent; he is both subtle and comprehensive.

It seemed that the critic in Santayana had absorbed both the poet and the moral philosopher. And yet the excellence of Santayana's criticism is largely due to the fact that he has never ceased being either a poet or a moral philosopher. What is his so generously admired irony but the moralist laughing humanity out of its folly and perversity? Santayana's humor may be biting, as in his description of William James's God as a "sort of young poet or struggling artist," and his reference to Royce as a "benevolent ogre" and "old child"; or it may more often be content to be gentle and whimsical, as in the well-known advice to philosophers not to teach but to "polish lenses like Spinoza, or to sit in a black skull cap and white beard at the door of some unfrequented museum, selling the catalogues and taking in the umbrellas." In either case, Santayana's "comic spirit" not only furnishes his readers with much delight, but also, like Molière's and Voltaire's, is definitely at the service of morality and reason. No critic has been more steadfast and sincere than Santayana in relating his criticism to an underlying attitude toward life. With Santayana criticism of literature, of philosophy, of culture and civilization is all part and parcel of the same criticism of life itself. As a critic Santayana is first, last, and always the moral philosopher. He believes that all life is of a piece, and that any part of it must be judged by the quantum of happiness it yields. Beauty, poise, serenity are the hallmarks of his morality, but he is a moralist for all that; the moral value of a book, a painting, a nation, or an ideal is to him the ultimate test of its greatness. And this moral worth must be ascertained not by the imagination but by the reason.

But Santayana is at the same time a poet, and beside his irony and invective are a remarkable insight and a power of synthesis which render his criticism positive and constructive. He can sketch in a few words or in several chapters the salient features of a man or a system or an age. We do not soon forget the brilliant studies of James and Royce, of Russell and Bergson, of the American and German and Briton, of Hellenism and Christianity and romanticism, of the ancient, medieval, and modern worlds. Some of Santayana's finest and most distinctive criticism is to be found in his analysis of the varied cultures which have been woven into the tapestry of civilization. He has made us understand the divergent genius of mankind, and he has made us see it from the central vantage point of reason. It takes a poet to bring a multiplicity of detail within a single focus, to penetrate through surface to essential core, to seize upon the significant term, like "barbarism" or "genteel tradition," which will transfix an epoch or a movement to eternity. The moral philosopher observes and judges, but the poet molds and creates.

We are still too near to Santayana to judge his ultimate worth as a critic. But we can see that he is a critic in the truest, deepest sense of the word. He does not stop at exposition or interpretation, rich as his criticism is in both these attributes; rather he presses on to judgment, evaluation, the most difficult function of criticism. And if his judgment is at times warped by sentiment, or a too specialized philosophical background, or an overindulgence in analogy, it has succeeded in challenging accepted and conventional estimates of even the greatest figures, and in forcing a reconsideration of venerable reputations. The full force of this achievement will be appreciated in an age less romantic and impressionistic than ours.

Santayana's place in contemporary criticism is perhaps nearest that of his recent enemies, the new humanists. In spite of recent unfriendly remarks on both sides, Santayana and the new humanists were during the first decade of our century performing much the same task for criticism. In fact, Professor Norman Foerster, looking backward in order to compile a bibliography of humanistic literature, heads his list with *Interpretations of Poetry and Religion.* Brownell, Babbitt, and More were laying siege to romanticism, were stressing the classical values, form, harmony, reason, with something of Santayana's vehemence. And they felt at first they had a strong ally in Santayana, whose *Interpretations of Poetry and Religion* Paul Elmer More considered the "wisest and most fascinating work in constructive criticism that has appeared in English for several years."

Although there has always been a radical philosophic difference between Santayana and the humanists, in literary criticism they have at times accomplished the same results. They have both struck out for an ethical interpretation of art and literature, have had much to say about the formal principle in art, and have looked backward to the ancient Greeks and to the Catholic tradition as in Dante for their models and support. They have both found considerable fault with modern romanticism and the cult of the indeterminate. They have both attempted to retain the moral and aesthetic inspiration of religion without committing themselves to religious dogma. They have united in bringing back to poetry the old conception of the poet as prophet, deeply obligated to the ultimate truths of life. In their criticism they have both been arbitrary and oracular, relying on absolute standards. And they have both been imbued with the feeling that they were preserving something essentially and preciously human as the touchstone of their critical philosophy. Certainly Irving Babbitt's *Rousseau and Romanticism,* Paul Elmer More's *The Drift of Romanticism* and his occasional studies of Shelley, Keats, Whitman, and other romantics, and Norman Foerster's scholarly *American Criticism* may be placed beside *Interpretations of Poetry and Religion* as substantial counterblasts against the whole romantic point of view in literature. Babbitt has carried the humanist point of view into ethics and political science, and More and G. R. Elliott have espoused a traditionalism in religion, all of them joining in an attack upon humanitarianism, liberalism, and modernism in terms strongly suggesting Santayana's treatment in *The Life of Reason* and *Poetry and Religion*. Despite *The Genteel Tradition at Bay*, 1931, and the humanists' disparaging reviews of Santayana's later books, they and he have gone over much the same ground in creating a permanent body of traditional, classical criticism in America.

So much have they had in common. But their differences have become even clearer over the years. The humanists' "ethical imagination," highest faculty of human nature, would be unacceptable to Santayana on two counts. It is wrought out of the freedom of the will, creating ideals and controlling impulses with an autonomy which seems illusory to the materialist Santayana. Moreover, in practice it is too often negative, an "inner check," as Paul Elmer More delights to call it. Now Santayana's "spirit" is less free in the metaphysical sense than the "ethical imagination"; it is, to him at least, more free in the moral sense, rising above impulse and matter to the plane of the ideal where it can enjoy the free contemplation which is its birthright. The humanists seem to Santayana both arrogant and impoverished in their moral absolutism. Their life is straitened by centuries of New England Calvinism, yet they would impose this narrow puritanism on the world at large. As Santayana has recently said, "I can find little in their recommendations except a cautious allegiance to the genteel tradition." Yet their conscience is so agonized "that they feel constrained to invoke a supernatural sanction for their maxims and to go forth and preach them to the whole world." The Renaissance humanists were more tolerant, more urbane, more humane. The new humanists are too often in practice puritans rather than humanists.

The difference between the humanists' ethics and Santayana's is important for literary criticism. They have both attacked romanticism and in particular Walt Whitman for what at first seem to be identical reasons. However, Santayana really objects to Whitman because the latter fails to see rising above the flux of existence those ideal peaks of aspiration which constitute the spiritual life. The humanists dislike Whitman because he reduces humanity to the level of natural impulse, the animal state from which man has gradually ascended. In either judgment Whitman has obliterated a dualistic distinction dear to the heart of the critic; but these dualisms are not quite identical. To Santayana Whitman has failed to mark off the ideal from the material; to the humanist he has failed to mark off the human from the natural. Now the natural *per se* is no evil to Santayana; Whitman's strength is rather in the very real tribute he pays to the natural springs of conduct. On the other hand, to the humanist there is no wrong in grounding the ideal in the actual if human values are not destroyed.

At a higher level of romanticism it is easier to see the divergence of the two points of view. The humanists, following Matthew Arnold, particularly object to Shelley; they find in him a vagrant individualism, a defiance of tradition, an utter indifference to discipline, and a shallow, Rousseau-like humanitarianism. On the other hand, a certain surface Christian orthodoxy and a moral energy in Browning blind them to the weaknesses Santayana finds in the latter's romanticism. They are also more enthusiastic than Santayana is over Goethe. These differences are explainable, I believe, by the divergent dualisms which underlie the two philosophies. The naturalism of Shelley, atheistic and materialistic, is not repugnant to Santayana, whereas he admires, as we have seen, Shelley's pure idealism. The idealism of Browning and Goethe, however, seems to him a weak Protestantism which misreads nature and completely distorts morality by grounding the ideal in the flux of matter and life. Browning and Goethe paint an ugly world in false colors; Shelley acknowledges the world as it is and escapes to something purer and finer. Essentially, Santayana's idealism is Catholic and Platonic, averted from life; humanism is concerned to find human values in life, and so looks with kindlier eye at Browning and Goethe —and Shakespeare, for that matter.

For this very reason humanism is sensitive to aspects of human nature, the romantic and passionate for instance, which are anathema to Santayana. In theory at least it welcomes the genuinely human wherever found, and thus has a greater breadth and perhaps humanity than Santayana's criticism. It is certainly more in sympathy with the Renaissance and the whole early modern period from Chaucer to Milton, more attuned to the English and German genius and to Protestantism and even to a moderate romanticism. Santayana is, however, more logical and rigidly classical, more philosophical in tone—for better or worse—, more aesthetic and more narrowly metaphysical than his humanist contemporaries. I think, too, he has a greater understanding of (though no more reverence for) the Graeco-Roman and medieval Catholic traditions, and has kept in more nearly perfect counterpoise the aesthetic and ethical strains in his critical judgment (as did the ancient Greeks). The swath cut by Santayana's criticism is deeper, less broad (and vague?) than that of humanism.

The resemblances between humanism and Santayana's criticism are less borrowings on either hand than the results of a common fund of traditional inspiration. Both draw heavily upon that ethical and formal conception of literature which has marked the classical tradition from Aristotle to Matthew Arnold. Santayana has points of resemblance to Arnold, Emerson, and Lowell in nineteenth-century criticism, and these men have influenced his work just as they have even more profoundly influenced that of the new humanists.

It might be said at the outset that Arnold, Emerson, and Lowell are all nearer to humanism than to Santayana because for all their classical protestations, they grew out of—at the same time as they outgrew—the Protestant, romantic tradition. Thus they do not share Santayana's almost scholastic distinction between ideal and actual, between spirituality and worldliness. Arnold is the nearest to Santayana because he exerted the most influence over Santayana's youth—this despite Santayana's recent derogatory remarks about Arnold. Santayana drew from Arnold his exaltation of poetry as prophecy or religion, his scorn for philistinism (his "barbarism" is close to Arnold's "provinciality"), his deference to the Greeks upon every occasion. He copied, too, something of Arnold's dogmatic, patronizing way, his oracular assurance, his stinging irony and lofty indignation. He adopted, too, some of Arnold's technique, pillorying Goethe because of his life as Arnold did Byron and Shelley, and justifying Shelley's love of beauty as Arnold did Keats's. Even his disparagement of Shakespeare, his praise of Leopardi, his measured judgment of Goethe have their hints in Arnold.* But there the parallel ends. Santayana could never have shared Arnold's enthusiasm for Wordsworth and Milton, just as he roundly attacked Arnold's belittlement of Shelley. In general, Arnold's taste is more catholic than Santayana's, less dominated by a particular metaphysics, more broadly humanistic. But Santayana's criticism is more rationalistically thought out, less dependent upon magic touchstones and mysterious remarks about the "grand style."

* Cf. "Shakespeare is divinely strong, rich, and attractive. But sureness of perfect style Shakespeare himself does not possess." "Leopardi . . . in his sense for poetic style is worthy to be named with Dante and Milton."

Emerson and Santayana as critics have many outward resemblances and, in spite of divergent philosophies and methods, often accomplish the same results in criticism. Emerson's criticism, like Santayana's, is predominantly ethical, moralistic; yet it holds forth beauty, conceived in a large, general sense, as the supreme objective of artistic creation. It is not mere rhetoric when Emerson says, "Beauty is its own excuse for being." Moreover, Emerson is just as rigorous as Santayana in demanding an ideal poet who will exceed any and all of the incomplete poets who have lived on earth. This ideal "poet-priest," very much like Santayana's poet-prophet, will express a wider spirituality than merely the creation of beautiful language, will be deeply religious in life and thought and works. Within the sphere of art proper, the poet must have range, dimension; he "traverses the whole scale of experience." He must be a form-giver, too; finding in the multitudinous impressions of life a pervasive synthesis and unity. "Art expresses the one or the same by the different. Thought seeks to know unity in unity; poetry to show it by variety." Poetry is thus the great liberator of the imagination. Poets "are free, and they make free." All of these statements read very much like Santayana's description of the third level of poetry in *Poetry and Religion*. Emerson's individual judgments, too, are often near to Santayana's. Like Santayana, he has scorn and contempt for modern art and is very hostile to the romanticists outside of Goethe and Wordsworth. Poe is a "jingle man," Tennyson a "lady's bower," Macaulay a "green-grocer." Emerson approaches the ancient Greeks, too, with something of Santayana's delight in their spontaneity and youthful freshness. In general Emerson reveals his Greek or Platonic side in his literary criticism, and this side of Emerson is of course nearest to Santayana's classical position. But there are many things over which Santayana and Emerson disagree; their similarities are after all perhaps incidental rather than basic. There are many enthusiasms of Emerson that Santayana, in the strict interests of classicism, could never share; he could not approve of Whitman and Wordsworth and Goethe and Swedenborg, and he could not call Shakespeare the greatest and most typical poet. Nor could he understand Emerson's faint praise of Dante and neglect of Lucretius. In fact, Emerson's individualism, scorn of tradition, transcendentalism, are so opposed to strict classicism that his criticism differs widely from Santayana's in spirit and in underlying philosophy. And certainly Santayana's naturalism could not agree with Emerson that "the beautiful rests on the foundations of the necessary," or that "the Universe is the externization of the soul," or that art springs spontaneously from a divine principle in nature:

> The passive Master lent his hand
> To the vast soul that o'er him planned.

And if Emerson sometimes speaks as if reason were to be the poet's guide to truth, it is hardly Santayana's reason that he refers to, but rather the higher Reason of the Germans, "the intellect released from all service and suffered to take its direction from its celestial life." The deeper spirit of Emerson's criticism is quite foreign to Santayana's.

Lowell as a literary critic has certain romantic inclinations and a certain armchair discursiveness, an inconsecutiveness that is foreign to Santayana's systematic criticism. He, too, has a ruddy enjoyment of Renaissance humanism and Elizabethan humor not shared by Santayana; in fact, his warmest sympathies are with the early moderns, not the ancients. Yet when he pauses to sum up a kind of critical credo, Lowell suggests Santayana more than do Arnold and Emerson. Like Santayana, Lowell places his greatest stress on the form-giving power of the imagination, its ability to reduce chaos to order, and, like Santayana, he differentiates levels upon which the imagination of the poet works. On the highest level it

. . . is the faculty that shapes, gives unity of design and balanced gravitation of parts. . . . It is only this higher form . . . which can unimpeachably assure to any work the dignity and permanence of a classic. . . . On a lower plane we may detect it in the structure of a sentence, in the limpid expression that implies sincerity of thought; but it is only where it combines and organizes, where it eludes observation in particulars to give the rarer delight of perfection as a whole, that it belongs to art. Then it is truly ideal.

This is Santayana's language; Santayana's method, too, of explaining an author in terms of his age is found time after time in Lowell, in the case of Shakespeare with much the same procedure. Lowell, too, attacks sentimentality in his article on Rousseau in a way that suggests Santayana's attack on the poetry of barbarism; and Lowell's indictment of modern literature is similar to Santayana's tirade against indeterminate art.

All of these parallels may be pressed too far, for Santayana is an original critic, and what he shares with Arnold, Emerson, and Lowell may be largely accounted for by the fact that all four men represent to some degree the classical tradition in criticism. Santayana, I believe, is the most classical of the four, the most uncompromisingly logical in his classical position. And from a humanistic standpoint he has a deficiency which may explain why Lowell and even Arnold come closer to real life than he does. The defect is pointed out as of Emerson (who shares it with Santayana) in a very interesting analysis of Professor Foerster's. Emerson "passed at one step from the life of the senses to the life of the spirit, virtually omitting that vast intervening realm of human emotions which is the main content of ordinary life and of literature." This realm is Santayana's second level of poetry, the level he mistrusts particularly; hence his inadequate appraisal of the humanity of Shakespeare, and perhaps of Browning and Goethe.*

While Santayana was gaining recognition as a critic of distinction, it was also dawning upon the reading public of the nineteen twenties that this Spaniard wrote the King's English with a purity and grace really astonishing in the light of his nationality. The philosopher of the Life of Reason had become, not over night, but gradually over a long period, master of an English prose of marked charm and individuality. Many observers, in fact, wondered whether the man of letters was not crowding out the philosopher. "It has been said," remarked Robert Bridges, "that George Santayana has imperiled the recognition of his philosophy by the fine robes in which he has consistently presented it; and that his readers have been distracted from the sincerity and depth of his purpose by the perpetual flow of his eloquence, his rich vocabulary, and the pleasant cadences of his sentences, with their abounding imagery, incisive epigrams, and jovial humour." Professional philosophers particularly would have none of him because he expressed himself gracefully and without recourse to the tools of the trade. But the very style which was holding the philosophers at bay was at the same time drawing to Santayana an ever increasing circle of cultivated readers and literary men, who, like Logan Pearsall Smith, were finding in Santayana "much writing like that of the older essayists on large human subjects . . . more interesting and in many ways more important than anything . . . in the works of other contemporary writers." "I soon fell into the way," said Mr. Smith, "of copying out the passages that

---

* However, when human emotions are unpretentious and blithely sensuous or sportive, as in Dickens and de Musset, Santayana is more given to admiration than are the Saxon Emerson and his humanist followers.

I liked, and thus I gradually found a collection of little essays on subjects of general interest—art and literature and religion, and the history of the human mind as it has manifested itself at various times and in the works of different men of genius." Mr. Smith's energy and Santayana's coöperation gave us the first volume of Santayana calling attention to his work as literature, the *Little Essays Drawn from the Works of George Santayana*. Robert Bridges wrote a lengthy, commendatory review of the volume for the *London Mercury*, and Santayana the essayist took his place beside Santayana the poet, critic, and philosopher.

Of course, sensitive readers had long been aware that Santayana's real distinction as a writer, and perhaps as a philosopher too, rested upon those flashes of poetic insight in the essay-like portions of the larger works. Santayana's method shows no marked architectonic skill; his full-length volumes are really collections of essays touching upon various aspects of his subject, not building up a logical construction of thought. Santayana's presentation does not suggest the analytical, progressive method of the textbook, but rather the synthetic method of poetry in which the idea is born entire and is developed by an illumination of now one aspect, now another. This method, as with Santayana's predecessor Emerson, confuses those who are used to the geometrical precision of textbook rhetoric. For instance, chapters in *The Life of Reason* such as "The Discovery of Natural Objects," "Nature Unified and Mind Discerned," and "The Discovery of Fellow Minds" do not form a chronological sequence of the growth and development of reason, but are individual topics, each one studied in its manifold implications throughout history even to the present day. "The Discovery of Fellow Minds" begins far back in prehistoric times with the "transposition of tertiary qualities," but before its close it has embraced the Hebrew prophets, Rousseau, and the British government in India. Perhaps orderly exposition suffers as a result, but this characteristic of Santayana's in its finest and most mature form, say in *Platonism and the Spiritual Life* (1927), leads to a series of loosely woven essays which in their lacy delicacy seem to be the prose equivalent of a sonnet sequence. There is a gentle forward movement as each chapter embroiders the common theme now with new, now with recurrent patterns. Rarely has philosophy been written with such grace and ease. And with all the free play, the turns and convolutions of Santayana's method, the thought in spite of its abstruseness becomes constantly clearer.

Santayana's formlessness is after all more apparent than real, if tested by result rather than method. If in reading Santayana one never seems to follow in a straight line the shortest distance between two points, upon conclusion one is seen to have reached a destination and one might as well have entrusted his guidance to Providence and the author and settled back to enjoy the beauties *en route*. What in Santayana seems formlessness to the uninitiate is but a surface laxness permitted by the very unity of the vision within. And, as Mr. Smith's book testifies, there are numbers of perfectly formed essays in Santayana not marked off as such, for example, the penetrating chapters on love; ideal immortality; piety, charity, and spirituality; free and ideal society, from *The Life of Reason*.

Yet when all is said and done, Santayana's treatment of the essay reaches its highest point in his *Soliloquies in England*. Before one has read very far into the book, one is aware that here is something refreshingly different in literature. The title of the first essay is "Atmosphere," but the reader finds neither a scientific study in meteorology nor a familiar ramble across country. Yet the title is not a misnomer; the atmosphere is made the basis of a fanciful yet serious essay on the short-sightedness of mankind, an essay philosophical in tone but entirely informal and effortless in argument. The application of the title is at once literal and figurative in Santayana's characteristic vein. The physical atmosphere of the planet blinds man's eyes to outer space, as the mental atmosphere of ignorance and fear in which he lives clouds his brain and shuts out reality. Man ignores and misconceives science and truth in general just as he ignores and misconceives the stars, a fragment of that reality which science investigates in its search for truth. The method is not allegory but a delicate poetic fusion of literal and figurative, both conceived as equally concrete in a philosophy where all is poetical and concrete. The essay is compact, close-woven; there is scarcely an extraneous word from the opening to the brief, stately close, "In those regions the shepherds first thought of God."

"Atmosphere" is a good specimen, by no means the best, of the soliloquies. The form is well named; the soliloquy is the prose equivalent of reflective poetry, grave, measured, earnest, as if the author were meditating aloud unconcerned about any possible hearers. Santayana's soliloquies are personal and lyrical, as is the familiar essay at its best, yet in their brevity and polished perfection of form they suggest rather the sonnet. They are unlike both in their metaphysical—technically metaphysical not merely reflective—foundation. The nearest prose parallels which come to my mind are Havelock Ellis' *Impressions and Comments* and Logan Pearsall Smith's *Trivia*. The former has the metaphysics, but the form is fragmentary and diaristic; the latter is nearer in form, but its tone is more gay and casual and unphilosophical. Santayana's soliloquies are really unique, and in this form he has expressed himself with the greatest artistry. Its brevity curbs his tendency to formlessness when working on a large scale, while it preserves his poetic inspiration at high pitch throughout. The flexibility of inner structure is a surety against monotony, yet the finest soliloquies are carefully put together and are wholes, however miniature. The sight of a skylark, a cloud castle, a war shrine, or perhaps the recollection of them in that "inward eye" of Wordsworth, starts a reverie which may sweep all nature and man into its ken before the spell is broken. There is not a uniform pattern in the soliloquies, but many have what might be termed a circular, or better yet, a spiral form. The point of departure is the object observed. The first half-circle traces the more obvious and usually depressing inference, e.g., the transiency of existence in "Cloud Castles." The return curve finds a deeper meaning in the permanence of form and the joy of contemplation. The circle is completed as the image of the cloud returns, but the thought is on a higher plane and we discover it is not a circle but a spiral the author has traced.

Not all the essays in *Soliloquies in England* are true soliloquies, as the author has by practice defined the form. Some, as we have seen, are critical essays, of Dickens, of philosophical tendencies, of the English character. On the other hand, there are soliloquies scattered here and there throughout the longer works. Chapter XXIII of *Platonism and the Spiritual Life* is a perfect example. Nor are all of the soliloquies of fine gold. "Atmosphere" has a slight tarnish of veiled sarcasm. "Praises of Water," which has somehow crept into the anthologies, seems to me nothing more than a lesson in physiography poetically varnished. "The Two Parents of Vision" suffers from didacticism and "The Psyche" from sentimentality. But there are some eight or ten as exquisite in workmanship as they are provocative in thought.

"Aversion from Platonism" shows that one paragraph is not too small to contain a complete soliloquy in which is compressed the essence of two civilizations and their differing response to nature.

Repetition is the only form of permanence that nature can achieve, and in those Mediterranean regions that nurtured the classic mind, by continually repeating the same definite scenes, nature forced it to fix its ideas. Everyone learned to think that the earth and the gods were more permanent than himself; he perused them, he returned to them, he studied them at arm's length, and he recognized their external divinity. But where the Atlantic mists envelop everything, though we must repeatedly use the same names for new-born things, as we continue to christen children John and Mary, yet we feel that the facts, like the persons, are never really alike; everything is so fused, merged, and continuous, that whatever element we may choose to say is repeated seems but a mental abstraction and a creature of language. The weather has got into our bones; there is a fog in the brain; the limits of our own being become uncertain to us. Yet what is the harm, if only we move and change inwardly in harmony with the ambient flux? Why this mania for naming and measuring and mastering what is carrying us so merrily along? Why shouldn't the intellect be vague while the heart is comfortable?

"Cloud Castles" is memorable for the beauty of the original metaphor and the skill with which it is woven into the tapestry of the soliloquy. Whenever metaphysical vapors threaten to shroud the landscape of thought, the original metaphor reappears, illuminating the scene. The soliloquy is cloud-like in the delicacy of its texture, suggesting Debussy's "Nuages" in music.

The following essay, "Cross-Lights," is a masterpiece. One of the most elusive, it is also one of the most profound. It is an essay in relativity, in perspective. Numerous contrasts are introduced, sun and earth, light and darkness, mind and matter, spirit and nature, and the unifying thread is the relativity of the point of view. Sun and mind are egotists and fancy that nothing exists save their brilliance, but were there no darkness and matter neither could be conscious even of its own existence.

When we are on the shady side of the earth we can, as a compensation, range in knowledge far beyond our painted atmosphere, and far beyond that little sun who, so long as he shone upon us, seemed to ride at the top of heaven.

The universe is the theater of this lyric, and its surge is felt in the lines. There is a passage of sheer poetry in this description of earth shine.

This earthlight, if we could only get far enough from the earth to see it, would seem strangely brilliant and beautiful; it would show sea-tints and snow-tints and sand-tints; there would be greens and purples in it reflected from summer and winter zones, dotted with cinder scars and smoke-wreaths of cities. Yet all these lights are only sunlight, received and returned with thanks.

"The Human Scale" is similarly concerned with the measure of man. The point of departure is the postern which is cut in great doors to reduce them to the human scale. Structurally the essay is perfect. Beginning with the postern, and its implication of human smallness, Santayana shows the proper place of the human scale and its expression in Oriental, Greek, and English architecture. Empire and church enlarged the perspective, and in the massiveness of their architecture the human scale was lost sight of. Finally even doors could not be opened and little doors had to be cut in them. Very neatly the spiral is completed.

"War Shrines" has the deep hues of a stained glass window. Or perhaps, its mood being minor, it suggests the tones of a full-throated organ. Death is its subject, the cross its symbol. The description of the wayside shrine is beautiful, the significance of it novel and impressive. The form here is loose-woven, with excursions into Pure Being and Buddhism. The main theme returns enriched at the end:

Death can do nothing to our lives except to frame them in, to show them off with a broad margin of darkness and silence; so that to live in the shadow of death and of the cross is to spread a large nimbus of peace around our littleness.

This soliloquy is one of the noblest applications of Santayana's philosophy to the problem of human suffering.

But the soliloquy of perhaps finest artistry is "At Heaven's Gate." Built on the bare metaphysical distinction between existence and essence, it shows the significance to human life and the possibilities of artistic treatment in that distinction. The parallel of skylark and English doughboy is admirable. The irresponsible clarion note of joy of each is caught, while the somber roll of the drums of nature is heard beneath. "At heaven's gate but not in heaven" the skylark falls back, but his song passes in. The text is stated last, "The length of things is vanity, only their height is joy," and there is a prayer-like coda of exquisite charm:

Of myself also I would keep nothing but what God may keep of me —some lovely essence, mine for a moment in that I beheld it, some object of devout love enshrined where all other hearts that have a like intelligence of love in their day may worship it; but my loves themselves and my reasonings are but a flutter of feathers weaker than a lark's, a prattle idler than his warblings, happy enough if they too may fly with him and die with him at the gate of heaven.

But there are some aspects of philosophy better presented by the give-and-take of dialogue than by the musings of soliloquy, and so in his next prose venture, *Dialogues in Limbo,* 1925, we find Santayana taking up one of the most hallowed of literary forms devoted to philosophy, the Socratic dialogue. Philosophically these dialogues are interesting, showing as they do the source of some of the ingredients of Santayana's system; artistically they are evidence that an eclectic system of philosophy is especially adaptable to the dialogue form. The characters are on the whole true to their originals, but since Santayana is writing Socratic dialogues, not imaginary conservations, they are subservient to the play of ideas and there is perhaps no impropriety in the author's speaking at times through the mouths of his characters. In fact, the characters are selected because in real life they stood for certain points of view which have been assimilated in Santayana's own philosophy. Democritus represents the naturalistic foundation; Socrates the moral and humanistic outlook; Alcibiades the "manly perfection" and "contentment in finitude"; Aristippus and Dionysius the sympathy with pure sensualism, the "easier attitudes." The dialogues seem to hark back to very early questionings in the mind of Santayana. Like *Lucifer,* they show us a good deal of the private Santayana, with dilemmas unresolved, loyalties transient, and no official system yet composed for public exhibition. But Santayana does more than put on the stage the ancient authorities for much of his thinking; he appears himself in the dialogues as a "stranger still living on earth" who has found his way to Hades to enjoy the company and absorb the wisdom of the ancients. They beguile eternity with incisive talk, and the Stranger is only too glad to listen, and at times to put in a word himself.

Artistically there are several weaknesses in the dialogues. In the first place, the fictional background is meager and undeveloped. There is no setting of palaestra or plane tree as in Plato to lend verisimilitude, no amusing by-play like the concealment of Lysias' oration in Phaedrus' cloak. The action is confined to Democritus' sniffing

Alcibiades' curly head, and a "measured dance" of the three devotees of Autologos, both of which incidents seem a trifle forced. And Limbo itself is ill defined. In "Normal Madness" it is described as a realm in which the shades of the dead take on the aspect of that time of life when the soul was most noble. Democritus sits "crowned with all the snows and wisdom of old age," while Alcibiades, Dionysius, and Aristippus walk "in the flower of their youth." "They are still ready for every folly, though luckily they lack the means." Are these ironical commentaries on a longing for material pleasures in an immaterial heaven? Socrates' description of Limbo is more philosophical; he makes it a part of the realm of essence, that portion which contains essences before and after their transit through existence.* Perhaps Santayana's treatment of Limbo is intentionally vague and whimsical because of his greater interest in the interplay of ideas.

There is an unevenness, too, in Santayana's handling of the dialogue form. Very few of his dialogues have the swift repartee which marks the Socratic method at its best. However, they are spared the tedium of cross-examination which this method falls into even in Plato. Two of Santayana's best dialogues from the standpoint of thought, "Normal Madness" and "Homesickness for the World," are almost soliloquies, showing that the dialogue form tended to slip from Santayana's hands. Others, like "The Scent of Philosophies," lack the movement of the true dialogue, which weaves through various convolutions, takes sudden and unexpected turns, yet at the end leaves the impression of something accomplished. It has the ease of good talk, but like the best conversation it arrives somewhere. "On Self-Government," satirizing majority rule in modern democracy, is too one-sided; the timid, cut-to-the-pattern answers of the Stranger are an insufficient foil to Socrates. On the other hand, in other dialogues the Stranger is too obviously Santayana acting as umpire at the end and putting the ancients in their places.

"Autologos," "The Philanthropist," and "Lovers of Illusion" are, however, notably successful dialogues. In the first, the controlling figure is Democritus, who consents to compose for the worshipers of Autologos a ritual which he makes out of high-sounding truisms, then upbraids them for worshiping such a fickle divinity as the ego, and finally admits to the Stranger that such worship is universal and that Autologos is "truly a great, a boundless, an irrepressible

* See below, p. 234.

spirit." There is depth of thought in the attack on romantic self-delusion, and from a formal standpoint the shiftings of mood and the turns of idea create the necessary suspense of the true dialogue.

Even finer is "The Philanthropist," most like the Platonic originals. Here the Stranger and Socrates argue the respective merits of Christian charity and Socratic philanthropy. Santayana has never settled this question to his satisfaction; consequently one feels that the deciding vote has not been cast before the dialogue begins. His rationalism points toward the perfectibility of man; his Catholicism and his temperament urge sympathy with man's imperfection. Throughout the course of the dialogue every aspect of the question is touched upon, and while there is no decision reached, there is a feeling left that the air has been cleared and the relationship of the two points of view shown once and for all. Philanthropy is defined as the "love of that beauty and goodness in man which if realized would make his happiness," while charity is "less than philanthropy in that it expects the defeat of man's natural desires and accepts that defeat; and it is more than philanthropy in that, in the face of defeat, it brings consolation." Socrates is the aggressor and delivers many nimble thrusts, but the Stranger remains unshaken and the dialogue ends a stalemate. Artistically, however, it leaves the impression of balance and completeness, and we feel that both Socrates and the Stranger have, with the reader, benefited by the experience. The handling of the material is as skilful as the content is profound. There are moods varying from light banter, where the Stranger touches the sore spot of Socrates—woman, to impassioned eloquence in the Stranger's plea for the recognition of all God's creatures and in Socrates' proud boast that he has been a man when manhood saw its finest flower. There is the charming indirection, the free play of fancy which keeps conversation from a set mold and allows it to be lifelike. The characters rather than the author appear to keep the reins of dialogue in their hands, and the argument proceeds slowly and carefully enough for the reader to enjoy each mental landscape as it passes.

"The Philanthropist" is also interesting in its relation to Santayana's own character and philosophy. There has always been a "stout" Santayana (especially before the war) who like Socrates believed in human perfectibility and strove to bring it to pass. But the "tender" Santayana has come more and more to accept the world as it is, leaving change to circumstance and relishing the pageant of existence with a sympathy tinged with irony. Quite fittingly, then, he identifies charity, an "easier attitude," with himself, the Stranger, and gives over all reform (and with it his Socratic self?) to Socrates and the Greeks. His own position is made even clearer in one of the most personal statements in the book. Democritus has been chiding Aristippus for his indifference to human welfare, to morality. "Man," says Democritus, "is a fighting animal, his thoughts are his banners, and it is a failure of nerve in him if they are only thoughts. A philosopher especially . . . is commissioned by the gods. . . . Ferocity becomes him, as it does the lion. . . . His mere example will be a power, or if not, at least his self-assertion will be an action. . . . If in sauntering through the marketplace and observing its villainies, because his nook is safe and his liver is in good order, he tolerates the spectacle, he is like a woman in the theatre shuddering at the tragedy and eating sweets." But Aristippus wonders whether it is not "worthier of a philosopher to eat sweets than to count the number of the atoms, and less foolish to smile or to shudder at the world than to attempt to reform it." And then comes the Stranger's verdict as referee, a justification once more of Santayana the ironic spectator, of his detachment and his sympathy.

Both of you, Democritus and Aristippus, seem to me to have spoken justly. . . . Intrepid virtue, O Sage of Abdera, is a gift of the gods, and how often do they bestow it? . . . As for me, disillusion was my earliest friend, and never were chagrin and hope strong enough to persuade me that anything was to be gained by rebelling against fortune. . . . I should honour heroic virtue if it were sane and beneficent; but I find satisfaction also, and perhaps oftener, in little things.

McStout has to give ground in ethics; he is also challenged in metaphysics. The stoutness of Santayana as philosopher has always been his confident naturalism; materialism has been the "adamant underneath" his whole burden of thought. Democritus takes up the cudgels of materialism in *Dialogues in Limbo,* and in the first four dialogues plays heavily about him, belaboring idealists both past and present. He maintains that all thought is illusion, but claims that scientific thought, in particular atomism, of all illusion most approximates reality, being brought into agreement with it by careful observation and experimentation. Of all madness naturalism is the most wholesome and "normal." It is not only true, if that word is to mean anything, but it is also the key to happiness.

Before dying in the arms of Punishment madness may be mitigated and tamed by Agreement. . . . The automatism of life, which is necessarily spontaneous and blind, may by adjustment with its occasions become a principle of health and genius, the parent of noble actions and beautiful works. . . . Thus the most deep-dyed illusion, if it be interwoven with good habits, may flourish in long amity with things, naming and saluting them, as we do the stars, or the gods, without understanding their nature.

Now Santayana (early in "A Religion of Disillusion," and *Reason in Science,* late in "The Moral Adequacy of Naturalism," 1931) has often said this very thing; therefore, one may suspect that Democritus speaks for him, at least one side of him. But in an early sonnet, in his personification of Lucifer, in his remarks on Lucretius and Shelley, Santayana has questioned whether happiness can come from the mind alone, from reason. And so in a most searching and beautiful dialogue, "Lovers of Illusion," Alcibiades, Aristippus, and Dionysius rise to attack Democritus and defend madness and illusion. "The value of madness," says Dionysius, "is not such as you attribute to the normal illusions of sense or opinion, which Punishment and Agreement bring into a blind and external harmony with nature. On the contrary, such madness is almost sane, and quite uninspired; but divine madness wafts the soul away altogether from the sad circumstances of earth, and bids it live like a young god only among its own chosen creations . . . to be mad is simply, in spite of gods and men, to be indomitably free." "Fancy is not a falsification of nature, because nothing in nature is worth noting, or even possible to note, save for the fancy which overlays it." Socratic morality is lame and earthbound; the spirit must fly with the wings of Plato. The dialogue is then seen to be a contest for supremacy between two systems of thought, naturalism and Platonism, both of which have profoundly influenced Santayana. Let us see, then, what the Stranger will say in conclusion. He first protests once more his allegiance to Democritus. But he is not without "a certain sympathy with Dionysius and Aristippus when they extoll the pleasures of the simple mind and cling passionately to immediate experience." And even as a revelation of reality there are limitations to science.

Your hypothesis, Democritus, may be absolutely right; but what assurance can you have of its truth? . . . Never was a theory of nature more chastened than yours or more harmonious with the practice of the arts; but can any thought kindled in a human brain burn with a light so infinitely powerful and pure as to reveal the whole universe in its uttermost reaches and exact constitution?

There is growing in the later Santayana a relativism, an agnosticism, Platonic and Indian in its complexion, which shies away from absolutes in science as in religion and morality, and which threatens to undermine all the adamant upon which his stoutness has been built.

But Democritus, and perhaps the Greek Santayana, is not ready to yield throughout. And since the dialogue is fiction, there is a dramatic propriety in giving Democritus a final chance for an impassioned tribute (like that of Lucifer) to truth and reality though the heavens fall.

I therefore stand alone [he says] and am content to do so. The universe is my sufficient companion. . . . I will dismiss and expel every remnant of illusion even in myself, in order that nothing of me may remain save the atoms that compose me, and to them I will transfer all my fond being, placing my treasure where my substance has ever been; so that dwelling wholly there, when you who are all vanity have perished and the part of me which is vain has also dissolved, my glad strength shall be the force that destroys me, and while the atoms are I shall be. . . . As for the Stranger, having a paler soul, if he salutes the atoms from a distance, it is only in condescension to the exigences of art or calculation, which he knows are not obedient to magic; but he honours reality only for illusion's sake, and studies in nature only pageants and perspectives, and the frail enchantments which are the food of love.

How remarkable an appraisal of the tender Santayana by the stout Santayana and by stout scientists and moralists everywhere!

It is clear, then, that the *Dialogues in Limbo,* like all of Santayana's more artistic work, exhibit the inner force of his personality more clearly than do the formal, systematic treatises. The freer play of the sonnets, soliloquies, and dialogues allows him to linger successively and more intimately over mental vistas which have side by side made up the landscape of his thought. Santayana is a man of strong attachments, and in this way he may pause to acknowledge these without the need of always reconciling and harmonizing and bringing them within the focus of a single system.

There is such a store of wisdom in the dialogues, and their incidental beauties are so many and so varied that any objections to them on the grounds of form seem but carping criticism. There is irony where the reference is to contemporary life; there is excellent sustained narrative where Avicenna tells of the "secret of Aristotle"; there is pleasantry and grace in the lighter moments; there are flashes of poetry such as Avicenna's description of his earthly possessions. But these are part and parcel of all Santayana and perhaps therefore assumed too casually. *Dialogues in Limbo* will continue to occupy an important place in any shelf of Santayana's works; it is one of his own favorites and I believe will always have a sympathetic following among those who enjoy wisdom tempered with irony and expressed with candor and grace.

Nature after all has been doubly generous to Santayana; she has granted him not only vision, but also a means of expressing what he sees. Not the least among his attainments is his admirable prose style. This has been commented upon so frequently that my remarks may be brief. Here again I believe his distinction is the result of that poetic faculty of seeing a thing in its concreteness. With most philosophers there is a groping for concrete illustration to clarify an abstract idea, but with Santayana the illustration seems born with the idea itself, a spontaneous creation of word and thought. His concepts are indeed so much a part of him that he sees them illustrated in nature all about him. There is more than rhetoric in his statement that "the stars, the seasons, the swarm of animals, the spectacle of birth and death, of cities and wars" are his philosophy.

Since he thinks clearly and since he has never relinquished the poet's grasp on language, his style possesses those traits which have been pointed out again and again by his admirers, fertility of metaphor, epigrammatic precision, a sense of the *mot propre*. Aphorisms are sprinkled throughout his pages, neatly turned, without a trace of forced paradox or stale truism. The success of Santayana's aphorisms is due partly to their balanced construction, partly to their illumination of a generally hidden truth, or, sometimes, half-truth. Thus both form and content contribute to their excellence. The following illustrate Santayana's fondness for balance and antithesis:

Those who cannot remember the past are condemned to repeat it.
Absent he is a character understood, but present he is a force respected.
Culture is on the horns of this dilemma: if profound and noble it must remain rare, if common it must become mean.
An artist may visit a museum, but only a pedant can live there.

Men have feverishly conceived a heaven only to find it insipid, and a hell to find it ridiculous.
Dying is something ghastly, as being born is something ridiculous.

The following have the novelty and charm which come whenever an unexpected truth is suddenly disclosed. It will be observed that a number of these aphorisms, like many of their kind, illuminate the novel underside of a truth so brilliantly that the conventional upper side is obscured. As a result a certain bias or exaggeration creeps in.

Perhaps the only true dignity of man is his capacity to despise himself.
It is easier to make a saint out of a libertine than out of a prig.
As man is now constituted, to be brief is almost a condition of being inspired.
Music is essentially useless, as life is.
Fanaticism consists in redoubling your effort when you have forgotten your aim.

These aphorisms are the nearest Santayana comes to the paradox. He is not like Chesterton a deliberate cultivator of paradoxes. Often with Santayana a truism is made to seem unusual by an unexpected figure of speech.

Scepticism is the chastity of the intellect.
Truth is frozen history.
Criticism surprises the soul in the arms of convention.
The philosophy of the common man is an old wife that gives him no pleasure, yet he cannot live without her.

On the other hand, Santayana will often take a novel thought and clothe it in the traditional robes of the epigram; so that it seems a maxim of long acquaintance.

There is no denying Santayana's mastery of the epigram. In Logan Pearsall Smith's *Treasury of English Aphorisms,* Santayana is represented by fifty-six quotations, being exceeded only by Lord Chesterfield, Emerson, Halifax, Hazlitt, and Samuel Johnson. With allowances for Mr. Smith's particular admiration of Santayana, the count is still significant.

Even more individual than the epigrammatic texture of Santayana's style is its abundance of metaphor. A figure is always at the tip of Santayana's tongue; the most abstract ideas come out bedecked in the most concrete garments. Take the vision of the spirit, the strange offspring of mother Psyche, the animal organism of man:

Always something irrelevant: a shaft of dusty light across the rafters, a blue flame dancing on the coals, a hum, a babbling of waters, a breath of heat or of coolness, a mortal weariness or a groundless joy—all dream-images, visions of a play world, essences painted on air, such as any poet might invent in idleness. Yet the child cares about them immensely: he is full of sudden tears and of jealous little loves. "Hush, my child," says good mother Psyche, "it's all nonsense." It is not for those fantastic visions that she watches: she knits with her eyes shut, and mutters her same old prayers. She has always groped amidst obstacles like a mole pressing on where the earth is softest.

Santayana's proof of a philosophical proposition is usually by analogy rather than logic. This tendency is confusing to philosophers, but to the general reader it is a perpetual source of satisfaction. And he meets old friends in Santayana's diction: nature, God, spirit, substance, words enriched by the experience of the race. They are sometimes given a new significance, but the old fragrance hangs over them like a delicate perfume.

The rhythms of Santayana's sentences are a pleasure to the ear as their form and incisive thought are a joy to the mind. He has been often compared to Emerson and Pater, but his prose is really individual and suggests these masters only upon occasion. Santayana has not, for all his epigrammatic skill, the vigorous phrase-making faculty of Emerson; Santayana's style is less virile, less racy, less plastic —although it has more urbanity and repose. On the other hand, it has not the mellifluousness, the luster, the delicate nuances of Pater at his best; beside Pater's prose it seems more solid and American, more crisp and decisive. Of course there are sentences in Emerson and Pater which sound like Santayana—to my mind, there are even more in Mill and Arnold and particularly Newman. Arnold's crackling irony, without his reiteration, is in Santayana, also at times Newman's quiet strength and simple dignity. But these resemblances are merely proof that Santayana learned English in the late Victorian tradition and read widely of the best models. His style, like his accent, is late Victorian, with just a dash now and then of more recent American idiom to give it color and mobility.

His humor, particularly, seems American; its heartiness, its sharp satire, its sense of sheer fun at times, mingling extravagant overstatement with ironical understatement, is in the cultivated American tradition. Nothing calls it forth as readily as the American scene either. "Advanced opinions on politics, marriage, or literature are comparatively rare in America; they are left for the ladies to discuss, and usually to condemn, while the men get on with their work." "For the American the urgency of his novel attack upon matter, his zeal in gathering its fruits, precludes meanderings in primrose paths; devices must be short cuts, and symbols must be mere symbols. If his wife wants luxuries, of course she may have them; and if he has vices, that can be provided for too; but they must all be set down under those headings in his ledgers." "All his life the American jumps into the train after it has started and jumps out before it has stopped; and he never once gets left behind, or breaks a leg." This is nearer Santayana the conversationalist, the dignity and high seriousness of the moral philosopher put aside, the poet submerged in the critic, and the latter in bright, holiday mood with a zest for kindly mischief and high spirits. It will make *The Last Puritan* as amusing as it is profound.

Santayana's weaknesses are merely the excesses of his virtues. He can be over-ornate, piling figure upon figure, or massing a formidable and sometimes puzzling array of adjectives after his nouns. He gives certain words ("humorous," for instance) special connotations which only become apparent to the reader upon long acquaintance. Moreover, as Herbert Read pointed out in his *English Prose Style,* 1928, Santayana's fondness for aphorisms leads to a "fatal lapidary style," in which "individual sentences may be rhythmical enough, but they do not form part of a more sustained rhythm; they follow in a series of minute percussions that finally weary the strained attention of the reader." I believe, however, Santayana has largely outgrown this defect, and if his style shows any change at all, it is in the gradual abandonment of the paragraph bristling with disconnected epigrams in favor of one showing more prolonged rhythmic development. At his best there is a delicate though pronounced movement, a swell and cadence not confined to the individual sentence.

Perhaps the finest tribute to style is after all Buffon's, that it is the revelation of the man himself. As Matthew Arnold puts it, "Style in my sense of the word is a peculiar recasting and heightening under a certain condition of spiritual excitement of what a man has to say, in such a manner as to add dignity and distinction to it." The high seriousness, the intellectual energy, the leisurely charm of Santayana are all reflected in his style; it is truly, as Frederic Harrison might have said, "hall-marked from the mint of one particular author." Many of the passages quoted above are evidence of Santayana's perfection of style, but I should like to close with a passage where style and thought are perfectly attuned, a passage which sums up Santayana's outlook on life at the same time as it demonstrates the mastery of his instrument. This may serve to bring to focus the poetry inherent in his vision, his method, and his manner of expression, all in reality differing manifestations of one temperament. In such a passage, and there are many in the Santayana of recent years, Matthew Arnold's ideal seems attained.

The world is not respectable; it is mortal, tormented, confused, deluded for ever; but it is shot through with beauty, with love, with glints of courage and laughter; and in these the spirit blooms timidly, and struggles to the light among the thorns.

Such is the flitting life of this winged thing, spirit, in this old, sordid, maternal earth. On the one hand, in its innocence, spirit is happy to live in the moment, taking no thought for the morrow; it can enjoy the least gift as gladly as the greatest; it is the fresh, the pure voice of nature, incapable of learned or moral snobbery. It ignores its origin, so buoyant is it; its miraculous light seems to it a matter of course. Its career is everywhere conditioned and oppressed from without, yet it passes through the fire with a serene incredulity, an indomitable independence. On the other hand, the eye of spirit, in its virtual omniscience, sees the visible in its true setting of the invisible; it is fixed instinctively on the countless moments that are not this moment, on the joys that are not this sorrow and the sorrows that are not this joy, on the thousand opinions that are not this opinion and beauties that are not this beauty; understanding too much to be ever imprisoned, loving too much ever to be in love. Spirit chills the flesh and is itself on fire; thought, as Dean Inge says, "becomes passionate, the passions become cold"; or rather they are confronted and controlled by a profound recollection, in which laughter and tears pulse together like the stars in a polar sky, each indelibly bright, and all infinitely distant.

CHAPTER FIVE

THE METAPHYSICIAN

Santayana is never the man to stay still. Just when everyone has planned for him a public place as critic and man of letters, he shuts himself up in Rome, loosens his ties with the outer world, and watches the Realms of Being rise tier upon tier down the long corridors of his imagination. Since 1922 Santayana has occasionally appeared in the journals, and now and then written upon topics of the day, but his energies have been mainly devoted to what he believes is the crowning achievement of his career. His life has been singularly uneventful during the last fifteen years. The winters he has spent in Rome, the summers in the cooler air of Cortona, or perhaps traveling in France. In 1932 he was drawn somewhat out of his orbit to deliver lectures at the Hague and in London as part of the tercentenary celebrations of the birth of Locke and Spinoza. "Though," he says, "I avoid congresses in general, I could not refuse in this case." This was the exception, not the rule. Santayana's activity has been preponderantly mental during the last fifteen years; comfort and leisure have been all he has demanded of the world, and out of his seclusion he has wrought what may be one of the great philosophical systems of modern times.

Not that he has worked entirely alone either. From his Italian retreat he has at times collaborated with other philosophers; in fact, his work may be said to play a prominent part in that quest which has called forth the chief efforts of American philosophers for the past thirty years; to discover the true nature of the external world, and to ascertain how knowledge of that world is possible. During the nineteenth century idealism had been entrenched in the colleges, but as the new century proceeded, realism began to storm the academic citadel, aided later by a dubious ally, pragmatism. In general one might say the realists have tried to bring back philosophy to the judgments of common sense, to restore to Doctor Johnson's stone something of its power to resist Doctor Johnson's kick, to break through the impasse of the idealist, that mind can know only mind, i. e., something of its own nature. In the early years of the century there was much groping around among panpsychism, tychism, radical empiricism, and various other -isms whose boundaries were not too clear even to their proponents. There was much jockeying about of philosophers, lining up now behind one banner, now behind another. But to Santayana there had never been any doubt about the reality of the external world or its materiality; that was one touchstone by which he judged all philosophies. Writing in 1904 to William James, he said, "The materials which experience is composed of must . . . be credited with an existence which makes them material elements and gives them a mechanical order, since they exist *also* permanently, potentially, and beyond our range." If one goes from a room in which a nine-inch candle is burning, and returns to find it six inches, a sane mind must insist that the candle existed at one time eight inches in length. And why? Because "the eight-inch candle is something to be believed in . . . in the material world which the intellect has discovered it is a needful element, that counts and rewards our confidence in its reality." Deny the eight-inch candle and you reduce the universe to James's "buzzing, blooming confusion"; you may as well throw science straightway out the window.

But, assuming an external real world, you are next puzzled to account for the way in which the mind ever becomes acquainted with it. What is consciousness and what is knowledge? Now Santayana had wrestled with this problem as early as *The Life of Reason;* in fact, the Realms of Being have grown with his growth, and materials for their construction may be found strewn along the course of Santayana's entire philosophy. In *Interpretations of Poetry and Religion* he had chosen the understanding rather than the imagination as the avenue to truth, but he had not inquired how the understanding operates. In *Reason in Common Sense* he went over the ground more thoroughly, inquiring and demonstrating how common is sense and how natural and inevitable is reason.

He maintained that in the early stages of man's acquaintance with the external world, the mind associates sensations in two different ways, by their similarity and by their continuity. The first precedes the second in time, and is a recognition of the recurrence of identical sense impressions. The "togetherness" of sense impressions is next noted and they are assigned a definite place and object which they may be said to constitute. Thus in man's discovery of the sun, roundness, whiteness, and heat were identified first as separate recurrent sensations, second as occurring together, whereupon the sun was marked out as a distinct external object. The child no doubt recapitulates here the procedure of primitive man. It will be observed that both types of association arise in sensation and hence are equally concrete; however, as perception proceeds the former impressions take on the nature of ideas, the latter, of things: concretions in discourse as opposed to concretions in existence.

Both concretions have important implications which Santayana very carefully points out. Concretions in discourse show how native to the mind is the construction of ideas, underlying as it does the construction of things, yet how irresponsible a faculty it may become if the fancy and the imagination are allowed to people the landscape of the mind with creatures of their own begetting, unchecked by reference to the external world. Idealism is hence a merry madcap, a lord of misrule, but a lord for all that; beside him naturalism is a sad and plodding taskmaster. In concretions in existence there is something alien to the essential nature of consciousness; the mind here feels the pulse of matter, which it cannot altogether fathom. Things exist in space, affect each other, remain while the back is turned, move and beget movement; in short, the ideality, the constancy the mind gives them is purely formal and adventitious.

Such is the general position of Santayana in *Reason in Common Sense*. In *Reason in Science* he probes more deeply into the distinction he has made. Concretions in discourse and concretions in existence are both in reality ways of ordering experience; one is no more mental than the other. Concretions in existence (not existence itself) are as ideal as concretions in discourse; they are but reports of things; what is mechanism but a dialectical principle read into nature?· On the other hand, both types of concretions furnish us with all that we know of the world. They are not the warm world of life and matter but that world frozen into forms discernible by human consciousness; forms, too, that have a way of doing justice to and standing stoutly for the processes in nature they conceal.

In his next books, the Everyman *Spinoza* and *Winds of Doctrine,* Santayana abandons the term "concretions" for the simpler and happier one, "essences," and uses "existence" to designate the physical substratum of essence, the flux of matter itself. From this time on his philosophy proceeds upon this dualism of essence and existence, a distinction not identical with that between mind and matter, rather bisecting it at right angles, cutting through both the mental and the material. Mind is material except for those luminous essences that float into consciousness; and they in turn are as distinct from matter as from mind, a *tertium quid* altogether, yet at the same time the only link between consciousness and the external world.

To understand Santayana's position, one must see it in the light of the general development of American realism from 1910 onwards. About 1910 one group of American realists, attacking the age-old problem of what is knowledge, cast their lot with the common man and maintained that objects are directly known, are stamped faithfully by the senses upon consciousness, which itself is little more than a sensorium. Now this view of knowledge seemed too naïve to another group of realists, who called themselves "critical" as opposed to the "new" realists, their adversaries. The second group felt that the first, in avoiding the snares of idealism, trusted too implicitly the report of the senses concerning external reality. Science proved that things are not really as we see them; to believe in substance was not to mistake appearance for it. The new realism, said one critic, "holds that the very stuff of reality is given in the field of experience. . . . There is the minimum element of skepticism and agnosticism in such an outlook." On the other hand, "while the new realist holds that knowing is the givenness of the object, its literal presence to inspection, the critical realist regards knowledge more as an interpreting of a selected and meant object by means of characters discriminated in the field of consciousness. Such knowing is a complicated affair with its meanings and its categories which have gradually been developed in the human mind in its continued response to things." Critical realism, in short, makes knowledge representative and symbolic.

Now Santayana during the war years had kept in touch with his professional colleagues by letter and by an occasional article in the *Journal of Philosophy*. With all of his interest in human affairs, he had never ceased to concern himself with the basic problems of metaphysics. And there had grown up a younger group of men, some of them his former students, who found much inspiration in his epistemology and in that of his friend C. A. Strong. These were the critical realists. In 1916 they projected a volume of essays which would be a "coöperative study of the problem of knowledge," and four years later the volume was published under the title *Essays in Critical Realism*. Durant Drake, who wrote the introduction, gave "especial credit . . . to Professor Strong and Professor Santayana, who, though overseas during this entire period, have kept up a constant correspondence with the rest of us, and thus shared with their cis-Atlantic colleagues the fruits of their many years of consideration of the vexing problem we had chosen to attack." Strong in turn acknowledged his indebtedness to Santayana in the following words:

I had long been convinced that cognition requires *three* categories for its adequate interpretation, the intermediate one—between subject and object—corresponding to the Kantian "phenomenon" or "appearance," . . . but, in my efforts to conceive it clearly, I was continually falling off either into the category of "object" or into that of "psychic state." What was my relief when at last I heard Mr. Santayana explain his conception of "essence," and it dawned upon me that here was the absolutely correct description of the looked-for category.

Santayana's place, then, in the critical realist movement is an important one, and his article in the collected essays, "Three Proofs of Realism," is one of the clearest, most incisive presentations of the critical realist point of view.

Santayana begins by posing two questions, the cardinal questions of all shades of realism, if not of all philosophic investigation: "What measure of independence or separate existence shall be ascribed to the object?" and "What degree of literalness and adequacy shall be claimed for knowledge?" He attacks the first problem not with the weapons of logic, but with those of common sense, what he was later to call "animal faith." Our whole life is founded upon the belief in an independent external world; without this world there is no ground for our assurance of the past, our confidence in the present, or our hope for the future. Even our differences of opinion take for granted a common denominator of fact about which opinions may differ. You cannot have error without truth. And truth is meaningless if there is not a transition from idea to fact. Truth is not identity, but representation. And so Santayana says,

It is evident that all animals have relevant and transitive knowledge of their environment; so that realistic knowledge is but another name for vital sensibility and intelligence. . . . Looking at the moon, one man may call it simply a light in the sky; another, prone to dreaming awake, may call it a virgin goddess; a more observant person, remembering that this luminary is given to waxing and waning, may call it the crescent; and a fourth, a full-fledged astronomer, may say (taking the aesthetic essence before him merely for a sign) that it is an extinct and opaque spheroidal satellite of the earth, reflecting the light of the sun from a part of its surface. But all these descriptions envisage the same object—otherwise no relevance, conflict, or progress could obtain among them.

The proof of realism, Santayana would agree with the pragmatists, is experience; but experience tests truth, it is not truth itself as pragmatism seems to aver.

Having demonstrated the existence of a real world to his satisfaction, Santayana goes on to define the character of knowledge. Just what is it the mind glimpses; what is the "datum" which Professor Strong felt had been a discovery on the part of Santayana? It is an "essence." In the simplest sensation, says Santayana, "we have come upon a present object without roots that we can see, without conditions, seat, or environment. It is simply an essence." We believe unless we are dreaming that such an essence represents and measures a real object, but this

. . . imputed existence is a dignity borrowed from the momentum of the living mind, which spies out and takes alarm at that datum (or rather at the natural process that calls it forth), supposing that there is something substantial there, something dangerous that will count and work in the world. . . . Even in the most excruciating pain, it is not the quality of the feeling that can injure us, but only the organic process that it betrays.

An angel, a madman, or a poet might be content to gaze upon the panorama of essence and never be troubled by the flux of existence beneath, but the world is a busy and a sorry place, and it is the fate of the human organism to be desperately pragmatic, and to look upon essences as the counters of existence, to work and fight and play as if the objects around it were discernible in their true nakedness and not veiled with an unsubstantial poetic sheen and glamour. And somehow the world responds to this innate trustfulness of man. Science proceeds to demonstrate what even rapt contemplation would disclose: that our vision is all a blur of cross-lights and false perspectives, our senses make no accurate report of reality. But neither is science's verdict, sobered and refined as it is, a copy of reality. We come no nearer in knowledge than to Plato's shadows in the cave; but we live on the assumption that these shadows are shadows and not hallucinations, and that their silhouette is a picture and guarantee of the behavior of matter.

Since "Three Proofs of Realism" Santayana has continued to elaborate his theory of knowledge and has constructed from it his four realms of being. An introduction to his system, *Scepticism and Animal Faith,* appeared in 1923, and two of the four *Realms* have recently been issued. Two other books are parts of this general whole: *The Unknowable,* 1924 (a first sketch of the realm of matter) and *Platonism and the Spiritual Life,* 1927, an approach to the realm of spirit. With these books may be placed two important periodical articles, "Some Meanings of the Word Is" and "Literal and Symbolic Knowledge," which go over the epistemological groundwork of Santayana's system. These books and articles contain much technical metaphysics, but if the lay reader goes to them with open mind and persistence, they will repay him the effort they cost.

Most difficult for the layman to grasp in Santayana's system is the conception of essence. There are several possible approaches to essence—dialectic, mathematics, the contemplation of beauty—but the one chosen by Santayana in his introductory volume is scepticism. Be a sceptic, he says in effect, doubt all you will; pare your universe down to the flash of the passing moment and in that sensation you have an essence. Deny if you will that the blue of the sky, the roundness of the sun, the crash of the thunder represent substantial objects, you still have the blue, the roundness, and the crash. Santayana has always loved to assume attitudes (in his youth he used to play the solipsist) and so his elastic imagination enables him to approach the central problem of his philosophy with something of the zest of the poet as well as the acumen of the metaphysician. His scepticism is, you see, tentative, Descartian. It is a prelude to discovery, to construction. And so he is able to announce:

The sceptic, then, as a consequence of carrying his scepticism to the greatest lengths, finds himself in the presence of more luminous and less equivocal objects than does the working and believing mind; only these objects are without meaning, they are only what they are obviously, all surface.

The relation of essences, thus discovered, to existence is then demonstrated. Matter of course is the motive force, the causative agent. An essence can in no wise produce itself or anything else; it has no material efficacy. Moreover, "to be able to become something else, to suffer change and yet endure, is the privilege of existence, be it in a substance, an event, or an experience." "Essences can be exchanged, but not changed." An essence is always the same to eternity; its identity gives it its character. To drop this identity would be to suffer annihilation. Furthermore, essence and existence are really two planes of being, two realms, Santayana calls them, and their interrelationship is as follows: "The flux flows by flowing through essences; and essences are manifested as the flux of matter or of attention picks them up and drops them." They in turn render existence intelligible. But there are other essences, too, in the mind, not realized in existence, fancies and abstractions and universals as well as sensations and perceptions; and there is an infinite realm of essences which neither man nor nature accidentally stumbles upon, all the possible forms of things conceivable and inconceivable. From the point of view of human knowledge this infinite realm is irrelevant, except the segments of it which may furnish future discoveries; that portion of the realm realizable in nature and experience, however, by its power of representation tells us all we know about ourselves, mankind, and the uttermost reaches of the universe. We can never form an idea that is not an essence, and whether this idea be truth or fiction depends upon whether it has or has not been picked up by the flux of existence. All essences, however, are equally concrete, luminous, and individual; they are changeless and imperishable, being altogether without the vicissitudes of existence.

The uninitiate finds two difficulties in trying to grasp Santayana's conception of essence. He is a little dubious about a *realm* of essences, and about the inclusiveness of such a realm. And perhaps the word "realm" has unfortunate spatial and temporal connotations; certainly Santayana does not mean that essences wait in some prehistoric or remote heaven for their incarnation in matter. Their plane of being is not material at all, nor temporal; it is purely formal. Existence traces certain patterns, matter falls into certain modes, perhaps its inner constitution determines which particular modes; and then the reason apprehends these modes and the imagination envisages others; but neither nature nor consciousness exhausts the realm of essence because that realm comprises every shade of possible modes, an infinity of forms. As for the inclusiveness of the realm of essence, most readers of Santayana agree with him in placing there concepts, universals, mathematical and physical laws, but they refuse to admit such variable things as sensations to such a frozen eternity. They maintain that each sense impression is born anew with each external stimulus; recurrence and identity are just a mental illusion. But Santayana has an answer to this objection which is quite convincing. He does not mean by essence either the mental or the neural act of sensation, but rather the quality sensed. And certainly that belongs no more in some brain cell or nerve tissue than in some sunbeam or thunderbolt outside the body. Moreover, although each act of sensation is unique, the quality sensed, straightness for instance,

. . . is absolutely identical at each recurrence. It is irrelevant that the material object evoking this essence may be different in each instance, and never quite straight: that context, even if vaguely pressing on the psyche, remains unsynthesised, unnoticed, and unintended. When, on looking at a palm tree, a Roman road, or the horizon, I say to myself, How straight! I have exactly the same clear feeling; and this pure essence, not its irrelevant context . . . is the essence apprehended.

Attention is not just passive, but selective, form-giving; it focuses and identifies within the field of sense perception. Santayana, then, would include in the realm of essence sense qualities as well as ideas and the forms of things; an architect's plans, the pattern of the house when completed, the redness of the bricks, the very "houseness" would all be essences, yet there would be at the same time the actual house, a physical object in the realm of matter.

To return to *Scepticism and Animal Faith,* having shown that even scepticism must admit essence, Santayana abandons doubt for "animal faith," which is that tendency to belief inherent in the very animal nature of the human being. We are all instinctively believers. Though scepticism can doubt any or all of the following things, animal faith proceeds blithely to take for granted the duration and identity of sensations, experience, memory, the self, external objects, and an external world. What is more, the arrogance of animal faith in so doing seems to be approved by nature, which submits to its judgment and sanctions the simplification of experience thus brought about. Santayana is, then, ready to return to a fuller development of the theory of knowledge he had worked out in "Three Proofs of Realism." Two factors, he says, are involved in knowledge: the intuition of essences and the representation of things. Animal faith lusts for things, but it has to be content to embrace essences. But the daily mart of life for all practical purposes can get along very well with them. Only the philosopher longs to penetrate behind the veil. For the most part, "we read Nature as the English used to read Latin, pronouncing it like English, but understanding it very well." "The ideas we have of things are not fair portraits, they are political caricatures made in the human interest, but very often, in their partial way, masterpieces of characterization and insight."

Santayana is now ready to turn to truth and its place in the scheme of things. Perhaps the reader has been wondering where truth would find a place in this dualism of essence and existence, in this representative knowledge of Santayana's. There is indeed room for truth, much room, a whole realm, or perhaps more strictly that segment of the realm of essence illustrated in existence. Truth, then, though part of essence, points always at existence and in a sense links the two major realms. In Santayana's words,

It is the splash any fact makes, or the penumbra it spreads, by dropping through the realm of essence. Evidently no opinion can embrace it all, or identify itself with it; nor can it be identified with the facts to which it relates, since they are in flux, and it is eternal. The word truth ought, I think, to be reserved for what everybody spontaneously means by it: the standard comprehensive description of any fact in all its relations.

This absolute truth of course outruns human comprehension; like Shelley's white radiance it is broken into many colors, refracted and distorted by the glass of human understanding, which is but the product of variable matter. But there is relative truth, degree of truth, as common sense affirms. And of true perspectives "the simplest and most violently foreshortened may be as good as the most complicated, the most poetical or pictorial as good as the most scientific, not only aesthetically but even cognitively; because it may report the things concerned on that human scale on which we need to measure them, and in this relation may report them correctly." And truth's concern with this real world of ours gives its realm a "tragic importance" denied the more imaginative and dialectical segments of essence.

Matter and spirit compose the other two realms in Santayana's metaphysics. In his more recent works Santayana abandons the terms "existence" and "substance" for the simpler and more concrete word "matter," but he uses all three words with practically the same significance. Now a belief in substance is at the very bottom of animal faith, yet with a representative knowledge substance can never be completely intelligible. Thus Santayana is at a greater loss to describe matter than to describe essence; he must fall back on symbols which by their very nature give only a vague, pictorial account of the underlying reality. But he says, "I see no necessity that our ideas of matter or of God should be truer than that"; if substance is essentially "unknowable," at least it is basic and "unequivocal." Matter is the matrix of all life and thought, the whole physical universe, perpetually in flux, yet given to habit-forming, its laws and principles being essences which illuminate but never quite exhaust its inscrutable behavior.

Spirit is given a more unusual connotation than matter in Santayana's philosophy. What most men call spirit, Santayana would call substance or matter, since they mean by it a universal or individual power capable of action and influence, an "efficient cause" in Aristotle's sense. Santayana's conception of spirit is very different. Spirit is the highest manifestation of consciousness, that which marks off the human mind, in its reflective capacity, from mere animal or vegetable consciousness. It is by no means a soul, no distinct entity corporeal or incorporeal. "Its peculiar sort of reality is to be intelligence in act. . . . By spirit essences are transposed into appearances and things into objects of belief . . . a moral actuality which in their logical being or their material flux they had never aspired to have." Passive in the material sense, epiphenomenal, it is at the same time an acute awareness, a glow of intelligence which the animal organism generates and which in turn transforms the whole outlook and environment of the organism. Spirit is not essence, for it is directed at essence. Nor is it matter, although it may be considered a function of matter, a radiance or iridescence playing over matter, matter at white heat. Spirit "is no phenomenon, not sharing the aesthetic sort of reality proper to essences . . . nor that other sort proper to dynamic and material things." It "accordingly forms a new realm of being, silently implicated in the apparition of essences and in the felt pressure of nature, but requiring the existence of nature to create it, and to call up those essences before it." It cannot quite be identified with consciousness either. It is more than "passive intuition"; it implies "intent, expectation, belief, and eagerness." And there are as many forms of it as there are essences, each being a distinct "spiritual fact."

Here, then, are the four realms of being: essence, matter, spirit, and truth. As we stand off and survey Santayana's creation, it impresses us as a work of art, ordered and symmetrical, complete with a place for everything. And what an interesting cosmos stretches out before us, essence so pure in its very intangibility, the ceaseless thrust of matter, intimate yet impenetrable, spirit brooding over all, transmuting everything with its brilliance. And this is no remote cosmos, but a description of the very world in which we live our daily lives.

Of the five volumes dealing with the realms of being, *Scepticism and Animal Faith* is the most technical and controversial. Here Santayana enters the metaphysical lists to defend his system, to parry objections and thrust home demonstrations. Just as the layman finds it the most bewildering of Santayana's works, the philosopher finds it the most satisfying; for once the seer descends to argument and logical analysis. Nevertheless, the book is not without its sprinkling of poetic passages, its gems of humor and wisdom that only Santayana could write, its store of pungent aphorisms. *The Realm of Essence* and *The Realm of Matter* return to Santayana's lofty, oracular style. The air is cleared of controversial dust, and the opinions are handed down with a kind of Olympian authority and elegance. *The Realm of Essence* seems to me the better book, for the conception of essence, being by nature poetical, is well suited to Santayana's temperament and method of demonstration. *The Realm of Matter,* like *Reason in Science,* suffers from a vagueness due to the avoidance of all scientific data. No Copernicus or Einstein enters its pages; in fact, the book is not science at all, but pure philosophy, a laying of certain foundations in regard to substance which science will build on in detail. And in spite of the interest and persuasiveness of some of the doctrines—pictorial space, sentimental time, "actual moment" —the treatment at times seems thin and devoid of concrete example. More lucid and gracious is the brief Herbert Spencer lecture, *The Unknowable,* one of Santayana's finest bits of writing; and even more striking as literary expression is *Platonism and the Spiritual Life*. In the latter the deepest loyalties of Santayana are touched; here is his contemplative ideal in its purity; naturally the style is kindled as the fervor of the moral philosopher is added to the subtlety of the metaphysician. For what could be more worth writing about than man's highest faculty directed at that which endures forever. "The existence of anything is a temporary accident, while its essence is an indelible variation of necessary Being, an eternal form. The spirit lives in this continual sense of the ultimate in the immediate."

Obviously in any system of philosophy as thoroughgoing as Santayana's there are bound to be borrowings from philosophers past and present; the distinction of Santayana's metaphysics is not that it is radically original but that it has assimilated so judiciously the truths and insights of other men. "My system is not mine, nor new," says Santayana at the beginning of *Scepticism and Animal Faith;* yet truly its eclecticism is less a patchwork than an integration of beliefs about "a certain shrewd orthodoxy which the sentiment and practice of laymen maintain everywhere." It is, so Santayana believes, common sense refined and made honest with itself. Such a chastened common sense will build upon its own intuitions and upon whatever philosophies happen to suit its purpose. It will bring into juxtaposition the most divergent points of view if they mutually illuminate any problem under consideration. Thus Platonism and naturalism, scholasticism and pragmatism, scepticism and rationalism have glimpsed reality in their own ways. Why should there not be room in a truly catholic mansion for strange bedfellows, if they are willing to renounce whatever of them is official and apologetic and keep only what is founded on honest intuition and observation? *The Realm of Matter* will then reflect a philosophical tradition quite different from that behind *The Realm of Essence,* and the other two *Realms* will reveal still different affinities and obligations.

The materialism of Santayana is related to all materialisms modern and ancient, yet in the long run it is the product of observation and common sense rather than of any particular philosophic tradition. As far back as he can remember, Santayana has always believed that his senses report to him an external material world, mechanical in operation, the matrix of mind and spirit. To this basic materialism other systems have lent refinements and corroborations. Thus, Spinoza in Santayana's college days demonstrated conclusively to the young man's satisfaction that nature is scientifically predictable, perhaps controllable, but at heart is also indifferent to and on another plane than human nature. Democritus and his followers early convinced Santayana that the inner structure of matter is atomic, however pictorial any particular atomic system may be. As he says in *The Realm of Matter,*

The atomic theory is . . . in one sense inherent in physics, and alone possible; because the very nature of existence is to be dispersed in centres, dislocated, corpuscular, granular; the parts must be particulars externally related. Any demand for a unity not a unity of arrangement, derivation, or conjunction turns its back on existence.

The early Greeks mistook symbol for reality, but their sense of direction was trustworthy, and science has followed it ever since.

Yet Heraclitus was also right in his way. Matter is dispersed, but it is also a continuum and is in constant flux. Change is a postulate of substance; Parmenides in denying motion had his eyes on essence, not matter. More and more has Santayana come to feel the ground swell of change in the world of existence, ever creating, ever destroying the forms which appear for a moment on its broad bosom. In many ways *The Realm of Matter* is nearer to Heraclitus than to Democritus.

However perfectly . . . a system might transcribe the flux of existence, it would not *be* that flux in person, or in its lapsing life; and science cannot well be truer of it, though true at a deeper level, than are all the vulgar essences which visibly give it character.

Substance is to Santayana a serpent writhing away in the dark; we feel its pulsations, but we cannot see it. Strange how in his hands matter, the immediate thing to common sense, has retreated into a lair from which it influences us at all points yet in its throbbing vitality defies our utmost efforts at penetration. Still modern science, as well as Heraclitus, confirms Santayana's intuitions. The more minutely scientists penetrate into atom and electron, the farther away they seem to get from the brute matter we brush against in daily life. And though they chart something of its behavior, their symbols become more and more erudite and matter itself remains as mysterious as ever.

Not that flux need be synonymous with chaos. There are strains and propulsions in matter (lateral and forward tensions Santayana calls them) which seem to recur and submit to measurement and prediction. We "have the assurance that the flux, for the time being, has been somewhat canalised in our parts of the universe, and that lateral tensions are partly held in check, and turned to sustenance, for the benefit of some persisting organisms." Matter, like people, has habits. We call them in our egotism "laws of nature," but they are merely "tropes," descriptive of certain habits which have been perpetuated long enough to stamp themselves upon our powers of observation. But even the most definitive of them, as in mathematics, may reveal a "margin of error" when applied to nature.

... for a law is an essence, eternally identical, and nature is in flux, and probably never the same. Very likely all the movements of matter are more or less elastic or organic: I mean responsive afresh to a total environment never exactly repeated, so that no single law would perfectly define all consecutive changes even in the plane of matter, and every response would be that of a new-born organism to an unprecedented world. ... But on the human scale, and for fashioning perishable human works, such fundamental instability in nature would remain negligible. Even in a land of earthquakes we live in houses.

Moreover, the most comprehensive of "tropes" does no more than describe matter; it exerts no control over matter.

Matter is no model devised by the human imagination ... but is a primeval plastic substance of unknown potentiality, perpetually taking on new forms; the gist of materialism being that these forms are all passive and precarious, while the plastic stress of matter is alone creative and, as far as we can surmise, indestructible.

There is, of course, in this later elaboration of Santayana's materialism a resemblance to that agnostic tradition of modern philosophy which began with Kant and found its fullest expression in Herbert Spencer. It is not mere accident that Santayana's first sketch of the realm of matter was entitled *The Unknowable* in tribute to Spencer. At the beginning of his lecture Santayana says, "On the whole ... I belong to Herbert Spencer's camp. ... When I rub my eyes and look at things candidly, it seems evident to me that this world is the sort of world described by Herbert Spencer, not the sort of world described by Hegel or Bergson," who convert "sharp facts" into "a clarified drama or a pleasant trance." But Santayana does not take pride in the inscrutability of matter; in fact, he feels Spencer was incautious in his choice of the term "unknowable." "Nothing can be intrinsically unknowable," can "antecedently defy description." "If substance remains largely unknown to mankind, the reason will not be any recalcitrancy on its part, but rather a casual coincidence in ourselves of curiosity with blindness, so that we earnestly desire to search the depths of substance, but cannot." Perhaps consciousness is fatally geared to the direct apperception of essence, a world of surfaces, whereas the real world has obviously depth and solidity. Why not rest content, then, with a knowledge of acquaintance which tells us very well what kind of world we live in and how to get along in it. Agnosticism moans for a kind of knowledge that is perhaps impossible and fails to appreciate the very adequate knowledge upon which all sane living is built. The positivists Mill and Comte were wiser in abandoning the Unknowable, once they had posited it, and in turning their whole attention to what could be known.

The limitations to our knowledge of matter should be neither a barrier to science nor a new avenue to religion. Modern science, in expanding the frontiers of knowledge so rapidly, has come upon a dilemma. The exact, positive science of the Victorians has retreated before a barrage of investigation which shows how pictorial this older science was and intimates that all science must of necessity be pictorial. Among puzzled laymen and among scientists themselves the confusion in modern science, the overthrow of authority, has seemed to lead either to an agnostic defeatism or to an encouragement of all sorts of idealisms and supernaturalisms which are seen rising out of the fancied ashes of materialism. Santayana approaches this dilemma in a recent essay, "Revolutions in Science," first published in the *New Adelphi* in 1928, and later reissued in *Some Turns of Thought in Modern Philosophy*, 1933. He argues that the revolution in science is "perfectly legal" and should be "welcomed." It should breed a new humility in scientists by showing them the truth: that science "yields practical assurances couched in symbolic terms, but no ultimate insight." As for religious consolation, the "softhearted" and "muddle-headed" maintain that "physics is no longer materialistic since space is now curved, and filled with an ether through which light travels at 300,000 kilometres per second—an immaterial rate," that electrons "dart and whirl with such miraculous swiftness that occasionally for no known reason, they can skip from orbit to orbit without traversing the intervening positions—an evident proof of free-will in them," that there are "astral bodies" "immaterial although physical," that "ether and electricity" are "the very substance of spirit." Santayana dismisses all these premature interpretations of the new science with a few words of timely, sobering advice. Instead of ushering in "the breakdown of scientific materialism," they seem to him to represent a breakdown of clear thinking, a loss of the "power to discern the difference between material and spiritual things"; and he would have scientists remember this distinction and turn their attention to the many things which remain for science to do on the material plane, the correlation and confirmation of data, that our picture of nature may be as lifelike and relevant as human agency can make it.

The Realm of Essence is a more original construction than *The Realm of Matter,* more of a "refinement in speculation," Santayana calls it, more "unfamiliar to the common man." Yet it too has antecedents in the history of philosophy, for many men have discovered essence if they have not always called it or even recognized it as such. Santayana himself seems to have clearly glimpsed essence early in his life, long before he gave it a name. The true poet, and Santayana is one, lives constantly in the presence of essences, and if he is clear-minded and disillusioned, he will know that the panorama of his world is all form and surface and that its elements are eternal and changeless. The poet is used to the symbolism of language, and by extension should read the same symbolism into nature until he realizes that the lovely cloak nature wears is but essence playing over the flux of existence. So when the young Santayana in his sonnets pondered whether

> . . . aught abideth of the things that seem

and affirmed that

> Truth is a dream, unless my dream is true

and that we behold

> The deathless beauty of all winged hours,
> And have our being in their truth alone,

he was discerning and paying tribute to the imperishability of the world of essence. Art and architecture showed him too that form can be imprinted on matter as well as truth on the mind, and that beauty can be rescued from the flux of existence and transfixed to eternity for our pleasure. Essence is the nearest thing in life to all of us. "I cannot read a book," says the mature Santayana, "or think of a friend or grieve or rejoice at any fresh event, without some essence rising sensibly before me, the sole actual harvest to me of that labour. At every moment the rattle of the machine of nature, and of my own engine, unless I lose the sense of it altogether, is at once revealed and hidden by some immediate essence, which it wears like a shining garment, or more often, perhaps, merely suggests to me as its meaning, its beauty, or its secret." Of course, admits Santayana, "this trick of arresting the immediate is in one sense an interruption to life; it is proper only to poets, mystics, or epicureans." But was not the youthful Santayana something of all three?

Certainly his Catholicism brought him close to essence, for from the earliest he looked upon theology as myth and fable, arresting and beautiful, but insubstantial. If we may believe the sonnets, he was troubled and saddened for a time by the realization that religion envisioned essence rather than existence, but disillusionment brought with it not only a greater respect for "eternal mother" nature, but also a deeper insight into the true nature of the spiritual.* I wonder, too, if Santayana's early acquaintance with medieval scholasticism did not lead him in the direction of essence. For the schoolmen had time and patience to erect immense structures in the realm of essence (which they generally mistook for existence), "universals" were their daily bread, and even their perpetual warfare between "nominalism" and "realism" was but a recognition of two different approaches to essence: "universals," being essences, are terms in discourse, but their reality from the standpoint of logic and form may be truthfully asserted even if existential reality be denied them. From the point of view of the realm of essence, a clear recognition of "universals" is more significant than differences of opinion concerning their nature. And certainly the great schoolmen, like Saint Thomas, in their distinction between the active and the contemplative life, clearly perceived the pathway to essence, and in their emphasis upon God as "the highest intelligible good," to be glimpsed only through the power of the intellect in contemplation, were close to the conception of deity as Pure Being, i. e., Essence. The very theory of knowledge of Thomas Aquinas, positing the finitude of man's intellect because of its immersion in the physical, has points of resemblance to the epistemology of the critical realists. "It is impossible," says Thomas, "that the mind, in the state of the present life, wherein it is joined to the passive body, should know anything actually except by turning itself to images. . . . The appropriate object of the human mind, which is joined to a body, is the essence or nature existing in material body; and through the natures of visible things of this sort it ascends to some cognition of invisible things."

Of course medieval scholasticism derives in great part from Aristotle, and when Santayana came upon the Greeks themselves he

---
* See above, pp. 27–29, 38, 39.

was brought even closer to a true recognition of essence. Aristotle's conception of form and, even more so, the Platonic "ideas" were clear intuitions of essence. Aristotle was entirely aware of the formal, essential element in things, and Plato, more mystical and poetical, saw with equal clarity that this element might be abstracted from things altogether and given an abode of its own, timeless and imperishable. All later recognition of essence is profoundly indebted to Plato and Platonic idealism. Santayana himself acknowledges, "My theory is a variant of Platonism, designed to render Platonic logic and morals consistent with the facts of nature." But herein is the rub. Both Aristotle and Plato were drawn by the "political, censorious temper" of the Greeks to turn from a study of essence to one of existence, and in Aristotle's "final cause" and Plato's myths (which he at times took seriously) essence enters the realm of force and matter and imposes its will as if it were a physical agent.

I am no pupil [says Santayana] of Plato's in all that phase of his thought in which he seems to supply the lack of a cosmology by turning moral and ideal terms into supernatural powers. The supernatural is nothing but an extension of the natural into the unknown, and there is infinite room for it; but when these deeper or remoter parts of nature are described in myths evidently designed for the edification or easier government of human society, I distrust the fiction.

Unfortunate it was that one of the truest visions of essence should have been blurred, and should have led mankind into centuries of confusing essence with existence. For with the triumph of Christianity Platonic insight was perpetuated, but even more "abusively," with essence again "pretending to be more than essence." "And mankind has been divided ever since between the impulse to admire the vision and the impulse to denounce the lie." ·

It is apparent, then, that his own poetic sensibility, Catholicism, Platonism, and later the Hindus would have sufficed to give Santayana a completely adequate notion of essence. But all these approaches to essence are intuitive or categorical; it was necessary for Santayana to go through the mill of modern psychologism before he was able to see how essence might be demonstrated systematically and with logical precision.

Santayana's work as a graduate student under Ebbinghaus, Simmel, and James brought vividly to his attention the physical substratum of mind and the phantasmagoria of sensation playing over it. William James particularly had a lively sense for the flux of existence, and encouraged Santayana to look upon consciousness as mercurial and protean, a flood in which rose and fell the objects of sense and thought. James had thus "a profound insight into existence" as well as a remarkable faculty of catching and describing essence. His psychology was "literary" rather than scientific, but just therein did it describe the realm of essence in its dual relation to matter and to mind. Platonism and scholasticism had marked out the permanence and universality of essence, but both had discredited the immediacy and contingency of essence as revealed through sensation. It remained for modern psychology (unknowingly) to discern the humblest, yet most easily demonstrable attribute of essence, and to reveal the physical dependence of essence upon existence. For a time it looked as if Santayana would be swayed by psychologism too far in the direction of the subjective; *The Sense of Beauty* is so intent upon disproving the objectivity of beauty that it looks upon beauty as emotion rather than essence. But the Platonism of *Interpretations of Poetry and Religion,* treating both poetry and religion as concretions of the imagination, is definitely a return to the study of essence.

I believe Santayana's grasp of the sceptical approach to essence was facilitated by his study and teaching of early modern philosophy, especially the British and French schools. The first courses he gave at Harvard were in these fields, and he has always felt that early modern philosophy was in possession of as acute an analysis of knowledge as that of the more recent schools, without the latter's tendency to mistake this analysis for reality itself. All early modern philosophers, being close to science or theology, retained through all their scepticism some grasp of a real external world; their scepticism was thus a method of reorientation; it never completely ravished common sense nor destroyed the real world only to build upon the ruins a new and transcendental edifice. Thus Descartes' scepticism reduced the world to nothing but the thinking self, but with an "animal faith" equal to Santayana's Descartes immediately proceeded to reëstablish other selves, matter, and God. It is true, Santayana's scepticism is more thoroughgoing than Descartes'; it does not stop with the self, nor with extension and motion as attributes of matter. The idealists Leibniz and Berkeley were nearer to Santayana in attacking Descartes' postulates regarding matter, and Hume was still nearer in questioning beliefs in causality and the self. Santayana's scepticism goes the whole way and stops, like Hume's, at last with the ultimate, irreducible sense impression. In fact, Hume's arguments against a belief in substance and in the self sound very much like Santayana's discovery of essence. "We have," says Hume, "no idea of substance distinct from that of a collection of particular qualities. . . . When I enter most intimately into what I call myself, I always stumble on some particular perception or other, of heat or cold, light or shade, love or hatred, pain or pleasure. I never can catch myself at any time without a perception." We can be sure of nothing, concludes Hume, but the passing sensation; ultimate reality forever eludes us.

To all this disintegration of knowledge Santayana would of course agree. He would even follow the paradoxical Scotchman when, after obliterating the real world, he proceeds to live and love as if the real world existed. But there is a striking difference between the scepticism of Santayana and that of Hume. With Santayana scepticism is constructive, a means to an end. It proves that there is a realm of essence, and retires from the scene to allow "animal faith" to posit a realm of matter and to act in accordance with it. Hume's animal faith governs his life, but, except for his concept of God, is held in abeyance in his philosophy. In fact, his intention in metaphysics was to attack and destroy, and one wonders whether, having discovered essence, he really knew what he had come upon and did not, following Locke, look upon sensation as a purely subjective phenomenon. Certainly, in failing to recognize the representative character of knowledge, he led the way to all subsequent psychologism and idealism. He sowed seeds of distrust in all knowledge of the external world, because such knowledge could not be direct and intuitive, and forced philosophy back upon "categories" and "postulates" wherever it tried to avoid the snares of his scepticism. Thus, what should have been the foundation of a chastened theory of knowledge and a permanent evaluation of essence became an avenue to the wildest flights of transcendentalism. For over a century essence was again to be lost in fogs of misunderstanding. There was really more common sense to Bishop Berkeley, who, having reduced the world to idea, turned about and gave it the same independence and actuality it had had as matter. Thus, Santayana's method is that of Hume, but his sympathies are rather with Descartes and Locke and Berkeley, who never for long allowed metaphysics to distort the vision of common sense.

But if the earliest British and French schools charted the psychological approach to essence, it remained for the earliest Germans to discover the infinity and multiplicity of the realm of essence—all the time believing they had penetrated to the reality of existence. Spinoza had a deep respect for existence in its inevitable disregard for human wishes; but his respect passed from recognition to a kind of pantheistic zeal and piety. And when he began to mark out lovingly the infinity of what he called substance and to attribute to substance an infinite number of modes, of which extension and thought (themselves capable of infinite variation) were the only two known to man, he assumed a familiarity with the real substance which is just impossible. Knowledge ceased to be representative and became intuitive and mystical. Nature is under no obligation to infinity; existence is dispersed and precarious; it need not exemplify all possible modes. What Spinoza had stumbled upon was the realm of essence "in its omnimodal immensity," in its capacity for infinite variations of form. Leibniz, too, saw the realm of essence in this light. Not only did he, as Santayana points out, in his myth of the creation envisage a creator who looked out upon "all possible worlds" and then chose this one, but his very "monadology," which split up reality into a multiplicity of spiritual entities, described essence rather than existence. If "every individual substance . . . is a world apart, independent of everything else except God," if it is impossible for a monad to be "altered or changed in its inner being by any other created thing," then Leibniz is describing the unique and irrefragable character of an essence rather than the continuum of existence. As Santayana says in the heading to one of his chapters, essences are all "primary"; they "have no family tree"; even "the essence of the whole is not compounded of the essences of the parts," but is "individual and distinct." The parts of substance, on the contrary, are interrelated, and tremors of causation run through the whole.

Post-Kantian idealists, though they swam among essences, were blind to the nature of the fluid in which they were immersed; "Both psychology and the criticism of knowledge ought to bring essence to light, since essences are the only objects of indubitable and immediate experience." Yet British empiricism treated appearance as the only reality, and German idealism, seeing no other way of getting at nature, concluded that anything known by the mind must be sentient, and cognate with the mind. Thus essence was mistaken for substance or treated as if it were purely subjective. Even the new realists, trained in the school of British empiricism, have found a new way of arriving at an old deception, for they have practically replaced substance by the sense qualities, which are, after all, but essences telling us something more or less pertinent about the behavior of matter.

But there is hope, says Santayana.

> Of late . . . various judicious persons, trained in these schools, have begun to confess that consciousness is not aware of itself but of objects variously styled sense-data or concepts or neutral entities (neither mental nor material), or simply "objects," meaning essences present to sense or thought as opposed to the events in nature which they symbolise.

And Santayana proceeds to point out three thinkers of three nationalities whose views seem to confirm his own. Alfred North Whitehead has come upon essence through mathematics and clearly marks out a realm of eternal, individual entities which he however calls by the adventitious and misleading terms, "sense objects" and "scientific objects." Edmund Husserl, an analytical psychologist and a transcendentalist to boot, has discovered what he calls "pure phenomena," "immediate data" which are "non-existent, and are situated out of all local relation to the 'real world.'" But both Whitehead and Husserl are still under the influence of the empirical schools, and consequently invest essence with too tight-fitting a subjectivity. The infinite realm of essence, tangential to nature and consciousness alike but not exhausted by either, is better described by René Guénon, "a pupil of the Oriental school." He, too, calls the study of essence by a misleading term, metaphysics, but he clearly distinguishes not only that portion of essence which is illustrated in existence (the realm of truth) but also that infinite reach of essence which goes beyond existence altogether and which Hindu philosophy, with weak earth-roots, very clearly envisions. All of these descriptions of essence are contemporary with Santayana's and may hardly be said to have influenced him; among the critical realists, too, he is a pioneer rather than a follower. But I believe he is indebted somewhat to Bertrand Russell and G. E. Moore, the English realists whom he described in 1911 as the vanguard of a new scholasticism. These two men, from the vantage point of mathematics, discerned very clearly a world of pure, immutable forms whose character was quite independent of existence; and although they gave to moral terms a rigid absolutism contrary to their dependence upon experience, Russell and Moore did bring back philosophy from its drift through sensationalism to a *terra firma* of truth and representative knowledge. After his study of Russell, Santayana uses the terms "essence" and "existence" more frequently and consistently.

With the volumes devoted to the realms of truth and spirit still unpublished, it is more difficult to trace the sources of these constructions. The realm of truth is so close to one assumption of common sense, that there is "a standard, comprehensive description" of everything, that it seems to have grown out of Santayana's mother wit rather than anything so erudite as a system of metaphysics. Yet common sense uses the word "truth" with a certain duplicity, often meaning relative or provisional truth, truth satisfactory for most human needs. Santayana's conception of truth is more rigid and rigorous. There is a realm of truth though no human being should ever discover it; and no human being from his immersion in the flux of existence could ever survey in its entirety something as austere and comprehensive as the realm of truth, or any segment of it *sub specie aeternitatis*. Truth is the marriage of essence and existence, and such holy nuptials are veiled to the profane eye of humanity. The realm of truth is thus seen to be Catholic, scholastic. All it needs is a God to preside over it, and it would be Saint Thomas all over again. Driven out of the world of existence by Santayana's materialism, Catholicism finds a back door to reënter his philosophy in truth. Santayana's realm of truth, therefore, may be looked upon as allied with the neo-scholastic attempt to dethrone modernism in the Catholic church and pragmatism outside it, and to restore a stern Thomist theory of knowledge which will make truth again absolute at the same time as it is objective and representative. This is not to say that there is an ulterior theological motive behind Santayana's work, or that neo-scholastics acknowledge or welcome so dubious an ally; but it does testify to the ineradicable impression Catholic habits of thought have made upon Santayana and explains why he always thinks of idealism, and subjectivism in general, as Protestant, and opposes them on religious as well as on philosophical grounds.

The realm of spirit is Platonic, but it is Platonism stripped of everything mythical and supernatural. In its elevation above matter and flesh, in the joy it furnishes the truly contemplative soul, it is close to Indian thought, and Santayana has of late admitted that of all peoples the Hindus have glimpsed spirit most clearly and cherished it most devoutly. The Indians saw that "substance is infinite, out of scale with our sensuous images and (except in the little vortex that makes us up) out of sympathy with our endeavors." They saw furthermore that "the spirit is at home in the infinite, and morally independent of all the accidents of existence." The Indians in their humility knew that "the thoughts of man and his works, however great and delightful when measured by the human scale, are but the faintest shimmer on the surface of being." Yet the Indians, intent "on the vanity of human life," "did not study the movement and mechanism of nature: they had no science," and "they also neglected the art of rational conduct in this world." Thus the freedom of the spirit was obtained at an unnecessary cost of worldly servitude; and being so completely divorced from its parent the psyche and from the material world, the spirit spun out its own macrocosm and microcosm, just as mythical as those of western civilization and even more monstrous. Thus where wholesome living is sought, the Greeks, not the Hindus, will furnish the model; yet at moments when the anxieties of life may be forgotten, man may find a true inspiration in the Indians—or in Plotinus and Emerson, their closest affinities.

I believe the realm of spirit is Santayana's most original construction, because in it the hitherto most contradictory elements come peaceably to rest. In the dependence of spirit upon psyche you have frank, unabashed materialism, yet at no loss of those *human* values transcendentalists have claimed for spirit. The finest flowering of human nature is provided for; in fact, that is just what spirit is: a loving absorption in form, aesthetic, mathematical, moral. Yet spirit is kept relevant to matter and to human life by its very roots in the psyche. Of course, spirit is an epiphenomenon, but it need give up nothing of the intellectual, moral, or aesthetic heritage that has been traditionally associated with the spirit of man. Only the freedom of the will and the spirit's mastery of the body need be abandoned, and these, says Santayana, reduce spirit to a material agency, anyhow, and make its position anomalous. They vitiate the true worth of the spiritual. In Santayana's philosophy a pragmatic ethics exists side by side with an encouragement of pure spirituality in art and life. From "What Is a Philistine" to *Platonism and the Spiritual Life* Santayana has tried to ennoble life by giving it fixed aims, ideals if you will; and these ideals are in no way deprived of their authority and charm by the fact that they are grounded in animal life. Herein, I believe, is the uniqueness and distinction of his philosophy. And then one may (for not too long) forget the material world and turn playfully to ideal worlds like mathematics or music; idealism is native to spirit; it is only the pulsating beat of the psyche within or the encroachment of matter without that would ever call away spirit from her idle fancies and raptures. As Santayana says,

> Spirit is bred in the psyche because the psyche, in living, is obliged to adjust herself to alien things: she does so in her own interest; but in taking cognisance of other things, in moulding a part of her dream to follow their alien fortunes, she becomes intelligent, she creates spirit; and this spirit overleaps the pragmatic function of physical sensibility —it is the very act of overleaping it—and so proves itself a rank outsider, a child rebellious to the household, an Ishmael ranging alone, a dweller in the infinite.

The Realms of Being has won for Santayana recognition as a metaphysician of the first rank. Professor D. S. Robinson, who is by no means an admirer of Santayana's philosophy, places *The Realms of Being* among the seven or eight most important philosophical works of the twentieth century, chosen from the standpoint of range and synthetic power. Certainly Santayana's system has made him the foremost champion of critical realism, a fact admitted by almost all commentators. He has taken what began essentially as a critique of knowledge and broadened it to a system which probes the nature of being itself; in philosophical terms, converted an epistemology into an ontology. The objection that critical realism is merely controversial and negative has largely been invalidated by Santayana's work.

Such commendation is not to say that philosophers in large numbers from opposing camps have flocked to the banner of critical realism. The ranks are aligned much as they were before *The Realms of Being;* in fact, the work has come in for its share of attack from all quarters of the philosophical compass. Idealists have objected not only to the underlying realism of Santayana's position but also to what they maintain is a sly theft of their own hard-won bounties. They declare that Santayana wishes to preserve man's spiritual prerogatives, yet grounds them illogically and unaccountably in an alien, materialistic universe. As to essence, they feel that Santayana's conception is abstract and barren, resulting in a realm which is denied any concern for man's welfare, yet at the same time rises inexplicably from the world of matter. An infinity of universals seems to Professor Hocking "a piece of modern mythology without Plato's excuse, a striking instance of the extreme fancifulness which marks the realists' resolve to be supremely matter-of-fact." If the realm of essence is infinite, there must be every conceivable shade and gradation in it, and that this crammed world is independent of human perception and is waiting for nature to embody and man to discover fragments of it is just inconceivable to the idealist. The pragmatist joins the idealist in objecting to the intuition of essence as if the datum were independent of human intent and the mind merely a passive spectator. "Knowledge," says John Dewey, "confers upon a non-cognitive material traits which *did* not belong to it." Professor C. I. Lewis particularly objects to Santayana's treatment of sense impressions as essences. He maintains that a sense impression is merely a blur, is often completely ignored unless the mind attends to it and judges its character by an active mental process. In general, the pragmatists maintain that critical realism has reintroduced Kant's "things-in-themselves" into modern philosophy, universals which are unreal, unnecessary, and removed from all experience. The new realists, of course, have always felt that critical realism complicated epistemology by positing a wholly unnecessary *tertium quid,* and Santayana's books have not altered their opinions in the least.* Even some of Santayana's associates in critical realism have struck out in directions which lead away from certain of Santayana's principles. There is a disposition on the part of most of them to draw back from Santayana's materialistic interpretation of the universe. Drake has come around to "meliorism" and Lovejoy to "emergent evolution," both of which are efforts to reintroduce a mild teleology into realism. Strong has flirted in and out with panpsychism, a philosophy which sees in all nature a mental counterpart of the physical. Pratt casts his vote for "interactionism," which permits the mind to influence matter, restores a semblance of the freedom of the will, and even renders immortality possible. Realism in contemporary philosophy does not commit one to materialism; but Santayana has remained obdurate within the nineteenth-century mechanistic view of nature. Among professional philosophers he is perhaps the Last Victorian, the direct and staunch heir of Comte and Huxley, a rock among the scientific quicksands of the modern world.

The varied objections to Santayana's system are proof that it is vulnerable at many points to philosophical attack. His materialism no longer has the shibboleths of Victorian science to bolster it: the

---

* Two outstanding English realists, Bertrand Russell and Samuel Alexander, have veered in the direction of new rather than critical realism.

indivisibility of the atom, the independence of matter and energy, mechanical causation, and gradual change. Modern science reveals a world in which the atom is a universe in itself, in which matter becomes energy and energy matter, in which change may be indeterminate, and in which time and space seem interdependent. In this novel and curious world all traditional postulates become untenable; although further knowledge may reveal merely a more intricate mechanism and causality. Such is Santayana's belief, but at the present time his materialism must become with all other -isms purely a faith and intuition. This it has always been at heart, a deep-seated conviction that idealism glozes over human suffering and evil, and teleology misreads the order of nature and the course of history.

Materialism has to fall back upon the miraculous to account for mind and spirit. How the psyche comes to generate the spirit, Santayana admits he is unable, in spite of the researches of his friend Strong, to explain. He merely attributes it to an impulse in the animal organism brought into play by the environment, which the animal must master if it is to survive. Santayana could perhaps argue his point further in terms of the biological survival of the fittest, but he is content merely to accept mind and spirit as facts which experience reveals. The appearance of essence, its relation to matter and to mind are also puzzles which Santayana has not tried fully to solve. In fact, Santayana's metaphysics is hardly speculative at all; it merely describes what seems given when looked at in different perspectives. To my mind, here is its strength—in its very humility. But those who prefer a metaphysics which leaps beyond the given to the hypothetical will undoubtedly find Santayana's earthbound and pedestrian.

And yet to describe adequately what is given of the universe is no mean feat of the imagination. As Santayana pointed out long ago in "A Religion of Disillusion," if the poet should turn from myth to reality, he would find ample exercise for his faculties; in fact, the real world might reveal a beauty and an intricacy far surpassing the world he could create out of his imagination. Lucretius was perhaps the true poet after all, only his range and insight at times fell short of his goal. *The Realms of Being,* then, like any great work of constructive philosophy, is an exercise of the creative imagination; it has the symmetry and grandeur of a great poem or a great symphony, and the further merit of being close to reality. Philosophy, as Santayana has often pointed out, is an art rather than a science, since all versions of truth are limited and pictorial; but there are degrees of truthfulness, and one man's vision, personal as it is, may be clearer than another man's.

Into *The Realms of Being* Santayana has put his most mature philosophical reflections. It is more abstract and abstruse than *The Life of Reason;* it is also more imaginative and creative. Its surface technicality and impersonality merely veil how personal a thing it is, and how intimately Santayana's own. The poet, crowded out by the critic and moralist, has silently crept back and donned the garb of metaphysician. In the twilight of his life the creator of the odes and sonnets has faced life again with something of his early rapture and with an increased dignity and repose. The style, forsaking rime and meter, has found an even finer poetical vein in the bedrock of metaphysics. For majesty and cadence some of the passages of *The Realm of Essence* and *The Realm of Matter* cannot be surpassed by anything else of Santayana's. Matter, spirit, essence lose their conceptual aridity in Santayana's hands because he views them not as mere logical terms but as the stuff out of which the world is made, and sees them with the concreteness of the poet's vision. What, after all, can be more grand and inspiring than the foundations of the world, what more suitable theme for poetry? And there is poetry in passages like these:

Thinking is like telling one's beads; the poor repeated mutterings of the mind compose, beyond themselves, a single litany, a path leading humbly step by step, past every mystery, up the mountain of knowledge.

In mature human perception the essences given are doubtless distinct and the objects which they suggest are clearly discriminated: here is the dog, there the sun, the past nowhere, and the night coming. But beneath all this definition of images and attitudes of expectancy, there is always a voluminous feeble sensibility in the vegetative soul. Even this sensibility posits existence; the contemplation of pure Being might supervene only after all alarms, gropings, and beliefs had been suspended—something it takes all the discipline of Indian sages to begin to do. The vegetative soul enjoys an easier and more Christian blessedness: it sees not, yet it believes. But believes in what? In whatever it may be that envelopes it; in what we, in our human language, call space, earth, sunlight, and motion; in the throbbing possibility of putting forth something which we call leaves, for which the patient soul has no name and no image.

It was well known to the ancients, and is confirmed daily, that when things die they leave heirs; the flies that seem to vanish every winter return every summer. And this pertinacity in substance is not always intermittent; a phase of latency, silent but deeply real, often connects the phases of activity. Sleep and night are not nothing: in them substance most certainly endures, and even gathers strength, or unfolds its hidden coils. Then the spirit, in withdrawing into slumber, seems to return into the womb, into a security and naturalness much deeper than its distracted life. It knows that while it sleeps all things wait, last, and ripen; they all breathe inwardly with that same peace which returns to it only in the night. Those heavenly bodies, which when gaped at seemed but twinkling specks, are in reality sleeping giants; they roll with an enormous momentum at prodigious distances, and keep the world in equilibrium. The rocks are rooted in their buried foundations, the bed of the sea stretches beneath it, and holds it; the earth broods over its ominous substance, like a fiery orange with a rind of stone. It is this universal pause and readiness in things, guarding us unwatched, that chiefly supports our sanity and courage. This constancy gives us security; the eyes may close in peace, while the child's dreaming hand, half closing, prepares to grasp a sword.

I hope that *The Realms of Being* will be more widely read. The plain man, it is true, will find there much to puzzle him; but he will find as well that philosophy may be wedded to poetry, that prose may be precise and definitive without loss of flavor or imagery. And if he is willing to face life without prejudice or reserve, he will find that a philosophy may be woven out of the most uncompromising naturalism and yet find room for all that he has come to value as the precious heritage of human nature.

CHAPTER SIX

SANTAYANA AND AMERICA

During the composition of *The Realms of Being* Santayana has continued to write occasionally for periodicals, rather more frequently of late. He has returned to aesthetics in a number of searching articles, which advance no new position although they are more tolerant of modernism; he has commented upon Freud and Proust, upon Leopardi and Spinoza and Locke; but his most extensive criticism has turned back to America for its theme. And of the articles dealing with America the most important are "Marginal Notes on Civilization in the United States," and the three articles comprising "The Genteel Tradition at Bay." The first is an informal review of *Civilization in the United States,* "an Inquiry by Thirty Americans," edited by Harold Stearns. Santayana's comments are in reality "marginal notes" and display him in his most witty, ironical vein, with of course glints of seriousness now and then. He foresees that he is to hear "the plaints of superior and highly critical minds, suffering from maladaptation," and will learn "more about their palpitating doubts than about America or civilization." For these critics are not truly Americans; they are perhaps emancipated from the "genteel tradition," but they in no way represent or show sympathy with that rough and ready philosophy of its practical, hard-headed successor. Their thrusts at America Santayana takes delight in parrying, sometimes, it must be confessed, out of sheer love of argument or out of scorn for their barbarous style. But more interesting than his thrusts at American critics are Santayana's own interpretations of the American scene. This description of American humor, for instance, suggests similar passages in *Character and Opinion:*

The heartiness of American ways, the feminine gush and the masculine go, the girlishness and high jinks and perpetual joking and obligatory jollity may prove fatiguing sometimes; but children often overdo their sports, which does not prove that they are not spontaneous fundamentally.

And here is an excellent summary of the spirit of modern America.

It is the present task, the present state of business, and present fashion in pleasure that create the hearty unity and universal hum of America—just the unity which these thirty individuals resent, and wish to break up. Why not be patient? Situations change quickly. Why not enjoy moral variety *seriatim* instead of simultaneously? A proof that Americanism is the expression of a present material environment, is that the immigrants at once feel themselves and actually become typical Americans, more instinct with an aggressive Americanism than the natives of Cape Cod or the poor whites in the South. Another consequence is that the whole world is being Americanized by the telephone, the trolley car, the department store, and the advertising press. Americanism, apart from the genteel tradition, is simply modernism—purer in America than elsewhere because less impeded and qualified by survivals of the past, but just as pure in Spanish-Italian Buenos Aires as in Irish Jewish New York.

And certain traits of American modernity are to be genuinely admired. Consider architecture, for instance.

The architects are intelligent and well-informed; they are beginning to be prudent; and public taste is very watchful and discriminating. It is not in churches nor in great official edifices that artistic success or originality can be expected, but rather in engineering works, such as skyscrapers, or else in ordinary private houses, such as in England are called cottages and in America "homes." Shaded streets of detached villas, each in its pocket-handkerchief of land, are distinctively American. With a little more solidity in the materials and a little more repose in the designs, they might be wholly pleasing; and if sometimes they seem chaotic and flimsy, as if they were a row of band-boxes laid on the ground and not houses built on foundations, perhaps they only express the better the shifting population which they shelter. They are the barracks of industrialism, which cannot live in the country, but is spilled out of the towns.

And if modernism is to be found in its most pure state in the large cities, the countryside is therefore not to be despised. Santayana says, "But what surprises me more than disbelief in democracy, is this hatred of the country-side. Is agriculture the root of evil? Naturally, the first rays of the sun must strike the east side of New York, but do they never travel beyond?" It is quite apparent from these remarks that Santayana is coming to admire America the more, the longer he says away from her shores. He is even resolved to defend her from the calumny of her own critics. And even if there are grains of truth in some of their indictments, can the situation be so desperate, can civilization be at such a low ebb, when "thirty such spirits can be brought together in a jiffy, by merely whistling for them"?

"The Genteel Tradition at Bay" is directed at the so-called new humanists, who like the critics above are militantly aroused to attack the prevailing order of things in America. But unlike the preceding critics, the humanists seem to Santayana the direct scions of conservative, traditional New England, in short "the genteel tradition." Santayana seems to enjoy all this critical warfare over humanism which has raged in America during the last few years. The genteel tradition, instead of melting "gracefully into the active mind of the country," as it seemed likely to do twenty years ago, is now "raising its head more admonishingly than ever, darting murderous glances at its enemies, and protesting that it is not genteel or antiquated at all, but orthodox and immortal. Its principles, it declares, are classical, and its true name is Humanism."

Santayana's comments on the new humanism are in many instances illuminating. He defines its pedigree more accurately than do the humanists themselves. It is not the humanism of the Renaissance that they derive from, but the medieval Christianity which the Renaissance burst asunder. Renaissance humanism, and the whole course of modern history, have been attempts at a "many sided insurrection of the unregenerate natural man, with all his physical powers and affinities, against the regimen of Christendom." The old humanists were "pleasantly learned men, free from any kind of austerity," who "believed in the sufficient natural goodness of mankind, a goodness humanised by frank sensuality and a wink at all amiable vices; their truly ardent morality . . . flashed out in their hatred of cruelty and oppression . . . their scorn of imposture."

There is, however, a justification for the new humanism in that the old humanism has spent its strength. It has ended at last

> . . . in a pensive agnosticism and a charmed culture, as in the person of Matthew Arnold. It is against this natural consequence of the old humanism that the new American humanists, in a great measure, seem to be protesting. They feel the lameness of that conclusion; and indeed a universal culture always tolerant, always fluid, smiling on everything exotic and on everything new, sins against the principle of life itself.

We exist by distinction, by integration round a specific nucleus according to particular pattern. Life demands a great insensibility, as well as a great sensibility. If the humanist could really live up to his ancient maxim, *humani nil a me alienum puto,* he would sink into moral anarchy and artistic impotence—the very things from which our liberal, romantic world is so greatly suffering. The three R's of modern history, the Renaissance, the Reformation, and the Revolution, have left the public mind without any vestige of discipline.

Whether Matthew Arnold, or even Charles Eliot Norton, was ever as fluid and tolerant as Santayana asserts, it is quite clear that Santayana is debating the old issue of culture versus *Kultur,* and is lining up the modern stout humanists against the tender ones of the past. Humanism, he feels, is a modern revival of *Kultur,* and it should openly seek supernatural support for its authoritative pronouncements. The humanists have made a step in this direction in their notion of an "ethical imagination" above natural explanation and natural control. And for the authority of the church they substitute the authority of tradition crystallized in the finest minds of civilization, hoping in this way to arrive at a universal moral criterion. But the Catholic Santayana holds such an "imagination" erroneous and such an authority at the mercy of the utilitarian and the relativist. The humanists would do better to "reinstate a settled belief in a supernatural human soul and in a precise divine revelation." Then, "instead of expiring of fatigue, or evaporating into a faint odor of learning and sentiment hanging about Big Business," the genteel tradition would be "mounting again to its divine source. In its origin it was a severe and explicit philosophy, Calvinism; not essentially humanistic at all, but theocratic."

Now Santayana has a certain sympathy with supernaturalism. His Catholic habits of thought hate a shoddy, spineless liberalism, and there would be something austerely grand and satisfying about an "eternal criterion, apart from all places, persons, and times, by which everything should be judged." "To reinstate absolutism philosophically would be a great feat, and would prove the hopeless perversity of relaxing integrity in any degree whatever." What consolation to stout moralists everywhere! But the naturalist in Santayana will not be stilled. Christianity's report of the cosmos is too human for it to be credible.

How shall any detached philosopher believe that the whole universe, which may be infinite, is nothing but an enlarged edition, or an expurgated edition of human life? This is only a daylight religion; the heavens in its view are near, and pleasantly habitable by the Olympians; the spheres fit the earth like a glove; the sky is a tent spread protectingly or shaken punitively over the human nest.

And is there need after all for a morality dependent upon supernaturalism? "The particular regimen sanctified by Platonic and Christian moralists" is not unacceptable; "but they did not require any supernatural assistance to draw it up. They simply received back from revelation the humanism which they had put into it."

Santayana's third article, "The Moral Adequacy of Naturalism," is in reality an epitome of his whole moral philosophy. In many ways it recapitulates the ethics of *The Life of Reason,* but with more emphasis upon spirituality and less upon utility. Santayana's preference is of course for a morality based on natural, not supernatural, sanctions. Such a morality will naturally be more humble, less disposed to dictate its mandates to all humanity. It will encourage variety and breed tolerance. "Nothing is more multiform than perfection. No interest, no harmony, shuts out the legitimacy or the beauty of any other." It will be individualistic because "the only natural unit in morals is the individual man.... The state is only a necessary cradle for the body of the individual, and nursery for his mind."

What, then, is binding about a naturalistic morality; wherein is its stoutness, its authority? "Is there anything compulsory in reason?" asks Santayana. And he answers unhesitatingly, Yes.

In the mindful person the passions have spontaneously acquired a sense of responsibility to one another; or if they still allow themselves to make merry separately—because liveliness in the parts is a good without which the whole would be lifeless—yet the whole possesses, or aspires to possess, a unity of direction, in which all the parts may conspire, even if unwittingly.

As in *The Life of Reason,* morality demands harmony, order, leads to perfection. And since human nature has its limits and its uniformity as well as its inner flexibility, a rational morality will not be merely wayward and variable. "The living organism is not infinitely elastic." A certain "animal obstinacy is the backbone of all virtue." But the rigidity of rational morality will be determined by its natural basis, nothing more.

Blindness to the biological truth about morality is not favorable to purity of moral feeling: it removes all sense of proportion and relativity; it kills charity, humility, and humor; and it shuts the door against that ultimate light which comes to the spirit from the spheres above morality. . . . Call it humanism or not, only a morality frankly relative to man's nature is worthy of man, being at once vital and rational, martial and generous; whereas absolutism smells of fustiness as well as of faggots.

And on the higher level of spirituality,

. . . pure reason in the naturalist may attain, without subterfuge, all the spiritual insights which supernaturalism goes so far out of the way to inspire. . . . That the fruition of happiness is intellectual (or as perhaps we should now call it, aesthetic) follows from the comprehensive scope of that intuition in which happiness is realised, a scope which distinguishes happiness from carnal pleasures; for although happiness, like everything else, can be experienced only in particular moments, it is found in conceiving the total issue and ultimate fruits of life; and no passing sensation or emotion could be enjoyed with a free mind, unless the blessing of reason and of a sustained happiness were felt to hang over it. . . . In raising truth to intuition of truth, in surveying the forms and places of many things at once and conceiving their movement, the intellect performs the most vital of possible acts, locks flying existence, as it were, in its arms, and stands, all eyes and breathless, at the top of life.

In these three articles, as shrewd and seasoned as any moral philosophy he has composed, Santayana restates in the light of his mature thought his early faith in a morality grounded in nature, dedicated to reason, and lighted up by an idealism as pure as it is disillusioned.

The criticism of America voiced in *The Genteel Tradition at Bay* is continued in *The Last Puritan,* Santayana's only novel, whose unexpected brilliance and timeliness brought a reticent philosopher within the glare of book clubs and best-seller lists. *The Last Puritan,* is not, however, something manufactured for the times or a mere bid for popularity. No living writer cares less than Santayana what his contemporaries think of him; and, besides, *The Last Puritan* is the work of a lifetime, a *jeu d'esprit* of a philosopher's idle moments, hardly intended for publication at all. Santayana tells us he conceived the idea of the novel in the early nineties, but allowed it to lie unfinished for want of invention until life in England during the War revived his interest in undergraduates and gave him the necessary perspective to carry out his original plan with some semblance of dramatic unity and upon a larger stage. Even as late as 1932, however, the book was still incomplete, and Santayana informed the present writer he was undecided whether to publish it. Fortunately for his readers he did so, for *The Last Puritan* adds to his stature as a literary artist, and reveals many of the facets of his philosophy in a new light which is at once objective and intimate.

As a study of American manners the book is acute and masterly. It attacks anew the "genteel tradition," but with more kindliness and humor than there was in the essays. The Boston of Santayana's youth is recreated before our eyes with a gentle irony which spares none of its asperities, yet somehow folds everything in a mellow haze of reminiscence. Old Nathaniel Alden, genteel to the bone yet angular and uncompromising, must have had his many counterparts in the Beacon Street of the nineties—with his taste for good business and bad art, his cramped enthusiasms and his agonized conscience. And Peter Alden, black sheep that he is, takes us down from that "red-brick world" of respectability to the dim purlieus of South Boston, where a freer and friendlier existence behind doors and around corners shocked the puritans on the Hill and occasionally enticed one of their number from the path of duty. Even the minor personages, the hearty doctor with more than a suggestion of Oliver Wendell Holmes, the bland Unitarian clergyman, are expressions of their age and their city. But the "genteel tradition" is not confined to Boston; watered with worldliness and provinciality, it is even more repulsive in the person of Harriet Alden, the mother of the "last puritan," who rules her Connecticut household with an ugly blend of feminine frailty and puritan strength. This suburban gentility, reconciled to material progress, fond of display and fearful of reputation, is a more unlovely thing than the starkness of Nathaniel Alden. But there were rebels in those days, and Peter Alden and Harold van de Weyer in their escape from the genteel tradition, in their refuge in irony and art, in their very frustration stand for some of Santayana's associates, perhaps the more emancipated of his classmates and students, who tried vainly to expatriate themselves from a *milieu* which, though they spurned it, had left its blight upon them too. They were of the world, but their exquisiteness was hothouse and soon perished. Santayana tells us his characters are not "full-length portraits from life"; their sources "were diffused widely and observed somewhat externally"; notwithstanding, *The Last*

Puritan is an indictment, no less vigorous for being gentle and fictitious, of that belated Calvinism whose moral fervor and incapacity for happiness Santayana had dealt with in *Character and Opinion in the United States* and in his various articles and lectures on the "genteel tradition."

Oliver Alden, the "last puritan," is a scion of the same stock, but he is something more, too. The genteel tradition had become gnarled and cross-grained in men like Nathaniel Alden, or fussy and respectable in women like Harriet Alden, or it might become so lax and so lighted with an inward irony as to produce a Peter Alden or a Charles Eliot Norton. But in Oliver there was a throwback to primitive strength and purity; like the new humanists he was "at bay," aroused against a world which he could not countenance or compromise with. He was a namesake not only of the gentle John Alden, but of the militant Oliver Cromwell as well.

In many ways Oliver is a product of his environment; his weaknesses are particularly American. He is the prey of every subscription list and every call to the colors; out of supposed duty he dissipates his energy in a constant round of things he does not want to do but does because it is expected of him. School, college, life itself make a conformist out of one who would dedicate himself to an original and worthy aim. Worse, the America of his day gives him no clue as to what that aim should be. With an independent income and a capacity for untiring labor, he can only browse among the dust of ancient philosophers, hoping for some light to dispel the darkness of his soul and point a path of action for him.

But Oliver is more than a bent twig of the genteel tradition in America; he would not enlist Santayana's admiration and sympathy if he were that and nothing more. Oliver is not the last puritan in a chronological sense; there will never be an end of puritans. Oliver is the ultimate puritan—logically and dynamically. "His puritanism," says Santayana in the prologue, speaking as one of the characters, "had never been mere timidity or fanaticism or calculated hardness: it was a deep and speculative thing: hatred of all shams, scorn of all mummeries, a bitter merciless pleasure in the hard facts." The grandeur of early puritanism looked out in his singlemindedness and integrity. Oliver's puritanism was a puritanism turned even against itself. "He convinced himself, on puritan grounds, that it was wrong to be a puritan." Yet this convincement could not make him any less a puritan, nor could it bring him any settled peace or happiness. For was not life itself a challenge to the puritan conscience, a summons to duty? And yet what duty? Life gave Oliver no clear pattern by which to order his own life or the lives of others. Thus he remained baffled and frustrated throughout his brief existence, and longevity would have left him unchanged, because, as Santayana is careful to point out, his wilful nature would never have profited by experience.

Beside Oliver is placed Mario van de Weyer, his cousin, of mingled American and Italian stock, but essentially Latin in his playful spirit and his amused acceptance of life.

Mario [says Santayana] like Oliver, was late-born. The two were differently aristocratic, and belonged to the past rather than to the future. Only Mario, being less serious and more adaptable, could make the best of his good luck, and sail before the wind without pretending to have any firm hold on reality. He was healthy and therefore bold, humble and therefore facile. His ability to laugh at everything, including himself, made it easy for him to put up with the mixed loose world in which he lived, and positively to enjoy it: easier, too, than for Oliver, much easier, to put up with himself.

Mario has his youthful flings, skirts the jagged edges of life, and grows gracefully into a respectable Roman with a charming family and a calm haven in the Church. "Gallantry in a gentleman"—and Mario, or Vanny as his admirers call him, is every inch a gentleman—"passes easily into chivalry, and chivalry into religion." He is the anti-puritan, the foil to Oliver; his destiny on earth is happiness, and the world, Santayana believes, is better off for him and his kind. "Any future worth having" will spring from such men, not from "weedy intellectuals or self-inhibited puritans."

The puritan is condemned before the bar of Santayana's judgment, but not without a fair hearing or even a secret sympathy. There is something admirable about the "pure" puritan, something beautiful in his simple grandeur. As Santayana says to Mario in the prologue,

You and I are not puritans; and by contrast with our natural looseness, we can't help admiring people purer than ourselves, more willing to pluck out the eye that offends them, even if it be the eye for beauty, and to enter halt and lame into the kingdom of singlemindedness. I don't prefer austerity for myself as against abundance, against intelligence, against the irony of ultimate truth. But I see that in itself, as a statuesque object, austerity is more beautiful, and I like it in others.

And in a way puritanism is perhaps one of the eternal and elemental attitudes of the human spirit. "Puritanism is a natural reaction against nature."

There is a kind of initial earnestness in all life which in some people remains predominant; a certain soulfulness and idealism which the Germans attribute especially to themselves, but which they would probably recognize also in the deeper intuitions of English poetry. It is a mood proper to youth; and youth in a race ... can only mean that at a given juncture sentiment, fancy, and dialectic have outrun external experience.

The Nordic, Santayana believes, has never outgrown this elemental earnestness, or the confused wilfulness which accompanies it. The Latin and the Catholic, beside this youthful cloudiness "were born clear," and do not have to "achieve clearness." "The mind of the East or South, the mind of fatigued and long-indoctrinated races" is "for the most part unblushingly subservient to interest, passion, or superstition ... yet in its reflective phase detached and contemplative, able occasionally to despise all entanglements, to dominate the will, and to look truth in the eye without blinking."

Mario and Oliver represent, then, two racial or geographical antipodes as well as two moral ones. Oliver fits almost perfectly Santayana's description of Hamlet, the supreme manifestation of Nordic genius. Oliver, like Hamlet, "is strong in his integrity and purity of purpose, but lost in floating emotion, perplexed by want of concentration and of self-knowledge." The puritanism of Oliver and Hamlet does not construct systems or dragoon peoples under the heavy yoke of *Kultur*. It is at once less blinded and less clear. It has too much of reason and sensitiveness to play the tyrant, even to follow doggedly a fixed idea; but it has not the insight into external nature or human nature to integrate wisely its own life, let alone the lives of others. It remains tender and puzzled, dreamful and futile.

It is true there is a strain of puritanism in all prophets and lawgivers, in Socrates, Buddha, Christ. The "stout" attitude everywhere is puritanical—arbitrary, compulsive, tyrannical even. Now Oliver was "pure" enough, but he was neither sufficiently rational nor sufficiently spiritual to be a leader of men. He remained tied to and dissipated by many little loyalties, filial, athletic, friendly, which sapped his strength and obscured his vision.

His great error was that he tried to be commonplace. His vocation remained vague: he had not the insight or the courage to make it definite. In vain the Vicar reminded him that Christ had not been a soldier or an athlete or a lover of women or a merchant or a statesman or even (though the Vicar did not say so) a professor of philosophy or a believing Christian.

If only Oliver had had Emerson's will to say no. In this lack lay his tragedy.

In certain respects *The Last Puritan* recalls *Dialogues in Limbo* and even *Lucifer*. Like them it is a dramatic presentation of profound contrasts of thought. Santayana's latest preface makes clear what the present writer, for one, had long surmised. Outwardly there is less autobiography in *The Last Puritan* than the prologue and epilogue and the presence of the author as one of the characters would lead the unwary to believe. Of course, the backgrounds are those of Santayana's varied residence, but the characters are composite and largely fictitious. Inwardly, however, the book is more intimately Santayana's than any mere "memoir" could be. The reason all of the characters speak like Santayana (a defect from a literary standpoint, as has been often pointed out) is that they actually speak his thoughts and feel his feelings. As in the dialogues, he can faithfully represent varied points of view not only because his sympathies are wide and elastic but also because he has himself held, if only temporarily, these points of view. The characters of *The Last Puritan,* says Santayana, "were originally contrasted and spontaneous potentialities" within him, and "by no means vehicles" for his own "later conventional personality or approved thoughts." Certainly Mario is his Latin "looseness," his bundle of "easier attitudes," with something of the sensuous Aristippus of the dialogues and the youthful, sportive Hermes of *Lucifer*. And just as certainly Peter Alden is his ironic detachment, his refusal to take everything seriously because it takes itself so. Peter is Santayana the critic, and of all the characters voices most of the sentiments which seem unmistakably Santayana's. His uncompromising intellect, tempered by his quiet resignation and his sympathy with even such irrationalities as English authority and Roman religion, brings him close to the mature Santayana, who feels that the world is a sorry, mad affair, but that the gentleman's lot is quietly to accept it. Peter is the "tender" Santayana, soft in regard to almost everything except romantic egotism. But firmer loyalties of Santayana are represented too: to Catholicism in crotchety old Caleb Weathertree, with his unabashed supernaturalism; to art in the aesthetic Harold van de Weyer. Even Santayana's delight in the English character finds expression in the robust manliness of Jim Darnley and the "contentment in finitude" of his father, the Anglican vicar, perhaps the most sympathetically drawn character in the book. I believe Oliver, too, is a part of Santayana, perhaps a throwback to those youthful days when the world was "ashes in the mouth," when romantic pessimism made truth or religion worth sacrificing oneself for, before Spinoza led Santayana to accept the universe as given and "go about the business of one's heart or one's country." We all have a puritan in us more or less; irony and tolerance are only late growths, the veneer of civilization. And there is something, too, of Santayana in the disavowals of Oliver, in his hatred of cheap worldliness, his frugality, his contempt for hypocrisy and sentimental illusion. Oliver at times recalls the melancholy austerity of Lucifer, lonely and embittered in his allegiance to truth, or the similar Democritus of the dialogues. I believe these recurrent attitudes express something deep and vital in Santayana himself, a "stoutness" which his later irony and tolerance have controlled but not entirely obliterated. It is not mere careless workmanship that Oliver, like the other major characters of *The Last Puritan,* speaks in the idiom of Santayana himself.

But what of *The Last Puritan* as a novel? If the characters are mental perspectives, cultural, national, even personal, have they the objectivity, the flesh and blood, of real persons? Yes, I should say, to an unexpected degree. Santayana in his novel is far more successful in creating the illusion of fiction than in either his play or his dialogues. *The Last Puritan* is a novel of ideas, but it is equally a novel of personalities, of real people living real lives. How accurately Santayana has drawn his backgrounds, and how dramatically he has sketched in his incidents. From the scrawny, cluttered landscape of suburban America to the quiet lushness of Iffley meadows we see these scenes, and if the characters speak a purer English than they would in real life, at least their language is charged not only with ideas but with overtones of emotion as well. Oliver in particular, the masterpiece of the book, lives before our eyes in all his perplexity, his sensitiveness, his youthful seriousness. And Mario, lovable Vanny, child and man in one, is every inch a real person, whom it would be a pleasure to meet and know, whom one seems to have known, so intimately is he presented. Even the women: timid, fluttery Letitia

Lamb; Mrs. Darnley, plebeian and motherly; the ruthlessly competent Harriet; Irma the German governess, buxom and sentimental, are more than abstractions or caricatures. And Santayana shows in Edith that he can understand and create a woman of refinement who in addition to her poise and judgment is every inch a woman. Her relationship to Oliver and the parallel relationship of Rose Darnley to Oliver are presented with an unexpected sensitiveness to the feminine mind and heart. Santayana understands love not only Platonically, but also, as *Reason in Society* might have intimated, in terms of its physical undercurrents and even its blandishments and evasions. Oliver's inability to charm either Edith or Rose because of his imperious egotism, for he is at bottom thoroughly self-centered, is certainly believable. Just as understandable is Vanny's power over women. Yes, one may enjoy *The Last Puritan* as a story without any theoretical interest in Puritanism, or the genteel tradition, or the Latin and Nordic minds. The surprising thing is that a philosopher should have written so good a story.

In fact, on the plane of fiction I see less to quarrel with the book than on the plane of philosophy. Even the puritan—as a fictional character—is presented fairly and sympathetically. But beneath the story stands a condemnation of the puritan, of the Nordic, of the genteel tradition, which is more categorical, perhaps because playful and dramatic, than were the essays devoted to the subject. Of course, to brand everything Nordic as cloudy and everything Latin as clear is a frank enthronement of the personal equation which, however honest it may be, is certainly unphilosophic. Just as personal and sentimental is Santayana's condonement of everything Catholic and harsh rejection of everything Protestant, his acceptance of illusion when mellowed by the English climate and contempt for it in the garish light of America. Beauty and grace go far with Santayana in molding his preferences. Puritanism is naturally an unlovely thing, wayward, formless, unaesthetic; but one may question whether the fluttering, bird-like existence of Vanny is any finer in the scale of moral values, any truer to the deeper impulses of man and his higher aspirations. To the Anglo-Saxon he will seem necessarily effeminate and frivolous; I suspect he would have seemed so too to the ancient Greeks. Moral earnestness, alone or ill directed, results in just such futility as Oliver's, but life without moral earnestness seems a tinkling of empty chimes. Has Santayana forgotten the deep refrain of his early poems "Midnight" and "In Grantchester Meadows," the "true unhappy human things"? At the risk of being considered another "last puritan," I must say Santayana's statement that "any future worth having will spring from" men like Mario is in my judgment simply unthinkable. Van Tender has merely forgotten the ineradicable stoutness in the human organism itself. The "initial earnestness in all life" re-forms the flux of consciousness and then the environment of the organism; to re-form is native to life at all its stages. Order and civilization itself are products of reform. Irony and playfulness and contemplation are fine things in their way, but they are less fundamental, less native to the human mind than reform. Observe, too, that Oliver is not merely a reformer of others' lives; his whole being cries out against the petty meddlesomeness of most puritans. His greatest task is to reform himself, to perfect his own life. He is in his puzzled way perfectionist as well as humanitarian. As Henry Seidel Canby says in his admirable review of *The Last Puritan,* "Santayana's puritans . . . are men and women resolved first of all to govern themselves and to consent only to such life as seems to them best. They carry a burning coal of perfection at their heart. And so they fail, or at least Oliver fails, because he would triumph fastidiously or not at all." I certainly feel with Ellen Glasgow that he is the only one in the book "who proves himself to be capable of a genuine passion for reality, of a bitter merciless pleasure in the hard facts."

In everything Santayana writes, a large part of the reader's pleasure is in the incidental beauties which frame in the main argument. These are particularly abundant in *The Last Puritan.* An old acquaintance will find in the novel many of Santayana's favorite themes of discourse, no less miniature essays for being put in the mouths of the characters. There is the familiar scorn of romantic genius and German metaphysics, the delight in rural England, the admiration for Latin grace and British manliness, the ironical laughter over American education. There is the thrill of football, the charm of quiet work, the sense of the ocean as "an ironical background," the passage of cloud castles, the longing for "pure spirit," the "human scale" of British architecture. The progress of Oliver's childhood even recapitulates the evolution of consciousness as described in *Reason in Common Sense.* Truly *The Last Puritan* is a kind of itinerary of Santayana's mental journeys; it really has soaked up the idiosyncrasies as well as the wisdom of a lifetime.

Yet it is not Santayana's masterpiece in point of style. Simpler and more readable than most of Santayana, it does not often attain to the unique excellence of his prose at its best. Lovers of Attic prose may prefer it to the royal purple of the soliloquies or *The Realms of Being,* but elaborateness and ornament rather become Santayana, and he is more at ease with them than with the simple transparency which fiction demands of style. But if *The Last Puritan* is less lyrical, less majestic than the recent Santayana, it has much of the snap and sparkle of his earlier epigrammatic style. "The music was classical and soothing, the service High Church Unitarian, with nothing in it either to discourage a believer or to annoy an unbeliever." "Even if you were doing nothing morally wrong, to be unobserved was always reassuring. It restored to you half of that negative blessedness which you would have enjoyed if you had been non-existent." And nowhere else has Santayana been freer to indulge his zest for ironical humor. Who will forget poor old Nathaniel Alden riding in a Boston street car.

[He] sat on the edge of the bench, looking fixedly before him, with his hands crossed over the handle of his umbrella and his knees pressed closely together in the vain effort to avoid contact with his neighbors. Beside him was a fussy woman with a baby and a large bundle, which —contrary to the principles of a just democracy—kept rolling about and trespassing on his narrow slice of the public space; but unpleasant as intrusions might be from that quarter, the motionless bulk that pressed against him on his other side was even more objectionable. There a huge red-faced Irish priest sat with one enormous paw spread on each knee; he positively exuded animal heat, and a sort of satisfied determination clinched his brutal jaw. What business, thought Mr. Alden, what business have these gross foreigners among us? Didn't we choose distance to avoid contagion and hard work to escape poverty and superstition? He had never, to his knowledge, actually touched a Catholic before. Probably there was little risk for the moment of *moral* infection, but who could tell what loathsome diseases this fleshly monster might conceal under an appearance of robust health? The man looked like a butcher. Hadn't all priests been butchers originally? What evil omens lay in that word! Yet the public danger of Popery and the Inquisition was perhaps a little distant: more immediate was Mr. Alden's apprehension that the poor woman's baby was about to cry, that it might have some scrofulous ailment, and needed a change of diapers.

Any reader might name his own favorites: perhaps the gushing, garrulous letters of Irma the governess, or the curious prenatal experience of Oliver's, or the ill-concealed love affair of Jim Darnley;

in all of these humorous episodes we are treated to something of the merry, ebullient wit that makes Santayana such a charming conversationalist. We are reminded once more that of all living philosophers Santayana is perhaps the most humorous.

But *The Last Puritan* is not a forced draught of either irony or wit. Mostly the language submerges itself in the main business of telling a story well and charmingly, and that is perhaps as the style of a novel should be. Santayana takes less time out to declaim or rhapsodize than do Pater and Meredith and other novelists who are philosophers and stylists as well. At the same time, we now and then regret that Santayana's prose has to tinker with so much of the machinery of moving people in and out and getting them ready to act their parts—which of course the technique of fiction necessitates. The amenities and absurdities of daily living are not the most suitable theme for Santayana's instrument, and perhaps he wisely reduces them to a minimum. In conversation he can be more truly and comfortably himself.

The Last Puritan, of course, sharpens one's interest in the long-standing question, what is the relation of Santayana to America, his home for forty years? How wise a judge is he of America? How well does he know this country? In any sense is he an American himself? We have seen how penetrating, how uncannily accurate are Santayana's many studies of America and Americans, how well he sifts out our cultural ingredients, how he understands both our gentility and our rough, raw aggressiveness, how he has done much to focus our attention on these two contrasted sides of our national character. Yet Santayana looks at America as a spectator, an observer of long residence with us, not as an indigenous part of the society he surveys. He is more aware of our contradictions and illogicalities than most Americans would be, but he somehow misses a certain unity which absorbs these contrarieties; dilemmas which seem so sharp to his Latin eyes somehow resolve themselves in that very hearty pragmatism which Santayana recognizes but is really a stranger to. Take his division of this country into the genteel tradition and practical, commercial America. To a logical Latin this distinction is ineradicable, yet in practice the two Americas exist side by side and interpenetrate without serious friction. A note of rebelliousness seems to sound through so much that Santayana writes of America. Walt Whitman and William James are rebels against the genteel tradition; the new humanists are the genteel tradition rebelling against both its former self and the other America. Yet is not this rebelliousness a good deal that of Santayana himself? The key to Santayana's treatment of America, I believe, is to be found in America's treatment of him.

Santayana was never quite at home in either of the two Americas. Practical, money-mad America seemed to him, as it did to his generation at Harvard, hopelessly brash and Philistine. His sensitiveness was bruised by the whirl of modern industrialism. Yet the gentility of Boston and Cambridge offended him as much as the hustle and bustle of New York. Something about smug old Boston got under his skin. He appreciated its kindliness and culture at arm's length, but he mocked it inwardly because, perhaps, he thought it mocked him. A whimsical remark of Santayana's in a recent paper throws more light on his relation to Boston than its genial pleasantry would at first suggest. Speaking of social visits, Santayana says,

Sometimes a sweet creature would ask you to call. With some trepidation you walked up the handsome flight of brown stone steps that led to the abode of Elegance. You were kept waiting a long time for that impossible door to open. . . . Within, all was solemnity and hush: thick carpets drowned your footsteps. . . . You had a terrible feeling that you were not expected and not wanted; the simplicity and naturalness of the inmates, when finally one or two appeared, surprised and reassured you. These ladies were gentle, they were witty, above all they were kind; yet somehow you felt that you had interrupted their nap, that they had changed their clothes and smoothed their hair before coming down to receive you. Moreover, you were sure they would have received anybody else with the same sweetness and the same civility. No, you didn't call again.*

I am afraid Santayana never quite penetrated the reserve of Beacon Street, was never quite taken into its heart. For the most part he accepted Boston with amused tolerance; only once do we learn of the impatient scorn which festered long in his bosom. Replying to William James's caustic remarks on *Interpretations of Poetry and Religion,* Santayana with unprecedented bitterness exclaims,

You tax me several times with impertinence and superior airs. I wonder if you realize the years of suppressed irritation which I have passed in the midst of an unintelligible, sanctimonious and often disingenuous Protestantism, which is thoroughly alien and repulsive to me, and the

* Represented by courtesy of the Boston Latin School Association.

need I have of joining hands with something far away from it and far above it.

It is true the dispute is over technical philosophy, but more than technical philosophy, a whole environment and social order must have struck such sparks of indignation from Santayana's temper. No wonder the irony of Santayana's backward glances at the genteel tradition. No wonder a rebelliousness nearer to that of Henry James and Peter Alden than to anything William James or Whitman could have felt. As a result, Santayana's criticism of America is at times more personal than judicious. He dyes his subject with his own feelings. The genteel tradition may be impoverished and sad, but it is not so to itself, as Santayana at times would almost imply. Nor does everyone who rises above it feel strangely blessed and yet strangely empty. I am sure Poe and Hawthorne and Emerson did not seem to themselves "employed on a sort of inner play, or digestion of vacancy . . . in danger of being morbid, or tinkling, or self-indulgent." Nor is the most sensitive and disillusioned heir of the genteel tradition, say an Oliver Alden, doomed to isolation and futility. As Henry S. Canby rightly says, Santayana "is thinking too much in terms of his selected Harvard experience. He knew his young Americans at the youthful peak of their intellectual intolerance. He knew America outside the college only as they knew it—a lovable country content with mediocrity. But surely it is by the wedding of such potential leadership as theirs and Oliver's with a hearty animal faith that civilizations are saved or made." Oliver, it is true, had not the "hearty animal faith," but he too was an intellectual of the nineties and of the Harvard stamp. "Surely not all the Olivers will die discouraged and futile," and I think Mr. Canby is right.

Now that Santayana has removed himself from America, he is kindlier toward the "gush and go" of American life, but his bitterness against the genteel tradition is a lifelong aversion. What, then, is the effect of Santayana's residence in America upon Santayana himself? Well, I believe America strengthened his detachment and irony by driving him the more within himself. It did not make him more European, but it made him fonder of Europe. For if Santayana is not American, neither is he European in any indigenous sense. As one commentator rightly points out, "Santayana's admiration for many . . . things remote in time and space has about it some of the enthusiasm of the expatriate. It is hard to imagine a lifelong resident of Europe becoming quite so lyrical about classicism, and for this America must be held responsible." But America affected Santayana positively as well as negatively. "Thoroughly American" and "the fruit of association with such men as William James" is his "almost pragmatic confidence in his own commonsense investigations of the universe, unshaken by all the terrifying discoveries of the epistemologists. . . . Thus to brush aside shelves of modern philosophy, and to evaluate all the realms of being, as it were right out of one's head, displays a daring that is Greek or Elizabethan or American, certainly not modern European." If Europe gave Santayana her traditions, America gave him something of her jaunty assurance, her frank self-confidence.

And yet one hardly thinks of America as one sees Santayana today. Except that his enunciation still carries something of the cultivated Bostonese of his day, one finds little in Santayana to associate with any particular country. He seems too much a man of the world, perhaps of another world more sane and detached and pure than ours. Not that Santayana today is out of touch with this world; though he travels little, he is intensely interested in the world at large, and still follows with curiosity the pageant of history. He is particularly interested in our own American scene, even, when I saw him, to the point of finding out the exact status of the Eighteenth Amendment. The progress of philosophy, of course, he follows closely; in fact, the only writings he seems entirely ignorant of are the numerous reviews and criticisms of his own work which have sprung up in the last few years. He says, "I don't hear of these things, which the authors seem too modest to send me. They probably think it inconceivable that I shouldn't be better informed." As for Santayana's own work, his mind works faster than his pen can record. Two volumes of *The Realms of Being* remain to be completed, although most of the material for them is already written out. Numerous smaller pieces are lying around, waiting to be gathered into a collection he would like to call "Symptoms." There is still a store of mental energy in Santayana. Large undertakings do not daunt him; he recently set out to reread the complete works of Shakespeare, to see how time had changed his estimate of the great Elizabethan.

Santayana is often described as unsocial. He does have few friends, especially of his own age, and does not go out of his way to seek acquaintance with other philosophers or men of letters. He admits that he has never had a French friend, the novelty of the experience would interest him, and he never met even his most distinguished compatriot, Miguel Unamuno. He says little men are more pleasant companions than great men, who are almost always insufferable bores. If some of those traits seem unsocial, Santayana is nevertheless a most jolly, good-humored person. He welcomes visitors even if he refuses to return their visits. He is fond of young people and takes great pleasure in showing them the sights of Rome, a delightful excursion with such a guide. In conversation his mirth is constantly ruffled into those silvery ripples of laughter which no one who has ever heard them will forget. He loves a good story, and tells one with gusto himself. For his wit is ever ready to illuminate an incongruity, and his eyes fairly sparkle as he recalls some incident of pompous affectation or ludicrous taste. The stern irony of his writing softens and unbends in personal intercourse; there is always bright laughter and a kindly twinkle to take away its sharp edge.

But Santayana is not always amused or amusing. He can be serious on occasion and in the middle of a luncheon conversation discuss the most abstruse philosophical problems—but with a wind-blown lightness and grace. For he is always urbane, even when he is most technical. And beneath the whimsicalities of his temperament there is a clear, steady outlook on life; the surface is all animation, light and sparkle, but beneath is the steady radiance of vision. Thus Santayana seems both old and young at the same time; in spite of his wisdom and his graying and thinning hair, there is something naïve and unspoiled in his manner, something fresh and youthful in his enthusiasms.

Outwardly his life is much the same as it was when he studied at Harvard and in Germany; there has been little to ruffle its even surface, and he would be the first to admit that the fates have smiled kindly upon him. He has chosen to live out his bachelorhood at Rome largely because Rome of all places on earth brings him closest to the twin traditions of the ancient and Christian worlds. Here is not only the antique past in ruin and monument but also a distillation of the classic and Catholic spirit dear to his Latin heart. His leisurely round of activities is well described by Van Meter Ames in a recent essay.

He says that walking is the best exercise for a philosopher, and usually strolls alone, unaware of traffic except when the difficulty of talking makes him realize the noise. In the middle of the street, with cars whizzing all around him, he said by way of reassurance, "They don't run over you." He likes to climb the Spanish Steps for a turn on the Pincio where he enjoys the view over the Piazzo del Popolo, with the dome of St. Peter's in the distance. He takes pleasure in the shade of the trees but does not know their names, because he is city-bred. To him the charm of the Borghese Gardens is their verdure. Here and there they suggest to him a passage in Virgil or Horace, and the stadium by the tall umbrella pines reminds him of a Greek tragedy he heard in Athens. He has a bench in the sun where he sits on cool days, and a shady one, against the rocks near the temple of Esculapius, that he saves for warm weather. As he likes to read in the open, he often cuts apart an unbound book and carries a section of it in his pocket—enough for one sitting. . . . Having seen all the show-places he has no curiosity about what is there, but he does like to go to the Pantheon, which is more religious to him than most churches.

Santayana is fond of conversation, and his *obiter dicta* are priceless for their sparkle and shrewdness. Yet Professor Ames's delightful record of them only confirms my own impression that they should not be taken too seriously. The significant utterances of Santayana have been put into print, and his chance opinions of this and that today are interesting as curios but are often merely the *badinage* of a man who is now content to sit back and enjoy this strange, hopeless muddle of a world. For the present Santayana is more tender than stout, and sentiment has more and more crept into his dislikes and enthusiasms. He seems now to admire modern dictatorships despite his careful analysis of their faults in *The Life of Reason* and his advocacy of "English Liberty" in *Character and Opinion in the United States*. At that, his partiality is to Italian dictatorships; not even a dictator can make Germany palatable. Italian conquest is classic imperialism; German conquest is barbaric *Kultur*. Communism is a detestable tyranny of mediocrity; he has forgotten it too might have what he once called "its splendid emotions." Even Santayana's firm rationalism of earlier days seems to have slipped a little. He asks in *The Last Puritan* why a man in his seventies should be as stark and relentless in the pursuit of truth as Lucifer and Oliver Alden.

Santayana today is playful and ironic and sentimental when he turns to life, and perhaps he is so because his heart is elsewhere. His delight is more and more in essence, in the realm of spirit, where he has found a timelessness and purity impossible on this earth.

> For we behold, from those eternal towers,
> The deathless beauty of all winged hours,
> And have our being in their truth alone.

Santayana is going to close his literary career as he began it—a poet. More and more *The Realms of Being* bring back the early Santayana with his otherworldliness, with his almost ascetic rapture over pure beauty and the ideal world. He has rediscovered in the heart of metaphysics that perfection he vainly sought in the church, in nature, and in reason. He has come full circle back to a Platonic insight that looks upon all life as fleeting and imperfect and somehow unsatisfactory. He is at last a "free soul," bound to this earth by only the slightest of ties, and ever ready to turn his back upon these. For spirituality means to Santayana, as it meant to the early Christians, a renunciation of the world—not literally, of course, rather a rising above all earthly attachments and contingencies. The "proper function" of spirit is

> ... to see such things as come in its way under the form of eternity, in their intrinsic character and relative value, in their transitiveness and necessity, in a word, in their truth. This contemplative habit evidently finds a freer course in solitude than in society, in art than in business, in prayer than in argument. It is stimulated by beautiful and constant things more than by things ugly, tedious, crowded, or uncertain.

This natural mysticism, if it be called such, is delightful to the disciplined yet sensitive mind. But Santayana is not willing to abandon himself completely to its allurements. His chosen field, he says, is moral philosophy, and pure spirituality is a disintoxication from even moral concerns. He is still enough of a Greek to be drawn occasionally to human affairs, and not enough of an Indian to turn his back utterly on this world. At that, he has become increasingly with the years a Platonic rather than a Socratic Greek; this change of direction of his later philosophy was well described by him when his publishers reissued *The Life of Reason* in 1922.

> What lay before in the background—nature—has come forward, and the life of reason, which then held the center of the stage, has receded. The vicissitudes of human belief absorb me less; the life of reason has become in my eyes a decidedly episodical thing, polyglot, interrupted, insecure. ... These things seem to me less tragic than they did, and more comic; and I am less eager to choose and to judge among them, as if only one form could be right.

And yet this change of direction does not mean that Santayana's early and late philosophies contradict each other. More recently he has said,

> Spirit and reason, as I use the words, spring from the same root in organic life, namely, from the power of active adaptation possessed by animals, so that the external world and the future are regarded in their action. Being regarded in action, absent things are then regarded in thought; and this is intelligence. [But] spirit is essentially simpler, less troubled, more lyrical than reason: it is not specifically human. . . . In its outlook, far from being absorbed in tasks and cares, like reason, it is initially universal and addressed to anything and everything that there may happen to be. . . . Thus there is a certain option and practical incompatibility between spirituality and humanism, between poetry and business, between sheer logic and sound sense; but the conflict is only marginal, the things are concentric, and spirit merely heightens and universalises the synthesis which reason makes partially, as occasion requires, in the service of natural interests.

The imagination, crowded out of Santayana's early philosophy by the understanding, returns in his later works to its rightful place in the realm of spirit; moreover, it returns enriched as well as chastened. The spiritual life is the supreme manifestation of Santayana's "religion of disillusion."

To some Santayana has seemed a shrinking, sensitive soul, only too ready to build for himself an ivory tower and let the rest of the world muddle through as best it can. Paul Shorey once called him "that dainty, unassimilated man," and William James spoke of his "moribund Latinity." Certainly Santayana was not cut to the bustling, strenuous Anglo-Saxon pattern. And it is true he has not had much sympathy with the active humanitarians or with those leaders of many-sided social movements throughout the modern world. I cannot recall a single reference in all his pages to Kagawa or Gandhi or Lenin. William James's "varieties of religious experience" seemed to him but cases of "religious slumming." He has always been more interested in developing good leaders than in raising the level of those who are to be led. The perfection of the individual rather than the amelioration of the crowd has been his goal—and of late it has seemed to many that he has even despaired of achieving that and turned within himself to a refuge in pure spirit.

All of which may be true, yet it cannot be maintained that Santayana is utterly indifferent to his fellow beings. If the "unhappy human things" of the early poems, the chapter on "Charity" in *The Life of Reason*, the sonnets introducing *Soliloquies in England*, the treatment of Oliver in *The Last Puritan* are not sufficient evidence of Santayana's sympathy and humanity, may I call the reader's attention to a recent letter of his which perhaps more than anything else he has written shows the warmth of feeling beneath his sculptured exterior. He replies to a letter of James concerning *The Life of Reason:*

You say I am less hospitable than Emerson. Of course. Emerson might pipe his wood-notes and chirp at the universe most blandly; his genius might be tender and profound and Hamlet-like, and that is all beyond my range and contrary to my purpose. I am a Latin, and nothing seems serious to me except politics, except the sort of men that your ideas will involve and the sort of happiness they will be capable of. The rest is exquisite moonshine. . . . What did Emerson know or care about the passionate insanities and political disasters which religion, for instance, has so often been another name for? He could give that name to his last personal intuition, and ignore what it stands for and what it expresses in the world. It is the latter that absorbs me; and I care too much about mortal happiness to be interested in the charming vegetation of cancer-microbes in the system—except with the idea of suppressing it.

But Santayana goes on in even more intimate vein:

I have read practically no reviews of my book so that I don't know if anyone has felt in it something which, I am sure, is there. I mean the *tears*. . . . Not that I care to moan over the gods of Greece, turned into the law of gravity, or over the stained glass of cathedrals, broken to let in the sunlight and the air. It is not the past that seems to me affecting, entrancing, or pitiful to lose. It is the ideal. It is that vision of perfection that we just catch, or for a moment embody in some work of art, or in some idealized reality; it is the concomitant inspiration of life, always various, always beautiful, hardly ever expressible in its fulness. And it is my adoration of this real and familiar good, this love often embraced but always elusive, that makes me detest the Absolutes and the dragooned myths by which people try to cancel the passing ideal, or to denaturalize it. That is an inhumanity, an impiety that I can't bear. And much of the irritation which I may betray and which, I assure you, is much greater than I let it seem, comes of affection. It comes of exasperation at seeing the only things that are beautiful or worth having, treated as if they were of no account.

Santayana's love of perfection is a powerful emotion, the aesthetic sensitiveness of the poet deepened and strengthened by the conscience of the moral philosopher. Suffering and misfortune are imperfect and unlovely things; there are certain scenes in literature—in Lear, in Dickens, in Proust—that Santayana skips because he cannot endure their horror. He feels the tragic pulse of life too keenly to enjoy the literary creation of tragedy, unless, as with the ancient Greeks, it is suffused with beauty. In some ways the whole burden of Santayana's philosophy has been to make mankind more genuinely happy by a fuller realization of both its limitations and its possibilities. Certainly the most exacting moralist cannot call that an unworthy aim. And if Santayana's methods are not those of the humanitarian and the reformer, his desire to build happiness from within is in the great humanistic tradition and is all the more precious for its rare emphasis upon beauty and harmony and repose.

And lest this attitude seem to be tender to the point of giving up all stoutness, Santayana would have us realize that his philosophy finds a place for both McStout and Van Tender and that their antithesis is more apparent than real:

The antinomy McStout—Van Tender has always had a clear solution—a Spinozistic solution—in my own mind. All my oscillations are within legitimate bounds. For the solution is this: Moral bias is necessary to life; but no particular form of life is necessary to the universe (or even to the human intellect, except the form of intellect itself). All contrary moralities are therefore equally acceptable *prima facie:* but the one organic to any particular species, or nation, or religion, or man must be maintained *there* unflinchingly, without compromise or heresy.

Or again:

If you take the political-moral point of view, and shout for your side in the football match, you are McStout. If you consider the place of shouting and football in the universe, you are Van Tender. The latter is therefore the deeper philosopher: yet the former is the more radical and ineradicable man, because man is an animal before he is a spirit, and can be a spirit only because he is alive, i. e., an animal. The nature of the human animal, however, is to be intelligent, to be speculative; and hence the vocation to transcend the conditions of his existence in his thought and worship.

There is a further reconciliation of the stout and tender points of view in Santayana's lecture, "Ultimate Religion," delivered at The Hague during the tercentenary celebration of Spinoza's birth. Man's ultimate religion must be truthful in a Spinozistic sense, humble and disillusioned and cosmic; yet it must have a feeling for "the moral urgency proper to some particular creature or some particular interest." In both directions it must cherish kindness and love. Its aim must be "to love things spiritually . . . to love the love in them, to worship the good which they pursue, and to see them all prophetically in their possible beauty. To love things as they are would be a mockery of things; a true lover must love them as they would wish to be."

Here is perhaps not only a reconciliation of the stout and tender points of view, but also a final solution to the conflict between charity and philanthropy which Santayana debated in *Dialogues in Limbo.* Charity must be part of an ultimate religion, but it must never degenerate to a mere worship of things as they are, as happened in Walt Whitman; on the other hand philanthropy must base its perfectionism on the needs and wishes of the individual and never be dragooned into a narrow, impoverished *Kultur.* Catholic Christianity and Hellenism find a harmony at last in the wisdom of "Ultimate Religion"; and both are nurtured in a sober, Spinozistic naturalism. This solution had of course been adumbrated in *The Life of Reason* and in *Platonism and the Spiritual Life,* but in "Ultimate Religion" it is set forth with something of the emotional warmth and the persuasiveness of a religion. It is as if Santayana, in giving this last will and testament to humanity, felt a return in the ripe wisdom of old age to the "breathlessness and unction" of his youthful poetry.

The influence of Santayana upon the modern world is steadily growing. It began back in the early years of the century when Santayana was leaving his mark upon a growing body of undergraduates and graduates at Harvard. It is impossible now to measure the debt of a generation of students to the "smooth-browed, frictionless being" who stood in front of them and gave them something of his own serene detachment. Horace Kallen describes him thus:

Those who remember him in the classroom will remember him as a spirit solemn, and sweet and withdrawn; whose Johannine face by a Renaissance painter held an abstracted eye and a hieratic smile, half mischief, half content; whose rich voice flowed evenly, in cadences smooth and balanced as a liturgy; whose periods had the intricate perfection of a poem and the import of a prophecy; who spoke somehow for his hearers and not to them, stirring the depths of their natures and troubling their minds, as an oracle might, to whom pertained mystery and reverence, so compact of remoteness and fascination was he, so moving, and so unmoved. . . . This detachment, which often seemed to me to have a tinge of sadness and insufficiency in it, is a quality of all Mr. Santayana's works and endows them with something of the passionate impersonality of great music.

Upon those who were to become professional philosophers Santayana's influence was varied and subject largely to the laws of personality. Some subsequent distinguished teachers of philosophy seem to have passed through Harvard without feeling any particular attachment to Santayana's person or to his philosophy: Professors Hocking and C. I. Lewis of Harvard, J. C. Boodin of California, and H. C. Brown of Stanford, for instance. Professor Hocking tells us he felt Santayana's "essence inwardly repugnant to my own" and "avoided him to my great loss." But there are others who gladly acknowledge that Santayana was to them a great inspiration, a seminal force. And not only the critical realists, whose relation to Santayana we have observed above. Professor Loewenberg of the University of California says, "Fresh impetus in the direction of Problematic Realism I received later from Mr. Santayana," who "has richly variegated the only theme that really matters in all philosophy: the relation between substantive reality and the translations of it in the polyglot terms of human reason and imagination. . . . Mr. Santayana taught me not to confuse the life of reason with the life of substance." The realism of Santayana was persuasive, too, to Professor Montague of Michigan. "It was a relief to hear Santayana, who had gone through that epistemological hell with his common sense unscathed, talk delightfully and quietly about the various substances of which the world might conceivably be composed." But I suspect Santayana's theory of value had a more widespread influence upon students than his more technical metaphysics. Professor Montague says,

It is to Santayana especially that I owe my realization of Plato's truth. I took his courses at about the same time that I read Huxley's *Evolution and Ethics* and Stevenson's *Pulvis et Umbra*. In all three the teaching was to the effect that value did not depend on existence, nor right on might, nor ethics on religion. An atheistic nature red with tooth and claw could in no sense absolve man from his obligation to actualize ideals of beauty and goodness; nor could it deprive him of the consolation of knowing that those ideals were always and eternally there, be the world what it might. The fact that I did not share the pessimism of Huxley and Santayana as to the existing world in no way lessened my debt of gratitude.

Professor DeWitt Parker of Michigan also attributes to his study under Santayana "an awakening to the problems of value (I still think Santayana's whole metaphysics, with its artifices of matter and essence, however original and beautiful in expression, a sad mistake, while his interpretations of culture remain incomparable in our generation)."

The influence of Santayana's lectures merges with the wider influence of his books, for many of his former students followed the progress of his thought after both they and he had left Harvard. In aesthetics, particularly, his name is still to be conjured with. His psychological approach to beauty and his extension of art to include most fields of human endeavor are acknowledged as permanent contributions by most recent writers on aesthetics. Some aestheticians admit a great personal indebtedness to Santayana. Professor C. J. Ducasse of Brown University, for instance, says, "My obligations to the writings of Mr. Santayana on aesthetics are overwhelming and gratefully acknowledged. His marvellously acute psychological insight has illuminated for me many an obscure problem," in particular, "the conditions under which 'expression,' or . . . aesthetic connotation, comes to be acquired by anything." "With Santayana, I hold that there is no human function that is not at least theoretically capable of contributing something to aesthetic pleasure." This last broadening of the aesthetic experience is also approved by Laurence Buermeyer, who acknowledges Dewey and Santayana as his chief creditors, and follows them in maintaining that "unless art is felt to be something growing out of the interests that supply driving force to our daily life, it will remain the object of concealed or avowed indifference on the public's part, and of academic or dilettante professionalism on the artist's." More specific passages in *The Sense of Beauty* are admired by other writers on aesthetics: the discussion of the relation of evil to beauty, by Helen Parkhurst; the section on multiplicity and uniformity, by Herbert Langfeld. But it would be futile to list all the times Santayana is referred to in recent books on aesthetics; even those who disagree with him often use his verbal felicity to emphasize a point. And traces of his influence are found even where his name is not mentioned. I feel sure much of D. W. Prall's *Aesthetic Judgment,* 1929, stems from Santayana. Not only is Santayana's concept of beauty as objectified pleasure found in Prall's interesting elaboration of the psychology of the aesthetic experience; more to the point, Prall's description of aesthetic judgment suggests both the thought and at times the language of Santayana, the later Santayana of *The Realms of Being* even more than the author of *The Sense of Beauty:*

Not only the physical world but all life is a flux. Beauty, if it is seen or heard or felt, is recognized as a quality supervening upon this flux in some particular situation. And situations are marked for human minds by these supervening qualities and by nothing else. . . . Beauties of all sorts are among determinate qualities. Hence, while beauty is obviously transitory in its occurrence, it is also a defined nature, a specific sort of being. . . . Every beauty is eternally itself, eternal, not as lasting through time, but as in its own nature what it is regardless of time. . . . It simply is what it means, and when and where it is embodied makes no difference to this meaning, nor whether it is ever embodied at all.

This is patently a description of beauty in terms of the realm of essence. Moreover, Prall's treatment of expression reminds one of Santayana, even to the distaste for indeterminate art and for a pale art for art's sake. And Prall's justification of art and the aesthetic experience as conducive to the most sustained and rational happiness, seems to come bodily out of *The Life of Reason.*

A reasonable order of living and of society would bend its energies towards making the surface of its own practical active world satisfactory to the perception that must in any case dwell on it for most of its waking hours. If the forms of human relation and the interactions of individuals also partook of such grace and satisfactoriness to the discriminating view, society would be living a more rational life in a more rationally controlled environment. . . . Such forms would beautify men's whole world, not by suggesting to them what it might be were it another world, but by offering them beauty as its actually present and apparent surface.

I do not mean that Prall's statements are deliberate borrowings; they attest rather to the permanent atmosphere Santayana's rationalism has cast over the whole field of aesthetics, so that many of his judgments have come to seem commonplaces, and the more sane and wise a recent work appears, the more it will seem imbued with his philosophy. So far, his first field of philosophic interest has been the one in which he has exerted the most decisive and sustained influence.

In general, one might say Santayana's attitudes have been more fruitful in recent philosophy than his specific beliefs. He has blown a breath of critical rationalism across the standing pool of metaphysics whose ripples have yet to die down. He has faced life with an uncompromising naturalism, yet has managed to preserve intact the essentially human values. And I believe the cogency of his calm assurance has led many another philosopher to bring to philosophy something of the same courage and reasonableness. This influence of Santayana has never been better acknowledged than by Professor Woodbridge of Columbia:

I may as well say now that the *Life of Reason* is a book I wish I could have written myself. . . . Telling the truth about the life of reason and trying to discover what that truth implies seem to me to be the business of philosophy. I had reached this conviction before I read the *Life of Reason,* but after reading it the conviction had received a force and an illumination which it had not had before. . . . Indeed, if I may use a chemical figure, the reading of Santayana has acted upon my thoughts like a catalysing agent, dissolving them and recombining them in ways better suited to my own satisfaction at least.

It may be that Santayana's most widely and deeply felt influence is just here. Like Socrates, and Emerson after him, he reveals to men more clearly their own half-formed ideas. To be a catalytic is a rôle not unworthy of Santayana the critic and moral philosopher. And I believe his philosophy is still having this effect here and there upon the younger group of American philosophers. If those recently gathered together under the banner, *American Philosophy Today and Tomorrow,* may be said to represent the newer currents of American thought, it is at once obvious that they no longer are exclusively Harvard trained and that they talk more of Dewey and instrumentalism and social objectives than did their so-called "pre-depression elders" of *Contemporary American Philosophy.* None the less, a few of them refer to Santayana, if less frequently; and even if their new, zealous search for happiness in practical life be due to James and Dewey rather than Santayana (*The Life of Reason* notwithstanding), their occasional emphasis upon aesthetic values and their new respect for value itself in an alien world may be traced to Santayana. For instance, when Horace Kallen stands up foursquare and plots the philosophy of the future in the following terms, I seem to hear his old teacher speaking through him:

Above all, it will be aware that nature is as neutral to man and to human values—especially her own unity and eternity—as to all other items which compose the infinitude of her teeming overflow. It will insist that human excellence and human destiny are matters of concern to man alone. Job's utterance regarding God will be its verdict regarding human good and human fate.

> I have no hope
> I know that he will slay me
> Nevertheless will I maintain my ways before him.

But of all the younger philosophers, the one most deeply touched by the wisdom of Santayana would seem to be Irwin Edman. There is good reason for his choice as editor of a recent collection of Santayana's writings; his own books are permeated by Santayana's doctrines. A brief examination of his opinions reveals these, often expressed in Santayana's terminology. Like Santayana, Edman believes that religion is poetry, "a lyrical and dramatic symbolism by which the significance of life, the movement of nature, the aim and direction of human life are represented." But so are philosophy and science poetry, "the product of a creative intelligence," "the work of synthesizing imagination." In fact, "we live in a world where all discourse is metaphor." None the less, the representative character of all knowledge, far from destroying its practicality, is a guarantee that philosophy may and should deal with a "common world of sun and stars, of birth and death, of war and peace, of hope and fear and love and hate." This common world, assumed by common sense at every step, is the basis of an inevitable naturalism.

The nature that man thinks about he admits long before he has thought and in the intervals when he is not thinking. It is the nature in which acorns grow into oaks, boys into men, relations into communications. It is the nature in which the tongue utters speech and the body flowers into the entelechy of the soul. It is the nature wherein bodily life comes to a glow of realization in consciousness, blossoms into dreams, ideals and purposes.

These higher values are of course contingent upon nature, but they are relative to human nature alone. And a more rational order of living, recognizing both these facts, would lead to a freer and happier humanity.

Faith in the possibilities of experience intelligently to redirect itself, to find the materials for its ideals in nature consciously controlled, to make the objects of faith the objects of fulfillment and realization that creative and imaginative thinking may first discern out of the suggestions Nature itself generates—this is the temper of the only possible naturalistic faith.

Santayana would call it a religion of disillusion. Edman is less severely materialistic than Santayana, more receptive to the newer science, but the cardinal points of his philosophic credo are unmistakably those of Santayana.

Upon men of letters Santayana's influence is more difficult to trace, for they are more likely to reflect his general attitudes than his specific beliefs. Two of his greatest students, from the standpoint of literary and public prominence, are T. S. Eliot and Walter Lippmann, and it is sometimes claimed that they have never outgrown the dispassionate sanity that permeated Santayana's classroom. I can see more of Santayana in Lippmann than in Eliot, despite a certain temperamental affinity the latter has with Santayana. Eliot of course shares Santayana's Catholicism and a certain scorn of the liberal movement in politics and the romantic in literature which are its natural concomitants. He is a classicist, an authoritarian, a dogmatist in principle and temper, with the Catholic assurance of the rightness of his judgment. But the best way to see Santayana's deviation from Catholicism is to place him beside a real Catholic, even an Anglo-Catholic. In their ultimate philosophies Eliot and Santayana are as wide as the poles; I believe Eliot is considerably nearer the non-Catholics Irving Babbitt and Matthew Arnold than the Catholic Santayana. With Lippmann the situation is different. He is a liberal and a modern, with a respect for and a kind of optimistic faith in the processes of democracy and organized industry. Yet when he turns to morals and philosophy, he echoes certain principles of his former teacher, in general, those we have already observed in Edman: the relativity of both science and religion, the value of religion as poetry, the inevitability of naturalism, the need for a reconstructed morality which will be true to nature and yet find ample room for the ideal aspirations of man. Lippmann's "high religion," or "religion of the spirit," is very close to Santayana's "religion of disillusion," with some of the overtones of his "spiritual life."

The religion of the spirit [says Lippmann] has no thesis to defend. It seeks excellence wherever it may appear, and finds it in anything which is inwardly understood; its motive is not acquisition but sympathy. . . . To understand is not only to pardon, but in the end to love . . . [Its professor] would have the whole universe, rather than the prison of his own hopes and fears, for his habitation, and in imagination all possible forms of being. . . . He might dwell with all beauty and all knowledge, and they are inexhaustible. Would he, then, dream idle dreams? only if he chose to. For he might go simply about the business of the world, a good deal more effectively than the worldling, in that he did not place an absolute value upon it, and deceive himself.

Santayana feels that there is implicit in *A Preface to Morals* an alliance of worldliness with spirituality, an identification of "high religion" with big business, but this possible departure from strict Santayana doctrine should not blind us to the many resemblances between *A Preface to Morals* and *The Life of Reason*.*

Turning to the influence of Santayana upon Robert Bridges, we see a relationship not of teacher and pupil but of contemporaries and friends. Bridges was one of Santayana's most intimate friends in England, and long conversations upon philosophy and life served to bring out the discoveries and insights they held in common. Thus, when Bridges made up his final *summa* for posterity, *The Testament of Beauty,* 1929, he voiced many of the opinions and at times used the terminology of Santayana. There are many traces of *The Life of Reason* in *The Testament of Beauty;* in fact, Reason is the protagonist of Bridges' poem, guiding man to a happier because more rational life. Bridges, following Santayana, pays full respect to the naturalistic groundwork of reason. To begin with, life on this planet is precarious:

> all its self-propagating organisms exist
> only within a few degrees of the long scale
> rangeing from measured zero to unimagin'd heat
> a little oasis of Life in Nature's desert;

Man is but part of nature, together with the plant and animal kingdoms. Even his intellect

> is nascent also in brutes, and of their bloodkinship
> as fair a warranty as our common passions are,
> our common bones and muscles, skin and nerves of sense.

---

* The reader interested in comparing Lippmann and Santayana should read Santayana's review of *A Preface to Morals* and Lippmann's reply. My own feeling respecting the controversy is that Santayana mistakes the letter of Lippmann's book, but is true to the underlying spirit of Lippmann's liberalism and modernity.

So far, Bridges might be merely echoing a kind of naturalistic piety which has been the stock of sceptical minds from Montaigne down. But when he traces the evolution of reason from animal consciousness to the loftiest contemplation, he seems unmistakably in Santayana vein.

> from blind animal passion to the vision of Spirit
> all actual gradations come of nature, and each
> severally in time and place is answerable in man.
> . . . .
>
> And Reason—being essentially (as in place 'twas found)
> the idea of Order, and thus itself the appurtenance
> of essences, with them passing from physical
> unto spiritual order in a mind endued
> with conscience of the higher spiritual essences—

Close to *The Life of Reason,* then, is the scheme of *The Testament of Beauty,* in Bridges' words, to show

> How the mind of man from inconscient existence
> cometh thru' the animal by growth of reasoning
> to'ard spiritual conscience . . .

and the orderly hierarchy of stages reason passes through, made common by the form-giving power reason exhibits at all stages, is presented very much in the manner of *The Life of Reason.* Even the two obstacles to reason, the spirited steeds of Plato's myth which Bridges calls Selfhood and Breed, seem based upon Santayana's classification in *Reason in Society* of the two primal instincts in man, the nutritive and the reproductive.

But in its higher reaches, *The Testament of Beauty* seems to me to depart far from Santayana's naturalism. The evolution of reason to Bridges is but symptomatic of a grander evolutionary process which makes nature in the long run teleological and justifies man's religious insights. I cannot conceive of Santayana writing lines like these which find a place for immortality:

> This mind perishes with this body, unless
> the personal co-ordination of its ideas
> have won to Being higher than animal life,
> at thatt point where the Ring cometh upward to reach
> the original creativ Energy which is God,
> with conscience entering into life everlasting.

The language of the latter part of *The Testament of Beauty* suggests an idealism which is sometimes neo-Hegelian, sometimes scholastic, but is most certainly not the idealism of Santayana. Bridges' rationism is brought into line with what a good Anglican might expect of his poet laureate. Witness his concluding remarks upon the nature of God:

> God is seen as the very self-essence of love,
> Creator and mover of all as activ Lover of all,
> self-express'd in not-self, without which no self were
> In thought whereof is neither beginning nor end
> nor space nor time; nor any fault nor gap therein
> 'twixt self and not-self, mind and body, mother and child,
> 'twixt lover and loved, God and man: but ONE ETERNAL
> in the love of Beauty and in the selfhood of Love.*

The purely literary influence of Santayana is even broader than the philosophical. I do not mean that authors have rushed to imitate the soliloquies or the dialogues or even Santayana's prose style. It is hard not to detect now and then in his most assiduous followers, in Edman when he is most eloquent, in Lippmann when he is most ironical, the cadences and patterns of Santayana's prose; but for the most part, writers have seen the folly of trying to imitate so individual and dangerous a model. I refer rather to the increasing frequency with which Santayana is quoted. Here, there, everywhere one meets a sentence or a paragraph from Santayana, often torn from its context, often in the midst of opinions quite foreign to its author. Like Emerson, Santayana may reach his widest public as a phrase-maker. Whether or not his is, as Ludwig Lewissohn says, "the most perfect English prose yet produced on this continent," more and more writers are coming to depend on him to slay an opponent or buttress an argument. And I believe this power of expression is circulating more widely his ideas.

Of course, Santayana has as many and as vociferous detractors as ever. What Professor Cohen said in 1920 of his philosophy is still true today, though perhaps less so. "Santayana has failed to draw fire because few people are interested in a frankly speculative and de-

---

* I have repeated here the original spelling of Robert Bridges. It is Santayana's opinion, as expressed to the present writer, that most of Bridges' ideas were formed before he met Santayana, and his acquaintance with the latter merely served to corroborate and strengthen them. But Santayana's usual modesty in matters of this kind must be remembered.

tached philosophy that departs radically from the accepted traditions and makes no appeal to the partisan zeal of either conservatives or reformers." Moreover, it alienates both the scientist and the religionist. To the former "Santayana is just a speculative poet who may value science very highly but does so as a well-groomed gentleman who knows it at a polite distance, afraid to soil his hands with its grimy details." To the latter "a combination of aetheistic catholicism and anti-puritanic, non-democratic aesthetic morality, lacking withal in missionary enthusiasm, typifies almost all that is abhorrent." Even his fellow Catholics shy away from him. James W. Lane in the *Catholic World* calls him "Averroistic," "an irritating Proteus in his beliefs and attachments," with an "Oriental love of the indecisive." Much the same opinion is voiced by another Catholic, Katharine Brégy, in a letter to the present writer which attributes her loss of interest in Santayana to his recent Orientalism. As Lane well expresses it, Santayana's philosophy lacks for a Catholic "the fixed cardinal point of the Christian spiritual life. . . . Faith has been left out." As a result, its whole burden is "sicklied o'er with the pale cast of intellectual images." And while traditionalists thus cast out Santayana, the radicals will have little of him too. He has too much contempt for reform, too little faith in their socialistic panaceas. As he once significantly put it,

Had there been some wise prophet in my day, summoning mankind to an ordered and noble life, I should gladly have followed him, not having myself the gift of leadership. . . . But I found no master. Those who beat the drum or rang the church-bell in my time were unhappy creatures, trying to deceive themselves. . . . Green, quiet places and boyish sports are more moralizing than these moralists.

And this detachment and irony alienate Santayana from the moderates and liberals as well as the radicals. They have not forgotten his essay on "The Irony of Liberalism," and they look upon his world as 'a kind of ivory tower, austere and beautiful perhaps, but remote from the exigencies of modern life. Ludwig Lewissohn calls his work "the Divine Comedy of a great artist forsaken in an alien age by both verse and God, but building on the frontiers of heathendom a last rampart to guard the ideals which he would make as imperishable as he believes them to be excellent." And Horace Kallen believes that he has not himself escaped "the contagion of the genteel tradition. . . . He conceives life . . . vertically, not horizontally. . . .

And that one kind of life only should be called a good life, and that of a fashion arising not from the soil of present life, but from a memory and estimate of life long gone, that perhaps is most romantic and American of all."

But Santayana has his ardent admirers too, and they are increasing. To O. Barfield he is "easily the greatest living critic," to J. Middleton Murry the author of the "only modern book of philosophy worthy the name . . . a champion and epitome of that true civilization . . . not an institution, but a spiritual possession." Ellen Glasgow calls him "the only modern philosopher . . . who has been able to make philosophy into an art . . . the greatest contemporary master of English prose." Archibald Macleish even maintains that his "art in poetry . . . should not have heaped the sacrifice to any god."

It will be noticed how the emphasis here is upon Santayana as man of letters as well as philosopher. His almost unique rôle in bringing to philosophy the artistry and grace of literature is now broadly acknowledged. The versatility of his pen, his mastery of numerous literary forms and styles is not matched among contemporary metaphysicians. He has consistently stuck to his principle that good writing will clarify the most abstruse point in philosophy, and that charm and graciousness will detract in no way from a philosopher's power to convince. But expression, however good, is only one of the attributes of Santayana; there is force in what he says as well as in how he says it.

What will his contribution be to the world of the future? Well, prophecies are dangerous; existence is, in Santayana's words, a flux, and its direction is on a human scale perhaps indeterminate. But I do not see where Santayana stands to lose at the bar of time. Few philosophies have in them so little that is transient and fashionable, so little that is pleading for special interests. Omniscience only knows how much of truth there is in the realms of being, but since they constitute a philosophy of perspectives rather than a cosmology, even a more precise knowledge of the nature of the universe might prove them incomplete rather than false. Their rendering of existence is figurative, poetical, but to me at least they seem to describe our world better than either idealism or crude realism. However, one's choice of philosophies is at the present stage of human knowledge largely preferential; at least of Santayana's it can be said that it faces nature four-square and will survive any defeat of human wishes.

Here, too, on a moral plane it seems to me to have an unusual pertinence to the modern world. Whether Whirl, in Mr. Lippmann's words, will continue to be king, whether the old ideals and values will return or whether they are banished forever, it seems to me the morality of the future must build on firmer foundations than those of the past. Civilization cannot stand many recurrences of the despair and frustration which Joseph Wood Krutch well describes as "the modern temper." Thomas Carlyle in one of those rare moments of insight said that if you reduce the denominator of the fraction of happiness to zero, you have the world at your feet. Santayana's philosophy does just that. His religion of disillusionment asks little of the universe; it accepts life perhaps on its lowest terms; then it proceeds to reconstruct human happiness upon a more secure because completely disillusioned basis. And surprisingly enough, most of the cherished values of mankind are still there. Their origins are seen to be natural, as if that were any harm, but they are still ideal in the truest sense of the word. The modern world has had to face the first truth, and its confusion is largely because it cannot find its way to the second. It has forgotten, or perhaps has yet to discover, that "while values derive existence only from their causes, causes derive value only from their results." "The error" is "profound and the contradiction hopeless if we should deny the ideal authority of human nature because we had discovered its origins and conditions." This is a bitter pill for the world to swallow, but it should be therapeutic. For there is still ground for morality, perhaps the only reasonable ground. There is still, there cannot help being, human nature being human, an "ineradicable practical difference between the better and the worse, the beautiful and the ugly, the trustworthy and the fallacious." True, these distinctions must be worked out through long labor and a sympathetic understanding which man has yet to evince; they can no longer be accepted as someone's *fiat*. But whether *The Life of Reason* be practicable today or merely a nostalgic effort to retrace the past, it seems to me inescapable that Santayana erected the ramparts of morality in the right place and that they have a stalwartness very nearly unique in this day and age.

And the outlook of a religion of disillusionment need not be pessimistic and barren.

We can turn from the stupefying contemplation of an alien universe to the building of our own house, knowing that, alien as it is, that universe has chanced to blow its energy also into our will and to allow itself to be partially dominated by our intelligence. Our mere existence and the modicum of success we have attained in society, science, and art are the living proofs of this human power. . . . The ideal is itself a function of the reality and cannot therefore be altogether out of harmony with the conditions of its own birth and persistence. Civilisation is precarious, but it need not be short-lived. . . . There is no impossibility, therefore, in the hope that the human will may have time to understand itself, and, having understood itself, to realise the objects of its rational desire. What we should do is to make a modest inventory of our possessions and a just estimate of our powers in order to apply both, with what strength we have, to the realisation of our ideals in society, in art, and in science. . . . We shall then be making that rare advance in wisdom which consists in abandoning our illusions the better to attain our ideals.

And who knows but that

. . . this gradually unfolding, intelligible, and real world would not turn out to be more congenial and beautiful than any wilful fiction, since it would be the product of a universal human labor and the scene of the accumulated sufferings and triumphs of mankind?

But there is another legacy of Santayana to the modern world just as wholesome and beneficial as his Socratic rationalism. Practical life is never so absorbing that it leaves no time for contemplation and spiritual growth. There would be times in even the best ordered society, in fact there would be more times, when the spirit would want to turn from the world to its true home in the eternal. And just here is the true worth of Santayana's soliloquies, his poems, and his *Platonism and the Spiritual Life.* Man is by nature otherworldly as well as worldly; the true greatness of Santayana's philosophy is that it allows for both of these human characteristics, in fact makes both possible without interference and conflict. The world of spirituality is clearly marked off, and it is possible for man to turn to it in the midst of life or in forgetfulness of life. Its peaks are always discernible above the flux, if man is really spiritually minded. And this long view of life does not minimize its evil and sorrow. Santayana is not an optimist with a penny whistle. No one can see life steadily and see it whole without detecting the tragic cast. As Santayana beautifully says in one of his soliloquies,

The foot of the cross—I dare not say the cross itself—is a good station from which to survey existence. In the greatest griefs there is a tragic calm; the fury of the will is exhausted, and our thoughts rise to another level. . . . The dark background which death supplies brings out the tender colours of life in all their purity . . . to live in the shadow of death and of the cross is to spread a large nimbus of peace around our littleness.

But philosophy, from Boethius down, is nothing if not a consolation, and there are other views than the long one, or perhaps it is really not long enough. "Time laughs at ambition, and Eternity laughs at time; and if we could relish this double irony, the great crime of existence, self-destruction, would cease to seem an outrage, and the violence of it would become like a lover's violence, tragic but welcome." For after all, says Santayana in perhaps his most notable line, "Everything in nature is lyrical in its ideal essence, tragic in its fate, and comic in its existence." The soul must of necessity at times takes the middle view; if it is wise it will gain comfort from the last; but its true measurement is the extent to which it rises to the first. These three stops on the organ of life give meaning and beauty to every note of the human scale; but the quality of the first is the supreme test of man's power of idealization. Most lovely is nature when viewed in its lyrical essence. Then can the truly contemplative mind lose itself in the song of the skylark, in the eucharist of the church, in the pure white light of mathematical truth or musical form, surmount its basis in nature and enjoy the free play which is the divine prerogative of spirit.

NOTES

NOTE: References are made at the end of quotations and include everything since the preceding citation. Full citations of works are given in the first reference to them in each chapter.

CHAPTER ONE

Page : line
1 : 21—"Santayana at Cambridge," *American Mercury*, I (1924), 73.
2 : 19—*Poems*, N. Y. and London, 1923, viii.
2 : 24—*Soliloquies in England and Later Soliloquies*, N. Y. and London, 1922, 188.
2 : 28—*Ibid.*, 4.
3 : 5—"Brief History of My Opinions," *Contemporary American Philosophy: Personal Statements*, edited by George P. Adams and Wm. Pepperell Montague, N. Y., 1930, II, 239.
3 : 18—*American Mercury*, I (1924), 69.
3 : 32—*Contemporary American Philosophy*, II, 242.
4 : 2—"Spain in America," "written after the destruction of the Spanish fleet in the battle of Santiago, in 1898," *Poems*, 1923, 118–129.
4 : 3—*Dial*, LXXXII (1927), 282–286.
4 : 4—*Poems*, 101–104.
4 : 5—"A Contrast with Spanish Drama," *Soliloquies in England*, 149–155.
4 : 6—"Spanish Opinion on the War," *New Republic*, II (1915), 252–253; *Library of the World's Best Literature*, edited by Charles Dudley Warner, N. Y., 1897, VI, 3451–3457; "Imitation of Calderon: The Lament of Segismundo in *La Vida es Sueño*," *London Mercury*, IX (1923), 13–14.
4 : 16—Boston, 1871, 5 (1903 edition).
4 : 19—"Avila," *Poems*, 101.
4 : 25—Preface to *Poems*, viii.
4 : 29—"Spain in America," *Poems*, 119, 120.
4 : 34—*Spain*, N. Y., 1930, 19.
5 : 3—Salvador da Madariaga, "Spain in America," *Forum*, LXXXI (1929), 131, 135.
5 : 6—*Englishmen, Frenchmen, Spaniards*, Oxford, 1928, 47.
5 : 10—*Europe*, N. Y., 1930, 19.
5 : 15—*Contemporary American Philosophy*, II, 239.
5 : 22—*Ibid.*, II, 240.
5 : 31—*Ibid.*, II, 240.

297

NOTES

Page : line
- 5 : 36—*Ibid.*, II, 240.
- 6 : 15—*Ibid.*, II, 240.
- 6 : 22—*Ibid.*, II, 239-240.
- 6 : 32—*Ibid.*, II, 241-242.
- 6 : 39—*Soliloquies in England*, 3.
- 7 : 19—*Contemporary American Philosophy*, II, 241.
- 7 : 25—*Ibid.*, II, 241.
- 8 : 3—See the school catalogues during the years Santayana attended Boston Latin School.
- 8 : 19—*Contemporary American Philosophy*, II, 241.
- 9 : 10—"Glimpses of Old Boston," *Latin School Register*, LI (Mar. 1932); No. 5; 8.
- 9 : 35—George E. Howes, in a letter to the *Latin School Register*, XXXIV (Feb. 1915), 23.
- 10 : 33—This poem may be found in the archives of the Boston Latin School or in the library of Harvard University.
- 10 : 35—*Latin School Register*, I (Oct. 1881); No. 1.
- 11 : 7—*Ibid.*, LI (Mar. 1932), No. 5; 8.
- 11 : 19—*Ibid.*, I (Dec. 1881); No. 3.
- 11 : 23—*Ibid.*, I (Mar. 1882); No. 6.
- 11 : 33—*Ibid.*, I (Nov. 1881); No. 2.
- 12 : 13—*Ibid.*, I (Oct. 1881); No. 1.
- 13 : 10—*Ibid.*, LI (Mar. 1932); No. 5; 9.
- 13 : 26—S. E. Morison, *The Development of Harvard University since the Inauguration of President Eliot, 1869–1929*, Cambridge, 1930, xliii.
- 13 : 37—"The Spirit and Ideals of Harvard University," *Educational Review*, VII (1894), 318.
- 15 : 1—*The Harvard Crimson 1873–1906*, Cambridge, 1906, 19–20, quoting from the issue of Jan. 8, 1885.
- 15 : 7—*Ibid.*, quoting from the issue of May 1, 1885. The instructors were Briggs, Clymer, and Wendell.
- 15 : 20—"The Founding of the Harvard Monthly," *Harvard Monthly*, XXI (Oct. 1895), 2.
- 16 : 24—*Daily Crimson Supplement*, VII (Feb. 25, 1885), No. 15.
- 16 : 36—*Ibid.*, VII (Mar. 26, 1885), No. 40.
- 18 : 12—*Character and Opinion in the United States*, N. Y., 1920, 50–51.
- 18 : 19—"A Glimpse of Yale," *Harvard Monthly*, XV (Dec. 1892), 91.
- 18 : 31—*Ibid.*, XV, 91.
- 18 : 39—*Character and Opinion in the United States*, 51.
- 19 : 13—"Spanish Opinion on the War," *New Republic*, II (1915), 253.
- 19 : 16—*The Soul of Spain*, Boston, 1913, viii.
- 19 : 21—"Avila," *Poems*, 1923, 102.
- 19 : 25—"Spain in America," *Ibid.*, 121.
- 19 : 31—See "Spanish Opinion on the War," *op. cit.*
- 19 : 39—*The Genius of Spain*, Oxford, 1923, 94.
- 20 : 3—*Essays and Soliloquies*, translated by J. E. Crawford Flitch, N. Y., 1924, 37.
- 20 : 14—*Contemporary American Philosophy*, II, 243.
- 20 : 24—*Ibid.*, II, 243.
- 20 : 31—Inaugural address, 1869, quoted in *The Development of Harvard University*, lxii.
- 20 : 35—*The Development of Harvard University*, 25.

NOTES

Page : line
- 21 : 11—*Contemporary American Philosophy*, II, 244.
- 21 : 28—*Ibid.*, II, 245.
- 22 : 3—*Ibid.*, II, 244.
- 22 : 11—*Ibid.*, II, 245–246.
- 22 : 20—*Ibid.*, II, 246–247.
- 22 : 28—*Ibid.*, II, 247.
- 22 : 33—*Ibid.*, II, 251.
- 23 : 17—See the college catalogues for the years Santayana was an undergraduate at Harvard.
- 23 : 32—*Egotism in German Philosophy*, London, 1916, 5.
- 23 : 39—*Recollections of My Youth (Souvenirs)*, translated by C. B. Pitman, N. Y., 1883, 245.
- 24 : 3—*Soliloquies in England*, 216.
- 24 : 6—*Ibid.*, 216.
- 24 : 12—*Egotism in German Philosophy*, 16–17.
- 24 : 36—*Recollections of My Youth*, 246.
- 24 : 39—*The Letters of Charles Eliot Norton*, edited by Sara Norton and M. A. De Wolfe Howe, Boston and N. Y., 1913, II, 43.
- 25 : 7—*Apologia pro Vita Sua*, 245 (1865 edition).
- 25 : 22—*Contemporary American Philosophy*, II, 248.
- 26 : 3—A. W. Benn, *A History of English Rationalism in the Nineteenth Century*, London and N. Y., 1906, I, 432.
- 26 : 20—*The Letters of Charles Eliot Norton*, II, 128, 211.
- 26 : 24—*Contemporary American Philosophy*, II, 244.
- 26 : 29—*Ibid.*, II, 246.
- 27 : 3—"The Ethical Doctrine of Spinoza," *Harvard Monthly*, II (June 1886), 145, 147.
- 27 : 26—*Ibid.*, II, 152.
- 27 : 41—*Daily Crimson Supplement*, VII (Feb. 25, 1885), No. 15.
- 28 : 9—*Poems*, 1923, 9. I have quoted the final versions of these poems. For the relation of these to the originals see pp. 338, 339.
- 28 : 14—*Ibid.*, 6.
- 28 : 19—*Ibid.*, 7.
- 28 : 24—*Ibid.*, 8.
- 29 : 3—*Ibid.*, 5.
- 29 : 16—*Contemporary American Philosophy*, II, 243.
- 29 : 23—*Ibid.*, II, 246.
- 29 : 25—Arnold, "Stanzas from the Grande Chartreuse," 1855; "Obermann Once More," 1867.
- 29 : 29—*Recollections of My Youth*, 281.
- 30 : 8—"The Spirit and Ideals of Harvard University," *Educational Review*, VII (1894), 320.
- 30 : 10—"A Glimpse of Yale," *Harvard Monthly*, XV (Dec. 1892), 95.
- 30 : 27—*Character and Opinion in the United States*, 54–55.
- 31 : 4—*Contemporary American Philosophy*, II, 248, 242.
- 31 : 30—Henry Vizetelly, *Berlin under the New Empire*, London, 1879, II, 97.
- 31 : 38—*Egotism in German Philosophy*, 159.
- 32 : 24—Jan. 2, 1888, quoted in Ralph B. Perry, *The Thought and Character of William James*, Boston, 1935, I, 403.
- 32 : 29—Jan. 28, 1888, *Ibid.*, I, 40.
- 32 : 32—*Ibid.*, I, 40.
- 32 : 34—April 22, 1888, *Ibid.*, I, 405.

NOTES

Page : line

32 : 37—Even the facilities for graduate work he felt to be inferior to those at Harvard. "The Harvard Graduate school . . . I should not hesitate, to judge from my own experience, to prefer . . . to those German universities to which American students flock in search of the last words of science. The number of professors is not so great, perhaps, but their quality is not inferior, and the facilities for study in the way of books and personal direction are much greater." *Educational Review*, VII (1894), 320.
33 : 9—See Santayana's letters of Dec. 18, 1887 and Jan. 28, 1888, in *The Thought and Character of William James*, I, 401, 404.
33 : 23—Dec. 18, 1887, *Ibid.*, I, 402.
33 : 32—For a full discussion of philosophical tendencies in Germany at about this time, see G. H. Howison, "Some Recent Aspects of German Philosophy," *Journal of Speculative Philosophy*, XVII (1883), 30–31 and Arthur Fairbanks, "Present Tendencies in German Philosophy," *New England Magazine*, LIV (o.s.) (1891), 341.
33 : 37—July 3, 1888, *The Thought and Character of William James*, I, 405.
34 : 7—July 3, 1888, *Ibid.*, I, 405, 406.
34 : 14—Dec. 18, 1887, *Ibid.*, I, 401.
34 : 18—*Introduction to Philosophy*, translated by F. Thilly, N. Y., 1895, 420.
34 : 25—*Contemporary American Philosophy*, II, 244, 249.
34 : 38—*Soliloquies in England*, 214.
35 : 3—*Contemporary American Philosophy*, II, 249.
35 : 9—*Ibid.*, II, 249.
35 : 15—*Ibid.*, II, 251.
35 : 32—"Lotze's Moral Idealism," *Mind*, XV (Apr. 1890), 191. This is a condensed and revised version of Santayana's thesis.
35 : 38—*Ibid.*, XV, 200.
36 : 13—*Ibid.*, XV, 212.
36 : 16—*The Thought and Character of William James*, I, 766.
36 : 20—*Mind*, XV, 212.
36 : 26—*Ibid.*, XV, 199, 200.
37 : 2—*Ibid.*, XV, 194, 197, 199.
37 : 23—*Harvard Monthly*, VI (May 1888), 95.
38 : 9—*Poems*, 1923, 19. I have quoted from the final version of these poems.
38 : 16—*Ibid.*, 16.
38 : 23—*Ibid.*, 18.
39 : 2—*Ibid.*, 21.
39 : 4—*Ibid.*, 20.
39 : 13—*Ibid.*, 20.

CHAPTER TWO

40 : 24—Benjamin Rand, *Philosophical Instruction in Harvard*, Cambridge, 1929, 42. (Reprinted from the *Harvard Graduates' Magazine*, XXXVII (1928–29).
41 : 4—See Rand, *Op. cit.*, and the college catalogues for these years.
41 : 20—"Santayana at Cambridge," *American Mercury*, I (1924), 71–72.
41 : 24—*Ibid.*, I, 72.
41 : 26—A statement of Santayana's to the present writer.
41 : 29—"Thomas Parker Sanborn," *Harvard Monthly*, VIII (Mar. 1889), 166–168.

Page : line
41 : 31—*Poems*, N. Y. and London, 1923, 60–63.
41 : 38—*American Mercury*, I, 72.
42 : 3—*Ibid.*, I, 73.
42 : 18—Statements of Margaret Münsterberg to the present writer.
42 : 26—*American Mercury*, I, 70.
42 : 29—See *New Republic*, XXXIV (1923), 102.
43 : 2—*American Mercury*, I, 70.
43 : 5—Ralph B. Perry, *The Thought and Character of William James*, Boston, 1935, II, 270.
43 : 12—*American Mercury*, I, 70. See also Margaret Münsterberg, *Hugo Münsterberg, His Life and Work*, N. Y., 1922, 46.
43 : 20—*American Mercury*, I, 70, 69.
43 : 27—Dickinson Miller, "Mr. Santayana and William James," *Harvard Graduates' Magazine*, XXIX (Mar. 1921), 352.
44 : 7—Reviews of John Owen, *The Sceptics of the Italian Renaissance*, III (Mar. 1894), 190–192; Lucien Lévy-Bruhl, *History of Modern Philosophy in France*, IX (June 1900), 357–359; James H. Woods, *The Value of Religious Facts*, IX (June 1900), 357–359; William W. Newell, *Sonnets and Madrigals of Michelangelo Buonarroti, Rendered into English Verse*, IX (Sept. 1900), 584–585.
44 : 10—I (Dec. 1892), 658–673; V (Dec. 1896), 681–691; VIII (Sept. 1899), 401–417. The last two were reprinted in *Interpretations of Poetry and Religion*, N. Y. and London, 1900, the third under the title of "The Dissolution of Paganism."
44 : 14—X (May 1890), 85–92; XIV (May 1892), 89–99; XV (Dec. 1892), 89–97; XVIII (July 1894), 181–190; XXVIII (Mar. 1899), 1–14; XXX (Mar. 1900), 1–13.
44 : 16—VII (Apr. 1894), 313–325.
44 : 17—LXVII (Apr. 1891), 552–556. Santayana also reviewed for the *Harvard Monthly* William A. Leahy, *The Siege of Syracuse: a Poetical Drama*, VIII (June 1889), 166–168; and William M. Fullerton, *In Cairo*, XIII (Jan. 1892), 172–174; and for the *Philosophical Review*, Otto Willmann, *Geschichte des Idealismus*, VI (Nov. 1897), 661–664; and Jules Martin, *Saint Augustin*, X (Sept. 1901), 515–526. An article of Santayana's on Cervantes accompanied the selections from Cervantes in the *Warner Library of the World's Best Literature*, N. Y., 1897 (VI, 3451–3457), and his lecture on "Platonism in the Italian Poets," delivered Feb. 5, 1896 before the Contemporary Club of Buffalo, was privately printed in Buffalo, 1896, and later included as one of the chapters of *Interpretations of Poetry and Religion*, 1900.
44 : 29—Review of W. M. Fullerton, *In Cairo, Harvard Monthly*, XIII (Jan. 1892), 174.
44 : 33—"What Is a Philistine," *Harvard Monthly*, XIV (May 1892), 89.
44 : 36—"The Decay of Latin," *Harvard Monthly*, XXX (Mar. 1900), 5.
44 : 37—Review of Wm. A. Leahy, *The Siege of Syracuse, Harvard Monthly*, VIII (June 1889), 168.
45 : 1—"A Glimpse of Yale," *Harvard Monthly*, XV (Dec. 1892), 90.
45 : 15—"What Is a Philistine," *Harvard Monthly*, XIV (May 1892), 90.
45 : 21—*Sonnets and Other Verses*, Cambridge and Chicago, 1894; *Ibid.*, 2nd. edition, 1896; *Lucifer*, Chicago and N. Y., 1899; *A Hermit of Carmel, and Other Poems*, N. Y., 1901; London, 1902.
45 : 27—See p. 75.

NOTES

Page : line
- 45 : 30—Preface to *Poems*, 1923, xii.
- 46 : 19—*Poems*, 1923, 4.
- 46 : 26—*Ibid.*, 10.
- 46 : 31—*Ibid.*, 12.
- 47 : 8—*Ibid.*, 13.
- 47 : 12—Sonnet 13, *Ibid.*, 15.
- 47 : 15—*Ibid.*, 16.
- 47 : 22—Sonnet 16, *Ibid.*, 18.
- 47 : 26—Sonnet 20, *Ibid.*, 22.
- 48 : 19—*Sonnets and Other Verses*, 1896, 85.
- 48 : 29—*Ibid.*, 88.
- 49 : 9—*Poems*, 1923, 71, 72.
- 49 : 18—*Ibid.*, 73.
- 49 : 25—*Poems*, 1923, 79.
- 50 : 2—*Ibid.*, 81.
- 50 : 28—*Ibid.*, 77, 78.
- 51 : 12—*Ibid.*, 74.
- 51 : 18—See p. 41.
- 51 : 25—XXV (1894), 99.
- 51 : 27—LXXV (1895), 412.
- 51 : 18—XXV (1894), 99.
- 51 : 21—II (June 1894), 597.
- 51 : 26—XXV (1894), 99.
- 52 : 41—*Culture and Anarchy*, 1869; 8, 98, 94 (N. Y., 1920).
- 53 : 5—*The Letters of Charles Eliot Norton*, edited by Sara Norton and M. A. DeWolfe Howe, Boston and N. Y., 1913, II, 8.
- 53 : 14—*The Symbolist Movement in Literature*, London, 1899, 170 (N. Y., 1908).
- 53 : 26—Margaret L. Woods, "Poets of the 'Eighties," in *The Eighteen-Eighties*, edited by Walter de la Mare, Cambridge, Eng., 1930, 1.
- 53 : 28—Irving Babbitt, *Modern French Criticism*, Boston and N. Y., 1912, 320.
- 53 : 30—Sonnet 17, *Poems*, 1923, 19.
- 54 : 4—*Ibid.*, 71.
- 54 : 18—"La Bonne Chanson," 1870.
- 54 : 22—"Sagesse," 1881, translated by Arthur Symons, *Poems*, Volume III, London, 1924, 130.
- 54 : 23—"The Hound of Heaven," 1890.
- 54 : 25—"A Rebours," 1884, translated and quoted in A. Symons, *The Symbolist Movement in Literature*, London, 1899, 139 (N. Y., 1908).
- 54 : 36—See Holbrook Jackson, *The Eighteen Nineties*, London, 1913, 65.
- 55 : 14—"To a Spanish Friend," *Poetical Works*, London, 1915, 101-102.
- 56 : 11—Preface to *Poems*, 1923, xi.
- 56 : 26—"The Present Position of the Roman Catholic Church," *New World*, I (1892), 659.
- 56 : 35—"Rolla," 1833, *The Complete Writings of Alfred de Musset*, N. Y., 1905, II, 3-4 (Vol. II translated by George Santayana, E. I. Forman, and M. A. Clarke).
- 57 : 13—"A se stesso," translated by Lorna de' Lucchi, in her *Anthology of Italian Poems*, N. Y., 1922, 291.
- 57 : 23—See note to 44: 17.
- 58 : 1—Statements of Santayana to the present writer.
- 58 : 16—*Interpretations of Poetry and Religion*, 120, 145.

NOTES

Page : line
58 : 34—*Poems*, 1923, 28.
59 : 4—*Ibid.*, 27.
59 : 8—*Ibid.*, 26.
59 : 19—*Ibid.*, 28.
59 : 22—*Ibid.*, 29.
59 : 30—*Ibid.*, 30.
60 : 11—*Ibid.*, 31.
60 : 19—*Ibid.*, 32.
60 : 29—Sonnet 34, *Ibid.*, 38.
60 : 38—Sonnet 35, *Ibid.*, 39.
61 : 4—Sonnet 36, *Ibid.*, 40.
61 : 18—Sonnet 37, *Ibid.*, 41.
61 : 30—Sonnet 44, *Ibid.*, 48.
61 : 34—Sonnet 49, *Ibid.*, 53.
62 : 3—See Rittenhouse, *The Younger American Poets*, Boston, 1904; Archer, *Poets of the Younger Generation*, London, 1902.
62 : 23—See note to 44: 7.
62 : 35—*Interpretations of Poetry and Religion*, 132.
62 : 37—Sonnet 52, translated by J. A. Symonds. *The Sonnets of Michael Angelo Buonarroti*, London, 1878, 57 (1926 edition).
63 : 14—Sonnet 54, *Ibid.*, 59.
63 : 28—Sonnet 43, *Poems*, 1923, 47.
63 : 30—Sonnet 47, *Ibid.*, 51.
63 : 36—Sonnet 39, *Ibid.*, 43.
64 : 8—Sonnet 38, *Ibid.*, 42.
64 : 13—*Interpretations of Poetry and Religion*, 130.
64 : 23—Sonnet 39, *Poems*, 1923, 43.
64 : 26—Sonnet 40, *Ibid.*, 44.
64 : 29—Sonnet 30, *Ibid.*, 34.
65 : 13—*Ibid.*, 137. Santayana has also translated Michelangelo's "Non so se s'è la desiata luce" and "Il mio refugio," *Ibid.*, 135, 136. There are also translations of Michelangelo, Cavalcanti, and Lorenzo de' Medici incidental to the discussion of "Platonic Love Poetry in the Italian Poets," in *Interpretations of Poetry and Religion*.
65 : 17—Sonnet 39, *Poems*, 1923, 43.
65 : 26—*Ibid.*, 36.
65 : 34—Sonnet 22, *Ibid.*, 26.
66 : 24—"Memories of King's College, Cambridge," *Harvard Monthly*, XXVIII (Mar. 1899), 4.
66 : 33—*Soliloquies in England and Later Soliloquies*, N. Y. and London, 1922, 3–4.
66 : 38—XXVI (Mar. 1898), 1–5; XXVIII (May 1899), 85–86; XXV (Oct. 1897), 1–2.
67 : 13—*Poems*, 1923, 105, 106, 108.
67 : 17—*Ibid.*, 109.
67 : 27—*Ibid.*, 103.
67 : 33—"Solipsism," *Ibid.*, 95.
67 : 38—*Ibid.*, 95.
68 : 4—*Ibid.*, 96.
68 : 26—"In Grantchester Meadows," *Ibid.*, 116–117.
68 : 33—*Ibid.*, 115.
69 : 13—*Ibid.*, 103.

NOTES

Page : line
- 69 : 18—"Premonition," *Ibid.*, 93.
- 69 : 35—*Ibid.*, 93–94.
- 70 : 9—"Avila," *Ibid.*, 103.
- 70 : 17—*Ibid.*, 66.
- 70 : 37—*Sonnets and Other Verses*, 1894, 58.
- 72 : 27—*A Hermit of Carmel and Other Poems*, 205–206; 213–214.
- 72 : 34—*Contemporary American Philosophy: Personal Statements*, edited by George P. Adams and Wm. Pepperell Montague, N. Y., 1930, II, 246.
- 73 : 8—Hutchins Hapgood in *New World*, VIII (1899), 575.
- 73 : 21—*Ibid.*, VIII, 574.
- 73 : 37—*Ibid.*, VIII, 576.
- 74 : 14—XXVIII (July 1899), 210–211.
- 74 : 17—*Ibid.*, XXVIII, 212.
- 74 : 29—XXXII (1902), 47–48.
- 74 : 31—VIII (Dec. 1899), 297–298.
- 74 : 32—LXXIII (1901), 439.
- 74 : 33—LXIV (1903), 81.
- 75 : 7—LIV (1902), 460–461.
- 75 : 14—"The Dioscuri: Two Interludes," XXIV (June 1902), 141–144; "The Flight of Helen, A Fragment," XXXVI (Apr. 1903), 53–56; "Philosophers at Court, from Act IV," XXXVIII (June 1904), 129–133.
- 75 : 27—*Century*, CV (1923), 684–685 (reprinted in *Poems*, 1923); *A Book of Homage to Shakespeare*, edited by Israel Gollancz, Oxford, 1916, 377; *London Mercury*, IX (1923), 13–14; "A Premonition," Cambridge, October 1913, "The Undergraduate Killed in Battle," Oxford, 1915, "The Darkest Hour," Oxford, 1917, *Soliloquies in England*, 7–8.
- 75 : 29—"On the Three Philosophical Poets," *The Works of George Santayana*, Triton Edition, N. Y., 1936–1937, VI, frontispiece (in facsimile).
- 76 : 9—Preface to *Poems*, 1923, 8–9, 11–12.
- 76 : 28—May 31, 1923.
- 76 : 31—XXIV (1923), 102.
- 76 : 33—VII (1923), 71.
- 78 : 5—*The Younger American Poets*, 104.
- 78 : 18—Preface to *Poems*, 1923, vii–viii.
- 78 : 21—*The Younger American Poets*, 105.
- 78 : 34—Louis Untermeyer, *American Poetry since 1900*, N. Y., 1923, 289, 290.
- 78 : 37—"To W. P.," sonnet III, *Poems*, 1923, 62.
- 79 : 7—Sonnet 3, *Ibid.*, 5.
- 79 : 9—"In Grantchester Meadows," *Ibid.*, 117.
- 79 : 11—"To W. P.," sonnet I, *Ibid.*, 60.
- 79 : 13—"Midnight," *Ibid.*, 115.
- 79 : 15—Preface to *Poems*, 1923, xiii.
- 79 : 19—"King's College Chapel," *Ibid.*, 106.
- 79 : 21—"In Grantchester Meadows," *Ibid.*, 116.
- 79 : 22—"Before a Statue of Achilles," sonnet III, *Ibid.*, 66.
- 79 : 23—"On a Volume of Scholastic Philosophy," *Ibid.*, 57.
- 79 : 24—Sonnet 5, *Ibid.*, 7.
- 79 : 33—Sonnet 8, *Ibid.*, 10.
- 80 : 2—Sonnet 12, *Ibid.*, 14.
- 80 : 4—Sonnet 15, *Ibid.*, 17.
- 80 : 5—Sonnet 17, *Ibid.*, 19.
- 80 : 6—Sonnet 27, *Ibid.*, 31.

NOTES

Page : line
- 80 : 9—Sonnet 28, *Ibid.*, 32.
- 80 : 18—*A Hermit of Carmel and Other Poems*, 122.
- 80 : 32—Preface to *Poems*, 1923, ix.
- 81 : 13—*Lucifer*, 70.
- 81 : 24—*Ibid.*, 116–119.
- 82 : 26—*Poems*, 1923, 79.
- 83 : 3—*The Sense of Beauty*, N. Y. and London, 1896, 173.
- 83 : 28—*Ibid.*, 173.
- 84 : 12—"The Knight's Return," *A Hermit of Carmel and Other Poems*, 72.
- 85 : 23—"Santayana the Poet," *Bookman*, LXII (1925), 189.
- 85 : 31—Preface to *Poems*, 1923, xii.
- 86 : 1—*The Younger American Poets*, 98.
- 86 : 5—Preface to *Poems*, 1923, xiv.

CHAPTER THREE

- 88 : 12—*The Life of Reason*, N. Y. and London, 1905–06, Vol. I, *Reason in Common Sense*, x–xi (preface to the revised edition of 1922).
- 88 : 28—*Ibid.*, I, xi (1922 edition).
- 89 : 15—*Soliloquies in England and Later Soliloquies*, N. Y. and London, 1922, 209.
- 89 : 37—*Harvard Monthly*, X (May 1890), 88.
- 90 : 17—*Ibid.*, X, 89, 90, 91. This whole discussion puts one in mind of a similar dialogue in Longfellow's novel, *Kavanagh*, 1849. There the speaker for the tender, romantic view urges "a national drama in which scope enough shall be given to our gigantic ideas . . . a national literature altogether shaggy and unshorn. . . . I insist on originality. . . . We do not want art and refinement; we want genius,—untutored, wild, original, free." How well this demand anticipates Whitman! But the "stout" speaker replies, "Excuse me!—are you not confounding things which have no analogy? . . . Literature is rather an image of the spiritual world than of the physical, is it not?—of the internal, rather than the external. Mountains, lakes, and rivers are, after all, only its scenery and decorations, not its essence and substance. . . . If this genius is to find any expression, it must employ art and refinement, for art is the external expression of our thoughts." *Longfellow's Prose Works*, Boston and N. Y., 1890, 365–367.
- 90 : 31—*Harvard Monthly*, X, 91.
- 91 : 4—"Mr. Santayana and William James," *Harvard Graduates' Magazine*, XXIX (Mar. 1921), 351.
- 91 : 17—*Harvard Monthly*, XIV (May 1892), 97, 98.
- 91 : 33—*Ibid.*, XIV, 97.
- 91 : 41—See especially *The Life of Reason*, Vol. II, *Reason in Society*, 63–67 and chapter XII.
- 92 : 8—Ode 2, *Poems*, 1923, 74.
- 92 : 25—*The Sense of Beauty*, N. Y. and London, 1896, 14.
- 92 : 32—*Ibid.*, 49.
- 93 : 31—*Ibid.*, 269, 270.
- 94 : 31—*Ibid.*, 78.
- 95 : 3—*Ibid.*, 131.
- 95 : 19—*Ibid.*, 133.
- 95 : 22—*Ibid.*, 150.

Page : line
96 : 6—*Ibid.*, 206, 207.
96 : 14—*Ibid.*, 207, 208.
96 : 25—*Ibid.*, 221.
96 : 27—*Ibid.*, 228.
96 : 32—*Ibid.*, 258–259.
96 : 35—*Ibid.*, 230.
97 : 10—*Ibid.*, 231–232, 233.
97 : 23—*Ibid.*, 260.
97 : 30—*Ibid.*, 260.
97 : 37—LXV (1897), 75.
97 : 38—VI (1897), 560.
98 : 12—LI (1897), 147.
98 : 30—*Interpretations of Poetry and Religion*, N. Y. and London, 1900, 91.
99 : 7—*The Sense of Beauty*, 56.
99 : 13—*Ibid.*, 269.
99 : 27—*Bookman*, N. Y., V (1897), 70.
99 : 35—*Ibid.*, V, 70.
100 : 2—See notes to 44:10 and 44:17.
100 : 10—*Interpretations of Poetry and Religion*, v.
100 : 19—*Ibid.*, 256.
100 : 27—*Ibid.*, 261.
101 : 2—*Ibid.*, 267.
101 : 12—*Ibid.*, 264.
101 : 22—*Ibid.*, 168.
101 : 26—*Ibid.*, 167.
101 : 32—*Ibid.*, 174–175.
101 : 38—*Ibid.*, 288.
102 : 9—*Ibid.*, 284, 290.
102 : 40—*Bookman*, N. Y., XII (1900), 190, 191.
103 : 20—*Interpretations of Poetry and Religion*, 72.
103 : 34—*Ibid.*, 90.
104 : 6—*Ibid.*, 116.
104 : 15—*Ibid.*, 116–117.
104 : 27—*Philosophical Review*, IX (1900), 533.
104 : 40—*Interpretations of Poetry and Religion*, 106.
105 : 1—*Ibid.*, 5.
105 : 11—*Ibid.*, 9.
105 : 24—*Ibid.*, 10.
105 : 32—*Ibid.*, 15.
105 : 36—*Ibid.*, 15, 18.
106 : 6—*Ibid.*, 18, 19, 20.
106 : 23—*Ibid.*, 20.
106 : 30—*Ibid.*, 22.
107 : 2—*Bibliotheca Sacra*, LVII (1900), 782.
107 : 4—LXXXV (1900), 51.
107 : 6—Santayana's attitude toward religion was unfavorably reviewed by journals as varied as *Harvard Graduates' Magazine* (Paul Elmer More), *Philosophical Review* (Ernest Albee), *Bookman*, N. Y. (Hutchins Hapgood), *Independent*, *American Journal of Theology*, and *American Journal of Psychology*. By way of exception, the *Critic* said the book "exhibits an ideality, cultivation, and literary skill that must charm

Page : line

at once every lover of poetry and every religious thinker whose creed is broader than that of Calvin." XXXVII (1900), 83.
107 : 11—Review by J. W. Chadwick, IX (June 1900).
107 : 14—Arnold, *Literature and Dogma*, 1873, 18 (N. Y., 1920); *Culture and Anarchy*, 1869; 16 (N. Y., 1920).
107 : 17—Mill, *Three Essays on Religion*, 1874, 103 (N. Y., 1884).
107 : 39—Ralph B. Perry, *The Thought and Character of William James*, Boston, 1935, II, 319.
108 : 10—*International Monthly*, V (Feb. 1902), 185–199; *International Quarterly*, VI (Sept. 1902), 13–28. Santayana also reviewed for the *Journal of Philosophy, Psychology, and Scientific Methods* E. Hershey Sneath, *Philosophy in Poetry, a Study of Sir John Davies' Poem "Nosce Teipsum,"* and *The Mind of Tennyson, His Thoughts of God, Freedom, and Immortality*, I (Apr. 1904), 216–217; for the *Journal of Comparative Literature* Croce, *Estetica come scienza dell' espressione e linguistica generale*, I (Apr. 1903), 191–195; and for the *Atlantic Monthly* Prince d'Essling and Eugene Müntz, *Pétrarque, ses études d'art, son influence sur les artistes, ses portraits et ceux de Laure, l'illustration de ses écrits*, XCIV (July 1904) 135–138. Santayana also delivered at Oberlin College in 1904 the commencement address, which was published as "Tradition and Practice," *Oberlin Alumni Magazine*, I (Oct. 1904), 4–14.
108 : 24—XIII (1904), 322.
108 : 30—XIII (1904), 324, 325.
108 : 32—*Reason in Common Sense, Reason in Society, Reason in Religion, Reason in Art*, N. Y. and London, 1905; *Reason in Science*, N. Y. and London, 1906.
108 : 38—*The Life of Reason*, I, 32.
109 : 9—*Ibid.*, I, 2, 6.
109 : 19—*Ibid.*, I, 3, 5–6.
109 : 40—*Ibid.*, I, 141–151.
110 : 16—*Ibid.*, I, 206.
111 : 10—*Ibid.*, I, 36–37.
111 : 24—Ode 3, *Poems*, 1923, 78.
111 : 33—See A. W. Moore, *Journal of Philosophy, Psychology, and Scientific Methods*, III (Mar. 29, 1906), 211–221.
112 : 9—*Ibid.*, III (July 19, 1906), 410–412.
112 : 25—*The Life of Reason*, I, 183.
113 : 27—*Ibid.*, IV, 168–169.
114 : 9—*Ibid.*, III, 211.
114 : 31—*Ibid.*, I, 5.
115 : 5—*Ibid.*, I, 260.
115 : 7—*Ibid.*, I, 261.
115 : 27—*Ibid.*, III, 216.
115 : 31—*Ibid.*, III, 217.
116 : 4—*Ibid.*, I, 256.
116 : 18—*Ibid.*, II, 195.
116 : 28—*Ibid.*, IV, 29–30.
116 : 35—*Ibid.*, I, 238.
117 : 3—*Ibid.*, I, 54–55.
117 : 7—*Ibid.*, V, 270.

Page : line
117 : 11—*Ibid.*, I, 238.
117 : 21—*Ibid.*, IV, 28.
118 : 5—*Ibid.*, II, 9.
118 : 27—*Ibid.*, II, 29–30.
118 : 32—*Ibid.*, II, 32.
118 : 36—*Ibid.*, II, 30.
119 : 3—*Ibid.*, II, 33.
119 : 21—*Ibid.*, II, 35.
119 : 30—*Ibid.*, II, 35–36.
119 : 34—*Ibid.*, II, 50.
119 : 38—*Ibid.*, II, 43.
120 : 11—*Ibid.*, II, 46, 45, 58.
120 : 13—*Ibid.*, II, 58.
120 : 21—*Ibid.*, II, 59.
120 : 33—*Ibid.*, II, 61.
120 : 37—*Ibid.*, II, 65.
121 : 2—*Ibid.*, II, 66–67.
121 : 10—*Ibid.*, II, 67–68.
121 : 31—*Ibid.*, II, 122.
122 : 3—*Ibid.*, II, 129, 130.
123 : 12—*Ibid.*, III, 10, 9.
123 : 17—*Ibid.*, III, 7.
123 : 29—*Ibid.*, III, 66.
123 : 37—*Ibid.*, III, 115.
124 : 13—*Ibid.*, III, 13.
124 : 23—*Ibid.*, III, 8.
125 : 24—*Ibid.*, III, 272–273.
125 : 34—*Ibid.*, III, 260, 272.
126 : 8—*Ibid.*, IV, 118–119.
126 : 11—*Ibid.*, IV, 45.
126 : 28—*Ibid.*, IV, 35–36, 37.
126 : 30—*Ibid.*, IV, 4.
126 : 35—*Ibid.*, IV, 32, 33.
127 : 8—*Ibid.*, IV, 177–178.
127 : 14—*Ibid.*, IV, 212.
127 : 28—*Ibid.*, IV, 56.
127 : 34—*Ibid.*, IV, 13.
127 : 36—*Ibid.*, IV, 222.
128 : 4—*Ibid.*, IV, 228, 229–230.
128 : 6—*Ibid.*, IV, 229.
128 : 38—*Ibid.*, V, 303.
129 , : 6—*Ibid.*, V, 25.
130 : 19—*Ibid.*, V, 318–319.
130 : 23—LXVIII (1905), 589.
130 : 25—III (1906), 471.
130 : 28—Aug. 26, 1905, 269.
130 : 30—XVII (1907), 248.
130 : 32—*Letters of William James*, edited by Henry James, Boston, 1920, II, 234, 235. James goes on to say: "Santayana's book is a great one, if the inclusion of opposites is a measure of greatness. I think it will be reckoned great by posterity. It has no *rational* foundation, being merely one man's way of viewing things: so much of experience admitted

NOTES

Page : line

and no more. He is a paragon of Emersonianism—declare your intentions, though no other man share them; and the integrity with which he does it is as fine as it is rare. But the same things in Emerson's mouth would sound entirely different. E. receptive, expansive, as if handling life through a wide funnel with a great indraught: S. as if through a pinpoint orifice that emits his cooling spray outward over the universe like a nose-disinfectant from an 'atomizer'!" *Ibid.,* II, 234–235.

130 : 33—*Science,* XXIII (1906), 225.
131 : 4—XVII (1907), 249. Cf. also Ernest Albee in *Philosophical Review,* XIV (1905), 604.
131 : 23—IV (1906), 462.
131 : 38—See pp. 26–27, 89–91.
132 : 15—*The Life of Reason,* V, 320.
133 : 8—*Three Essays on Religion,* 1874, 29, 65 (N. Y., 1884).
133 : 11—*Ibid.,* 64.
133 : 17—"Empedocles on Etna," 1852.
133 : 26—*Apologia pro Vita Sua,* 1865, 267, 268.
133 : 29—Marjorie Harris, *The Positive Philosophy of Auguste Comte,* Cornell University, 1923, 79–80.
133 : 32—A. W. Benn, *The History of English Rationalism in the Nineteenth Century,* London and N. Y., 1906, II, 172.
133 : 38—"On the Advisableness of Improving Natural Knowledge," 1866; "On the Physical Basis of Life," 1868. *Methods and Results,* N. Y., 1902. 164, 38.
134 : 7—"On the Advisableness of Improving Natural Knowledge," *Ibid.,* 31–32.
134 : 13—Preface to *Vorlesungen über die Menschen und Thierseele,* quoted in Th. Ribot, *German Psychology of Today,* N. Y., 1886, 191.
134 : 18—*An Enquiry concerning the Principles of Morals,* Appendix I.
134 : 23—*Introduction to Philosophy,* translated by F. Thilly, N. Y., 1895, 121.
134 : 28—A. Mamelet, "La Philosophie de Georg Simmel," *Revue de Metaphysique et de Morale,* XX (1912), 157.
134 : 33—"The Place of Pater," *The Eighteen-Eighties,* edited by Walter de la Mare, Cambridge, Eng., 1930, 97.
134 : 38—*Three Essays on Religion,* 103, 105.
134 : 40—Chapter IX.
135 : 3—*Three Essays on Religion,* 119.
135 : 23—*The Life of Reason,* I, 9.
135 : 31—*Soliloquies in England,* 205. Cf. Mill's famous statement: "It is better to be a human being dissatisfied, than a pig satisfied," "Utilitarianism," 1863.
135 : 36—*The Life of Reason,* I, 9.
135 : 40—Cf. especially the following passages: "The religion of one age is often the poetry of the next. Around every living and operative faith there lies a region of allegory and imagination into which opinions frequently pass, and in which they long retain a transfigured and idealised existence after their natural life has died away. . . . Religious ideas die like the sun; their last rays, possessing little heat, are expended in creating beauty." *A History of Rationalism in Europe,* N. Y., 1867, 268, 269. "Modern Unitarianism is, I conceive, unfortunate on the one hand in refusing to allow its legitimate force to the exercise of reason and criticism; on the other hand, in having by its past exercise

NOTES

Page : line

of reason and criticism thrown aside treasures of pure religious tradition because of their dogmatic exterior." *The Prose Remains of Arthur Hugh Clough*, edited by his wife, London, 1888, 419.

136 : 8—See *The Tragic Sense of Life in Men and Peoples*, N. Y., 1921.
136 : 10—*The Genius of Spain*, Oxford, 1923, 24.
137 : 6—*Soliloquies in England*, 257-258.
137 : 10—See p. 178.
137 : 17—"The Spaniard is an empire and God unto himself. The perfected Spanish person makes permanent the social Spanish chaos." Waldo Frank, *Virgin Spain*, N. Y., 1926, 24. "The Englishman's norm is virtue, the Spaniard's norm is honour; the Englishman seeks action in order to conquer things; the Spaniard in order to conquer men." Salvador da Madariaga, *The Genius of Spain*, 17. Havelock Ellis cites numerous testimonies of Spaniards to the same effect, notably Macias Picavea, Donna Emilia Bazan, and Rafael Altamira. *The Soul of Spain*, Boston and N. Y., 1913.
137 : 21—*Interpretations of Poetry and Religion*, 98, 99.
138 : 13—*The Life of Reason*, I, 17, 29.
139 : 5—*Outlines of the History of Ethics*, London, 1886, 147. Cf. also "Greek conceptions, while indeed conversant with the great problems of mind in its relation to the surrounding world, know nothing of serious inner conflicts. . . . Here there reigns a secure and joyful faith in the power and glory of the human mind. The intellectual faculties, just as we have them, are recognised to be good; all that is needed in order to ward off everything hostile and to subordinate man's sensuous nature, is their vigorous development and a clear consciousness." Rudolf Eucken, *The Problem of Human Life*, N. Y., 1916, 125.
139 : 15—For an interesting discussion of this problem, see B. A. G. Fuller, *A History of Greek Philosophy*, Vol. II, *The Sophists, Socrates, Plato*, N. Y., 1931, 213.
139 : 32—Cf. Fuller's statement of Plato's ethics: "The proportion in which the ingredients of the good life must be mixed is a fixed quantity as deeply and directly inherent in the nature of reality as the properties of the circle or the triangle, and it has all the authority and rigidity of a truth once and for all delivered unto all mankind. . . . It is not provisional, relative, and flexible, rinsed clear of metaphysical starch, as later Aristotle was to develop it." *Ibid.*, 287.
139 : 36—*The Life of Reason*, I, 20, 21.
140 : 4—*Ibid.*, I, 27, 18.

CHAPTER FOUR

143 : 30—Chapter VII, "The Poetry of Barbarism" (Whitman, Browning); Chapter VIII, "Emerson;" Chapter VI, "The Absence of Religion in Shakespeare."
144 : 13—*Interpretations of Poetry and Religion*, N. Y. and London, 1900, 175, 177, 178, 181.
144 : 23—*Ibid.*, 208.
144 : 37—*Ibid.*, 198.
144 : 16—*Ibid.*, 181.
145 : 19—*Robert Browning* (English Men of Letters Series), London, 1903, 183 (1926 edition).

NOTES

Page : line
146 : 10—*Interpretations of Poetry and Religion*, 204, 206.
146 : 14—"Speculative," 1889.
146 : 26—"Christmas Eve," 1850.
146 : 28—*Interpretations of Poetry and Religion*, 211.
146 : 35—*Ibid.*, 213.
147 : 7—*Ibid.*, 186-187.
147 : 17—*Ibid.*, 213, 214.
147 : 26—*Ibid.*, 184.
147 : 38—*Ibid.*, 184.
148 : 3—*Ibid.*, 184.
148 : 16—"Seeing James one day shortly after his *Varieties of Religious Experience* had come out, Mr. Santayana crossed the street and said to him with a friendly smile, 'You have done the religious slumming for all time.' 'Really?' answered James genially; 'that is all slumming, is it—all these experiences are of the slums?' 'Yes,' was the answer, 'all.' In repeating this James chuckled to himself. 'Santayana's white marble mind!'" Dickinson Miller in a review of *Character and Opinion in the United States*, Dial, LXX (1920), 578.
148 : 28—*Interpretations of Poetry and Religion*, 195.
150 : 13—*Ibid.*, 222, 223.
150 : 32—*Ibid.*, 217, 233.
151 : 2—*Ibid.*, 221.
151 : 25—"Ode inscribed to W. H. Channing," 1846.
151 : 32—*The Journals of Ralph Waldo Emerson*, edited by Edward Waldo Emerson and Waldo Emerson Forbes, Boston and N. Y., 1909-1914, V. 205, 473 (entries of May 26, 1839 and Oct. 17, 1840).
152 : 13—*Interpretations of Poetry and Religion*, 147.
152 : 29—*Ibid.*, 162, 163.
153 : 3—*Ibid.*, 163.
153 : 17—*Ibid.*, 164, 165.
154 : 37—*Three Philosophical Poets*, Cambridge, 1910, 4.
155 : 2—*Ibid.*, 14.
155 : 5—*Ibid.*, 133.
155 : 15—*Ibid.*, 208.
155 : 20—*Ibid.*, 204.
155 : 36—*Ibid.*, 206-207.
156 : 4—*Ibid.*, 212.
156 : 14—*Ibid.*, 213.
156 : 34—*Ibid.*, 213, 214.
157 : 14—*Ibid.*, v.
157 : 35—*Ibid.*, 57, 61.
158 : 3—*Ibid.*, 66, 67.
158 : 8—*Ibid.*, 61
158 : 26—*Ibid.*, 115.
158 : 30—*Ibid.*, 129.
158 : 36—*Ibid.*, 131.
159 : 5—*Ibid.*, 132, 134.
159 : 19—*Ibid.*, 157.
159 : 26—*Ibid.*, 171.
159 : 35—*Ibid.*, 182.
159 : 38—*Ibid.*, 183.
160 : 7—*Ibid.*, 190.

NOTES

Page : line
160 : 10—*Ibid.*, 195.
160 : 20—*Ibid.*, 193.
160 : 26—June 1831, *Conversations with Eckermann;* quoted in Bayard Taylor's notes to his translation of *Faust,* II, 459.
161 : 23—*Three Philosophical Poets,* 187.
161 : 33—*Ibid.*, 185.
161 : 36—*Ibid.*, 185.
162 : 18—*Ibid.*, 196, 199.
162 : 30—LXXIX (1910), 563.
162 : 34—VIII (1911), 133, 134. Santayana's dismissal of all scholarly apparatus, citations, references, etc., was taken amiss by some critics, however. Thus a German reviewer wrote: "Wem nun eben im ersten Doppelbande von Vossler's meisterhafter Entwicklungsgeschichte die religiosphilosophischen und ethisch-politischen Grundlagen von Dante's System erlautert worden sind, der wird aus Santayana's Skizzierung wenig entnehmen können, wie auch die Betrachtung des Faust deutschen Lesern kaum etwas bieten dürfte." *Literarisches Zentralblatt für Deutschland,* Leipzig, May 20, 1911, 673. So also Lane Cooper took Santayana to task for implying that "scholarship and pedantry are the same thing," and that literary criticism can "be founded on something short of a first-hand knowledge." *Philosophical Review,* XX (1911), 443. The reader may also be interested in the following reviews and articles Santayana wrote from 1905 to 1910: for the *Journal of Philosophy, Psychology, and Scientific Methods*—reviews of Thomas Davidson, *The Philosophy of Goethe's Faust,* IV (Feb. 14, 1907), 106–108; Edith H. Johnson, *The Argument of Aristotle's Metaphysics,* IV (Mar. 28, 1907), 186–187; James Adam, *The Religious Teachers of Greece,* VI (Jan. 7, 1909), 23–25; G. Lowes Dickinson, *Is Immortality Desirable?* VI (July 22, 1909), 411–415; for the *New England Magazine* —"Sculpture," XXXVIII, n. s., (Mar. 1908), 103–111. He also furnished introductions to *Hamlet* in the Harper edition of Shakespeare, 1908, and to the Everyman's Library edition of Spinoza's *Ethics* and *De Intellectus Emendatione,* London and N. Y., 1910. The introduction to *Hamlet* has been recently reprinted in *Obiter Scripta,* edited by J. Buchler and B. Schwartz, N. Y. and London, 1936. It continues the theme of "The Absence of Religion in Shakespeare," but with much excellent analysis of the play.
163 : 2—"Shelley: or the Poetic Value of Revolutionary Principles," *Winds of Doctrine,* London and N. Y., 1913; "Dickens," *Soliloquies in England and Later Soliloquies,* N. Y. and London, 1922.
163 : 22—*Essays in Criticism,* 1865, II, 252 (N. Y., 1924).
163 : 36—*Winds of Doctrine,* 157.
164 : 3—*Ibid.*, 161, 183.
164 : 6—*Ibid.*, 182.
164 : 11—*Ibid.*, 176.
164 : 26—*Ibid.*, 182.
164 : 28—*Ibid.*, 183.
164 : 35—*Ibid.*, 184.
165 : 20—*Soliloquies in England,* 60–61.
165 : 24—*Ibid.*, 62.
165 : 29—*Ibid.*, 63.

NOTES   313

Page : line
165 : 35—*Ibid.*, 64.
166 : 3—*Ibid.*, 66–67.
166 : 6—*Ibid.*, 69.
166 : 10—*Ibid.*, 67.
166 : 16—*Ibid.*, 69.
166 : 19—*Ibid.*, 61.
166 : 24—*Ibid.*, 62.
166 : 25—*Ibid.*, 70.
166 : 34—*Ibid.*, 70–71.
167 : 24—The only change in Santayana's criticism has been a gradual extension of sympathy to literature which is less lofty and ethical than the standards of *Three Philosophical Poets* call for. In *Soliloquies in England* he says, "So anxious was I, when younger, to find some rational justification for poetry and religion, and to show that their magic was significant of true facts, that I insisted too much, as I now think, on the need of relevance to fact even in poetry. . . . I maintained that the noblest poetry also must express the moral burden of life and must be rich in wisdom. Age has made me less exacting, and I can now find quite sufficient perfection in poetry, like that of the Chinese and Arabians, without much philosophic scope, in mere grace and feeling and music and cloud-castles and frolic." 254.
168 : 7—See the Harvard catalogues for these years.
168 : 8—He spent this year traveling in Europe. He writes to William James: "Since I left America I have had glimpses of England, Belgium, Holland, Germany, and France, besides six weeks . . . in Avila, and almost a month in Florence. . . . From here I mean to go to Naples and Sicily, Egypt and Greece—all new ground for me." R. B. Perry, *The Thought and Character of William James*, II, 396.
168 : 12—Letter to William James, Dec. 5, 1905, *Ibid.*, II, 400.
168 : 25—Dickinson Miller, "Mr. Santayana and William James," *Harvard Graduates' Magazine*, XXIX (Mar. 1921), 352.
168 : 29—In a letter to the present writer.
168 : 33—*Character and Opinion in the United States*, N. Y. and London, 1920.
168 : 38—In a letter to the present writer.
169 : 2—In a conversation with the present writer.
169 : 26—I am indebted to the late Professor Palmer for these details.
169 : 40—*Soliloquies in England*, 256.
170 : 22—"The Intellectual Temper of the Age," *Winds of Doctrine*, 5.
170 : 32—*Ibid.*, 6.
170 : 37—*The Life of Reason*, V, 320.
171 : 3—*Ibid.*, V, 320.
171 : 14—*Winds of Doctrine*, 23.
171 : 32—*Ibid.*, 1.
171 : 41—*Ibid.*, 1–2.
172 : 7—*Ibid.*, 2.
172 : 25—*Ibid.*, 10.
172 : 30—*Ibid.*, 10, 11.
172 : 39—*Ibid.*, 12.
173 : 8—"Russell's Philosophic Essays," *Journal of Philosophy, Psychology, and Scientific Methods*, VIII (Feb. 3, Mar. 2, Aug. 3, 1911), 57–63, 113–124, 421–434.

Page : line

173 : 11—April 25, 1911, before the Philosophical Union of the University of California, Berkeley, Calif. Printed in *University of California Chronicle*, XIII (1911), 357-380.
173 : 29—*Winds of Doctrine*, 108.
173 : 38—*Ibid.*, 109.
174 : 4—*Ibid.*, 109.
174 : 7—*Ibid.*, 110.
174 : 38—*Ibid.*, 24.
175 : 4—*Poems*, 1923, 15.
175 : 8—*Winds of Doctrine*, 23.
175 : 15—Mar. 29, 1913, 353.
175 : 19—XCVI (1913), 574, 575.
175 : 21—XI (1913), 655.
175 : 22—XCVII (1913), 536.
175 : 33—From a letter of Logan Pearsall Smith to the present writer.
175 : 38—"The Logic of Fanaticism," I (Nov. 28, 1914), 18-19; "Goethe and German Egotism," II (Jan. 2, 1915), 15-16 (reprinted in *Egotism and German Philosophy*, London and N. Y., 1916); "Shakespeare: Made in America," II (Feb. 27, 1915), 96-98; "Spanish Opinion on the War," II (Apr. 10, 1915), 252-253; "Heathenism," II (Apr. 24, 1915), 296-297 (reprinted in *Egotism in German Philosophy*); "The Indomitable Individual," III (May 22, 1915), 64-66; "Genteel American Poetry," III (May 29, 1915), 94-95; "Natural Leadership," III (July 31, 1915), 333-334; "Classic Liberty," IV (Aug. 21, 1915), 65-66; "German Freedom," IV (Aug. 28, 1915), 94-96; "Liberalism and Culture," IV, (Sept 4, 1915), 123-125 (the last three reprinted in *Soliloquies in England*, 1922); "The Alleged Catholic Danger," V (Jan. 15, 1916), 269-271; "The Human Scale," V (Jan. 29, 1916), 326-328 (reprinted in *Soliloquies in England*). With the articles on America should be placed "Materialism and Idealism in America," *Landmark*, I (Jan. 1919), 28-38 (reprinted in *Character and Opinion in the United States*, 1920). During this time Santayana was also writing an occasional article for the *Journal of Philosophy*, see 230 : 34.
176 : 27—*New Republic*, II, 296-297.
176 : 36—*Ibid.*, II, 252.
177 : 8—*Ibid.*, II, 253.
177 : 24—*Ibid.*, III, 65, 66.
177 : 31—"Liberalism and Culture," *Ibid.*, IV, 123; *Soliloquies in England*, 174.
178 : 5—"Liberalism and Culture," *Ibid.*, IV, 124; *Ibid.*, 175.
178 : 23—"Classic Liberty," *Ibid.*, IV, 65; *Ibid.*, 166.
178 : 30—*Ibid.*, IV, 65; *Ibid.*, 168.
178' : 36—"German Freedom," *Ibid.*, IV, 94; *Ibid.*, 171.
179 : 7—*Ibid.*, IV, 95; *Ibid.*, 170-171.
179 : 16—"Liberalism and Culture," *Ibid.*, IV, 124; *Ibid.*, 176, 177.
180 : 8—"The Logic of Fanaticism," *Ibid.*, IV, 18.
180 : 13—*Ibid.*, IV, 19.
180 : 22—"Liberalism and Culture," *Ibid.*, IV, 125; *Soliloquies in England*, 177-178.
180 : 36—"Classic Liberty," *Ibid.*, IV, 66; *Ibid.*, 168-169.
181 : 15—"On My Friendly Critics," *Soliloquies in England*, 258.
182 : 1—"The Irony of Liberalism," *Ibid.*, 188.
182 : 9—"Liberalism and Culture," *New Republic*, IV, 124; 176.

Page : line

182 : 17—See above, pp. 89–91.
182 : 33—*Egotism in German Philosophy*, London, 1916, 5.
183 : 6—*Ibid.*, 12.
184 : 6—Ralph B. Perry, in a review for *Journal of Philosophy, Psychology, and Scientific Methods*, XIV (1917), 639.
184 : 10—Kojoro Sugimoro, in *International Journal of Ethics*, XXVII (1917), 383.
184 : 18—*Egotism in German Philosophy*, 6.
184 : 22—*Dial*, LXIII (1917), 65.
184 : 24—*Journal of Philosophy, etc.*, XIV (1917), 639.
186 : 10—*Egotism in German Philosophy*, 167–168.
186 : 18—*Ibid.*, 103.
186 : 20—Curiously enough, both Santayana and Dewey reviewed each other's books. See for Dewey's review of Santayana, *New Republic*, IX (1916), 155–156; for Santayana's review, *Journal of Philosophy, etc.*, XII (1915), 645–649. Dewey's is really one of the most favorable reviews of Santayana's book. "That which no one else could have produced is the combination of searching criticism with a pathetic sense of something basically sound and hopeful in reversion from authority and tradition to basic human interests.... At all events, he does justice with the sensitiveness of an artist to whatever he finds true in the doctrine which he condemns." *New Republic*, IX, 155. Santayana's review is also enthusiastic.
187 : 2—*Winds of Doctrine*, 196.
187 : 6—*Ibid.*, 212.
187 : 28—*Ibid.*, 187–188.
187 : 39—*Ibid.*, 192.
188 : 11—*Ibid.*, 212–213.
188 : 38—*Character and Opinion in the United States*, 1920, 143.
189 : 9—*Ibid.*, 163.
189 : 29—*Ibid.*, 188.
190 : 3—*Ibid.*, 175, 176.
190 : 13—*Ibid.*, 178–179.
190 : 24—*Ibid.*, 188.
190 : 30—*Ibid.*, 190.
191 : 10—Letter to George Herbert Palmer, April 2, 1900. *The Letters of William James*, edited by Henry James, Boston, 1920, II, 122, 123.
191 : 21—*Character and Opinion in the United States*, 76.
191 : 28—*Ibid.*, 82.
192 : 6—*Ibid.*, 101.
192 : 10—*Ibid.*, 137, 138.
192 : 14—*Harvard Graduates' Magazine*, XXIX (Mar. 1921), 361.
192 : 25—*Character and Opinion in the United States*, 85.
192 : 36—*Dial*, LXX (1921), 578.
193 : 1—II (1920), 378.
193 : 10—*Character and Opinion in the United States*, 65.
193 : 22—*Ibid.*, 95, 96.
193 : 41—XXVIII (1920), 346.
194 : 10—*Character and Opinion in the United States*, viii.
194 : 15—The soliloquies appeared originally in the *New Republic*, *Athenaeum*, and *Dial*. The *Journal of Philosophy* and the *London Mercury* also contained one each. For dates see "Bibliography of the Published

Page : line

Writings of George Santayana," *Obiter Scripta,* edited by Justis Buchler and Benjamin Schwartz, N. Y. and London, 1936.
194 : 36—*Soliloquies in England,* 1.
195 : 24—*Ibid.,* 103-104, 101.
195 : 30—*Ibid.,* 30.
196 : 4—*Ibid.,* 5.
196 : 11—*Englishmen, Frenchmen, Spaniards,* Oxford, 1928.
196 : 29—*Soliloquies in England,* 6, 5.
196 : 37—*Ibid.,* 53-54.
197 : 3—*Ibid.,* 54.
197 : 18—*Ibid.,* 54-55.
197 : 34—*Ibid.,* 30-31, 32.
197 : 42—*English Traits,* 1856, 127, 129, 130 (Boston, 1885).
198 : 19—*Soliloquies in England,* 74-75.
198 : 25—*Ibid.,* 75.
199 : 2—*Ibid.,* 21-22.
200 : 5—*Ibid.,* 140-141.
200 : 16—*Ibid.,* 22.
200 : 20—*Ibid.,* 142.
200 : 36—LXXIII (1922), 559.
201 : 3—*Nation and Athenaeum,* XXXI (1922), 474. See also *Freeman,* VI (1922), 164.
201 : 10—*Soliloquies in England,* 6.
201 : 18—*Dial,* LXXIII (1920), 562.
201 : 37—See pp. 349-351.
202 : 13—*Freeman,* II (1920), 378.
202 : 29—XXXI (1922), 474.
202 : 37—*Winds of Doctrine,* 210.
202 : 38—*Character and Opinion in the United States,* 99.
203 : 3—*Ibid.,* 96.
204 : 11—*Humanism and America,* edited by Norman Foerster, N. Y., 1930, 291.
204 : 17—*Harvard Graduates' Magazine,* IX (Sept. 1900), 19.
204 : 40—*Democracy and Leadership,* Boston and N. Y., 1924.
205 : 1—See especially Elliott, "The Pride of Modernity," *Humanism and America;* More, *Shelburne Essays,* Eighth Series, Boston and N. Y., 1913.
205 : 9—No work of Santayana's beyond *Interpretations of Poetry and Religion* is included in Norman Foerster's bibliography of humanistic literature. In fact, even by 1910 the humanists sense disturbing elements in Santayana's writings. The *Nation,* under the editorship of More, finds *Three Philosophical Poets* marred by "a lack of central veracity in the critic's own philosophy," "a disquieting touch of make-believe," and *Winds of Doctrine* a fine example "of the modern tendency to 'burrow downwards toward the primitive.'" XC (1910), 419; XCVI (1913), 575.
205 : 28—*The Genteel Tradition at Bay,* N. Y. and London, 1931, 69.
206 : 9—See especially P. E. More, "Shelley," *Shelburne Essays,* Seventh Series, Boston and N. Y., 1910, 1-28.
207 : 17—See "Brief History of My Opinions," *Contemporary American Philosophy,* edited by George P. Adams and Wm. Pepperell Montague, N. Y., 1930, II, 244.
207 : 20—See *The Genteel Tradition at Bay,* 7, 69; *Winds of Doctrine,* 182.
207 : 38—"Milton," *Essays in Criticism, Second Series,* 1865, 62, 69 (N. Y., 1924).

NOTES 317

Page : line
208 : 7—"The Rhodora," 1839.
208 : 12—See "The Poet," *Essays, Second Series*, 1844.
208 : 14—*Ibid.*, F. I. Carpenter, *Ralph Waldo Emerson: Representative Selections*, N. Y., 1934, 210.
208 : 17—"Plato: or the Philosopher," *Representative Men*, 1850; *Ibid.*, 240.
208 : 18—"The Poet," *Ibid.*, 224.
208 : 24—See Norman Foerster, *American Criticism*, Boston and N. Y., 1928, 58.
209 : 1—"The Poet," *Ralph Waldo Emerson: Representative Selections*, 214.
209 : 4—"The Problem," 1840.
209 : 8—"The Poet," *Ralph Waldo Emerson: Representative Selections*, 221.
209 : 27—"Shakespeare Once More," *Among My Books*, Boston, I, 175–176 (1886 edition).
209 : 31—See especially "Rousseau and the Sentimentalists," *Among My Books*, Vol. I.
210 : 10—*American Criticism*, 104.
210 : 28—Review of *Little Essays Drawn from the Writings of George Santayana*, edited by Logan Pearsall Smith, with the collaboration of the author, N. Y., 1920, *London Mercury*, II (1920), 411.
210 : 30—See particularly: Morris Cohen, "On American Philosophy—George Santayana," *New Republic*, XXIII (1920), 221–223, which accounts for Santayana's neglect at the hands of philosophers.
211 : 4—*Little Essays, etc.*, v.
212 : 33—*Soliloquies in England*, 13.
214 : 18—*Ibid.*, 18–19.
214 : 36—*Ibid.*, 26.
215 : 6—*Ibid.*, 24.
215 : 26—*Ibid.*, 99.
215 : 37—*Ibid.*, 116.
216 : 7—*Ibid.*, 116.
216 : 25—See *Soliloquies in England*, 2.
217 : 2—*Dialogues in Limbo*, N. Y. and London, 1925, 5, 66.
217 : 8—*Ibid.*, 36.
218 : 1—*Ibid.*, 69.
218 : 19—*Ibid.*, 139.
219 : 2—See above, pp. 89–91.
219 : 16—*Dialogues in Limbo*, 31.
219 : 19—*Ibid.*, 31.
219 : 29—*Ibid.*, 32, 33.
219 : 33—See *Soliloquies in England*, 2.
220 : 11—*Dialogues in Limbo*, 47, 48.
220 : 13—*Interpretations of Poetry and Religion*, 1900, Chapter IX; *The Life of Reason*, Volume V; *The Genteel Tradition at Bay*, 1931, Chapter III.
220 : 17—Sonnet 3, *Poems*, 1923, 5; *Three Philosophical Poets*, 1910, Chapter I; *Winds of Doctrine*, 1913, Chapter V.
220 : 30—*Dialogues in Limbo*, 72–73, 74.
220 : 38—*Ibid.*, 84.
221 : 6—*Ibid.*, 84, 85.
221 : 14—*Lucifer*, 1899.
221 : 28—*Dialogues in Limbo*, 88.
222 : 4—*Ibid.*, 173–193.
222 : 6—*Ibid.*, 164–168.

NOTES

Page : line
222 : 25—*Scepticism and Animal Faith*, 1923, x.
223 : 3—*The Life of Reason*, I, 284; *Interpretations of Poetry and Religion*, 273; *The Life of Reason*, II, 111; *Ibid.*, IV, 129; *Ibid.*, IV, 190; *Three Philosophical Poets*, 51. Quoted in Logan Pearsall Smith, *A Treasury of English Aphorisms*, London, 1928.
223 : 15—Introduction to *Spinoza*, viii; *The Life of Reason*, III, 201; *Three Philosophical Poets*, 11; *The Life of Reason*, IV, 118; *Ibid.*, I, 13. Quoted in Smith, *op. cit.*
223 : 24—*Scepticism and Animal Faith*, 69, 271, 11.
224 : 10—*Soliloquies in England*, 223.
225 : 2—*Character and Opinion in the United States*, 180.
225 : 8—*Ibid.*, 174.
225 : 11—*Ibid.*, 175.
225 : 26—*English Prose Style*, N. Y., 1928, 53.
225 : 36—*On the Study of Celtic Literature*, 1866, 106 (1895 edition).
226 : 30—*Platonism and the Spiritual Life*, 85, 86.

CHAPTER FIVE

227 : 15—From a letter to the present writer.
228 : 16—Nov. 29, 1904, Ralph B. Perry, *The Thought and Character of William James*, Boston, 1935, II, 397.
228 : 22—*Ibid.*, II, 397.
228 : 34—Chapter I, "Understanding, Imagination, and Mysticism."
229 : 11—See *The Life of Reason*, N. Y. and London, 1905-06, I, Chapter VII.
229 : 26—See *Ibid.*, V, Chapters III, VI.
229 : 39—Introduction to Everyman Library edition of Spinoza's *Ethics* and *De Intellectus Emendatione*, London and N. Y., 1910; *Winds of Doctrine*, London and N. Y., 1913.
230 : 31—R. W. Sellars, "Current Realism," in D. S. Robinson, *An Anthology of Recent Philosophy*, N. Y., 1929, 287, 288.
230 : 34—*Journal of Philosophy, Psychology, and Scientific Methods*, "Dr. Fuller, Plotinus, and the Nature of Evil" (Review of B. A. G. Fuller, *The Problem of Evil in Plotinus*), X (Oct. 23, 1913), 589-599; "The Coming Philosophy" (Review of E. B. Holt, *The Concept of Consciousness*), XI (Aug. 13, 1914), 449-463; "Some Meanings of the Word 'Is,'"; XII (Feb. 4, 1915), 66-68; "Philosophic Sanction of Ambition," XII (Mar. 4, 1915), 113-116; "Philosophical Heresy," XII (Oct. 14, 1915), 561-568; Review of Dewey, *German Philosophy and Politics*, XII (Nov. 25, 1915), 645-649; "Two Rational Moralists" (Review of John Erskine, *The Moral Obligation to be Intelligent* and E. B. Holt, *The Freudian Wish*), XIII (May 25, 1916), 290-296; "Notes Written on the Flyleaf of a Copy of the Life of Reason," XV (Jan. 31, 1918), 82-84; "Literal and Symbolic Knowledge," XV (Aug. 1, 1918), 421-424. "Philosophical Heresy" and "Literal and Symbolic Knowledge" have been reprinted in *Obiter Scripta*, edited by Justus Buchler and Benjamin Schwartz, N. Y. and London, 1936.
231 : 1—Subtitle of *Essays in Critical Realism*, by Durant Drake, Arthur Lovejoy, James Bissett Pratt, Arthur K. Rogers, George Santayana, Roy Wood Sellars, and C. A. Strong, London, 1920.
231 : 8—*Ibid.*, v.
231 : 18—"The Nature of the Datum," *Ibid.*, 224.

Page : line

231 : 27—*Ibid.*, 163.
232 : 9—*Ibid.*, 173, 172.
232 : 19—*Ibid.*, 179.
232 : 28—*Ibid.*, 180.
233 : 15—"Literal and Symbolic Knowledge," *Journal of Philosophy, Psychology, and Scientific Methods*, XV (Aug. 1, 1918), 1918; *Scepticism and Animal Faith*, N. Y. and London, 1923; *The Unknowable* (Herbert Spencer Lecture, Oxford, Oct. 24, 1923), Oxford, 1923; "Some Meanings of the Word 'Is,'" *Journal of Philosophy*, XXI (July 3, 1924), 365–377; *Platonism and the Spiritual Life*, N. Y. and London, 1927; *The Realm of Essence*, N. Y. and London, 1927; *The Realm of Matter*, N. Y. and London, 1930; *The Realm of Truth*, N. Y. and London, 1937.
233 : 37—*Scepticism and Animal Faith*, 70.
234 : 5—*The Realm of Essence*, 23.
234 : 11—*Ibid.*, 40.
235 : 17—*Ibid.*, 37–38.
236 : 4—*Scepticism and Animal Faith*, 88.
236 : 8—"Literal and Symbolic Knowledge," *Journal of Philosophy*, XV, 436.
236 : 22—*Scepticism and Animal Faith*, 267–268.
236 : 32—*The Realm of Essence*, xiv.
237 : 8—*The Unknowable*, 24, 25.
237 : 24—*Scepticism and Animal Faith*, 274.
237 : 40—*Ibid.*, 274.
238 : 29—See Chapter IV.
239 : 3—*Platonism and the Spiritual Life*, 83.
239 : 12—*Scepticism and Animal Faith*, v.
239 : 31—See above, p. 25.
240 : 5—*The Realm of Matter*, 39.
240 : 19—*Ibid.*, 98.
240 : 37—*Ibid.*, 99.
241 : 11—*Ibid.*, 110–111.
241 : 18—*Ibid.*, 100.
241 : 29—*The Unknowable*, 3–4.
241 : 36—*Ibid.*, 8, 9.
242 : 20—I, n. s. (Mar. 1928), 206–211.
242 : 25—*Some Turns of Thought in Modern Philosophy*, Cambridge, Eng. and N. Y., 1933, 79.
242 : 34—*Ibid.*, 82.
242 : 39—*Ibid.*, 83.
243 : 6—*Scepticism and Animal Faith*, vii.
243 : 19—Sonnet V, *Poems*, 1923, 7.
243 : 21—*Idem*.
243 : 24—Sonnet 19, *Poems*, 21. These sonnets were written originally during Santayana's student days at Harvard. See above, pp. 27–29, 38, 39.
244 : 2—*The Realm of Essence*, 156.
244 : 37—*Summa Theologiae*, pars prima, qu. lxxxiv, art. 7. Cited in Henry Osborn Taylor, *The Medieval Mind*, II, 496 (third American edition).
245 : 10—*The Realm of Essence*, 155.
245 : 22—*Ibid.*, 155.
245 : 29—*Ibid.*, 157.
246 : 5—*Contemporary American Philosophy: Personal Statements*, edited by

Page	: line	
		George P. Adams and Wm. Pepperell Montague, N. Y., 1930, II, 251.
247	:	9—*Treatise on Human Nature*, 1739, Book I, part IV, section 6.
247	:	39—The relation of Santayana to Hume is admirably treated in Hardy Hoover, *The Philosophy of Santayana*, 1928, a Harvard dissertation.
248	:	16—See *The Realm of Essence*, 160–161.
248	:	23—*Ibid.*, 162–163.
248	:	24—"Letters to Arnaud," IX; "Monadology," section 7. Quoted in Calkins, *The Persistent Problems of Philosophy*, N. Y., 1907, 82 (3rd, edition).
248	:	29—*The Realm of Essence*, 138, 143.
248	:	35—*Ibid.*, 165.
249	:	10—*Ibid.*, 166.
249	:	16—*Ibid.*, 169.
249	:	19—*Ibid.*, 173.
249	:	29—*Ibid.*, 174–180.
250	:	5—Since the composition of this chapter *The Realm of Truth* has been published.
250	:	7—*Scepticism and Animal Faith*, 268.
250	:	19—See *Scepticism and Animal Faith*, Chap. XXV.
251	:	6—*Soliloquies in England and Later Soliloquies*, N. Y. and London, 1922, 210.
251	:	9—*Ibid.*, 210.
251	:	34—*Harvard Monthly*, XIV (1892), 89–99. For discussion, see p. 91.
252	:	11—*Platonism and the Spiritual Life*, 66–67.
252	:	17—*Introduction to Living Philosophy*, N. Y., 1932, 362.
253	:	1—*The Types of Philosophy*, N. Y., 1929, 366.
253	:	9—*Experience and Nature*, Chicago, 1925, 370.
253	:	13—See Robinson, *An Introduction to Living Philosophy*, 234.
253	:	40—See R. W. Sellars, "Current Realism," in D. S. Robinson, *An Anthology of Recent Philosophy*, 283–284.
254	:	12—See "Brief History of My Opinions," *Contemporary American Philosophy*, II, 248.
254	:	18—*Ibid.*, 253.
254	:	31—*Interpretations of Poetry and Religion*, N. Y., 1900, Chapter VII.
255	:	25—*The Realm of Essence*, 73.
255	:	39—*The Realm of Matter*, 24–25.
256	:	20—*Ibid.*, 35–36.

CHAPTER SIX

257 : 5—"Penitent Art," *Dial*, LXXIII (July 1922), 25–31; ""The Mutability of Aesthetic Categories," (Review of Henry R. Marshall, *The Beautiful*), *Philosophical Review*, XXIV (May 1925), 281–291; "An Aesthetic Soviet," *Dial*, LXXXII (May 1927), 361–370. Santayana is still as insistent upon the relation of art to life and its obligation to moral values. He has little sympathy with an "soviet" of "emancipated" artists. They announce that art must be emancipated from nature, and appreciation of art from literature. This is possible (though by no means exclusively right) if by literature we understand romantic history or fiction, and by nature visual appearances; but there is a moral world of which literature is the verbal expression; and from these no human art can be emancipated. All values are natural in their origin, and they all become moral in their harmony." Dial LXXXII 369. "The

| Page : line | |

pleasures which are called aesthetic turn out, I think, to be intellectual, historical, and moral in the end and in their chief substance; but this circumstance is nothing against them. It makes for their dignity, as for that of human happiness, that they should be broadly based." *Journal of Philosophy,* XXXIV, 290–291. Yet there are signs of penitence in modern art. Cubism, even if it "can daub a cross-eyed section of the entire spectrum or a compound fracture of a nightmare," is "by no means an inexpert or meaningless thing," and not without "a very deep and recondite charm." It reverts to "what the spinal column might feel if it had a separate consciousness, or to what the retina might see if it could be cut off from the brain: lights, patterns, dynamic suggestions." *Dial,* LXXIII, 27–28. And another form of modern art is childlike in its effort to give no more than "a pregnant hint, some large, graphic sign, some profound caricature" which is "indication" rather than "reproduction." "The distortion, the single emphasis, the extreme simplification may reveal a soul which rhetoric and self-love had hidden in a false rationality." *Dial,* LXXIII, 28–29.

257 : 6—"A Long Way Round to Nirvana; or Much Ado about Dying," (Freud), *Dial,* LXXV (Nov. 1923), 435–442; "Proust on Essences," *Life and Letters,* II (June 1929), 455–459; "Locke and the Frontiers of Common Sense" (Paper read before the Royal Society of Literature on the occasion of the tercentenary of the birth of John Locke); "Ultimate Religion" (Paper read at the Hague on the occasion of the tercentenary of the birth of Spinoza); Foreword to Iris Origo, *Giacomo Leopardi, A Biography,* Oxford, 1935. The first and third papers are reprinted in *Some Turns of Thought in Modern Philosophy,* Cambridge, Eng. and N. Y., 1933; the second and fourth in *Obiter Scripta,* N. Y. and London, 1936. Locke seems to Santayana a "sort of William James of the seventeenth century" . . . possessing an amiable "romanticism united with a scientific conscience and power of destructive analysis balanced by moral enthusiasm. . . . His system was no metaphysical castle, no theological acropolis: rather a homely ancestral manor house built in several styles of architecture. . . . There was no greater incongruity in its parts than in the gentle variations of English weather or in the qualified moods and insights of a civilised mind." *Some Turns of Thought, etc.,* 25, 26. Santayana has lost none of his early admiration of Spinoza, and uses him as a text for a disquisition upon what man may expect of an ultimate religion. See p. 282. Spinoza "solved the problem of the spiritual life after stating it in the hardest, sharpest, most cruel terms. . . . Let us nerve ourselves today to imitate his example, . . . by exercising his courage in the face of a somewhat different world, in which it may be even more difficult for us than it was for him to find a sure foothold and a sublime companionship." *Obiter Scripta,* 281. Proust is to be commended for having discovered the realm of essence and for having ably demonstrated its presence in his remarkable novel. Freud is to be commended for having "broadened his conception of sexual craving" and "his new myths . . . about life, like his old ones about dreams, are calculated to enlighten and to chasten us enormously about ourselves." *Some Turns of Thought, etc.,* 88, 92–93. As for Leopardi, he is still to Santayana, for all his frustration and pessimism, one of the truest, most genuine poets who have ever sung.

Page : line
257 : 7—"America's Young Radicals," *Forum*, LXVII (May 1922), 371–375; "Marginal Notes on Civilization in the United States" (Review of *Civilization in the United States*, edited by Harold Stearns), LXXII (June 1922), 553–568; "The Genteel Tradition at Bay," *Saturday Review of Literature*, VII (Jan. 3, 10, 17, 1931), 502–503, 518–519, 534–535; *Adelphi*, series 3, I (Jan., Feb., Mar., 1931), 309–321, 389–400, 466–479. Reprinted as a book, N. Y., 1931. The reader may also be interested in the following miscellaneous articles of Santayana: "Living without Thinking," (Review of John B. Watson, *Psychology from the Standpoint of a Behaviorist*), *Forum*, LXVIII (Sept. 1922), 731–735; *"Dewey's* Naturalistic Metaphysics," (Review of John Dewey, *Experience and Nature*), *Journal of Philosophy*, XXII (Dec. 3, 1925), 673–688; "Overheard in Seville," *Dial*, LXXXII (April 1927), 282–286; "Revolutions in Science," *New Adelphi*, I, n. s. (March 1928), 206–211; "Fifty Years of British Idealism," *New Adelphi*, II, n.s., (Dec. 1928), 112–120; "A Few Remarks," (on Crime, Prudence, Money, Self-Sacrifice), *Life and Letters*, II (Jan. 1929), 29–35; "Spengler" (Review of Spengler, *The Decline of the West*), *New Adelphi*, II n. s. (Mar. 1929), 210–214; "Enduring the Truth," *New Adelphi*, III, n. s., (Dec. 1929), 120–124, *Saturday Review of Literature*, VI (Dec. 7, 1929), 512; "The Prestige of the Infinite" (Review of Julien Benda, *Essai d'un discours coherent sur les rapports de Dieu et du monde, Journal of Philosophy*, XXIX (May 26, 1932), 281–289; "Alternatives to Liberalism," *Saturday Review of Literature*, X (June 23, 1934), 761–762, *Life and Letters*, X (Aug. 1934), 541–545; "Many Nations in One Empire," *New Frontier*, I (Sept. 1934), 6–10; "Why I Am Not a Marxist," *Modern Monthly*, IX (Apr. 1935), 77–79; Review of Bertrand Russell, *Religion and Science, American Mercury*, XXXVII (Mar. 1936), 377–379.
257 : 17—*Dial*, LXXII (1922), 554.
258 : 3—*Ibid.*, LXXII, 556.
258 : 19—*Ibid.*, LXXII, 555.
258 : 35—*Ibid.*, LXXII, 556–557.
258 : 41—*Ibid.*, LXXII, 560.
259 : 6—*Ibid.*, LXXII, 568.
259 : 19—*The Genteel Tradition at Bay*, New York and London, 1931, 1, 4.
259 : 27—*Ibid.*, 17–18.
259 : 32—*Ibid.*, 4–5.
260 : 8—*Ibid.*, 7, 8.
260 : 11—See pp. 178–180.
260 : 28—*Ibid.*, 23, 24.
260 : 35—*Ibid.*, 28–29.
261 : 4—*Ibid.*, 45.
261 : 9—*Ibid.*, 46–47.
261 : 19—*Ibid.*, 57.
261 : 23—*Ibid.*, 54.
261 : 32—*Ibid.*, 61.
261 : 38—*Ibid.*, 54.
262 : 8—*Ibid.*, 73–74.
262 : 24—*Ibid.*, 66–67.
263 : 2—"I call this book *A Memoir in the Form of a Novel*, because it was never planned as a story with an artificial dramatic unity, but was

Page : line

meant from the beginning to be the chronicle, half satirical, half poetic, of a sentimental education. In the early 1890's, when I had returned to Harvard to teach but still lived among undergraduates, it occurred to me to contrast the moral development of two friends, one gay and the other demure, who should be drawn in opposite directions, such as to test their mutual affection and lend it a tragic touch. . . . *How They Lived* was indeed the title which I gave to my first sketches." Preface to *The Last Puritan, The Works of George Santayana*, Triton Edition, N. Y., 1937, XI, ix.

263 . 40—*Ibid.*, XI, x, xi.
264 : 35—*The Last Puritan*, N. Y. and London, 1936, 7.
264 : 39—*Ibid.*, 6.
265 : 19—Preface to *The Last Puritan*, Triton Edition, XI, xiii–xiv.
265 : 24—Epilogue to *The Last Puritan*, 600.
265 : 28—*Ibid.*, 600.
265 : 39—*Ibid.*, 6–7.
266 : 3—*Ibid.*, 7.
266 : 10—Introduction to *Hamlet*, Harper edition of Shakespeare, 1908, reprinted in *Obiter Scripta*.
266 : 14—*The Last Puritan*, 9.
266 : 19—Introduction to Hamlet, *Obiter Scripta*, 62.
266 : 25—*Ibid.*, 62.
267 : 6—Preface to *The Last Puritan*, Triton Edition, XI, xv.
267 : 28—*Ibid.*, XI, viii.
267 : 29—As he describes himself in *Soliloquies in England*.
268 : 4—See p. 219.
268 : 11—See pp. 20, 27.
269 : 30—"I could not help feeling that what dominated America was a passing fever, a heresy, a forced enthusiasm, not really satisfying the heart and destined to end in emptiness." In England "all strain was relaxed; the eye and the ear were softly flattered; the imagination was stirred by living remnants of medieval Christendom; and something wholesome and Spartan in the air seemed to neutralise the affectations and crotchets of the inhabitants." Preface to *The Last Puritan*, Triton Edition, XI, xi.
270 : 5—See pp. 89–91.
270 : 20—*Saturday Review of Literature*, XIII (Feb. 1, 1936), 4, 12.
270 : 23—*New York Herald Tribune Books*, XII (Feb. 2, 1936), 2.
270 : 33—See p. 5.
270 : 35—See p. 215.
271 : 10—*The Last Puritan*, 19.
271 : 13—*Ibid.*, 32.
271 : 38—*Ibid.*, 24–25.
273 : 28—"Glimpses of Old Boston," *Boston Latin School Register*, LI (1932), 10.
274 : 2—Easter, 1900, Ralph B. Perry, *The Thought and Character of William James*, Boston, 1935, II, 321.
274 : 16—*Winds of Doctrine*, London, 1913, 192. See p. 187 above.
274 : 28—*Saturday Review of Literature*, XIII (Feb. 1, 1936), 12. Santayana himself admits that a considerable impetus toward the writing of his book came from the untimely deaths of several of the young Harvard poets of his day. See Preface to *The Last Puritan*, Triton Edition, XI, ix, x.
275 : 2—Harold A. Larrabee, "George Santayana: American Philosopher?" *Sewanee Review*, XXXIX (1931), 220.

NOTES

Page : line
275 : 10—*Ibid.*, XXXIX, 220.
275 : 16—See Henry S. Canby, "The American Santayana," *Saturday Review of Literature*, XV (Apr. 17, 1937), 3, 4+, for a different point of view.
275 : 28—From a letter to the present writer.
277 : 16—*Proust and Santayana*, Chicago, 1937, 54–55.
277 : 27—See *The Life of Reason*, II, 106–107.
277 : 29—Chapter VII.
277 : 33—*Soliloquies in England and Later Soliloquies*, 1922, 188.
277 : 37—*The Last Puritan*, 600.
278 : 3—Sonnet 19, *Poems*, 1923, 21.
278 : 22—*Platonism and the Spiritual Life*, N. Y., 1927, 33.
278 : 26—See p. 136.
279 : 17—"Preface on the Unity of My Earlier and Later Philosophy," *The Works of George Santayana*, Triton Edition, VII, x, xii.
278 : 39—Preface to *The Life of Reason*, 1922 edition, I, i–ii.
279 : 22—See *Interpretations of Poetry and Religion*, Chap. IX.
279 : 26—Quoted in Van Meter Ames, *Proust and Santayana*, 63. Santayana's remark is interesting: "If a piece of food can't be assimilated it must have some bone to it." *Ibid.*, 63.
279 : 27—See letter quoted from on p. 107.
279 : 33—See p. 311.
280 : 21—Dec. 6, 1905. R. B. Perry, *The Thought and Character of William James*, II, 401–402.
280 : 39—*Ibid.*, II, 403.
281 : 6—See *Soliloquies in England*, 67; Ames, *Proust and Santayana*, 65.
281 : 19—See above, pp. 89–91.
281 : 27—From a letter to the present writer.
281 : 36—*Idem*.
282 : 4—*Obiter Scripta*, 290.
282 : 9—*Ibid.*, 292.
282 : 12—See above, pp. 218, 219.
282 : 25—See above, p. 76.
282 : 30—Horace Kallen, "America and the Life of Reason," *Journal of Philosophy*, XVIII (1921), 534.
283 : 5—*Ibid.*, XVIII, 534, 535.
283 : 11—At least, they make no mention of Santayana among the teachers at Harvard who most influenced their thought. See *Contemporary American Philosophy: Personal Statements*, N. Y., 1930, passim.
283 : 14—*Ibid.*, I, 389.
283 : 24—*Ibid.*, 79, 80.
283 : 28—*Ibid.*, II, 138–139.
284 : 2—*Ibid.*, II, 138.
284 : 8—*Ibid.*, II, 164.
284 : 24—*The Philosophy of Art*, N. Y., 1929, iv, 186, 235
284 : 31—*The Aesthetic Experience*, Merion, Pa., 1924, 12.
284 : 33—*Beauty*, N. Y., 1930.
284 : 34—*The Aesthetic Attitude*, N. Y., 1920.
285 : 17—*Aesthetic Judgment*, N. Y., 1929, 7–9.
285 : 33—*Ibid.*, 44.
286 : 19—*Contemporary American Philosophy*, II, 415, 416.
286 : 27—*American Philosophy Today and Tomorrow*, edited by H. M. Kallen and S. Hook, N. Y., 1935.

NOTES

Page : line
287 : 9—*Ibid.*, 271.
287 : 13—*The Philosophy of Santayana*, with a critical introduction by Irwin Edman, N. Y., 1936.
287 : 18—"Religion and the Philosophical Imagination," *Adam, the Baby and the Man from Mars*, Cambridge, 1929, 227-228.
287 : 21—*Ibid.*, 222, 225.
287 : 25—"The Naturalistic Temper," *American Philosophy Today and Tomorrow*, 142.
287 : 33—*Ibid.*, 147.
288 : 3—*Ibid.*, 152.
288 : 23—Cf. Santayana's recent remark concerning Eliot's admiration for the Philosophy of Dante: "We can understand why Mr. Eliot feels this to be a 'superior' philosophy; but how can he fail to see that it is false?" "Tragic Philosophy," *Triton Edition of the Works of George Santayana*, II, 285.
289 : 7—*A Preface to Morals*, N. Y., 1929, 328, 330.
289 : 29—*The Testament of Beauty*, Oxford, 1929, 8.
289 : 34—*Ibid.*, 9.
289 : 36—See *Saturday Review of Literature*, VI (1929), 512-513.
290 : 13—*The Testament of Beauty*, 124, 176.
290 : 18—*Ibid.*, 176.
290 : 37—*Ibid.*, 184-185.
291 : 14—*Ibid.*, 192.
291 : 28—*Nation*, CXI (1920), 221.
291 : 40—For further discussion of the relation of Bridges to Santayana see H. A. Larrabee, "Robert Bridges and George Santayana," *American Scholar*, I (1932), 167-182.
292 : 9—"On American Philosophy—George Santayana," *New Republic*, XXIII (1920), 223.
292 : 12—"The Dichotomy of George Santayana," *Catholic World*, CXL (1934), 23, 27, 24.
292 : 19—*Ibid.*, 28, 27.
292 : 28—*Dialogues in Limbo*, 33.
292 : 37—*Nation*, CXI (1920), 222.
293 : 4—"America and the Life of Reason," *Journal of Philosophy*, XVIII (1921), 536, 570.
293 : 16—*New Statesman*, XVI (1921), 730.
293 : 9—*Nation* (London).
293 : 12—*New York Herald Tribune Books*, XII (Feb. 2, 1936), 1.
293 : 13—*Bookman* (N. Y.), LXII (1925), 189.
294 : 22—*The Life of Reason*, IV, 22; I, 277.
294 : 28—Review of Jules Martin, *Saint Augustin*, *Philosophical Review*, X (1901), 521.
295 : 13—*Interpretations of Poetry and Religion*, 245, 246, 250.
295 : 18—*Ibid.*, 22.
296 : 4—"War Shrines," *Soliloquies in England*, 98, 99.
296 : 11—"A Few Remarks," *Obiter Scripta*, 267.
296 : 13—*Soliloquies in England*, 142.

APPENDIX

VERSE FORMS USED BY SANTAYANA

LIST OF ABBREVIATIONS:

    H. M. *Harvard Monthly*
    1894 *Sonnets and Other Verses*, 1st. ed.
    1896 *Sonnets and Other Verses*, 2nd. ed.
    1899 *Lucifer* (2nd. ed., 1924)
    1901 *A Hermit of Carmel and Other Poems*
    1923 *Poems* (selected by the author and revised)
    +   in later reprints, e. g., 1894 + = 1894, 1896, 1923

I. STANZAS USED IN SERIOUS POEMS

1. *The sonnet*   "Sonnets, 1883-93," H. M., 1885-86, Jan. 1892 (10); 1894 + (20)
                           "Sonnets, 1895," H. M., Oct. 1895 (10); 1896 + (30)
                           "On a Volume of Scholastic Philosophy," 1894 +
                           "On the Death of a Metaphysician," 1894 +
                           "On a Piece of Tapestry," 1894 +
                           "To W. P.," 1894 + (4)
                           "Before a Statue of Achilles," H. M., Oct. 1897; 1901 + (3)
                           "The Rustic at the Play," 1901 + #
                           "The Power of Art," 1894, 1896
                           "Gabriel," 1894, 1896
                           "Invocation," 1899
                           "Futility," 1901
                           "Odi et Amo," 1901 (2) #
                           "Cathedrals by the Sea," 1901

"Mont Brevent," 1901
"Sonnet on Shakespeare," in *Homage to Shakespeare,* edited by Israel Gollancz, 1916
"A Premonition," Cambridge, Oct. 1913, in Prologue to *Soliloquies in England,* 1922
"The Undergraduate Killed in Battle," Oxford, 1915, *Ibid.*
"The Darkest Hour," Oxford, 1917, *Ibid.*
"On the Three Philosophical Poets," in Vol. VI, *Triton Edition of the Works of G. S.,* 1936–37
Total sonnets, 74; Italian, 71; English, 3
\# English sonnets

2. The quatrain
   (*abab*)
   5

"Premonition," 1901 +
"Avila," 1901 +
"King's College Chapel," H. M., Mar. 1898; 1901 +
"On an Unfinished Statue," 1901 +
Lucifer, conversation of Michael and Lucifer, Act IV, 1899

3. The "Sapphic" ode
   (*abcd*)
   52

"Odes I–V," 1894 + (5)

4. The irregular ode

"In Grantchester Meadows," H. M., May 1899; 1901 +
"Athletic Ode," 1901 +
"Chorus," 1894, 1896
"Resurrection," 1901
"A Minuet on Reaching the Age of Fifty," 1923

5. The Spenserian stanza
6. *abab*
   4
7. *abab*
   5353
8. *aabbb*
   5
9. *abbaab   ababba*
    4   4
10. *abccba*
    353353

"Spain in America," 1901 +
"Easter Hymn," 1894, 1896
"Good Friday Hymn," 1894, 1896
"Solipsism," 1901 +

"Sybaris," 1901 +

"Midnight," 1901 +

"Two Moralities," H. M., Oct. 1894

APPENDIX

11. *abababab abababcc*   "Two Voices," H. M., May 1888
          4   5
12. *abbbaaccc*   "The Dioscuri," Interlude II, H. M., June
    355335535   1902
13. *abbaaccddc*   "Decima," 1894, 1896
         4
    double, falling (trochaic)
14. *abbaabbacdcede*   "Lenten Greeting to a Lady," 1894, 1896
           4
    double, falling (trochaic)
15. *aabbccddeeffgghhii*   "President Garfield," *Latin School Regis-*
              5   *ter*, Sept. 1881
16. *aab ccb*   "Cape Cod," 1894 +
    443 443
    triple, rising (anapestic)

NOTE: The stanzas devoted by Santayana to serious poems are, with few exceptions, in rising, double (iambic) meter. The bulk of the verse is in conventional forms, and the exceptions seem merely attempts to vary these slightly. I have included "In Grantchester Meadows" among the odes since, in spite of its short stanzas, it has no uniform rime scheme and no uniform line or stanza length. Like the other odes, it has a preponderance of five and three stress lines. This partiality to five and three stress lines in combination Santayana probably derived from Spanish drama (see his "Imitation of Calderon," *London Mercury,* IX (1923), 13-14) and from the Italian *canzone*. The rime scheme in the odes is highly irregular, but falls into occasional couplets and quatrains. Of the unusual stanzas perhaps the most interesting are those of "Sybaris." Shelley, Moore, and Rossetti have used the same rime scheme, but with four and not five stress lines. The monotone of line length and successive rimes reminds one of Tennyson, and the lulling, soothing effect produced is excellent atmosphere for the Oriental pageantry of the poem. In "Solipsism" the alternation of five and three stress lines gives a curious hesitancy of movement, perhaps suggestive of the uncertainty of the philosophical position described. "Two Moralities" is an interesting experiment in a kind of circular pattern of both rime and meter. The inner lines form a couplet, and the symmetry of the whole structure is pleasing to the ear. The "decima" is a frequent verse form in Spanish drama, with instances as early as the fifteenth century. Lope de Vega speaks of it as the proper form for expressions of complaint. (See J. P. Crawford: *The Spanish Pastoral Drama*, Phila., 1915.) The last two forms are experiments with the sonnet, "President Garfield" being a kind of combination of sonnet and heroic couplet.

II. STANZAS USED IN HUMOROUS POEMS

DOUBLE, RISING (IAMBIC) METER

1. The ballad stanza   "Six Wise Fools," "The Scholar," 1901
   (abab)
   4343
2. abab   "Six Wise Fools," conclusion, 1901
   4
3. ababc(a)b   "Six Wise Fools," "The Sport," 1901
4. ababccaa   "Six Wise Fools," "The Pessimist," 1901
   4

TRIPLE, RISING (ANAPESTIC) METER

5. abab   "Fair Harvard," 1901
   4343
6. aaabbbC   "College Drinking Song," 1901
   4²

DOUBLE, FALLING (TROCHAIC) METER

7. abaB   "Prosit Neujahr," 1901
   4²
8. abacbc   "Six Wise Fools," "The Lover," 1901
   4
9. ababaabbcc   "Six Wise Fools," "The Critic," 1901
   4343433⁴2

NOTE: Santayana's humorous and occasional poems on the score of meter show many ingenious and appropriate devices. "Six Wise Fools" is especially interesting, with a different metrical scheme for each fool. There is more experimentation here than in the serious verse. Santayana is particularly fond of lines with feminine endings for ludicrous and mock-dignified effects. "The Pessimist's" stanza is one of the most effective, the unexpected couplets giving at the end a flippant, epigrammatic note. "The Critic's" stanza begins with the solemn, ponderous tread of legions of poems of the "Psalm of Life" *genre,* but with the seventh line the burlesque intention is apparent, for the seventh and eighth lines reverse the order of stresses and rimes and lead up to a merry little quip in the short last line.

APPENDIX

III. LYRICS FROM THE DRAMATIC VERSE

DOUBLE, RISING (IAMBIC) METER

1. aaa   *Lucifer,* Act III, song of the first devil, 1899
   4
2. abbab   *Lucifer,* Act IV, song of the angels, 1899
   34533
3. abbacd   "A Hermit of Carmel," song of the knight, 1901
   434343
4. abaabab   "The Knight's Return," Flerida's song, 1901
   3

TRIPLE, RISING (ANAPESTIC) METER

5. abc abcc abaa   *Lucifer,* Act III, song of the witches, 1899
   2   24   24
6. aaab   *Lucifer,* Act III, song of the witches and devils, 1899
   23
7. aabaaab   *Lucifer,* Act III, song of the first devil, 1899
   2

DOUBLE, FALLING (TROCHAIC) METER

8. aaa   *Lucifer,* Act IV, song of the angels, 1899
   4
9. abbaa ababa   *Lucifer,* Act III, song of the first devil, 1899
   4342^4 4342^4

NOTE: Many interesting and effective metrical devices are in these lyrics. The songs in triple time have movement and gusto, and a kind of grotesqueness in the long last line. The knight's song with its combination of alternate line lengths and enclosed rimes is pleasing. On the other hand, the line in Flerida's song seems abrupt and monotonous for a love song. Magic and supernatural are well indicated by the duplication of rime in the *Lucifer* lyrics.

IV. POEMS IN CONTINUOUS METER

1. *Blank verse*   "A Hermit of Carmel," 1901
   "The Knight's Return," 1901
   "Philosophers at Court," H. M., June 1904
2. *Irregular rime*   *Lucifer,* 1899
   "The Dioscuri," Interlude I, H. M., June 1902
   "The Flight of Helen," H. M., Apr. 1903

3.	*Heroic couplet*	"Lines on Leaving the Bedford Street Schoolhouse," 1880
		"The Aeneid," (parody), *Latin School Register*, 1881–82
		"The Poetic Medium," 1901
4.	*ababcdcd–* 53535353⁻	"A Hermit of Carmel," incidental passages, 1901 "The Knight's Return," " ", 1901
5.	*abbacddc–* 35353535⁻	*Lucifer,* Act I, song of Hermes, 1899
6.	*aabbccdd–* 4 (*double, falling*)	"A Toast," 1894 + *Lucifer,* occasional passages, especially speeches of the lesser devils, 1899
7.	*ababcdcd–* 4 (*double, falling*)	"Six Wise Fools," Introduction, 1901 "The Bottles and the Wine," 1901 "Uncle Sammy's First Wild Oats," 1901 "Youth's Immortality," 1901

NOTE: Santayana's fondness for rime is clearly evidenced in these poems; he particularly likes the meter of (2), where the rime is irregular but falls frequently into couplets and quatrains and sometimes more intricate patterns. For continuous meter he prefers the five stress line, although in (2) there are occasional shorter lines. (4) and (5) are interpolations for more lyrical effect. "A Toast" suggests Milton both in diction and in meter. (7) is a traditional humorous meter of eight and seven syllables in alternation and thus seems inappropriate for the dignity of "Youth's Immortality."

SANTAYANA'S TREATMENT OF THE SONNET

Santayana's preference for the Italian form of the sonnet is to be expected in the light of his fondness for traditional forms in general. However, he makes no attempt to follow the strict Italian practice of partitioning the sonnet into four distinct logical units. Only nineteen sonnets could possibly be placed in this category. Two sonnets have not even a full grammatical pause anywhere in them; six more have no full stop in the octave; twenty-two have none in the sestet. The sestet, however, is sharply set off from the octave by a full grammatical pause in almost all the sonnets, and in over fifty sonnets there is some attempt at rhetorical division as well. The octaves of Santayana's Italian sonnets are all regular in form, but the sestets afford him an opportunity for much interesting experimentation. He does not violate the requirements for the

APPENDIX

Italian sestet, but he does use an unusually large number of different rime schemes, as the following table shows:

	1st. sequence	2nd. sequence	Miscellaneous	Total
ccd ccd	2	2	1	5
cdd cdd	2	2	1	5
ccd cdd	2	1	0	3
cdd ccd	2	2	3	7
cdc dcd	3	9	5	17
cdc cdc	3	3	0	6
cdc dcc	1	0	2	3
cdd cdc	4	1	1	6
cdc ddc	0	2	2	4
cdd cee	1	0	0	1
cdc dee	0	4	0	4
cde cde	0	1	0	1
ccd eed	0	2	0	2
cdc ede	0	1	4	5
cdd ece	0	0	1	1
cdc eed	0	0	1	1
	20	30	21	71

Santayana in his fondness for two-rime sestets follows Italian rather than English practice, although the *cdcdcd* form has always been popular among English sonneteers. Some of his two-rime schemes have been rarely employed in English; out of 6,000 sonnets selected from British writers of four centuries only 42 employ the three arrangements which appear first in the table above; and there are not enough American instances of these to be included in the most exhaustive study of the American sonnet so far made. (See L. T. Weeks, "The Order of Rimes of the English Sonnet," *Modern Language Notes,* XXV (1910), 176–180; L. G. Sterner, *The Sonnet in American Literature,* Phila., 1930, 142.) On the other hand, Santayana does not confine himself to arrangements popular in the Italian sonnet. Although he frequently uses the popular *cdcdcd* form, the equally popular *cdecde* (favorite with Petrarch, Michelangelo, and Tasso) appears only once in Santayana. He employs ten schemes not found at all in Dante, Petrarch, Michelangelo, or Tasso, and omits the *cdeedc* form used by these authors 38 times and the *cdedce* form used 103 times. (See J. Schipper, *A History of English Versification,* Oxford, 1910, 372; Tomlinson, *The Sonnet: Its Origin, Structure, and Place in Poetry,* London, 1874, 4–8.)

Santayana is not only an experimenter in rime schemes in the sonnet; he is also to be commended upon his adaptation of these schemes to the thought he is expressing. It is his contention that "a sonnet in which the thought is not distributed appropriately to the structure of the verse has no excuse for being a sonnet," (*The Sense of Beauty*, 173) and he makes every effort to live up to this standard in his handling of the sestets. Where the thought of the sestet is neatly divided into halves of three lines each, he is most likely to use a rime scheme in which the first three lines and the second three lines are symmetrical (32 out of 39 such sonnets, 12 with rimes in each half identical). Thus the melody of rime parallels the idea. Instances are the sestets of sonnets 22 and 44:

> For the same breath that did awake the flowers,
> Making them happy with a joy unknown,
> Kindled my light and fixed my spirit's goal:
> And the same hand that reined the flying hours
> And chained the whirling earth to Phoebus' throne,
> In love's eternal orbit keeps the soul.
>
> For thee the labour of my studious ease
> I ply with hope, for thee all pleasures please,
> Thy sweetness doth the bread of sorrow leaven;
> And from thy noble lips and heart of gold
> I drink the comfort of the faiths of old,
> And thy perfection is my proof of heaven.

Where Santayana wishes to express a series of three related ideas, he almost always (7 out of 8 sonnets) employs the *cdcdcd* arrangement, dividing the sestet into three equal parts, one for each idea. But since this rime scheme is also symmetrical when divided into two groups of three rimes each (*cdc dcd*), 10 other sonnets employ it where the rhetorical division comes in the middle of the sestet. Even more interesting is Santayana's practice where his rhetorical pause divides the sestet into two parts with four lines in the first and two in the second. In the 13 such sonnets, 11 contain perfect quatrains for their first four lines, 6 with alternate rime (*cdcd*) and 5 with enclosed rime (*cddc*). Of these 13 sonnets, 8 end with a couplet, contrary to all rules of Italian sonnet-writing. But Santayana is careful to reserve the couplet for occasions when he desires a pithy, epigrammatic conclusion, as in sonnets 21 and 14:

> But, O ye beauties I must never see,
> How great a lover have you lost in me!
>
> They threat in vain; the whirlwind cannot awe
> A happy snow-flake dancing in the flaw.

Where, however, an epigram would be ineffective, Santayana is very careful to avoid it. The sestet of sonnet 16 is a case in point:

> 'Tis a sad love, like an eternal prayer,
> And knows no keen delight, no faint surcease.
> Yet from the seasons hath the earth increase,
> And heaven shines as if the gods were there.
> Had Dian passed there could no deeper peace
> Embalm the purple stretches of the air.

If the last two lines were a couplet, the resulting jingle would spoil the melody and give a false sententious effect. Yet Santayana can afford a duplication of rime in lines two and three since the two separate sentences prevent any running together of idea; in fact the enclosed rime is pleasing to the ear. This division of sestet between the fourth and fifth lines is extremely rare in Italian poetry, but is found more frequently in English and is, in fact, an approach to the English, or Shakespearean, sonnet.

Not that Santayana relates his rimes to his ideas with mathematical precision, with too studied an ingenuity. Careful reading of the sonnets, however, reveals many subtle adaptations which enforce the meaning as they add to the melodic beauty. One final example will suffice, from sonnet 13:

> Farewell, my burden! No more will I bear
> The foolish load of my fond faith's despair,
> But trip the idle race with careless feet.
> The crown of olive let another wear;
> It is my crown to mock the runner's heat
> With gentle wonder and with laughter sweet.

At first glance there seems no particular point, other than melody, for the unusual *ccdcdd* scheme, but closer examination reveals that all the *c*-rimes express one idea, which is contrasted with the second idea of the *d*-rimes. Thus the negative and affirmative assertions of the sestet are contrasted by rime as well as by rhetoric.

METRICAL ANALYSIS OF SANTAYANA'S LINE

A metrical analysis of Santayana's favorite five stress (pentameter) line shows, as would be expected, few variations from the normal five stress, ten syllable pattern. In the following table I have placed the results of a scansion of all the sonnets (1,036 lines) and comparable portions from the blank and the irregularly rimed verse of Santayana's longer poems (1,000 lines from "A Hermit of Carmel" and "The Knight's Return," and 1,000 lines from *Lucifer*, representing various parts of these poems.)

	Sonnets	Narrative Poems Blank Verse	Lucifer Rimed Verse
Initial inversion of accent	224	220	231
Internal inversion of accent	49	84	67
Extra syllable (resolution)	20	25	26
Feminine endings	51	147	22
Run-on lines	259	443	420
Two marked pauses in line (double caesura)	29	46	73

NOTE: Santayana's line does not vary appreciably in these three forms, the dramatic poems necessitating more freedom than the sonnets but still being exceedingly regular for such verse. The five sonnets published since 1910 are considerably freer than the early ones (10 out of 20 resolutions; 6 out of 29 double caesuras) and make us wonder how Santayana might have developed his sonnets had he continued to write them in any number.

To say that Santayana's line is regular is not to imply, however, that he fails to make full use of those minute and subtle variations that have always lent charm to the English pentameter: the half-stressed syllable, leveling out the marked difference between the normally stressed and unstressed syllables; counter falling rhythms interrupting the normal rising rhythm (wherever the stress falls upon the first of two syllables regularly pronounced together, as in a two-syllabled word accented on the first syllable, so that the second syllable is linked to the preceding, not, as normally, to the following stress; or wherever, following the medial pause, the line resumes on the beat.) Such falling rhythms result in a slower, softer line than the bold, forthright iambic pattern, and Santayana employs them whenever he wishes his lines to have a more lingering effect. Contrast the emphatic assertiveness of the first passage below, from sonnet 29, with the more flowing lines from sonnet 12 in the second passage:

> I know no deeper doubt to make me mad,
> I need no brighter love to keep me pure.
> To me the faiths of old are daily bread;
> I bless their hope, I bless their will to save,
> And my deep heart still meaneth what they said.

> But thou, glad river that hast reached the plain,
> Scarce wak'st the rushes to a slumberous sigh.
> The mountains sleep behind thee, and the main
> Awaits thee, lulling an eternal pain
> With patience; nor doth Phoebe, throned on high,
> The mirror of thy placid heart disdain.

The first lines have the simplicity and earnestness of a creed; they enforce their point with monosyllabic precision and little deviation from a marked rising rhythm. The second group has its normal metrical movement constantly interrupted by words like *river, rushes,* and *lulling* (one cannot read *glad-riv/er-thát* or *thee-lull/ing-án*) and by a tendency in the first five lines to place the medial pause so that an accent occurs on the first syllable following and a temporary falling rhythm is set up. The result is a lovely softening of poetic texture aided of course by the profusion of labial and sibilant consonants.

More subtle adaptations of meter to meaning may be found if one examines the sonnets closely. One instance will serve as example, the sestet of sonnet 13:

> Farewell, my burden! No more will I bear
> The foolish load of my fond faith's despair,
> But trip the idle race with careless feet.
> The crown of olive let another wear;
> It is my crown to mock the runner's heat
> With gentle wonder and with laughter sweet.

In the first line the medial pause allows the vehemence of the opening assertion to be fully felt. The line resumes with monosyllables in falling rhythm to give the effect of exertion. These continue into the second line, but the gradual change to rising rhythm indicates the overcoming of resistance, and after struggling through the consonants of the second line, the rhythm breaks loose in the third line with its quick succession of beats. The last four lines with their alternation of rising and falling rhythms bring the sonnet to a close in a kind of antiphony.

In attributing to Santayana a command of the nuances of five stress meter, I do not mean to imply his possession of anything not found in the verse of any skilled English poet. My interest is in demonstrating that he does have a feeling for just those things that have given charm and beauty to English verse. He writes not as a foreigner counting feet and syllables, but with an instinctive grasp of the accentual principle of English verse which has distinguished it from Anglo-Saxon times to the present.

SANTAYANA'S CORRECTIONS OF HIS OWN VERSE

That Santayana is a careful critic of his own verse is proven by the changes he has made in it from edition to edition. These are less striking in number than in quality. No reissue of Santayana's poems has appeared without some few changes, but most of the changes took place between the appearance of the poems in the *Harvard Monthly* and their later appearance in book form. A few of the more important emendations will show Santayana's workmanship and the almost uniform gain in excellence:

SONNET VII

(H. M. version in italics and above corresponding lines in later version. First published Oct. 1885, revised in *Sonnets and Other Verses*, 1894.)

I would I might forget that I am I,
And break the heavy chain that binds me fast,
   my soul
Whose links about myself my deeds have cast.
Then would the spirit, through a boundless sky,
What in the body's tomb doth buried lie
Upon the wings of contemplation fly,
Is boundless; 'tis the spirit of the sky,
Free from the galling slavery, at last,
Lord of the future, guardian of the past,
Of unborn future and unburied past.
And soon must forth, to know his own at last.
Would that my thought might live and I might die!
In his large life to live, I fain would die.
Happy the dumb beast, hungering for food,
   its its
But calling not his suffering his own;
Blessed the angel, gazing on all good.
But knowing not he sits upon a throne;
Wretched the mortal, pondering his mood,
And doomed to know his aching heart alone.

NOTE: The revision here is to my mind a distinct improvement. The conventional imagery of the original lines 4 and 5 is replaced by a more direct and less hackneyed simplicity. *Galling slavery* is rightly cut out as superfluous, and the neat but slightly prosaic antithesis of line 7 in the original is turned into the more imaginative one of line 6 in the revision. But the greatest improvement occurs in line 8, which is noticeably flat in the original. Observe that the well-known lines of the sestet are virtually unchanged.

SONNET IV

(H. M., Nov. 1885 in italics and above 1894 +)

O would we
I would I had been born in nature's day,
                 thoughtless
When man was in the world a wide-eyed boy,
    woes were clouds that crossed a sky
And clouds of sorrow crossed his sky of joy
And showered   *fields*
To scatter dewdrops on the buds of May.
    men could
Then could he work and love and fight and pray,
Nor heartsick grow in fortune's long employ.
More blest in crying for a broken toy
    Mighty to build and ruthless to destroy
Than we who weep not and forget to play,
    He lived, while masked death unquestioned lay.
But bowed with all this weight of sinful years,
    Now ponder we the ruins of the years,
How shall the world its childish heart regain.
    And groan beneath the weight of boasted gain;
A thrice disproved faith reprove our sneers
    No unsung bacchanal can charm our ears
    the   *hallowed*
And lead our dances to the woodland fane,
    Or   *sanctify our*
No hope of heaven sweeten our few tears
And hush the importunity of pain.

NOTE: These changes seem uniformly for the better. The singular in line 1 is more direct and intimate than the original plural, and *wide-eyed* is more expressive than *thoughtless*. The involved structure of the original line 3 is awkward, and the plural *men* not only conflicts with the earlier singular *man*, but clashes in sound with the preceding *then*. But the most important innovations are the deletions of the trivial figure in lines 7 and 8 and the pompously stiff line 11.
    Many of these changes are of course a mature poet correcting a col-

lege boy. But throughout his later life Santayana continued to change words here and there which did not suit him, even the 1923 edition containing slight changes in seven poems. These are generally for the better; e. g., in "On a Piece of Tapestry" line 4, "Her beauties in their freedom disagree" is certainly more epigrammatic than the original "Her mingled beauties never quite agree," and the concluding "O, I am far from home" of "Cape Cod" is certainly more fluent than the original "O, I am sick for home." In the same poem the British rook is replaced by the American crow, and the poetic bark of the 3rd. sonnet to W. P. becomes just a plain ship. Generally the changes represent a gain in concreteness and simplicity, though I prefer the original opening of sonnet 15, "A wall, a wall around my garden rear," to the rather conventional, Popeian successor, "A wall, a wall to hem the azure sphere." Only one emendation of Santayana's was reconsidered and later withdrawn. In sonnet 17 Santayana wrote originally, in the *Harvard Monthly* for January 1892, what is the final and familiar version of line 9: "O subtle Beauty, sweet persuasive worth." In 1894, however, he changed this line to "O Beauty, quelling chaos! mighty worth," apparently feeling that it led more suitably to the following line: "That didst the love of being first inspire." In an effort to secure strength, Santayana secured merely rhetoric, and spoiled the limpid flow of the lines. The wisdom of the change must have soon seemed dubious to him, for in the 1896 edition the lines were restored to their original form and have so remained ever since.

SANTAYANA AND THE TRADITION OF PLATONIC LOVE

Platonic love, at least on the philosophical side, was described essentially by Plato himself in numerous passages, particularly the lengthy tribute to it in the *Symposium*. From Plato the conception passed on into the middle ages through Neo-Platonic philosophers and through Christian mystics such as Bonaventura and Bernard of Clairveaux, who were able to blend it with the Catholic love of God and of the Virgin Mary. These religious overtones carried over into much medieval secular poetry, and in Chrétien de Troyes, in *The Romaunt of the Rose,* and in many of the later troubadours love was idealized in a way which, even if instinctive, was essentially Platonic. In their attitude that love was an all-absorbing good, that it worked in the lover a complete spiritual transformation, that it demanded a devout humility in the presence of the beloved, and that it was not incongruous with a worship of God, these medieval writers were setting the stage for the later Platonic love poetry. They, too, gave such poetry its delight in sensuous beauty and in the physical attributes of the loved one, its buoyancy and youthful charm. All these attributes, combined with a new interest in philosophy, marked the flourishing of the *stil nuovo* in the love poetry of Guido Guinicelli, Guido Cavalcanti, and preëminently Dante. But a more consciously Platonic love poetry was still to come in Italy of the fifteenth century, the outgrowth of a systematic translation of Plato's works by Marsilio Ficino at the behest of Cosimo de' Medici. Again the concepts of the *Symposium* were united or reconciled with Catholic teachings, and love of woman and of beauty was merged with a love of the Trinity. Benivieni's "Canzona dello Amore celeste et divino" gave the movement a philosophical canon, and in the hands of Lorenzo de' Medici, Pietro Bembo, and particularly Michelangelo, the Platonic impulse received suitable lyrical expression. The aspirations and many of the conventions of this love poetry are not different from the more naïve poetry of the "new style," but it is more conscious of its origins in Plato, it is more sophisticated and aware of its underlying symbolism, and it is more apt to pass quickly from the concrete to ideal beauty and to pure being. (See J. B. Fletcher: *Literature of the Italian Renaissance,* New York, 1934, Chap. V, XIII.)

Santayana's love poetry is nearest that of the period just described, perhaps because he too writes with a full knowledge of the Platonic tradition behind him. In this detachment he most resembles Michelangelo, as in the quality of his idealization. Both poets condemn and resist earthly, sensual love:

> The one love soars, the other downward tends;
> The soul lights this, while that the senses stir,
>   (Michelangelo. Sonnet 53)

> This is not love: it is that worser thing—
> Hunger for love, while love is yet to learn.
>   (Santayana, Sonnet 23)

They turn from a perishable love of the flesh to an enduring love of the spirit:

> Sense is not love, but lawlessness accurst:
> This kills the soul; while our love lifts on high
> Our friends on earth—higher in heaven through death.
>   (Michelangelo, Sonnet 52)

> When all loves die that hang upon a kiss,
> And must with cavil and with chance contend,
> Their risen selves with the eternal blend
> Where perfect dying is their perfect bliss.
>   (Santayana, Sonnet 39)

> But, finding these so false, we pass beyond
> Unto the Love of Loves that never dies.
> (Michelangelo, Sonnet 52)

For the Platonist the beauties of this world are but intimations of what the eternal holds:

> Lo, all the lovely things we find on earth,
> Resemble for the soul that rightly sees,
> That source of bliss divine which gave us birth:
> Nor have we first-fruits or remembrances
> Of heaven elsewhere. Thus, loving loyally,
> I rise to God and make death sweet by thee.
> (Michelangelo, Sonnet 54)

> And when thou comest, lady, where I dwell,
> The place is flooded with the light of heaven
> And a lost music I remember well.
> (Santayana, Sonnet 43)

In a surge of feeling the lover may even be carried to a vision of the eternal:

> And since by nature fire doth find its sphere
> Soaring aloft, and I am all ablaze,
> Heavenward with it my flight must needs be sped.
> (Michelangelo, Sonnet 59)

> Thou wouldst come down, forsaking paradise
> To be my comfort, but by Heaven's ruth
> I go to burn beside thee in the skies.
> (Santayana, Sonnet 48)

True love is celestial and has no end.

> For he who harbors virtue, still will choose
> To love what neither years nor death can blight.
> (Michelangelo, Sonnet 56)

> One love sufficeth an eternity.
> (Santayana, Sonnet 50)

The themes of Michelangelo's "celestial love" sonnets are very close to the concluding sonnets of Santayana's second series. (Translations of

APPENDIX 343

Michelangelo by J. A. Symonds, from *The Sonnets of Michael Angelo Buonarroti*, London, 1878.)

Yet in other sonnets Santayana echoes the more naïve, more Catholic Platonism of Dante and suggests the latter's concepts and occasionally his language. Both poets place their mistress in a close association with heavenly beings, speak of her as being, or having been in Paradise. Of course, this theme is paramount in Dante's *Paradiso*, but it is implied in his sonnets:

> Because the pleasure of her beauteousness,
> Taking itself away from out our sight,
> Became a spiritual beauty great,
> Which through the heaven spreads
> A light of love that doth the angels greet,
> And makes their high and keen intelligence
> To marvel, of such gentleness is she.
> (Dante, Miscellaneous sonnets)

> For once, methinks, before the angels fell,
> Thou, too, didst follow the celestial seven
> Threading in file the meads of asphodel.
> (Santayana, Sonnet 43)

And through her heavenly attributes the loved one has the power to lead her lover to Paradise:

> Beyond the sphere encircling all the spheres
> Passeth the sigh that from my heart doth rise;
> And a new wisdom learns from Love in tears,
> By which it is drawn up into the skies.
> (Dante, *Vita Nuova*, Sonnet 31)

> And might I kiss her once, asleep or dead,
> . . . .
> That kiss would help me on to paradise.
> (Santayana, Sonnet 39) *

Translation of Dante's sonnets by Lorna de' Lucchi. See *The Minor Poems of Dante*, Oxford, 1926, 74, 41.

Thus the beloved is able to confer upon him who has truly loved, a state of blessedness, grace. As Dante says in the second ode of the *Convivio*,

---

* Cf. the following lines of Petrarch's ninth ode:
> Lady mine high and gentle, there's a sweet
> Light, showing me the path that leads to God,
> Which meets me in the movement of your eyes.

Translation by Cayley, *Sonnets and Stanzas of Petrarch*, London, 1879.

"Her pure soul which receiveth this salvation from Him doth make Him manifest in that which she bringeth with her." (Cf. Santayana's ". . . shade of Him / Who only liveth, giveth, and is fair." Sonnet 47.) "Here where she doth speak there cometh down a spirit from heaven, who inspireth belief that the lofty worth which she owneth is beyond that which is allotted to us. . . . Things in her aspect appear which reveal to us some of the joys of Paradise, in her eyes I say and in her sweet smile." And, concludes Dante, "this is the same as to be blest." So Santayana:

> And as I see her in her kneeling-place,
> A Gabriel comes, and with inaudible breath
> Whispers within me: Hail, thou full of grace. (Sonnet 38)

The perfection of such a love and of such a loved one ("as completely perfect as the essence of man can possibly be," says Dante) is a proof of faith. Or with Santayana, "thy perfection is my proof of heaven."— Sonnet 44. (Translation of the *Convivio* by W. W. Jackson, Oxford, 1909, 124–125, 146, 153.)

Personal love in Dante can be so compelling because love after all is the motive force of the universe. This medieval conception finds a place also in the famous ode of Benivieni and in one of Tasso's sonnets, but Dante's phrasing at the close of the *Divine Comedy* is most like Santayana's rendition of the same idea in Sonnet 22:

> But yet the will rolled onward, like a wheel
> In even motion, by the love impelled,
> That moves the sun in heaven and all the stars.
>   (*Paradiso*, canto 33, lines 133–135, Cary's translation)

> 'Tis love that moveth the celestial spheres
> In endless yearning for the Changeless One,
>   (Santayana, Sonnet 22)

Just as Michelangelo's influence points toward pure Platonism, Dante's influence leads Santayana more in the direction of Catholic images and scholastic ideas.

But there is in the early part of Santayana's sequence a quality quite different from the poetry of either Dante or Michelangelo. The sonnets expressing doubt and despair represent a different strand of Platonism, which Santayana found in the love poems of Guido Cavalcanti. Of course, the lover from the time of the troubadours on had had moments of profound despair, but this literary tradition, spiritualized by the *stil nuovo,* had attributed his despair to his mistress' refusal of mercy, of grace, not to the disillusionment he had experienced in loving her. Now Guido at times voices the more conventional lover's complaint, but at other times he dwells upon the deep yearning which earthly love cannot possibly satisfy. As his lady leaves him, he speaks thus of her eyes:

> Alas! they shot an arrow as she turned,
> And with a death-wound from the piercing dart
> My soul came sighing back into my heart.
> (Santayana's translation, *Poetry and Religion,* p. 125)

Compare Santayana's "Hath the deep heart of me been satisfied?" (Sonnet 24) "While Guido's 'death-wound' was perhaps in reality nothing but the rebuff offered him by a prospective mistress, yet the sting of it, in a mind of Platonic habit, served at once to enforce the distinction between the ideal beauty, so full of sweetness and heavenly charm, which had tempted the soul out of his heart in its brief adventure, and the particular and real object against which the soul was dashed, and from which it returned bruised and troubled to its inward solitude." (*Poetry and Religion,* p. 125) Now this is not only a convincing interpretation of Guido's sonnet; it is also an accurate description of Santayana's own experience as revealed in the early sonnets. Guido's sceptical irony is well described by Jefferson Fletcher: "In degree as his desire was ideally exalted, so its grace, its *merzede,* became an irony, a tragic paradox. His must be a passionate loneliness forever teased by an illusion, a phantom mate of its own conjuring. . . . Guido's mood is essentially one with Leopardi's when the latter exclaims:

> Only my heart pleased me, and, with my heart
> In a communing without cease absorbed,
> Still to keep watch and ward o'er my own smart.

. . . The only love of which grace is born, entire possession granted, is love of the dim, immaterial idea, 'la figlia della sua mente.'" (*The Religion of Beauty in Women,* N. Y., 1911, 93-94) Philosophically Santayana would agree with Guido and Leopardi, but before this realization takes place, the soul goes through a period of torment (Italian *ira*) which Santayana describes in his first six sonnets. Death seems the only solution, as often to Guido and Leopardi. "Joy lies behind me. Be the journey brief." (Sonnet 26)

Santayana is particularly close to Leopardi in the more pessimistic moods of his sonnets, sometimes paralleling the latter's themes and incidents. Both poets contrast the sadness of their lives with the joyful innocence of youth and nature:

> To thee, light-hearted boy, I say
> That as a clear and tranquil day
> Is this thy spring, with blossoms rife,
> Before the festival of life:
> (Leopardi, "Il sabato del villaggio")

> I would I had been born in nature's day,
> When man was in the world a wide-eyed boy,
> And clouds of sorrow crossed his sky of joy
> To scatter dewdrops on the buds of May.
> (Santayana, Sonnet 4)

> O flock of mine, reposing, happy thou,
> Thy misery, I think, thou dost not know!
> (Leopardi, "Canto notturno di un pastore errante nell' Asia")

> Happy the dumb beast, hungering for food,
> But calling not his suffering his own:
> (Santayana, Sonnet 7)

Neither poet expects any consolation from external nature. The inevitable sorrow of the human lot must be accepted, even if at times with pain and regret:

> O virgin Moon, even so
> Is this our life below!
> With suffering man is born,
> Death at his birth stands near;
> (Leopardi, "Canto notturno . . .")

> Immortal is the soul that sings
> The sorrow of her mortal birth.
> O cruel beauty of the earth!
> O love's unutterable stings!
> (Santayana, "Midnight")

And the spirit may at times find peace where the quieter moods of nature are attuned to contemplation. Santayana's sonnet 15 is very near to Leopardi's "L'infinito."

> I always loved this solitary hill,
> This hedge as well, which takes so large a share
> Of the far-flung horizon from my view;
> But seated here, in contemplation lost,

APPENDIX

My thought discovers vaster space beyond,
Supernal silence and unfathomed peace;
Almost I am afraid; then, since I hear
The murmur of the wind among the leaves,
I match that infinite calm unto this sound
And with my mind embrace eternity,
The vivid, speaking present and dead past;
In such immensity my spirit drowns,
And sweet to me is shipwreck in this sea.
    (Leopardi)

A wall, a wall to hem the azure sphere,
And hedge me in from the disconsolate hills!
Give me but one of all the mountain rills,
Enough of ocean in its voice I hear.
Come no profane insatiate mortal near
With the contagion of his passionate ills;
The smoke of battle all the valleys fills,
Let the eternal sunlight greet me here.
This spot is sacred to the deeper soul
And to the piety that mocks no more.
In nature's inmost heart is no uproar,
None in this shrine; in peace the heavens roll,
In peace the slow tides pulse from shore to shore,
And ancient quiet broods from pole to pole.
    (Santayana)

(Translations from Lorna de' Lucchi's *Anthology of Italian Poems*, N. Y., 1922, pp. 275, 285, 281, 271.)

BIBLIOGRAPHY

WRITINGS ABOUT SANTAYANA

(*Exclusive of book reviews, notes, and letters*)

Aaron, D., "Postscript to *The Last Puritan*," New England Quarterly, IX (Dec. 1936), 683-686.
Ames, Van Meter, *Proust and Santayana,* Chicago and N. Y., 1937, 49-80.
Archer, William, *Poets of the Younger Generation,* London, 1902, 373-384.
Barfield, O., "George Santayana," (Review of *Character and Opinion* and *Little Essays*), New Statesman, XVI (Mar. 26, 1921), 729-730.
Canby, Henry S., "The Education of a Puritan" (Review of *The Last Puritan*), Saturday Review of Literature, XIII (Feb. 1, 1936), 3-4+.
Canby, H. S., "The American Santayana," *Ibid.*, XV (Apr. 17, 1937), 3-4+.
Clemens, Cyril, *George Santayana: An American Philosopher in Exile,* International Mark Twain Society. Webster Groves, Mo., 1937.
Clemens, C., *A Visit to George Santayana, Ibid.*, 1937.
Clyne, A., "George Santayana," *Bookman* (London), LXX (Apr. 1926), 11-13.
Cohen, Morris R., "On American Philosophy—George Santayana," New Republic, XXIII (July 21, 1920), 221-223. Reprinted in *Cambridge History of American Literature,* edited by W. P. Trent and others, N. Y., 1917-21, IV, 258-262.
Conger, George P., "Santayana and Modern Liberal Protestantism," Journal of Philosophy, XVIII (Jan. 6, 1921), 5-10.
Cory, D. M., "A Study of Santayana," Journal of Philosophic Studies, II (July 1927), 349-364.
Dewey, John, "Philosophy as a Fine Art" (Review of *The Realm of Essence*), LIII (Feb. 15, 1928), 352-354.
Dickinson, G. Lowes, "The Newest Philosophy," Independent Review, VI, No. 4 (1906), 177-190.

Edman, Irwin, "Santayana at Seventy," *Saturday Review of Literature,* X (Dec. 16, 1933), 349-350.

Edman, I., Introductory essay to *The Philosophy of Santayana* (selections from the works of G. S.), N. Y., 1936, i-lvi.

Gilbert, Katharine, "Santayana's Doctrine of Aesthetic Expression," *Philosophical Review,* XXXV (May 1926), 221-235.

Hoover, Hardy, *The Philosophy of George Santayana,* 1927. Harvard dissertation (unpublished).

Howgate, George W., "Santayana and Humanism," *Sewanee Review,* XLIII (Jan. 1935), 49-57.

Kallen, Horace M., "America and the Life of Reason," *Journal of Philosophy,* XVIII (Sept. 29; Oct. 13, 1921), 533-551; 568-575.

Lamprecht, S. P., "Naturalism and Agnosticism in Santayana," *Journal of Philosophy,* XXX (Oct. 12, 1933), 561-574.

Lane, J. W., "The Dichotomy of George Santayana," *Catholic World,* CXL (Oct. 1934), 20-28.

Larrabee, Harold A., "George Santayana: American Philosopher?" *Sewanee Review,* XXXIX (Apr. 1931), 209-221.

Larrabee, H. A., "George Santayana: Philosopher for America?" *Sewanee Review,* XXXIX (July 1931), 325-339.

Larrabee, H. A., "Robert Bridges and George Santayana," *American Scholar,* I (Mar. 1932), 167-182.

MacCampbell, Donald, "Santayana's Debt to New England," *New England Quarterly,* VIII (June 1935), 203-214.

MacCarthy, Desmond, *Criticism,* London, 1932, 17-24.

MacLeish, Archibald, "Santayana, the Poet," *Bookman* (N. Y.), LXII (Oct. 1925), 187-189.

McDowall, Arthur, "Three Philosopher-Prophets" (Inge, Russell, Santayana), *London Mercury,* IV (June 1921), 164-172.

Miller, Dickinson S., "Mr. Santayana and William James," *Harvard Graduates' Magazine,* XXIX (Mar. 1921), 348-364.

Munson, Gorham, *Style and Form in American Prose,* N. Y., 1930, 100-111.

Münsterberg, Margaret, "Santayana," *Nation,* CIX (July 5, 1919), 12-13.

Münsterberg, M., "Santayana at Cambridge," *American Mercury,* I (Jan. 1924), 69-74.

Münsterberg, M., "Santayana and His Pilgrim's Progress," (Review of *The Last Puritan*), *Ibid.,* XXXVIII (May 1936), 115-120.

Murry, J. Middleton, "Mr. Santayana on the United States" (Review of *Character and Opinion*), *Living Age,* CCCVIII (Jan. 29, 1921), 300-303.

Noxon, Frank W., "College Professors Who Are Men of Letters—Harvard," *Critic,* XLII (Feb. 1903), 124-135.

O'Neill, G., "Poetry, Religion, and Professor Santayana," *Studies,* X (Sept. 1921), 451-463.
Priestley, J. B., *Figures in Modern Literature,* London, 1924, 165-187.
Ransom, John Crowe, "Santayana's Palm Tree," *New Republic,* LXIV (Oct. 22, 1930), 262-263.
Ransom, J. C., "Art and Mr. Santayana," *Virginia Quarterly Review,* XIII, No. 3 (1937), 420-436.
Ratner, J., "George Santayana's Theory of Religion," *Journal of Religion,* III (Sept. 1923), 458-475.
Ratner, J., "George Santayana: a Philosophy of Piety," *Monist,* XXXIV (Apr. 1924), 236-259.
Rittenhouse, Jessie B., *The Younger American Poets,* Boston, 1904, 94-109.
Saglio, H. T., "Implications of the Life of Reason," *Journal of Philosophy, XXVIII* (Sept. 24, 1931), 533-544.
Smith, H. W., "George Santayana," *American Review,* I (Mar. 1923), 190-204.
Smith, T. V., *The Philosophic Way of Life,* Chicago, 1930, 144-176.
Stone, G., "Om! Theosophy and the Life of the Spirit at Bay," (Essay in the style of Santayana), *Sewanee Review,* XLV (Apr. 1937), 212-215.
Ten Hoor, Martin, "George Santayana's Theory of Knowledge," *Journal of Philosophy,* XX (Apr. 12, 1923), 197-211.
Trueblood, C. K., "The Rhetoric of Intuition," LXXXIV (May 1928), 401-404.
Van Doren, Carl, "Tower of Irony: George Santayana Ambassador to the Barbarians," *Century,* CVI (Oct. 1923), 950-956. Reprinted in *Many Minds,* N. Y., 1924, 83-101.
Watkin, E. J., "The Philosophy of George Santayana," *Dublin Review,* CLXXXII (Jan. 1928), 32-45.
Wecter, Dixon, "Harvard Exiles," *Virginia Quarterly Review,* X (Apr. 1934), 244-257.
Weirick, Bruce: *From Whitman to Sandburg in American Poetry,* N. Y., 1924, 124-127.
Wickham, Harvey, *The Unrealists,* N. Y., 1929, 94-104.
Woodworth, Helen D., "Santayana on Browning: a Pessimist Criticism," *Poet-Lore,* XIII (Jan. 1901), 97-111.
Yarros, V. S., "Philosophy and Animal Faith, Matter, and Essence; Santayana's Realms of Being," *Open Court,* XLV (Jan. 1931), 43-47.

NOTE: I have included a few book reviews where they are titled or particularly comprehensive. In biographical study, the most helpful sources are Münsterberg, Noxon, and Miller for Santayana's life and career at Harvard, and Ames and Clemens for Santayana's present residence in

Italy. All of these furnish interesting anecdote and personal material. For Santayana's relations with his colleagues at Harvard, see, in addition to Münsterberg and Miller, Kallen and R. B. Perry's review of *Character and Opinion*. (See p. 192). For the broader question of Santayana's relation to America, see especially Kallen and Larrabee. Canby claims considerably more American influence upon Santayana than do the others— rather too much, in my judgment. Santayana as a poet is well treated in MacLeish, Archer, and Rittenhouse, the last containing the most detailed analysis of individual poems. Münsterberg also has some stimulating remarks concerning Santayana's poetry. Santayana's mastery of prose is considered in Munson (somewhat unfavorably, but with interesting analysis), and to some extent in Kallen and Larrabee and Edman's introductory essay. See also Bridges' review of *Little Essays* (p. 211). On the philosophical side, the most detailed analysis of the more technical aspects of Santayana's work is to be found in Hoover, although at times Santayana is made a springboard for the author to jump to his own speculations, as is perhaps necessary in a dissertation in philosophy. For the average reader the most competent review of Santayana's philosophy is in Edman's introduction, an admirable summary in every way. Kallen and Smith also give excellent analyses of Santayana's philosophy, although the latter leans a little too much to an aesthetic interpretation. Murry is one of the most enthusiastic and penetrating critics of Santayana's significance to the modern world. The influence of Santayana's studies of religion upon Protestantism and Catholicism respectively is well considered in Conger and Lane. Individual volumes of Santayana are most fully treated in the various reviews of them, those in the philosophical journals being especially detailed and analytical. Popular, though sound, interpretations of Santayana are to be found in Priestley and Van Doren, but Wickham is decidedly inaccurate and superficial.

For Santayana's own published writings see the numerous entries in the notes. The bibliography in *Obiter Scripta,* edited by Buchler and Schwartz, N. Y., 1936, except for two or three minor omissions, is admirable in thoroughness and format.

INDEX

(q) = quoted from, but not mentioned; (r) = referred to, but not named.

A

"Absence of Religion in Shakespeare, The," 44, 310.
Academy, The, 74, 98, 130, 162.
"Aeneid, The," (parody), 11.
Aesthetic Judgment (Prall), 284, 285.
"Aesthetic Soviet, An," 320.
Aesthetics, 40, 41, 92, 93, 96-98, 108, 167, 168, 257, 284, 285, 321. *See also* Santayana, aesthetics; art; beauty.
Agnosticism, 33, 107, 191, 221, 230, 241, 242, 259.
Albee, Ernest, 104, 306.
Alcibiades, 216, 217, 220.
Alexander, Samuel, 253.
"Alleged Catholic Danger, The," 188.
Allen, Grant, 97, 98.
Allston, Washington, 151.
America, 2-4, 7, 13, 49, 53, 77, 91, 170, 176, 186-190, 193, 194, 225, 257-260, 262-264, 268, 269, 272-275, 323.
American character, 187, 189, 190, 193, 225, 264.
American Criticism (Foerster), 204.
American philosophy, 188, 189, 191-193, 230-232, 283-288. *See also* James; Royce.
American Philosophy Today and Tomorrow, 286.
Ames, Van Meter, 276.
Animal faith, 231, 235, 237, 246, 247.
Aquinas, Thomas, 244, 250.
Archer, William, 62, 74.
Architecture, 6, 18, 215, 243, 258, 270.

Archiv für Systematische Philosophie, 132.
Aristippus, 216, 217, 219, 220, 267.
Aristotle, 89, 103, 112, 139, 140, 158, 168, 207, 222, 237, 244, 245, 310.
Arnold, Matthew, 26, 29, 45, 52, 107, 133-135, 146, 163, 164, 206, 207, 209, 210, 224-226, 259, 260, 288.
Art, 51, 54, 62, 70, 77, 85, 92, 93, 95-99, 108, 125-128, 131, 141, 146, 156, 157, 172, 190, 204, 208, 209, 243, 251, 263, 284, 285, 295, 320, 321. *See also* aesthetics.
"At Heaven's Gate," 69, 296(q).
Athenaeum, The, 130, 175, 176.
"Athletic Ode," 78.
Atlantic Monthly, The, 44, 51.
"Atmosphere," 195, 212, 213.
"Autologos," 217, 218.
Averroes, 292.
"Aversion from Platonism," 213, 214.
Avicenna, 222.
"Avila," 4, 19(q), 53, 67, 69, 70(q), 77, 81, 125.

B

Babbitt, Irving, 53(q), 204, 288.
Bain, A., 25.
Baldwin, Wm. W., 15.
Barbarism, 22, 54, 101, 102, 115, 132, 142-150, 203, 207, 209.
Barfield, O., 293.
Bascom, John, 98.
Beauty, 50, 53, 60, 62, 68, 77, 85, 92-99, 108, 128, 156, 202, 208, 233, 246,

INDEX

278, 283-285, 291. *See also* aesthetics.
"Before a Statue of Achilles," 66, 70, 79(q).
Benn, A. W., 26(q), 133(q).
Bentham, Jeremy, 139.
Berenson, Bernhard, 98.
Bergson, 173, 203, 241.
Berkeley, 246, 247.
Berlin, University of, 31-35, 66.
Bibliotheca Sacra, The, 107(q).
Blank verse, 81, 83, 84, 331, 336.
Boethius, 56, 295.
Boodin, J. C., 283.
Bookman, The (N. Y.), 99, 102.
Boston Latin School, 7, 12.
Bowen, Francis, 23, 40.
Brégy, Katharine, 292.
Bridges, Robert, 175, 210, 211, 289-291, 325.
"Brief History of My Opinions," quoted, 3, 5-8, 20-22, 25, 26, 29, 31, 34, 35; 72, 207(r), 246(q), 254(r).
Briggs, LeBaron R., 14, 298.
Brimmer Elementary School, 7.
"British Character," 196.
Brown, H. C., 283.
Brownell, W. C., 204.
Browning, 22, 100-102, 143-149, 154, 163, 206, 210.
Buckle, H. T., 25.
Buddha, 266.
Buddhism, 215.
Buermeyer, Laurence, 284.
Buffon, 225.
Butler, Joseph, 139.
Byron, 207.

C

Calderón, 4.
Calvinism, 22, 186, 187, 205, 260, 264.
Cambridge University, 41, 66, 88.
Canby, Henry S., 270, 274, 324.
"Cape Cod," 340.
Carlyle, Thomas, 173, 294.
"Carnival," 199.
Carpenter, George Rice, 15.
Castilian Days (Hay), 4.
"Cathedrals by the Sea," 80.
Catholic World, The, 175, 292.
Catholicism, 6, 20, 21, 24, 25, 27-29, 34, 46, 48, 54, 56, 57, 63, 66, 67, 77, 90, 136, 137, 160, 181, 183, 204, 206, 218, 244, 245, 250, 260, 266, 268, 276, 282, 288, 292.
Catullus, 154.
Cavalcanti, Guido, 64, 344, 345.
"Cervantes," 4(r).
Character and Opinion in the United States, 18(q), 30(q), 168(r), 176, 189-194, 201-203, 225(q), 257, 264, 277.
Chesterton, G. K., 145, 223.
Child, Francis J., 14.
Christ, 266, 267.
Christianity, 19, 24, 29, 44, 72-74, 89, 100, 104, 116, 123, 124, 134, 137, 145-148, 151, 158, 171, 177, 178, 180, 182, 183, 185, 203, 206, 245, 255, 259-261, 278, 282, 292. *See also* Catholicism; Protestantism.
Civilization in the United States (Stearns, ed.), 257.
"Classic Liberty," 178(q), 179, 180(q).
Classicism, 73, 142, 143, 151, 153, 163, 205, 208, 210, 275, 288.
"Cloud Castles," 213, 214.
Clough, Arthur, 29, 135, 309, 310.
Cohen, Morris, 291, 317.
Colenso, J. W., 25.
Comte, Auguste, 26, 133, 134, 242, 253.
Contemporary American Philosophy (Adams and Montague, eds.), 283(r)(q), 284(q), 286(q). *See also* "Brief History of My Opinions."
"Contrast with Spanish Drama, A," 4(r).
Cooper, Lane, 312.
Coubertin, 107.
Critic, The, 306.
"Cross Lights," 214.
Culture, 179-182, 259, 260.

D

Dante, 58, 63, 64, 66, 102, 119, 148, 153-159, 167, 204, 208, 312, 325, 333, 343, 344.
Day, Henry N., 98.
Debussy, 214.
"Decay of Latin, The," 44(q).
Democracy, 121, 122, 145, 171, 174, 288.
Democritus, 138, 140, 157, 216, 219-221, 240, 268.
Descartes, 40, 233, 246, 247.

INDEX

Dewey, John, 44, 130, 186, 253, 284, 286, 315.
Dial, The, 74, 200.
Dialogues, 85, 89, 90, 216-218, 221, 222, 267.
Dialogues in Limbo, 75, 216-222, 267, 268, 282, 292(q).
Dickens, 163-167, 210, 213, 281.
"Dickens," 165, 166.
Dionysius, 216, 217, 220.
"Dioscuri, The," 75(r), 84.
"Distinction in Englishmen," 196.
Divine Comedy, The (Dante), 155-158.
Dowson, Ernest, 54, 55.
Drake, Durant, 253.
Drama, The, 71-75, 81, 84.
Drift of Romanticism, The (More), 204.
Ducasse, C. J., 284.
Dühring, 26, 33.

E

"Easter Hymn," 47.
Ebbinghaus, Hermann, 33, 34, 245.
Edman, Irwin, 287, 291.
Educational Review, The, 44.
Edwards, Jonathan, 186.
Egotism in German Philosophy, quoted, 23, 24, 31; 108, 176, 182-186.
Eliot, Charles W., 13, 20, 32, 42, 43.
Eliot, T. S., 134, 288, 325.
Elliott, G. R., 204, 316.
Ellis, Havelock, 19, 213, 310.
Emerson, 24, 100, 115, 143, 148-152, 154, 187, 197, 198, 207-211, 223, 224, 251, 267, 274, 280, 286, 291, 309.
"Emerson," 149-152.
Empiricism, 172, 188, 191, 248, 249.
England, 2, 4, 64, 66, 67, 169, 175, 188, 193, 194, 198, 200, 262, 270, 289, 323.
English character, 44, 166, 195-198, 200, 213, 268, 270, 310.
English philosophy, 135, 246-249, 253. See also Russell, Bertrand; Locke; Hume; Mill; Whitehead.
English poetry, 8, 65, 78, 266.
English Prose Style (Read), 225.
English Traits (Emerson), 198.
Epicurus, 157.
Essays in Critical Realism (Drake, ed.), 231, 232.

Essence, 198-200, 215, 216, 229-241, 243-250, 252, 253, 255, 277, 284, 285, 290, 296. See also *Realm of Essence, The*.
"Ethical Doctrine of Spinoza, The," 17, 26-27(q).
Eucken, Rudolf, 310.
Existence, 198-200, 215, 229-234, 239, 243-245, 248, 250, 296. See also matter.

F

Fairbanks, Arthur, 300.
Family, The, 117-119, 120.
Faust (Goethe), 159-162.
Fichte, 183, 185.
Figures in Modern Literature (Priestley), 201.
Fiske, Arthur Irving, 8.
Fiske, John, 16.
Fletcher, Jefferson, 162, 345.
"Flight of Helen, The," 75(r), 84.
Florentine Painters of the Renaissance (Berenson), 98.
Foerster, Norman, 204, 208(r), 210, 316.
Form, 70, 73, 93, 94, 99, 204, 208, 209, 243.
France, Anatole, 53.
Frank, Waldo, 310.
"Free Will," 27.
Freeman, The, 76, 192, 202.
French philosophy, 40, 246, 247.
Freud, 257, 321.
Fuller, B. A. G., 168, 310.

G

"Gabriel," 47.
Garfield, James, 11, 12.
"Genteel American Poetry," 188.
Genteel tradition, The, 186-188, 203, 205, 257, 259-264, 269, 272, 273, 292.
Genteel Tradition at Bay, The, 205, 207(r), 220(r), 257, 259-261.
"Genteel Tradition in American Philosophy, The," 173, 174, 186-188, 190.
"German Freedom," 178(q), 179.
German people, 31, 176, 184, 186, 262.
German philosophy, 23, 24, 32-36, 40, 105, 108, 151, 152, 160, 182-186, 208, 248, 270, 300, 315.

356   INDEX

German Philosophy and Politics (Dewey), 186.
Germany, 34, 175, 177, 181, 186, 276, 277.
Gizycki, G., 33.
Glasgow, Ellen, 270, 293.
"Glimpse of Yale, A," 18(q), 30(q), 44, 45(q).
"Glimpses of Old Boston," quoted, 9, 11, 13, 273.
Goethe, 115, 155-157, 159-163, 167, 183, 206-208, 210, 312.
"Good Friday Hymn," 47.
Greek philosophy, 34, 35, 88, 89, 167, 181, 240, 244. *See also* Aristotle; Democritus; Heraclitus; Plato.
Greek poetry, 79, 181.
Greek religion, 100, 103.
"Greek Religion," 44, 100(r).
Greeks, The, 34, 35, 37, 57, 70, 77, 87, 112, 113, 136-141, 147, 160, 178, 182, 192, 203, 204, 207, 219, 245, 251, 269, 281, 282, 310.
Grimm, E., 34.
Groce, Byron, 8.
Groos, Karl, 98.
Guenon, René, 249.

H

Haeckel, 26, 33.
Hamlet (Shakespeare), 266.
Hamlet, Introduction to, 266(q).
Hapgood, Hutchins, 73(q), 102, 306.
Harris, Marjorie, 133(q).
Harrison, Frederic, 225.
Hartmann, 33.
Harvard College and University, 1-3, 13-19, 20-23, 26-32, 35, 40-43, 92, 169, 170, 190, 246, 273, 274, 276, 282-284, 286, 300, 323.
Harvard Crimson, The, 14-16.
Harvard department of philosophy, 20-23, 37, 168. *See also* James; Palmer; Royce.
Harvard Graduates' Magazine, 51, 74.
Harvard Lampoon, The, 17.
Harvard Monthly, The, 15, 16, 27, 37, 41-46, 57, 73, 75, 98, 131, 338, 339.
Hawthorne, 187, 274.
Hay, John, 4.
"Heathenism," 176.
Hedonism, 36, 113, 116, 117.

Hegel, 22, 23, 87, 88, 183, 185, 241.
Heraclitus, 138, 198, 240.
"Hermit of Carmel, A," 70, 71, 83, 84, 331, 336.
Hermit of Carmel and Other Poems, A, 45(r), 66-72, 80(q), 83(q), 84(q).
Hibbert Journal, The, 131, 175.
History of Rationalism · in Europe, A (Lecky), 135.
Hobbes, 40.
Hocking, W. C., 252, 283.
Holmes, Oliver Wendell, 263.
Homer, 95, 96, 101, 102, 153, 154, 202.
"Homesickness for the World," 217.
Hoover, Hardy, 320.
Horace, 8, 277.
Houghton, Alanson B., 15.
Hovey, Richard, 52.
Howes, George E., 9(q).
Howison, G. H., 300.
Humanism, 153-155, 164, 204-207, 209, 210, 259-261, 272, 273, 279, 281.
Humanitarianism, 147, 148, 160, 205, 206, 270, 279, 281.
"Human Scale, The," 215, 270.
Hume, 40, 134, 246, 247.
Humor, 94, 166, 180, 181, 190, 209, 210, 224, 257, 258.
Husserl, Edmund, 249.
Huxley, Thomas H., 26, 133, 134, 253, 283, 284.
Huysmans, 54.

I

Idealism, 22-24, 57, 70, 77, 91, 103, 105, 112, 113, 115-119, 125, 135, 158, 163, 164, 183, 184, 189, 190, 206, 227-230, 242, 245, 247, 248, 250-254, 262, 266, 291, 293.
Imagination, 100, 101, 104-106, 150-152, 154, 208, 209, 228, 229, 246, 254, 260, 279, 283, 287.
"Imitation of Calderón," 4, 75, 329.
Impressions and Comments (Ellis), 213.
"In Grantchester Meadows," 66, 68, 69, 79(q), 82, 269, 329.
Independent, The, 74.
Indians, The, 89, 150, 221, 245, 249-251, 255.
Individualism, 136, 137, 140, 141, 177, 180, 206, 208.
"Indomitable Individual, The," 177, 179.

INDEX

Inge, Wm. Ralph, 226.
"Intellectual Temper of the Age, The," 170-172, 174, 175.
International Journal of Ethics, The, 130, 131.
International Monthly, The, 108.
Interpretations of Poetry and Religion, 58, 62(q), 64(q), 74, 90, 92, 98(q), 99-107, 115, 123, 125, 127, 131, 134, 137(q), 142-154, 204, 205, 208, 220(r), 223(q), 228, 246, 254(r), 273, 295(q), 316.
"Irony of Liberalism, The," 182(q), 292.
Italian Poetry, 57, 58, 62-66, 118, 332-335.
Italy, 2, 184.

J

Jackson, Henry, 88.
James, Henry, 274.
James, William, 14, 21-23, 25, 26, 32, 33, 36, 40, 43, 44, 107, 113, 114, 130, 148, 168, 174, 186, 188, 191-193, 202, 203, 228, 245, 246, 272, 273-275, 279, 280, 308, 311, 321.
Johnson, Lionel, 54, 55.
Johnson, Samuel, 228.
Journal of Philosophy, 130, 162, 173, 230.

K

Kallen, Horace, 168, 184, 282, 286, 292.
Kant, 33, 183, 185, 231, 241, 253.
Keats, 97, 100, 154, 204, 207.
Keyserling, 5.
"King Lear as the Type of Gothic Drama," 16.
"King's College Chapel," 66, 67, 79(q), 81.
"Knight's Return, The," 70, 71, 75, 83, 84(q), 331, 336.
Knowledge, 104-106, 227-236, 244, 247, 253, 287. *See also* Santayana, theory of knowledge.
Krutch, Joseph Wood, 294.
Kultur, 176, 178-180, 182, 260, 266, 277, 282.

L

Landmark, The, 189.
Lane, James W., 292.
Lange, Friedrich, 33, 107.
Langfeld, Herbert, 284.
Larrabee, Harold, 275(q).
Last Puritan, The, 225, 262-272, 277, 281, 322, 323.
Last Puritan, The, Preface to the Triton Edition, 265(q), 267(q), 323.
Latin character, 265, 266, 267, 269, 270, 272, 279, 280. *See also* Spanish character; Santayana, Spanish traits.
Latin School Register, 8, 10, 11.
Lecky, W. H., 135, 309.
Leibniz, 40, 185, 246, 248.
Leopardi, 29, 56, 57, 207, 257, 321, 345-347.
Leopardi, Giacomo (Origo), Foreword to, 321.
Letters of Santayana to the present writer, quoted, 168, 227, 275, 281.
Letters of Santayana to William James, quoted, 32-34, 43, 107, 168, 228, 274, 280, 313.
Lewis, C. I., 253, 283.
Lewissohn, Ludwig, 291, 292.
Liberalism, 170, 172, 177-182, 205, 260, 288, 289, 292.
"Liberalism and Culture," 179, quoted, 177, 178, 180, 182.
Life of Reason, The, 87, 90-92, 104, 108-141, 167, 170-171(q), 201, 205, 211, 212, 220(r), 223(q), 228, 229(r), 261, 277, 278(q), 280, 282, 286, 289, 290, 294(q), 308-309(r).
"Lines on Leaving the Bedford Street Schoolhouse," 9, 10.
Lippmann, Walter, 288, 289, 291, 294.
"Literal and Symbolic Knowledge," 233, 236(q).
Literarisches Zentralblatt für Deutschland, 312.
Literary criticism, 90, 92, 108, 162, 163, 167, 203-210. *See also* Santayana, criticism.
Literary World, The, 51.
Littell, Philip, 42.
Little Essays from the Works of George Santayana (Smith), 201, 211.
Locke, John, 247, 257, 321.
"Locke and the Frontiers of Human Knowledge," 321.
Loewenberg, J., 283.
"Logic of Fanaticism, The," 176, 180(q).
Logic of Plato, The (Lutoslawski), 108.

London Mercury, The, 211.
London Times, The, 76.
"Long Way Round to Nirvana, A," 321.
Longfellow, 147, 305.
Lotze, 35, 36.
"Lotze's Moral Idealism," quoted, 35-37. See also "Philosophy of Lotze, The."
Love, 54, 59-66, 73, 77, 117-119, 141, 146, 148, 269, 291. See also Platonic love.
Love poetry, 57-66, 340-345.
Lovejoy, A. O., 253.
"Lovers of Illusion," 217, 220.
Lowell, A. Lawrence, 169.
Lowell, James Russell, 207, 209, 210.
Lucifer, 29(r), 42, 45(r), 72-75, 77, 81, 216, 220, 221, 267, 268, 277, 331, 336.
Lucretius, 55, 140, 153-158, 167, 208, 220, 254.
Luther, 183, 185.
Lutoslawski, 108.
Lyric poetry, 71, 81, 331.

M

Macaulay, 208.
MacLeish, Archibald, 85, 293.
Madariaga, Salvador de, 4, 5(q), 19, 136, 197, 310.
Mamelet, A., 134(q).
Many Minds (Van Doren), 201.
"Marginal Notes on Civilization in the United States," 257.
Marshall, H. R., 97, 98.
Materialism, 25, 26, 33, 131, 135, 138, 175, 189, 190, 219, 239-243, 250, 251, 253, 254, 288. See also naturalism.
"Materialism and Idealism in America," 189, 190.
Matter, 70, 116, 131, 157, 229, 233, 235-243, 245-252, 254, 255, 284. See also existence.
"Memories of King's College, Cambridge," 44, 66(q).
Meredith, George, 272.
Merrill, Moses, 9.
Michelangelo, 58, 62, 63, 65, 119, 333, 341, 342.
"Midnight," 68, 69, 79(q), 125, 269.
Mill, John Stuart, 25, 26, 107, 132-135, 224, 242, 309.

Miller, Dickinson, 43(q), 91, 168(q), 192, 311.
Milton, 78, 102, 207, 332.
Mind, 37, 97.
Mind, The, 22, 23, 104-106, 109-114, 133, 134, 228-235, 237, 239, 243-246, 248, 254. See also reason; knowledge; Santayana, theory of knowledge.
"Minuet on Reaching the Age of Fifty, A," 75, 82.
Modern art, 95, 208, 257, 321.
Modern philosophy, 89, 172-175, 188, 189, 192, 245-250. See also Bergson; Russell.
Modern world, The, 49, 50, 67, 76, 77, 101, 170-172, 175, 193, 194, 258, 282-296.
"Modernism and Christianity," 173.
Molière, 203.
Montague, W. P., 283.
Montaigne, 290.
Moore, A. W., 111(r).
Moore, G. E., 131, 174, 249, 250.
"Moral Adequacy of Naturalism, The," 220, 261.
Morality, 89, 90, 92, 114-117, 134-141, 147-149, 158, 166, 180, 185, 186, 199, 200, 203, 206, 221, 261, 262, 281-283, 288, 292, 294. See also Santayana, ethics.
More, Paul Elmer, 44, 115, 204, 205, 306, 316.
Morison, S. E., 13(q).
Münsterberg, Hugo, 42, 43.
Münsterberg, Margaret, 1, 3, 41-43.
Murry, J. Middleton, 193, 293.
Music, 95, 126, 127, 163, 190, 223, 251.
Musset, Alfred de, 16, 29, 56, 210.
"Mutability of Aesthetic Categories, The," 321.
Mysticism, 105, 106, 147, 150, 160, 278.

N

Nation, The (London), 193.
Nation, The (N. Y.), 74, 97, 175, 316.
Naturalism, 27, 46, 47, 53, 55, 72, 73, 77, 88, 89, 93, 106, 111, 112, 119, 135, 157, 188, 206, 208, 216, 219, 220, 239, 261, 282, 286-290. See also materialism.
New Adelphi, The, 242.

INDEX 359

New Republic, The, 76, 175, 176, 182, 188, 202.
New World, The, 43, 44, 98, 107.
Newman, Francis, 25.
Newman, John Henry (Cardinal), 25, 133, 224.
Nietzsche, 22, 183.
"Normal Madness," 217.
Norton, Charles Eliot, 14, 24, 26, 52, 53, 260, 264.

O

Obiter Scripta (Buchler, Schwartz, eds.), 266(q), 282(q), 321(q).
Ode, The, 49-51, 53, 67, 81, 82, 92(q), 111(q), 255, 328.
"On a Piece of Tapestry," 340.
"On a Volume of Scholastic Philosophy," 79(q).
"On an Unfinished Statue," 70, 82.
"On My Friendly Critics," 181(q).
"On Self-Government," 217.
"On the Three Philosophical Poets," 75(r).
"Overheard in Seville," 4.
Oxford University, 175.

P

Palmer, George Herbert, 14, 20, 21, 23, 34, 40, 107, 168.
Paradiso (Dante), 63.
Parker, DeWitt, 284.
Parkhurst, Helen, 284.
Parmenides, 198, 240.
Pater, Walter, 51, 53, 54, 224, 272.
Patmore, Coventry, 82.
Patriotism, 45, 117, 122.
Paulsen, 34, 134.
Peabody, Francis J., 23.
"Penitent Art," 321.
Perry, Ralph B., 168, 184, 191, 192.
Pessimism, 29, 50, 51, 57, 72-74, 77, 268, 283.
Petrarch, 60, 64, 333, 343.
Phaedrus (Plato), 65.
"Philanthropist, The," 217-219, 282.
"Philosophers at Court," 75(r), 83.
"Philosophical Opinion in America," 188.
Philosophical Review, The, 98, 108.
Philosophisches Jahrbuch, 132.
"Philosophy of Lotze, The," 35-37.

Philosophy of Santayana, The (Edman, ed.), 287(r).
Philosophy of Santayana, The (Hoover), 320.
"Philosophy on the Bleachers," 44, 49.
Plato, 57, 58, 65, 75, 108, 139, 140, 216, 217, 220, 230, 245, 252, 283, 310.
Platonic love, 57-66, 100, 140, 340-345.
"Platonic Love in Some Italian Poets," 58.
Platonism, 37, 38, 47, 51, 58, 61-66, 77, 89, 90, 92, 93, 102, 107, 112, 116, 118, 119, 131, 150, 151, 158, 163, 208, 220, 221, 239, 245, 246, 250, 261, 278.
Platonism and the Spiritual Life, 213, 226(q), 233, 238, 239(q), 252(q), 278(q), 282, 295, 296.
Plotinus, 251.
Poe, 143, 187, 208, 274.
Poems, quoted, 2, 4, 19, 28, 29, 38, 39, 45-47, 49-51, 53, 54, 56, 58-61, 63-65, 67-70, 76, 78, 79, 80, 82, 85, 86, 92, 111, 175; 201, 220(r), 243(rq), 278(q), 334-347.
"Poetic Medium, The," 71.
Poetry, 89, 95, 100-103, 107, 127, 134, 140-167, 204-210, 313. See also blank verse; ode; sonnet; Santayana, poetry.
"Poetry of Barbarism, The," 143-149.
Positivism, 26, 134, 135, 242.
Powell, Baden, 25.
"Power of Art, The," 70.
Pragmatism, 131, 170, 172, 189, 227, 232, 239, 250, 251, 253, 272.
"Praises of Water," 213.
Prall, D. W., 284, 285.
Pratt, James B., 253.
"Preface on the Unity of My Earlier and Later Philosophy," 279(q).
Preface to Morals, A (Lippmann), 289.
"Premonition," 69, 77, 81.
"Present Position of the Roman Catholic Church, The," 44, 56(q).
"President Garfield," 11, 12, 17, 329.
Priestley, J. B., 201.
Principles of Psychology, The (James), 35, 44.
"Problem of the Freedom of the Will, The," 16.
"Progress of Philosophy, The," 89.
Prose Remains of Arthur Hugh Clough, The, 135.

Prose style, 224-226, 291. *See also* Santayana, literary style.
Protestantism, 21, 22, 24, 123, 183, 184, 192, 206, 273.
Proust, 257, 281, 321.
"Proust and Essence," 321.
Psyche, The, 199, 223, 224, 251.
"Psyche, The," 213.
Psychology, 22, 25, 40, 108, 129, 134, 246.
Puritanism, 17, 91, 136, 157, 158, 186, 192, 205, 207, 264-270.

R

Rand, Benjamin, 40(q).
Rationalism, 25, 106, 132, 135, 157, 159, 218, 239, 277, 285, 286, 290, 291, 295. *See also* reason.
Read, Herbert, 225.
Realism (philosophical), 188, 189, 227, 228, 230-232, 244, 248, 249, 252, 253, 283, 293.
Realm of Essence, The, 77, 238, 239, 243; quoted, 234-236, 244, 245, 248, 249, 255.
Realm of Matter, The, 236, 239-241, 243, 255-256(q).
Realm of Truth, The, 319, 320.
Realms of Being, The, 87, 233, 239, 252, 255-257, 271, 275, 278, 285, 293.
Reason, 87, 104, 109, 112-115, 132, 134, 139, 152, 154, 157, 171-174, 195, 197, 203, 204, 208, 211, 220, 228, 261, 262, 266, 278, 279, 283, 289. *See also Life of Reason, The.*
Reason in Art, 108, 117, 125-128, 129; quoted, 113, 116, 223, 294.
Reason in Common Sense, 108-118, 184, 228, 270; quoted, 135, 138, 139, 140, 223, 278, 294; 229(r).
Reason in Religion, 123-125, 129, 137; quoted, 114, 115, 223.
Reason in Science, 128-130, 220, 238; quoted, 117, 170, 171; 229(r).
Reason in Society, 91, 117-123, 137, 269, 290; quoted, 116, 223; 277(r).
Religion, 77, 100, 102-104, 107, 123-125, 134, 141, 152, 153, 170, 172, 197, 204, 205, 221, 242, 244, 246, 260, 261, 280, 282, 287, 289, 294. *See also* Catholicism; Protestantism; Santayana, religion.

"Religion of Disillusion, A," 220, 254, 288.
Renaissance, The, 53, 57, 58, 62, 77, 89, 152, 205, 209, 259, 260.
Renan, 23, 24, 26, 29.
Republic, The (Plato), 140.
Reviews of Fiske, *The Idea of God*, 16; Fullerton, *In Cairo*, 44(q); James, *Psychology*, 44; Leahy, *Siege of Syracuse, The*, 44(q); *Lucifer*, 73. *See also* Santayana, reviews.
"Revolutions in Science," 242.
Revue des Deux Mondes, 26.
Ritschl, 107.
Rittenhouse, Jessie B., 62, 74, 77, 85, 86.
Robinson, D. W., 253(r).
Romanticism, 25, 72, 73, 89, 95, 115, 132, 142-154, 159-167, 203-206, 270, 288, 321.
Rousseau, 113, 206, 209, 211.
Rousseau and Romanticism (Babbitt), 204.
Royce, Josiah, 14, 21-23, 25, 26, 43, 168, 191-193, 202, 203.
Ruskin, 53, 54.
Russell, Bertrand, 106, 173, 174, 200, 201, 203, 249, 250, 253.
"Russell's Philosophic Essays," 173(r).

S

Sanborn, Thomas P., 15, 41.
Santayana, Augustin, 5-7, 30.
Santayana, George.
  Birth, 1, 49, 60.
  Parents, 3, 5-7, 20, 30, 169.
  Family, 5-7, 41.
  Childhood, 4-6, 20.
  Education, elementary, 7; high school, 7-12; college, 13-23, 26-30, 35, 274; graduate school, 31-35, 300.
  Teaching, 40, 42, 43, 167-169, 246, 282-284, 286, 288, 323.
  Travels, 30, 41, 66, 168, 169, 227, 313.
  Residence in Spain, 1, 2, 4, 30, 169.
  Residence in America, 1-3, 6, 7, 29, 30, 35, 41, 42, 169, 274.
  Residence in Germany, 31-35.
  Residence in England, 41, 66, 262, 263.
  Residence in Italy, 227, 275-277.
  Appearance, 3, 9, 282.
  Character, 2, 9, 42, 43, 51, 62, 77, 85,

INDEX

Santayana, George (*continued*)
 137, 175, 181, 267, 268, 276, 277, 279-281, 292.
Humor, 224, 225, 238, 272.
Pessimism, 50, 51, 59, 72, 73, 77.
Religion, 6, 20, 46-48, 54-56, 62, 137, 268, 282, 294.
Spanish traits, 3-5, 19, 136, 137.
American traits, 224, 272-275, 293.
Catholic influences, 6, 20-22, 27-29, 46-48, 54-56, 63, 65-67, 73, 74, 136, 137, 181, 182, 204, 206, 244, 250, 282. *See also* Catholicism.
Greek influences, 34, 35, 37-39, 47, 57, 58, 61-65, 73, 75-77, 88-90, 136-141, 204, 206, 208, 220, 221, 239, 240, 244-246, 250, 251, 278, 282. *See also* Greeks, the; Greek philosophy; Platonism.
Oriental influences, 5, 165, 278, 292. *See also* Indians, the.
Victorian influences, 25, 26, 54-57, 111, 132-135, 224, 242, 253.
Relation to the 1890's, 52-57.
Aesthetics, 92-103, 108, 125-128, 142, 143, 154-157, 181, 257, 284, 285, 313.
Ethics, 114-123, 134-141, 181, 199, 203, 205, 206, 218-220, 261, 262, 267, 281, 282, 292, 294.
Theory of knowledge, 104-106, 109-114, 134, 228-236, 250, 253-255.
Metaphysics, 109-114, 198, 227-256, 283, 284.
Literary training, 8, 9, 14.
Literary style, 36, 73, 130, 131, 162, 200, 202, 222-226, 238, 255, 270-272, 291.
Poetry, 45-86, 201, 243, 244, 280, 295, 326-347.
Poetic diction, 78-80, 338-340.
Versification, 80-85, 326-337.
Essays, 44, 45, 49, 210-218.
Criticism, literary, 142-167, 175, 202-210, 313; cultural, 170-172, 175-188, 190, 193-198, 202-205, 225, 259, 260, 272, 284; philosophical, 172-174, 182-186, 188-193, 315, 321.
Reviews by Santayana, 43, 44, 73, 301, 307, 312, 315, 318, 322.
Articles by Santayana not mentioned in text, 312, 314, 318, 320-322.
Translations, 16, 64, 65.

Santayana, George (*continued*)
 Reviews of Santayana, 51, 74-76, 97-99, 102, 106, 107, 130-132, 175, 200, 201, 306, 315.
Influence upon the modern world, 282-296.
Sapphic odes, 49-51, 53, 67, 82, 328.
"Scent of Philosophies, The," 217.
Scepticism, 56, 230, 233, 235, 239, 246, 247.
Scepticism and Animal Faith, 201, 233, 235, 238, 239; quoted, 222, 223, 236, 237, 250.
Schiller, 154.
Scholasticism, 24, 40, 89, 168, 207, 239, 244, 246, 250, 291.
Schopenhauer, 29, 33, 183.
Science, 77, 89, 106, 128-131, 140, 220, 221, 232, 238, 240, 242, 246, 251, 254, 287, 292, 295.
"Search for the True Plato, The," 108.
Sellars, R. W., 230(q), 253(r).
Seneca, 6.
Sense of Beauty, The, 40, 54, 74, 83, 92-99, 101, 102, 107, 108, 127, 131, 156, 184, 246, 284, 285.
Shakespeare, 44, 75, 78, 81, 100-102, 107, 143, 149, 152, 167, 207, 210, 275, 281.
"Shakespeare Made in America," 188.
Shaw, George Bernard, 187.
Shelley, 53, 78, 100, 163, 164, 167, 174, 175, 204, 206, 207, 220, 236.
"Shelley, or the Poetic Value of Revolutionary Principles," 163-164(q), 173, 175.
Shorey, Paul, 279.
Sidgwick, Henry, 138, 139.
Simmel, Georg, 33, 34, 134, 245.
"Six Wise Fools," 71.
Smith, Logan Pearsall, 175(q), 210-211, 213, 223.
Socrates, 139, 216-220, 266, 286.
Soliloquies, 85, 88, 194, 195, 199, 212-217, 221, 271, 295.
Soliloquies in England, 3, 45, 69, 75, 125, 176, 178-181, 194-201, 212-216, 280; quoted, 2, 6, 24, 34, 66, 89, 135, 137, 165, 166, 169, 177-182, 224, 251, 277, 296; 219(r), 267(r), 281(r).
"Solipsism," 67.
"Some Meanings of the Word 'Is,'" 233.

Some Turns of Thought in Modern Philosophy, 242(q), 321(q).
Sonnet, The, 81-83, 221, 243, 255, 327-328, 332-335.
Sonnets, First series, 17, 27-29, 37-39, 45-47, 53(q), 79-80(q), 175, 220(r), 278(q), 334-339(q).
Sonnets, Second series, 57-66, 77, 80(q), 334-337(q).
Sonnets, Miscellaneous, 47, 66, 70, 75, 78-79(q), 80, 201, 280.
Sonnets and Other Verses, 45-51, 57-66, 70, 340. See also Poems.
"Sonnets to W. P.," 41, 51, 78-79(q).
Spain, 1-4, 19, 30, 60, 77, 136, 137, 169, 176.
"Spain in America," 4(q), 19(q), 78.
Spaniard, The, 3-5, 19, 136, 137, 310.
"Spanish Opinion on the War," 4(r), 19(q), 176, 177.
Spencer, Herbert, 23, 25, 26, 133-135, 238, 241.
Spinoza, 17, 23, 26, 27, 33, 35, 40, 89, 131, 203, 239, 248, 257, 268, 281, 282, 321.
Spinoza's *Ethics* and *De Intellectus Emendatione,* Introduction to, 223(q), 229.
Spirit, 37, 131, 165, 200, 205, 223, 224, 226, 236-239, 250-252, 254-256, 277-279, 281, 290, 295.
"Spirit and Ideals of Harvard University, The," 13(q), 30(q), 44.
Stearns, Harold, 192, 202, 257.
Stephen, Leslie, 26.
Stevenson, Robert Louis, 283.
Stickney, Joseph Trumbull, 41.
Stoicism, 138, 139, 150.
Strauss, David, 25.
Strong, C. A., 169, 230-232, 253, 254.
Sturgis family, 7.
Sugimoro, Kojoro, 184(q).
"Sybaris," 53, 68, 329.
Symbolists, The, 52, 54.
Symons, Arthur, 53, 54.

T

Taine, 25, 26.
Tasso, 333, 344.
Teleology, 35, 110, 111, 126, 253, 254, 290.
Tennyson, 78, 146, 208, 329.

Testament of Beauty, The (Bridges), 289-291.
Thompson, Francis, 54.
Three Philosophical Poets, 154-162, 166, 168, 220(r), 223(q), 313, 316.
"Three Proofs of Realism," 231-233, 235.
Timocracy, 121, 122.
"Tipperary," 195.
"To W. P." See "Sonnets to W. P."
"Toast, A," 332.
"Tragic Philosophy," 325.
Transcendentalism, 24, 145, 147, 149, 150, 183-187, 208, 247, 249.
Translations of De Musset's *"The May Night,"* 16; Michelangelo's "Gli occhi miei delle cose belle," 65.
Treasury of English Aphorisms, A (Smith), 223.
Trivia (Smith), 213.
Troubadours, The, 65, 340.
Truth, 73, 77, 96, 97, 104, 155, 174, 212, 223, 231, 232, 236, 238, 243, 250, 255, 262, 278. See also knowledge; Santayana, theory of knowledge; Realm of Truth.
Turner, 6.
"Two Idealisms," 108.
"Two Moralities," 329.
"Two Parents of Vision, The," 213.
"Two Voices," 37.
Tylor, C. B., 25.

U

"Ultimate Religion," 281.
Unamuno, 19, 136, 276.
University of Berlin, 31-35, 66.
"Unknowable, The," 233, 237(q), 238, 241.
Untermeyer, Louis, 78(q).
Utilitarianism, 135, 139.

V

Van Doren, Carl, 201.
Varieties of Religious Experience, The (James), 191, 311.
Verlaine, 54.
Victorians, The, 25, 53, 111, 224, 242, 253.
Villiers de l'Isle Adam, 53.
Virgil, 154, 277.

Vitalism, 170, 172, 173.
Vizetelly, Henry, 31(q).
Voltaire, 203.

W

"Walt Whitman: a Dialogue," 44, 89-92, 143.
"War Shrines," 215.
Warren, Bentley, 12.
Wendell, Barrett, 14, 298.
"What Is Aesthetics?" 108.
"What Is a Philistine?" 44, 45(q), 49, 53, 91, 121.
Whitehead, Alfred N., 249.
Whitman, Walt, 44, 89, 90, 100-102, 143-150, 153, 154, 163, 165, 167, 174, 183, 188, 204-206, 208, 272, 274, 282, 305.
Wilhelm, Kaiser, 183.
Williams College, 12.
Winds of Doctrine, 163-164(q), 170-175, 187-188(q), 202(q), 207(r), 220(r), 229, 274(q), 316.
Woodbridge, F. J. R., 286.
Woods, A. L., 53(q).
Wordsworth, 78, 132, 158, 207, 208, 213.
Wundt, 134.

Y

Yale College, 18.
"Young Sammy's First Wild Oats," 71.
"Youth's Immortality," 332.